HUGH MILTON McILHANY, JR.
§ 131

SOME
Virginia Families
Being
GENEALOGIES OF THE

KINNEY
STRIBLING
TROUT
McILHANY
MILTON
ROGERS
TATE
SNICKERS
TAYLOR
McCORMICK

AND OTHER FAMILIES OF VIRGINIA

By
HUGH MILTON McILHANY, JR., M. A., Ph. D.

1903

STAUNTON, VA.:
Stoneburner & Prufer, Printers,
1903.

Notice

In many older books, foxing (or discoloration) occurs and, in some instances, print lightens with wear and age. Reprinted books, such as this, often duplicate these flaws, notwithstanding efforts to reduce or eliminate them. The pages of this reprint have been digitally enhanced and, where possible, the flaws eliminated in order to provide clarity of content and a pleasant reading experience.

Originally published
Staunton, Virginia
1903

Reprinted by:

Janaway Publishing, Inc.
732 Kelsey Ct.
Santa Maria, California 93454
(805) 925-1038
www.janawaygenealogy.com

2013

ISBN: 978-1-59641-103-6

Made in the United States of America

PREFACE.

The facts contained in the following pages have been collected at leisure moments during the past eight years largely because of my desire to know something of my more immediate relatives. As my materials have increased rapidly in value and extent, and as others have become interested in my investigations from time to time, I have had numerous requests to put the results of my work into permanent form. Accordingly my first intention was to publish the history of each family in a separate volume. But as the numerous intermarriages among the families would have required the reprinting of a great deal of the material in each volume, I finally determined to include all the records in one book, cross references being made from one part to another.

As the work on the different families has been carried on largely at different times and in different ways, it will perhaps be noticed that the facts concerning the individuals are more detailed in some places than in others. Yet I have refrained from eulogizing any one, and have simply stated the facts as far as I could obtain them. Hence no literary merit need be expected in the work. Only in the earlier generations have I given many details of the lives of those concerned. The order in which the families are arranged in the book has been determined solely by the order in which they were completed, much of the information having been collected since the printer began work upon the first family some eight months ago. For this reason it may happen that some changes have occurred during the last year which are not recorded in the book.

It is important to note the following explanations:

Each generation is indented to the right of the preceding generation, and in addition is distinguished by the letters or figures preceding the names of the members of that generation. For example, the children of Taliaferro Stribling (p. 35) are preceded by capital letters, A., B., etc. (pp. 36, 76, 84 and 85); the children of each of these by Roman numerals, I., II., etc. (pp. 37, 48, 52, etc.); the next generation by Arabic numerals, 1, 2, etc. (pp. 39, 41, 42, etc.); the next by Arabic numerals in parentheses, (1), (2), etc. (pp. 39-41, etc.); the next by the small letters, a, b, c, etc.; the next by the same in parentheses, (a), (b), etc.; and the next by small italic letters, *a*, *b*, etc. By this arrangement relationships and direct lines of ancestry can be easily traced. Thus, Mary Virginia Ellett Cabell (p. 155) is the second child of Mrs. Nannie Powell McCormick Cabell, who is the second child of Dr. Cyrus McCormick (p. 154), who is the third child of Mrs. Rose Mortimer Ellzey McCormick (p. 153), who is the sixth child of Mrs. Rosannah McIlhany Ellzey (p. 149), who was the second child of James McIlhany (pp. 135 and 137) who was the second child of John McIlhany and Rosannah Stuart (p. 133). All members of the six main families are printed in SMALL CAPS, and those whom they married in *italics*. It will be observed also that in the family outlines given in the Notes, the names of the direct ancestors of those who married into any of the principal families are given in *italics*. All places mentioned are in Virginia, unless otherwise noted. Children are living with their parents, when no other place of abode is given. The following abbreviations are used extensively; b.= born, e.= educated, m.= married, d.= died, l.= living, ib.= the last mentioned place, p.= parents, gr. p.= grand parents.

I take this opportunity to express my hearty thanks to all who have rendered me any assistance in compiling these records. My letters of inquiry have met with uniform courtesy and attention. Every date and other fact has been given upon what ought to be trustworthy authority; yet I have discovered that some of my informants are not as reliable as they might be, especially in the matter of dates; and to this source can be traced most of the errors in the book. In cases where authorities have differed, I have had to use my own judgment in deciding which should be followed. Although particular care has been taken to avoid errors by correcting the proof sheets twice, I am sure some mistakes will be detected, particularly in the Notes, which are approximately correct, though by no means complete. I shall greatly appreciate it, therefore, if any reader who discovers a mistake, no matter how small it may be, will inform me of it at once, stating upon what authority the change should be made. I am especially anxious to get any additional facts not given here, particularly regarding the earlier members of the families. One side of each page has been left blank, so that each person can enter in his own book at the proper place any addition or correction that may be necessary from time to time. An index, in which only the heads of families are listed, is given at the end of the book.

HUGH MILTON McILHANY, JR.

The University of Virginia,
    April 15, 1903.

LIST OF ILLUSTRATIONS.

Hugh Milton McIlhany, Jr., § 131,	*Frontispiece*
Jacob Kinney, § 2,	1
Mrs. Matilda Kinney Stribling, § 3,	5
Nicholas Cabell Kinney, § 7,	9
William Kinney, § 10,	13
Mrs. Rebecca Porterfield Kinney, § 10,	17
Jefferson Kinney, § 14,	25
Gen'l. Robert Porterfield, § 20,	29
Erasmus Stribling, § 25, aged 62,	33
Erasmus Stribling, § 25, aged 21,	37
Dr. Francis Taliaferro Stribling, § 27,	41
Dr. Taliaferro Stribling, § 33,	49
Capt. Francis Stribling, § 38,	53
Admiral Cornelius Kincheloe Stribling, § 76,	89
Mrs. Sarah Whitesides Trout, § 99.	113
Nicholas Kinney Trout, § 101,	117
Capt. Hugh Milton McIlhany, § 131,	161
Hugh Rogers, § 210,	229
Mrs. Mary Coombs Rogers, § 211,	233
Col. Hamilton Rogers, § 218,	245
Gen'l. Asa Rogers, § 223,	249
Rev. Arthur Barksdale Kinsolving, § 224,	253
Rt. Rev. Lucien Lee Kinsolving, S. T. D., § 224,	257

JACOB KINNEY
§ 2

THE KINNEY FAMILY.

§1 **William Kinney**, with whom this record begins, owned property, purchased October 13, 1779, on the south side of Hardware River, near Scottsville in Albemarle County, and adjacent to the Fluvanna County line. Here he reared his family consisting of three sons and one daughter—Jacob, Ann, Chesley and William. Where his home was prior to 1779 is not known. He was born about 1725, and was most probably a son of Capt. William Kenney of Blisland Parish, New Kent County, who was a vestryman of the parish from 1724 to 1735, church warden in 1721 and 1729, and a magistrate of the County. The maiden name of his wife Mary Kinney is said by some to have been Chesley, in which way Chesley became a family name with the Kinneys; others think her name was Moon: but of her ancestry nothing definite has yet been learned. The old Family Bible was destroyed by fire shortly after the Civil War, making it impossible to give all dates exactly; but William and Mary Kinney were married about the year 1764. They took great care to give their children as good an education as could be secured in those troubled times of the Revolution, for in after life they showed the results of such early training. Their two sons Jacob and Chesley removed to Augusta County early in life, and while on a visit to them about the year 1794 William Kinney, Sr., was taken sick and died. On February 16, 1795 his property in Albemarle County was sold by "Chesley Kinney and Mary his wife, Jacob Kinney and Ann his wife, of the County of Augusta, and William Kinney, James Whitesides and Nancy his wife, of the County of Amherst, heirs of William Kinney, dec'd." His wife then moved to Augusta to be with her sons, and about the same time William

Kinney, Jr., and Nancy Whitesides also settled there. Mary Kinney died "Jan⁷ 3rd. 1805, aged about 78 years", and was buried by the side of her husband in the Tinkling Spring Church yard, about seven miles east of Staunton.

Only one-fifth of the nearly six hundred descendants of William and Mary Kinney have borne the name of Kinney. Eight of the family have served as clerks of the county and circuit courts of Augusta, five have been Mayors of Staunton, and four have represented the county in the two houses of the Virginia Legislature. In Johnston's "Memorials of Virginia Clerks" Judge Hugh W. Sheffey says of this "remarkable family of clerks.": "The Kinneys were, as it were, born clerks. The qualities and attributes which make up the characters of good clerks seem to have been hereditary and belonged to the race. They all wrote well; they had memories unsurpassed in tenacity and accuracy; and were methodical and orderly; and were as faithful and true to their official duties as any men who ever filled offices of any sort in the Valley or the State. They enjoyed the unwavering confidence of the people and of the bar and the bench .... These men—including Erasmus Stribling—constituted a class of citizens of great conservative influence in the community, and I verily believe they contributed largely to the tone and characteristics of the people of this county. They were honored, followed, looked up to for advice and guidance, and swayed the public sentiment and opinion of the county in favor of right. justice and civil integrity; and they helped greatly to make the citizens of old Augusta what they certainly once were, and I trust will ever be—that is, reverential respecters of law and order, and promoters of private honor and public welfare. I could mention many instances of their great influence as leaders of public opinion, and of their marked success in guiding it aright. Death and dispersions have broken up the brotherhood, and the influence so powerful and salutary is dissolved and gone."

For twenty years after coming to Augusta the Kinneys were connected with the Presbyterian church; but on the reorganization of the Episcopal congregation between 1811 and 1820, they returned to that communion. "None of them in early life", says Mr. Sheffey, "became communicants of the church; amid the shadows of declining years they made their profession of faith. But from 1828 down, they were the very bulwarks and supporters of the Episcopal church, and by their influence and large moneyed contributions, sustained it as if they had been confirmed members of the same, and they all lived to see their labors of love crowned with abundant blessings, and to share in its benedictions''.

§2 A. JACOB KINNEY, b. Albemarle County, July 24, 1765; d. "Oak Hill", near Staunton, March 15, 1812; m. Albemarle County, in 1788, *Ann Morris*, usually called *Nancy* (b. ib. in 1766; d. "Oak Hill", Dec. 13, 1824; for her ancestry see §16).

Jacob Kinney moved from Albemarle to Augusta about the time of his marriage. On Aug. 21, 1792, he gave bond for one thousand pounds as Clerk of the County Court of Augusta, in which position he served for eight years. He was a lawyer by profession, and was very prominently connected with various affairs of town, county and state. He served as a member of the Staunton Board of Aldermen in 1804; as Recorder of the town in 1805; and as Mayor in 1806. From 1805 to 1809 he was a member of the Virginia House of Delegates, and was intimately associated with the first men of the time, once being prominently mentioned for the governorship. As an intimate friend of William Wirt, the historian, he often stayed at the latter's home when visiting Richmond. The following is part of a business letter, written one week after Mr. Kinney's death, of which the writer had not heard, thus illustrating the slowness with which information could then be communicated:

Richmond, March 22, 1812.

My dear Kinney.

....

How are you my dear old friend— the memory of former times comes over me as I write to you, and fills me with a kind of pleasing melancholy— Are we ne'er to see you more in these precincts— O! the days and I may add the nights too, that we have seen! — But grieving's a folly— You have many friends here, whose hearts beat most warmly towards you— We often *talk* you over — I wish you would come down and let us *rub* you over—God bless you and all who are dear to you— My love to Mrs. Kinney—your daughter, Mr. S. [Stribling.]

Your friend till death,

WM. WIRT.

It is said that Mr. Wirt also wrote the following epitaph, the original draft of which is still preserved, and which is inscribed upon the stone that covers Mr. Kinney's grave in Trinity Church yard at Staunton:

> Here lies the body
> of
> JACOB KINNEY
> nat. 24th. July 1765,
> ob. 15th. March 1812.
> He was born in the county of Fluvanna [?]
> and Emigrated to this county
> shortly after he reached the years of
> manhood.
> The public utility of his life is acknowledged
> by all who knew him.
> A heart
> of great sensibility and benevolence
> formed for friendship the most
> sincere and disinterested;
> A temper
> gay and ardent;
> A disposition
> frank and generous;
> A mind
> prompt, vigorous, fertile, and original
> in all its sallies;
> A soul
> intrepid, noble and magnanimous,
> Once animated the dust that moulders here.
> The affection of a wife
> and the filial love of a daughter & only child
> have placed this stone
> ' to his memory.

In 1795 Mr. Kinney bought the property now known as the Virginia Waukesha Springs about two miles from Staunton, and built the house which still remains. This home called "Oak Hill" descended to his only child Mrs. Matilda Stribling. Besides other property in Staunton, he owned a stone tavern in the town of Warren in Albemarle, and a ferry on the James River at the same place, which he leased at a large sum annually.

The profile portrait of Mr. Kinney given herewith was made in the year 1808, by the famous French artist St. Memin, several original copies of which are in the possession of his descendants.

MRS. MATILDA KINNEY STRIBLING

THE KINNEY FAMILY.

Mrs. Nancy Kinney was a woman of great force of character, and was a prominent member of the Presbyterian church. It is said that she and Judge Archibald Stuart were the only two persons in the county at one time who owned a four-wheeled carriage. The annual license costing eleven dollars was made out in the name of her son-in-law in 1815. She survived her husband twelve years, and is buried by his side in the Trinity Church yard.

§3 I. MATILDA KINNEY, b. near Staunton, Nov. 18, 1789; d. Staunton, Apr. 17, 1829; m. ib. Apr. 23, 1807, *Erasmus Stribling;* for his ancestry and descendants see STRIBLING FAMILY, §§25-32.

§4 B. ANN KINNEY, usually called NANCY, b. Albemarle County, Sept. 22, 1766; d. Port Republic, Rockingham County, June 26, 1845; m. Amherst County, Aug. 7, 1792, *James Whitesides*, of the County of Amherst. See §17.

Mrs. Nancy Whitesides was always considered a remarkable woman. "She was possessed of a vigorous intellect, and agreeable and entertaining conversational powers, ever enlivening her companions with original humor and happily told anecdotes, of which she had an unabating fund. She remembered with historical accuracy and narrated with interest facts and incidents of the eventful era in which she was reared", recalling particularly the raid of the British under General Tarlton, when the army passed before her father's house.

About 1795 James Whitesides went with his brother Samuel from Amherst County to purchase land in Tennessee. They obtained land near Bean Station in Grainger County, where his brother remained; but as he was returning for his family he was drowned in crossing the Tennessee River. His brother stayed in Tennessee and prospered, but died unmarried. After her husband's death Nancy Whitesides removed with her infant daughter Sarah from Amherst to Augusta County, and lived near Tinkling Spring Church until her daughter's marriage, and thereafter with her son-in-law Joseph Trout.

§5 I. SARAH WHITESIDES, b. Amherst County, April 18, 1793; d. Port Republic, Aug. 15, 1873; m. Augusta County, Dec. 24, 1812, *Joseph Trout;* for his ancestry and descendants see TROUT FAMILY, §§99–107.

§6 C. CHESLEY KINNEY, b. Albemarle County, about 1768; d. "Walnut Grove", near Staunton, in 1829; m. Amherst County, Sep. 17, 1791, *Mary Edmunds* of that County, who died at "Walnut Grove", Aug. 14, 1831.

For several years in early life Mr. Kinney taught school near Jonesboro, now in Nelson County but then in Albemarle. After his marriage he removed to Augusta County, where at first he continued to teach. He lived in Staunton till 1808, when his home called "Walnut Grove", about two miles to the west of Staunton, was purchased. It is still in the possession of his family. In 1807 he served as Mayor of Staunton, and was several times elected to the Board of Aldermen previous to his removal to "Walnut Grove". He was Clerk of the County Court of Augusta from 1800 to July 1, 1812; was Clerk of the District Court of Law, succeeding Micajah Coulter some time during the same period; and was first Clerk of the Circuit Court of Law from 1809 till 1828, though after 1812 he was obliged to retire from all active service, having been stricken with paralysis about that time. While for nearly twenty years before his death he suffered in bed, his oldest son, Nicholas C. Kinney, performed the duties of his office. He was quite intimate with Thomas Jefferson, who visited Staunton on several occasions, and for whom he named one of his sons. His will made Oct. 5, 1811 was proved in court Jan. 26, 1830.

Mrs. Kinney was a daughter of Samuel Edmunds of Amherst. It is said that her mother was a Miss Lewis of Albemarle. She and her husband were buried in Trinity Church yard, but their graves were effaced in making room for the walk which leads to the Parish Building. They had six children, as follows:

§7 I. NICHOLAS CABELL KINNEY, b. Staunton, Feb. 29, 1793; d. ib. Nov. 16, 1859; m. *1st.* Amherst County, in 1817, *Eliza Catherine Slaughter Penn Thornton Holloway* (b. ib. March 11, 1801; d Staunton, Aug. 14, 1831; for her ancestry see §18); m. *2nd.* Richmond, March 19, 1835, *Mary Ann Ambler Fisher* (b. ib. June 1, 1811; d. Staunton, Aug. 27, 1863; for her ancestry see §19).

Mr. Kinney served as a lieutenant in the regular army in the War of 1812. After his return from the war, he

THE KINNEY FAMILY. 7

served as deputy to his bedridden father, as Clerk of the Circuit Court of Law, and succeeded him as Clerk from March 24, 1828 to 1831. He was then appointed the first Clerk of the Circuit Superior Court of Law and Chancery, in which capacity he served for twenty-eight years till the time of his death, when he was buried with military and masonic honors. At the final reorganization of the Episcopal Church in 1820, he was one of its first vestrymen. He was a member of the town Council in 1827 and 1828, and was Recorder of the town in 1829. In the "Memorials of Virginia Clerks" Judge Sheffey wrote of him,—"He was surpassed by no clerk in the State of Virginia as a lucid writer and an accurate draftsman of decrees and orders of the court............ He was a patient laborer, a most popular officer, and as true a friend as man ever had. His memory was marvellous; and this valuable faculty has descended to his children and grand-children to a remarkable degree." His obituary speaks of him as "the brave soldier, the accomplished gentleman, the kind, tender friend, the pleasant, cheerful, and sympathizing companion, and above all, the pure Christian". He had four children by each marriage, as follows:

§8   1. ROBERT HENRY KINNEY, b. "Walnut Grove", July 16, 1818; d. "Cherrymont", Grant County, Ky., May 20, 1881; m. Augusta County, May 20, 1841, *Rebecca Rachael Wayland* (b. ib. July 22, 1822; d. "Cherrymont", July 15, 1870; for her ancestry see §20). He served in the Mexican War as lieutenant in an Augusta company of volunteers. He was a civil engineer, and moved from Augusta to Grant County, Ky., in 1857.

      (1). ELIZABETH CHASTAIN KINNEY, b. Augusta County, Sep. 13, 1842; d. "Cherrymont", Ky., Aug. 26, 1863.

      (2). LOUIS NICHOLAS KINNEY, b. Augusta County, June 15, 1844; m. Knoxville, Ky., March 6, 1879, *Rosetta Tomlin* (b. Gardnerville, Ky., Feb. 22, 1853); l. Memphis, Mo; he is serving his second term as Treasurer of Scotland County.

The Kinney Family.

a. Louis Nicholas Kinney, b. Knoxville, Ky., March 24, 1880.
b. Alma Bernice Kinney, b. ib., Aug. 31, 1881.
c. Charles Roy Kinney, b. ib. April 15, 1883.

(3). Mary Ann Kinney, b. Augusta County, March 1, 1846; d. Memphis, Mo., Feb. 12, 1899.

(4). Charles Porterfield Kinney, b. Augusta County, July 9, 1849; m. *1st.* Knoxville, Ky., March 23, 1873, *Emma Virginia Simpson* (b. ib. April 22, 1857; d. ib. Jan. 17, 1874); m. *2nd.* ib. March 20, 1878, *Henrietta Race* (b. ib. Feb. 18, 1862); he had five children by the second marriage; 1. Crossville, Ill., where he is a physician.

a. Robert Porterfield Kinney, b. Phillipstown, Ill., Oct 9, 1879; m. Crossville, Ill., Sept. 6, 1899, *Nora Elizabeth How* (b. ib. Nov. 7, 1881); 1. ib.; he is cashier of a bank.

(a). Ruby Opal Kinney, b. ib. May 18, 1901.

b. Crawford Earl Kinney, b. Phillipstown, Ill., Jan. 22, 1883.
c. Mary Ada Pearl Kinney, b. ib. March 27, 1885.
d. Guy Louis Kinney, b. ib. Mar. 22, 1890.
e. Gladys Virginia Kinney, b. Crossville, Ill., Jan. 13, 1897; d. ib. July 19, 1897.

(5). Sarah Matilda Kinney, b. Augusta County, Jan. 15, 1852; d. "Cherrymont", Ky., Oct. 20, 1857.

(6). Kenton Harper Kinney, b. Augusta County, July 19, 1853; m. *1st.* Knoxville, Ky., Jan. 6, 1875, *Oberie Florence Simpson* (b. ib. Sep. 8, 1852; d. Hitt, Scotland Co., Mo., Jan. 1, 1895); m. *2nd.* Covington, Ky., Feb. 15, 1899, *Augusta Virginia Webb* (b. Knoxville, Ky., July 6, 1862); he had six children by the first marriage; 1. Hitt, Mo.; he is a farmer.

NICHOLAS CABELL KINNEY

The Kinney Family.

a. Chesley Chapman Kinney, b. Knoxville, Ky., Feb. 20, 1877; 1. Hitt, Mo.
b. Leonidas Bell Kinney, b. Knoxville, Ky., Jan. 5, 1879; m. Hitt, Mo., Sept. 7, 1899, *Minnie Pearl Bowman* (b. Elliott, Iowa, Jan. 3, 1885); 1. Hitt, Mo.
  (a). Mabel Neoma Kinney, b. Killwining, Mo., Aug. 17, 1900.
c. Robert Porterfield Kinney, b. Knoxville, Ky., Aug. 23, 1881; 1. Hitt, Mo.
d. Rosetta Louisa Kinney, b. ib. Oct. 23, 1884.
e. Frederick Hillman Kinney, b. ib. Mch. 15, 1888.
f. Bessie Florence Kinney, b. ib. Dec. 9, 1891.

(7). John Stribling Crawford Kinney, b. Augusta County, Feb. 4, 1856; m. Memphis, Mo., Nov. 10, 1892, *Lillian Isabelle Miller* (b. ib. Nov. 9, 1869); 1. ib.; he is in the jewelry business.
  a. Bernice May Kinney, b. ib. May 6, 1895.
  b. Robert Miller Kinney, b. ib. Sep. 14, 1898.

(8). Rebecca Holloway Kinney, b. "Cherrymont", Grant County, Ky., Nov. 2, 1859; d. Memphis, Mo., June 2, 1889; m. Scotland County, Mo., March 26, 1882, *Jonathan Dawalt* (b. Knoxville, Ky., Oct. 8, 1857; 1. ib.; he is a farmer).
  a. Mary Edna Chastain Dawalt, b. Hitt, Mo., Jan. 10. 1883; d. ib. June 3, 1886.
  b. John Crawford Dawalt, b. ib. Aug. 7, 1886; d. Memphis, Mo., Feb. 16, 1891.

(9). Virginia Beauregard Kinney, b. "Cherrymont", Grant County, Ky., Feb. 27, 1862; m. Carmi, Ill., April 16, 1883, *James Winder Daniel* (b. near Knoxville, Ky., Feb. 9, 1858; he is a farmer); 1 ib.
  a. Mary Claudia Rebecca Daniel, b. ib. June 7, 1884.

b. CHARLES KINNEY GUY DANIEL, b. Phillipstown, Ill., Feb. 13, 1888.

c. SARAH BEULAH ALTA DANIEL, b. Hitt, Mo., May 13, 1894.

2. CHESLEY KINNEY, b. Staunton, Sep. 27, 1819; d. Stribling Springs, July 10, 1886; m. *1st.* Augusta County, May 21, 1844, *Betsy Ann Bell* (b. ib. Dec. 29, 1821; d. Stribling Springs, March 3, 1869); m. *2nd.* Richmond, Jan. 15, 1874, *Mrs. Josephine Myers Allen-Wickliffe* (b. ib. Dec. 21, 1840; l. Staunton); he had five children by his first marriage; he was for many years proprietor of the Stribling Springs.

(1). JAMES BELL KINNEY (1st), b. Augusta County, May 31, 1846; d. ib. July 4, 1846.

(2). WILLIAM CRAIG KINNEY, b. ib. May 27, 1847; d. Stribling Springs, April 25, 1865.

(3). ELIZABETH CATHERINE SLAUGHTER PENN HOLLOWAY KINNEY, b. Augusta County, April 29, 1850; l. Staunton.

(4). MARGARET SUSAN KINNEY, b. Augusta Co., June 7, 1852; d. Stribling Springs, Jan. 18, 1862.

(5). JAMES BELL KINNEY (2nd), b Augusta Co., Jan. 14, 1855; d. Staunton, June 24, 1894.

3. GEORGE NICHOLAS KINNEY, b. Staunton, in 1823; d. Parnassus, Augusta County, April 30, 1896; m. Highland County, May 22, 1849, *Elizabeth Wallace Sivington* (b. ib. March 19, 1825; d. Deerfield, Oct. 13, 1884); he was a physician, and a graduate of Jefferson Medical College, Philadelphia; he lived for some years at Sherman, Tex., and then at Parnassus.

(1). MARY BARBARA KINNEY, b. Highland County, April 5, 1851; d. Deerfield, June 11, 1882.

(2). JOHN NICHOLAS CHAPMAN KINNEY, b. Ft. Washita, I. T., Sep. 27, 1857; d. Sherman, Tex., May 26, 1860.

(3). BETTIE AMANDA KINNEY, b. ib. Dec. 27, 1859; d. ib. July 23, 1867.

(4). JOHN NICHOLAS KINNEY, b. ib. June 5, 1866; d. Parnassus, Jan. 18, 1871.

THE KINNEY FAMILY. 11

4. CHAPMAN JOHNSON KINNEY, b. Staunton, in 1828; d. ib. March 16, 1885. He was a Major on the staff of Gen. Armstrong of the Army of the Tennessee in the Civil War. He also served in the Legislature and as Treasurer of Montana.

§9 5. ALEXANDER FISHER KINNEY, b. Staunton, May 12, 1836; m. ib. Oct. 26, 1858, *Jean Malcomb Galt* (b. "Glenarven", Fluvanna County, Sep. 25, 1839); 1. Staunton; he is Paying Teller of the National Valley Bank.

(1). WILLIAM GALT KINNEY, b. ib July 27, 1859; m. *1st*. Memphis, Tenn., Nov. 22, 1882, *Gertrude Corinth Brooks* (b. ib. Sep. 9, 1862; d. Staunton, April 12, 1884); m. *2nd* Washington, D. C., Dec. 5, 1889, *Willie Margaret Robertson* (b. Augusta Ga., April 16, 1866); 1. New York City; he has two children by the second marriage; he is in the insurance business.

   a. FLORINE FLEMING KINNEY, b. Staunton, Sep. 1, 1890.
   b. JEAN GALT KINNEY, b. Staunton, Nov. 11, 1893.

(2). MARY AMBLER KINNEY, b. Staunton, Aug. 25, 1862; m. ib. Feb. 9, 1887, *McHenry Holliday* (b. Winchester, Dec. 4, 1851; he is a merchant); 1. Staunton.

   a. MALCOMB ALEXANDER HOLLIDAY, b. ib. Nov. 10, 1887.
   b. HELEN McHENRY HOLLIDAY, b. ib. Jan. 1, 1893.

(3). THOMAS COLSTON KINNEY, b. ib. Feb. 20, 1866; m. *1st*. New Orleans, La., April 24, 1893, *Caroline Hancock Johnston* (b. Lexington, Aug. 8, 1866; d. Louisville, Ky., July 31, 1895); m. *2nd*. Peoria, Ill., March 12, 1902, *Maud Ingle Francis*, of Peoria; 1. London, England, where he is connected with the "Anglo-American Magazine".

(4). LUCY GALT KINNEY, b. Staunton, May 6, 1868; 1. ib.

(5). MATILDA TROUT KINNEY, b. ib. June 18, 1873; 1. ib.
6. JOHN MARSHALL KINNEY, b. ib. Dec. 31, 1837; m. ib. July 11, 1861, *Mary Frances Beirne* (b. Union, W. Va., June 15, 1840); 1. Staunton; he is a lawyer, and Librarian of the Court of Appeals.
   (1). MARIE ANTOINETTE KINNEY, b. ib. April 12, 1863; m. ib. Oct. 29, 1889, *Edward Valentine Harman* (b. ib. March 28, 1862; he is a manufacturer); 1. St. Louis, Mo.
      a. MARY BEIRNE HARMAN, b. Staunton, Jan. 15, 1891.
   (2). CABELL CARRINGTON KINNEY, b. Staunton, April 3, 1866; m. Detroit, Mich., Feb. 18, 1892, *Annette Peabody Trowbridge* (b. Huntsville, Ala., June 10, 1869); 1. Dallas, Tex.; he is a General Adjuster of Insuance.
      a. KATHLEEN TROWBRIDGE KINNEY, b. ib. Jan. 15, 1899.
   (3). EVELINE MARSHALL KINNEY, b. Staunton, Aug. 12, 1869; m. ib. Oct. 20, 1896, *John Alfred Renahan* (b. Sandusky, Ohio, Dec. 23, 1865; he is a member of the Hesser-Milton-Renahan Coal Company); 1. Chicago, Ill.
   (4). BEIRNE KINNEY, b. Staunton, April 17, 1875; 1. ib.; he is in the insurance business.
7. THOMAS COLSTON KINNEY, b. near Staunton, April 27, 1841; d. Staunton, July 28, 1863; he was Assistant Engineer on Gen. Jackson's staff, and died as a result of exposure.
8. EDWARD CARRINGTON KINNEY, b. ib. March 28, 1845; 1. ib.

§10 II. WILLIAM KINNEY, b. Staunton, May 18, 1795; d. ib. Nov. 25, 1863; m. Augusta County, Dec. 7, 1816, *Rebecca Farrar Porterfield* (b. ib. April 13, 1798; d. Staunton, Oct. 14, 1870; for her ancestry see § 20).

Mr. Kinney was a lawyer by profession. He served on the Staunton Board of Aldermen from 1821 to 1844, with the exception of two years, being Recorder of the Town in 1823, '25, '27, and '36. He was Mayor of Staun-

WILLIAM KINNEY
10

THE KINNEY FAMILY. 13

ton in 1824, '27, '28, and '43. In 1838 he was elected to the House of Delegates, having as colleague Mr. A. H. H. Stuart, and was re-elected in 1841 as colleague of Mr. Brisco G. Baldwin. He was State Senator from Augusta from 1847 to 1850, being in 1850 a member of the Committee of the Legislature which met President Taylor at the Potomac River on his way to Richmond to lay the corner stone of the Washington monument. He was also President of the old Central Bank of Staunton, and served as District Attorney under Mr. Harrison's administration.

1. MARY EDMUNDS KINNEY, b. Staunton, Nov. 15, 1817; d. ib. April 19, 1886; m. ib. Dec. 7, 1837; *James Alfred Chapman* (b. Orange County, June 29, 1813; d. Alexandria, July 2, 1876; he was a lawyer, and had the degrees of both M. D. and B. L. from the University of Virginia).

(1). REBECCA PORTERFIELD CHAPMAN, b. Staunton, Oct. 13, 1838; d. ib. July 15, 1898; m. Washington, D. C., Dec. 29, 1858, *James Ker*, (b. Eastville, Sep. 4, 1836; d. Staunton, Oct. 15, 1896; he was an accountant).

    a. MARY LEA KER, b. Washington, D. C., Nov. 20, 1859; d. Staunton, May 2, 1872.

    b. JAMES KER, b. Orange C. H., Nov. 11, 1862; m. Staunton, April 16, 1890, *Mary Winters McCue* (b. Fincastle, June 17, 1869); 1. Staunton; he is City Ticket Agent of the C. & O. Ry.

       (a). MARGARET PORTERFIELD KER, b. ib. March 19, 1891.

       (b). FANNIE MCCUE KER, b. ib. March 8, 1897.

    c. ALFRED CHAPMAN KER, b. Alexandria, April 22, 1869; d. Staunton, Aug. 4, 1869.

    d. ANNA BELL KER, b. Alexandria, April 22, 1869; d. Staunton, Dec. 2, 1882.

    e. MARY RUTH KER, b. ib. June 4, 1872; d. ib. Aug. 2, 1872.

    f. MARGARET YOUNG KER, b. ib. May 5, 1875; d. ib. May 11, 1878.

(2). WILLIAM KINNEY CHAPMAN, b. ib. March 23, 1840; d. Sanford, Fla., June 20, 1894; m. Clifton Forge, June 23, 1868, *Mary Jane Sarah Haynes* (b near Covington, March 1, 1849; l. Ashland, Ky.).
    a. FLORENCE MAY CHAPMAN, b. Clifton Forge, Jan. 26, 1870; m. ib. Oct. 29, 1890, *Charles Lucian McDaniel* (b. Shenandoah, Dec. 15, 1866; he is a grocer); l. Ashland, Ky.
        (a). JAMES EZRA MCDANIEL, b. ib. Sep. 21, 1891.
    b. EUGENIA JONES CHAPMAN, b. Clifton Forge, Feb. 21, 1873; m. ib. Jan. 12, 1894, *Francis William Henry O'Meara* (b. Port Hope, Ontario, Canada, Jan. 12, 1871; he is Chief Clerk to the Superintendent of the C. & O. Ry.); l. Clifton Forge.
    c. ALFRED CHAPMAN, b. ib. March 25, 1884; l. Ashland; Ky.
(3). EMMA CHAPMAN, b. Staunton, Feb. 25, 1842; d. ib. Feb. 22, 1843.
(4). ANNA CHAPMAN, b. ib. April 2, 1844; m. ib. Dec. 19, 1866, *Joseph Deakins McGuire* (b. Washington, D. C., Nov. 26, 1842; he is a lawyer and archæologist); l. ib.
    a. JAMES CLARK MCGUIRE, b. Ellicott City, Md., Sep. 21, 1867; l. New York City; he is a civil engineer and contractor.
    b. MARY MADISON MCGUIRE, b. Ellicott City, Md., Nov. 30, 1868; l. Washington, D. C.
(5). MARY ELLA CHAPMAN, b. Staunton, June 14, 1847; m. Brooklyn, N. Y., Feb. 1, 1876, *Glenn Brown* (b. Fauquier County; he is an architect); l. Washington, D. C.
    a. GLENN MADISON BROWN, b. Boston, Mass., 1876; l. Washington, D. C.
    b. BEDFORD BROWN, b. Alexandria, 1880; l. Washington, D. C.
    c. ROSALIE BROWN, b. Alexandria, Sep. 10, 1886; d. ib. Feb. 27, 1887.

THE KINNEY FAMILY. 15

(6). ROSALIE CHAPMAN, b. Staunton, June 12, 1849; m. Alexandria, June 18, 1874, *Andrew Hetherton Nott* (b. Richmond, Dec. 31, 1846); 1. Richmond.

(7). FANNIE STUART CHAPMAN, b. Staunton, Feb. 19, 1851; d. Lexington, Nov. 23, 1901; m. Clifton Forge, Feb. 5, 1883, *John Thornton Williams* (b. Keswick, June 9, 1854; d. South River, Rockbridge County, Oct. 29, 1885).

    a. JOHN STUART WILLIAMS, b. Lexington, Jan. 17, 1884; 1. ib.

    b. CAROLYN WILLIS WILLIAMS, b. Lowmore, Dec. 14, 1885; 1. Staunton.

(8). MARY KINNEY CHAPMAN, b. Washington, D. C., Oct. 31, 1853; 1. Staunton.

(9). FLORENCE CHAPMAN, b. Washington, D. C., May 16, 1856; 1. Staunton.

§11   2. JANE ELEANOR KINNEY, b. Staunton, June 25, 1819; d. ib. March 27, 1885; m. ib. June 18, 1839, *Edwin Mygatt Taylor* (b. New York City, Aug. 18, 1814; d. Staunton, Oct. 29, 1870; he was a banker in Staunton.

(1). SUSAN CARRINGTON TAYLOR, b. ib. May 1, 1840; d. Richmond, Dec. 30, 1842.

(2). ELEANOR HETH TAYLOR, b. Staunton, July 3, 1842; 1. Richmond; m. Staunton, Aug. 9, 1866, *Robert Haxall Fisher* (b. Richmond, June 16, 1842; d. ib. Feb. 17, 1897; see §19; he was in the railroad business, transportation department).

    a. EDWIN TAYLOR FISHER, b. Staunton, Nov. 18, 1867; d. Richmond, June 30, 1897.

    b. ANNE AMBLER FISHER, b. ib. April 10, 1871; m. ib. June 26, 1895, *Virginius Hall* (b. ib. Dec. 31, 1863); 1. ib.

    c. ELEANOR FISHER, b. Staunton, Feb. 24, 1873; m. Richmond, Jan. 22, 1896, *James McCaulay Higginson* (b. County Kildare, Ireland, Jan. 27, 1860; he is a farmer); 1. Ivy Depot.

THE KINNEY FAMILY. 16

d. ROBERT HAXALL FISHER, b. Richmond, May 18, 1880; d. ib. Sep. 14, 1880.
e. JANE TAYLOR FISHER, b. ib. Sep. 18, 1882; 1. ib.

(3). REBECCA PORTERFIELD TAYLOR, b. Staunton, June 5, 1844; d. ib. Jan. 5, 1895; m. ib. Nov. 28, 1867, *James Johnston Foster* (b. Ireland, May 24, 1834; d. Staunton, Nov. 19, 1900).
 a. JANE TAYLOR FOSTER, b. ib. Nov. 7, 1868; d. ib. Jan. 18, 1871.
 b. ELEANOR FISHER FOSTER, b. ib. April 26, 1870; 1. ib.
 c. JAMES CARRINGTON FOSTER, b. ib. Jan. 12, 1872; m. ib. Oct. 10, 1901, *Julia Boyd Baker* (b. ib. Sep. 18, 1876); 1. ib.; he is a book-keeper in the Valley Bank.
 d. ROBERT ERSKINE FOSTER, b. ib. Feb. 23, 1873; m. New York City, Sep. 20, 1900, *Lulu Gorsline* (b. Herkimer, N. Y., Aug. 16, 1869); 1. San Francisco, Cal.; he is a book-keeper.
 e. MARGARET JOHNSTON FOSTER, d. Staunton, March 23, 1874; 1. ib.
 f. EDWIN TAYLOR FOSTER, b. ib. Aug. 18, 1876; 1. Homestead, Pa
 g. JOSEPH FOSTER, b. Staunton, Aug.9, 1878; 1. Covington.
 h. CARRINGTON FOSTER, b. Staunton, Dec. 5, 1879; 1. Richmond.
 i. MARY MOORE FOSTER, b. Staunton, Oct. 20, 1883; d. ib. Nov. 11, 1886.

(4). CARRINGTON TAYLOR, b. ib. Dec. 1, 1845; d. Richmond, Oct. 28, 1875.

(5). ARABELLA SHERMAN TAYLOR, b. Staunton, July 19, 1847; d. Richmond, Nov. 6, 1879; m. Staunton, Oct. 10, 1872, *Edward Higginbotham Fisher* (b. Richmond, Aug. 31, 1846; d. Verona, Augusta County, Aug. 22, 1892; see §19).
 a. ELIZABETH HIGGINBOTHAM FISHER, b. Richmond, Aug. 5, 1877; 1. ib.

THE KINNEY FAMILY. 17

(6). ELIZA TAYLOR, b. Staunton, March 26, 1849; 1. Norfolk.
(7). ROBERT SKIPWITH TAYLOR, b. Staunton, June 29, 1851; d. ib. Oct. 25, 1878.
(8). WILLIAM KINNEY TAYLOR, b. ib. Aug. 1, 1854; d. ib. May 22, 1855.
(9). JAMES RICHARDS TAYLOR, b. ib. March 1, 1858; m. ib. April 27, 1887, *Maria Marshall Baldwin* (b. ib. March 10, 1861; see §93); 1. ib ; he is in the insurance business.
    a. NAJAH TAYLOR, b. ib. Feb. 7, 1888.
    b. MARTHA BARTON TAYLOR, b. ib. May 16, 1891.
    c. STUART BALDWIN TAYLOR, b. ib. May 14, 1893.
(10). EDWIN MYGATT TAYLOR, b id. March 16, 1861; d. Louisville, Ky., June 5, 1901; m. *1st.* Augusta, Ga , April 15, 1885, *Sarah Carter Jessup*, of Augusta; m. *2nd.* Alexandria, Sep. 23, 1900, *Eunice H. Duduit* (1. Washington, D. C.); he had two children by the first marriage.
    a. EDWIN MYGATT TAYLOR, b. Augusta, Ga., Jan. 15, 1886; 1. New York City.
    b. CHARLES QUINTARD TAYLOR, b. Staunton, Sep. 5, 1887; 1. New York City.

§12 3. ROBERT PORTERFIELD KINNEY, b. Staunton, Feb. 12, 1821; d. ib. Dec. 7, 1856; m ib. June 6, 1844, *Isabel Ann Stevenson* (b. ib. April 23, 1824; 1. Wilmington, Del.; for her ancestry see §21).
(1). ELIZABETH STEVENSON KINNEY, b. Staunton, June 20, 1845; m. ib. March 7, 1872, *Thomas Wing Sparrow* (b. Gambier, O., Aug. 28, 1840); 1. Washington, D. C.
    a. LEONARD LANSDALE SPARROW, b. Philadelphia, Pa., Nov. 17, 1872; m. Martinsburg, W. Va., Sep. 12, 1900, *Henrietta Kodrick* (b. Frederick County, Md., Feb. 8, 1875); 1. Washington, D. C.
    b. THOMAS WING SPARROW, b. Brooklyn, N. Y., Oct. 16, 1875; 1. Washington, D. C.

(2). EDWIN TAYLOR KINNEY, b. Staunton, July 18, 1846; m. ib. Feb. 22, 1872, *Viola McGuffin* (b. Augusta County, Oct. 10, 1852); 1. St. Louis, Mo.
    a. MARGARET ISABEL KINNEY, b. Garret, Ind , Nov. 9, 1876; m. St. Louis, Mo., Dec. 28, 1896, *Joseph Paul Louis Zanone* (b. Rome, Italy, Nov. 10, 1875); 1. St. Louis, Mo.
    b. DORA MCGUFFIN KINNEY, b. Nevada, Mo., Oct. 22, 1878; 1. St. Louis, Mo.
    c. HANNAH STEVENSON KINNEY, b. ib. May 14, 1882.
    d. GRACE ARNOLD KINNEY, b. ib. Nov. 20, 1887.
(3). MARY CHAPMAN KINNEY, b. Staunton, June 11, 1848; d. ib. Feb 14, 1851.
(4). CAROLINE VIRGINIA KINNEY, b. ib. April 10, 1850; d. ib. Dec. 1, 1851.
(5). REBECCA PORTERFIELD KINNEY, b. ib. Oct. 10, 1851; m. ib. Feb. 25, 1873, *William Abbott Pratt* (b. Richmond, June 16, 1850; he is a civil engineer, and professor in Delaware College); 1. Wilmington, Del.
(6). ROBERT PORTERFIELD KINNEY, b. Staunton, Sept. 13, 1854; d. St. Louis, Mo., March 25, 1896.
4. REBECCA FARRAR KINNEY, b. Staunton, March 14, 1822; d. Richmond, Aug. 8, 1899; m. Staunton, April 14, 1853, *Silas Augustus Richardson* (b. Worcester, Mass., about 1824; d. Staunton, March 7, 1867).
    (1). MARY EMMA RICHARDSON, b. ib. Sep. 16, 1856; d. ib. Jan. 19, 1862.
    (2). ROBERT PORTERFIELD RICHARDSON, b. ib. April 24, 1859; d. Southern Pines, N. C., Dec. 22, 1894.
    (3). WILLIAM AUGUSTUS RICHARDSON, b Staunton, Nov. 16, 1862; m. *1st.* Longdale, June 24, 1891, *Katie Farrar Alvis* (b. near Richmond, Feb. 12, 1869; d. Longdale, April 9, 1893); m. *2nd.* Halifax, N. C., June 6, 1894, *Sadie Denton Alvis*, (b. near Richmond, Dec. 13, 1878); he has had

THE KINNEY FAMILY. 19

two children by the first marriage and three by the second; 1. Richmond.
   a. MARY EMMA RICHARDSON, b. Longdale, March 22, 1892; d. ib. March 31, 1892.
   b. WILLIAM MACON RICHARDSON, b. ib. April 9, 1893.
   c. KATIE ALVIS RICHARDSON, b. ib. July 6, 1895.
   d. EDITH RANDOLPH RICHARDSON, b. Covington, March 11, 1897.
   e. ROBERT PORTERFIELD RICHARDSON, b. ib. March 31, 1900.
5. WILLIAM KINNEY, b. Staunton, March 25, 1824; d. Baltimore, Md., Dec. 19, 1851; he was a physician.
6. ANNE MARIA KINNEY, b. Staunton, Aug. 5, 1826; d. ib. March 21, 1885; m. ib. April 27, 1852, *Henderson Moffett Bell* (b. near Staunton, July 3, 1826; d. Staunton, Oct. 9, 1899; he was a lawyer).
  (1). RICHARD PHILLIPS BELL, b. ib. May 6, 1853; m, ib. April 25, 1876, *Emma Lyle Frazier* (b. ib. July 7, 1853); 1. ib.; he is a lawyer.
    a. JANETTE TAYLOR BELL, b. ib. Jan. 8, 1877; 1. ib.
    b. WILLIAM FRAZIER BELL, b. ib. May 11, 1878; d. Pocahontas, W. Va., Nov. 22, 1901.
    c. MARGARET LYNN BELL, b. Staunton, Dec. 8, 1879; d. Rockbridge Alum Springs, July 16, 1881.
    d. RICHARD PHILLIPS BELL, b. Staunton, Sep 28, 1881.
    e. LEWIS PORTERFIELD BELL, b. ib. Nov. 8, 1883.
    f. ANNE BELL, b. ib. Aug. 28, 1885.
    g. SUE LEWIS BELL, b. ib. Dec. 7, 1887.
  (2). JANETTE TAYLOR BELL, b. ib. Oct. 10, 1857; d. ib. Jan. 1, 1870.
  (3). ANNE BELL, b. ib April 30, 1859; m. *1st.* ib. Nov. 13, 1889, *John Robert Liggett* (b. Salem, Aug. 23, 1859; d. Huntington, W. Va., May 6,

1894); m. *2nd.* Staunton, April 21, 1897, *Gilpin Willson* (b. Rockville, Md., Jan. 3, 1860; he is a druggist); 1. Staunton; she has had one child by the first marriage and two by the second.
    a. HENDERSON BELL LIGGETT, b. ib. Aug. 22, 1890.
    b. GILPIN WILLSON, b. ib. Dec. 27, 1898.
    c. ANNE BELL WILLSON, b. ib. Dec. 13, 1901.
(4). FANNIE BELL, b. ib. May 29, 1861; d. ib. Aug. 7, 1861.
(5). HENDERSON MOFFETT BELL, b. ib. Aug. 23, 1862; m. ib. Feb. 6, 1889, *Mary Waddell* (b. ib. June 1, 1862); 1. Bramwell, W. Va.; he is a mining engineer.
    a. MARTHA VIRGINIA BELL, b. Staunton, March 19, 1890.
    b. MARY WADDELL BELL. b. Bramwell, W. Va., Jan. 15, 1892.
    c. ANNE KINNEY BELL, b. ib. Dec. 20, 1893.
    d. HENDERSON MOFFETT BELL, b. ib. Feb. 9, 1895.
    e. JAMES ALEXANDER BELL, b. ib. Sep. 28, 1896.
    f. ROBERT PORTERFIELD BELL, b. ib. May 4, 1898.
    g. JOHN BERRY BELL, b. ib. July 1, 1899.
(6). MARY KINNEY BELL, b. Staunton, Nov. 5, 1863; d. ib. June 19, 1864.
(7). FRANCIS STRIBLING BELL, b. ib. Nov. 27, 1866; d. ib. Dec. 7, 1866.
(8). PORTERFIELD KINNEY BELL, b. ib. March 29, 1868; d. ib. Sep. 18, 1868.
7. ELIZA HOLLOWAY KINNEY, b. ib. Feb. 5, 1828; 1. Richmond.
8. CHARLES NICHOLAS KINNEY, b. ib. Jan. 25, 1832; d. ib; Dec. 17, 1881.
9. JOHN CHESLEY KINNEY, b. ib. Dec. 4. 1836; d. ib. Oct. 20, 1859.

§13 III. CHESLEY KINNEY, b. ib. Dec. 30, 1803; d. ib. Feb. 7, 1851; m. ib. Jan. 8, 1835, *Margaret Ruth Stevenson* (b. ib. Nov. 2, 1816; d. San Antonio, Tex., April 5, 1896; for her ancestry see §21).

By profession Mr. Kinney was a lawyer, and lived at Staunton. He was a member of the Staunton Board of Aldermen in 1841, '42, '44, and '45. He was elected three times to the Virginia House of Delegates (1829, '30, and '37), and was in other ways prominently connected with the affairs of his time.

1. MARY EDMUNDS KINNEY, b. Staunton, Oct. 24, 1835; d. ib. June 2, 1872; m. ib. Nov. 30, 1858, *Heber Ker* (b. Eastville, Northampton County, Sep. 4, 1836; he was a twin brother of James Ker, §10; l. Staunton; he is chief office deputy of the United States Marshal of the Western District of Virginia.

(1). JOHN CHESLEY KER, b. Northampton County, Aug. 6, 1860; m. *1st*. Chicago, Ill., June 19, 1884, *Margarette Ada Collins* (b. Oswego, N. Y., Aug. 2, 1863; d. Chicago, Ill., April 24, 1888); m. *2nd*. Pekin, Ill., April 27, 1892, *Minnie Haines* (b. ib. Nov. 4, 1863); l. St. Louis, Mo.; he is a traveling salesman.

(2). HEBER KER, b. Richmond, Sep. 23, 1861; m. Baltimore, Md., May 27, 1886, *Isabelle Stuart Ball* (b. Stephens City, March 25, 1864); l. Sewickley, Pa.; he is in the insurance business.

    a. CHESLEY STUART KER, b. Nashville, Tenn., April 12, 1887.

    b. HEBER KER, b. Nashville, Tenn., Jan. 30, 1893.

(3). SEVERN PARKER KER, b. Richmond, Feb. 17, 1864; m. Nashville, Tenn., Sep. 10, 1891, *Annie Williams Gray* (b. Hickman County, Ky., Oct. 5, 1869); l. Pittsburg, Pa.; he is Vice-President of the American Steel Hoop Company.

    a. MARY RUTH KER, b. ib. Oct. 30, 1892.
    b. ANNIE GRAY KER, b. ib. Oct. 29, 1894.
    c. SEVERN PARKER KER, b. ib. Jan. 23, 1897.

(4). RICHARD STEVENSON KER, b. Staunton, Aug. 4, 1866; m. ib. May 11, 1898, *Jessie Shepherd McNeill* (b. Fayetteville, N. C., Dec. 1, 1876); 1. Staunton; he is a lawyer.
    a. RICHARD STEVENSON KER, b. ib. Sep. 5, 1899.
    b. GEORGE MCNEILL KER, b. ib. March 31, 1901.
(5). EDMUND BAYLY KER, b. ib. April 8, 1869; d. ib. May 3, 1876.
(6). KINNEY KER, b. ib. May 30, 1872; d. ib. Oct. 4, 1872.

2. JACOB CHESLEY KINNEY, b. ib. Sep. 22, 1837; m. Farmington, Ark., Sep. 24, 1877, *Eliza Jane Allen*, (b. ib. Aug. 3, 1851; d. ib. Sep. 17, 1879); 1. Prairie Grove, Ark.; he is manager of a hard-wood plant.

3. RICHARD STEVENSON KINNEY, b. "Walnut Grove", near Staunton, Feb. 28, 1841; m. Sweet Springs, Mo., Aug. 19, 1869, *Mattie Elizabeth Walton* (b. Lexington, Mo., Sept. 20, 1845); 1. San Antonio, Tex.; he is in the Commissary Department of the U. S. Army.

    (1). MARY WALTON KINNEY, b. Fort Fred Steele, Wyoming, Oct. 11, 1870; d. Sweet Springs, Mo., Dec. 2, 1870.

    (2). JOHN CHESLEY KINNEY, b. ib. Jan. 10, 1872; m. San Antonio, Texas, June 30, 1896, *Mattie Harriett Dougherty* (b. Shelbyville, Mo., March 21, 1871); 1. San Antonio, Texas; he is an electrician.
        a. ELIZABETH WALTON KINNEY, b. ib. Jan. 27, 1901.

    (3). WILLIAM WALTON KINNEY, b. Fort Fred Steele, Wyoming, July 4, 1874; d. ib. Aug. 22, 1874.

    (4). CLIFTON COMLY KINNEY, b. San Antonio, Tex., Nov. 22, 1876; he is an officer in the Regular Army in the Philippines.

    (5). JANET KINNEY, b. Fort Clark, Tex., Oct. 8, 1883; d. ib. Oct. 22, 1883.

§14 IV. JEFFERSON KINNEY, b. Staunton, April 4, 1805; d. ib. Dec. 21, 1866; m. ib. Nov. 26, 1829, *Sarah Robert Holloway* (b. Amherst County, Nov. 1, 1808; d. "Walnut Grove", July 9, 1875; for her ancestry see §18).

Mr. Kinney was Clerk of the County Court of Augusta for twenty-seven years (1831-1858). In the "Memorials of Virginia Clerks" Judge Sheffey wrote of him, that he was "one of the most patient and methodical workers I ever saw,............and one of the most agreeable talkers and anecdote *reconteurs*. He was a true and conscientious man, a most loving and affectionate husband and father, and a citizen without reproach". He served as an Alderman of Staunton for fourteen years, being Recorder of the Town in 1838 and 1847; and was five times elected Mayor (1839, '42, '46, '49, and '50). He was a Director of the Central Railroad, now the C. & O., and was also a Director of the Valley Bank.

   1. VIRGINIA KINNEY, b. Staunton, Aug. 30, 1830; d. Richmond, July 7, 1887; m. Staunton, Oct. 24, 1854, *Henry Donald Whitcomb* (b. Eastport, Maine, Feb. 19, 1826; 1. Richmond; he was a topographical and civil engineer, but is now retired).

      (1). MARY EDMUNDS WHITCOMB, b. Staunton, July 25, 1856; m. Richmond, Oct. 4, 1881, *Dr. Hugh McGuire Taylor* (b. Clarke County, Nov. 11, 1855; see §185; he is a physician and surgeon); 1. Richmond.

      (2). KATE HOLLOWAY WHITCOMB, b. Staunton, July 27, 1858; d. Richmond, Oct. 28, 1883; m. ib. Dec. 28, 1882, *Dr. William Perrin Nicolson* (b. Middlesex County, Feb. 4, 1855; he is a physician in Atlanta).

         a. PERRIN WHITCOMB NICOLSON, b. Richmond, Oct. 24, 1883; d. ib. Nov. 15, 1883.

      (3). VIRGINIA KINNEY WHITCOMB, b. Staunton, Sep. 20, 1860; m. *1st.* Richmond, April 29, 1885, *Charles McGruder* (b. ib. May 1, 1856; d. ib. Dec. 28, 1888); m. *2nd.* ib. Sep. 10, 1895, *Edgar Dalby Taylor* (b. Accomac County, Aug. 21, 1848; he is a wholesale druggist); 1. Richmond.

(4). ALICE WHITCOMB, b. ib. Sep. 16, 1866; m. ib. Nov. 15, 1892, *George Llewellyn Nicolson* (b. Deerchase, Middlesex County, Jan. 14, 1864; he is General Manager of the C. & O. Canal Company); l. Washington, D. C.
    a. HENRY WHITCOMB NICOLSON, b. Richmond, May 5, 1895.
    b. LLEWELLYN DUDLEY NICOLSON, b. ib. Jan. 29, 1897.
    c. KATHARINE HOLLOWAY NICOLSON, b. Georgetown, D. C., Aug. 17, 1900.
(5). HENRY DONALD WHITCOMB, b. Richmond, Sep. 26, 1869; m. St. Louis, Mo., Sep. 27, 1899, *Daisy Adelaide Cohen* (b. ib. Aug. 22, 1878); l. Philadelphia, Pa.; he is connected with the United Gas Improvement Company.
    a. HENRY DONALD WHITCOMB, b. Richmond, Sep. 26, 1900.

2. THOMAS HOLLOWAY KINNEY, b. Staunton, Aug. 19, 1835; d. Newport News, Feb. 25, 1894; m. "Buckeye", Hanover County, June 2, 1858, *Mary Todd Pollard* (b. ib. May 17, 1838; d. Longdale Furnace, Feb. 28, 1890); he was a physician.
    (1). THOMAS POLLARD KINNEY, b. Hanover County, Dec. 29, 1859; m. Danville, Oct. 18, 1887, *Emma Lancaster Brown* (b. ib. June 12, 1865); l. ib.; he is superintendent of the W. U. Telegraph office.
    (2). HARRY WHITCOMB KINNEY, b. Hanover County, Sep. 5, 1861; m. Winfield, W. Va., May 14, 1884, *Ellen Marguerite Stevens* (b. Meigs County, O., Dec. 27, 1861); l. Lynchburg.
        a. THOMAS HOLLOWAY KINNEY, b. Longdale Furnace, June 3, 1885.
        b. HARRY VINTON KINNEY, b. Clifton Forge, May 8, 1887.
        c. JUDSON STEVENS KINNEY, b. Knoxville, Tenn., Jan. 1, 1892.
        d. ELLEN MARGUERITE KINNEY, b. Lynchburg, Dec. 22, 1895.

JEFFERSON KINNEY
#14

(4). Betsy Ann Holloway, b. Sept. 22, 1805; m. *1st.* Maj. William Henley, and had four children; m. *2nd.* Wilkins Watson, and had three children.
(5). Sarah Robert Holloway, m. JEFFERSON KINNEY; see §14.
(6). Mary Ann Henry Holloway, b. Sept. 1, 1811; d. Oct. 11, 1811.
(7). Susan Crump Holloway, b. July 20, 1820; m. Guyandotte, W. Va., March 29, 1838, Carr W. Lane. The eighth of their thirteen children was *Susan A. Lane* who married ARCHIBALD KINNEY, her half first cousin; see §15.
(8). Thomas Slaughter Holloway, b. May 22, 1822.
2. *George Holloway*, who had among other children,
(1) *Eliza C. Holloway*, first wife of NICHOLAS C. KINNEY; see §7.

Note 4. Fisher and Ambler Families.

§19. (Compiled from Geo. D. Fisher's pamphlet, "Descendants of Jaquelin Ambler", and from Paxton's "Marshall Family", p. 42.)

Daniel Fisher, of Brunswick County, was the father of *George Fisher* (d. March 25, 1857), who married, May 29, 1795, Ann Ambler (b. Nov. 16, 1772; d. June 28, 1832); and had the following ten children:
1. Mary Rebecca Fisher; d. in infancy.
2. John Alexander Buchanan Fisher; d. young.
3. Elizabeth Jaquelin Fisher, m. Thomas Marshall Colston.
4. Jaquelin Ambler Fisher; d. in infancy.
5. Jane Ravenscroft Fisher, m. Carter H. Harrison.
6. *George Daniel Fisher*, b. Dec. 11, 1804; m. *1st.* Elizabeth Garrigues Higginbotham of Albemarle County; m. *2nd.* E. Harriet Haxall of Richmond; his children, by the first marriage, were:
(1). Mary Elmslie Fisher, m. Peyton Randolph.
(2). Ann Fisher, m. Geo. W. Camp of Norfolk.
(3). *Robert Haxall Fisher*, m. ELEANOR HETH TAYLOR; see §11.

origin, and the strong probability is they were brothers". On June 30, 1743 *Jacob Morris*, patented 437 acres in Goochland County, afterwards Albemarle. In his will, made Nov. 25, 1801, and approved in court in June 1806, he mentions his wife Jane Morris, his sons Powell and Benjamin Morris, and his granddaughter MATILDA KINNEY, child of his daughter *Ann Morris* wife of JACOB KINNEY. See §2. His personal estate was appraised at $4,587.00 at the time of his death. He and his brother Hugh both left large families, but it is said that none of their descendants remain in the County to-day.

Note 2. Whitesides Family.

§ 17. *William Whitesides*, evidently of English parentage, patented two tracts of land in Albemarle County, one of 400 acres March 15, 1741, and the other of 181 acres July 20, 1768. He and his wife Elizabeth afterwards sold both of these properties and removed to Amherst County. They had a family of several children, one of whom was unquestionably *James Whitesides* who married ANN KINNEY. See §4.

Note 3. Holloway Family.

§ 18. *George* (d. 1770) and *Betsy Holloway* of Caroline County were the ancestors of the two of that name that intermarried with the Kinneys. They had at least two sons:

1. *Thomas Slaughter Holloway*, b. May 27, 1765; d. June 28, 1824; m. *1st.* Sep. 27, 1796, Elizabeth Moore (b. Sep. 27, 1779; d. May 12, 1812, daughter of Capt. Reuben and Catherine Moore); m. *2nd.* March 28, 1819, Ann M. Crump, daughter of Benjamin and Eliza Crump. He had six children by the first marriage and two by the second.
    (1). Susanah Moore Holloway, b. March 1, 1798; m. Benjamin Harrison, and left no children.
    (2). George Holloway, b. Jan. 17, 1801; d. Huntsville, Ala., Aug. 4, 1826.
    (3). Catherine Price Holloway, b. Feb. 26, 1803; m. John G. Wright and left two children.

THE KINNEY FAMILY. 26

  a. FANNIE DUNBAR MURRAY, b. ib. Dec. 9, 1901.
  (2). ALEXANDER WADDELL KINNEY, b. "Walnut Grove", March 28, 1881.
  (3). VIRGINIA WHITCOMB KINNEY, b. ib. June 4, 1889.
  (4). SUSAN LANE KINNEY, b. ib. June 30, 1891.
 4. SARAH HOLLOWAY KINNEY, b. Staunton, March 15, 1842; 1. ib.
 5. WILLIAM NICHOLAS KINNEY, b. ib. Nov. 1, 1844; m. ib. Oct. 26, 1882, *Amelia Boykin Haile* (b. Camden, S. C., Sep. 19, 1855); 1. Staunton.
  (1). AMELIA HAILE KINNEY, b. ib. Oct. 3, 1883.
V. MATILDA RUTH KINNEY, b. ib. July 30, 1807; d. ib. July 20, 1884; m. ib. about 1830, *William Craig* (b. Augusta County, in 1799; d. Staunton, May 17, 1869; he was a merchant in Staunton, and a pillar in the Presbyterian Church); they had no children.
VI. ARCHIBALD STUART KINNEY, b. "Walnut Grove", April 19, 1809; d. Staunton, March 19, 1881. He was at different times Deputy Clerk of the Court under Nicholas and Jefferson Kinney, a civil engineer, treasurer of the C. & O. railroad, and a business man. He never married.

D. WILLIAM KINNEY, b. Albemarle County, about 1770; d. Staunton, about 1836. He was a teacher in early life, and came from Amherst to Augusta about 1795. In 1802 he was "Sargeant-at-arms" of the Chancery Court "He was a bachelor, and pursued no regular business during the latter years of his life, but was noted for genial traits which made him a welcome guest in many homes". He was especially fond of talking on theological and kindred questions. He was commonly known as "Uncle Billy".

Note 1. Morris Family.

§ 16. Rev. Edgar Woods in his "History of Albemarle County", p. 286, says that "two persons named Morris obtained patents for land in 1743, Hugh on the lower Hardware, and Jacob on Totier Creek. They were, as their names indicate, of Welsh

The Kinney Family.

e. POLLARD WINSTON KINNEY, b. ib. July 19, 1898.
f. JEFFERSON BADGELEY KINNEY, b. ib. Aug. 24, 1900.

(3). SUSAN WINSTON KINNEY, b. Hanover County, Aug. 10, 1865; m. Longdale, June 18, 1889, *James Meredith Williams* (b. Athens, Tenn., June 22, 1867; he is a bookkeeper); 1. Danville.
    a. MARY KINNEY WILLIAMS, b. Longdale, June 11, 1890.
    b. JAMES MEREDITH WILLIAMS, b. Danville, Aug. 20, 1897.

(4). JEFFERSON KINNEY, b. Hanover County, March 5, 1867; m. Roanoke, Dec. 22, 1890, *Elizabeth Alice Duerson* (b. Nelson County, Oct. 5, 1871); 1. Roanoke; he is an eye, ear and nose specialist.
    a. ALICE VIRGINIA KINNEY, b. ib. July 24, 1892; d. ib. June 21, 1893.
    b. JEFFERSON KINNEY (1st), b. ib. Dec. 11, 1893; d. ib. June 14, 1896.
    c. JEFFERSON KINNEY (2nd), b. ib. Feb. 19, 1896.
    d. EDWARD POLLARD KINNEY, b. ib. Jan. 11, 1898.

(5). SARAH HOLLOWAY KINNEY, b. Hanover County, Dec. 30, 1868; d. ib. Aug. 23, 1870.

(6). MARY TODD KINNEY, b. ib. Jan. 21, 1871; d. ib. Oct. 19, 1875.

(7). ALICE KINNEY, b. ib. Feb. 28, 1877; 1. Roanoke.

(8). WILLIAM NICHOLAS KINNEY, b. Hanover County, Apr. 12, 1880; 1. Danville; is a bank clerk.

§15 3. ARCHIBALD KINNEY, b. Staunton, Feb. 12, 1838; m. Carrolton, Mo., Oct. 9, 1877, *Susan Augusta Lane* (b. ib. July 23, 1853; see §18); 1. Staunton.
    (1). FANNIE SMITH KINNEY, b. "Walnut Grove", near Staunton, Sep. 22, 1878; m. Staunton, June 28, 1899, *Hugh Dunbar Murray* (b. Suffolk, Aug. 26, 1868; he is a photographer); 1. Staunton.

GENERAL ROBERT PORTERFIELD
% 20

The Fisher and Ambler Families.

(4). *Edward Higginbotham Fisher*, m. *1st* ARABELLA SHERMAN TAYLOR; see §11; m. *2nd*. Eliza Leroy Daingerfield of Augusta County.
7. Lucy Marshall Fisher, m. Daniel Norbourn Norton.
8. Edward Carrington Fisher, m. Lavinia Page.
9. *Mary Ann Ambler Fisher*, m. NICHOLAS CABELL KINNEY; see §7.
10. Charles Fenton Mercer Fisher, m. Mary Eskridge of Mississippi.

John Ambler and Elizabeth Burkadike of the City of York, England, had a son *Richard Ambler*, b. Dec. 24, 1690; d. Feb. 1766; came to Virginia in 1716; m. in 1724, Elizabeth Jaquelin (b. Oct. 1709; d. 1756; daughter of Edward Jaquelin,—son of John Jaquelin and Elizabeth Craddock of the County of Kent, England,—and Martha Cary,—daughter of William Cary, Gent., of Warwick Co., Va.), and had nine children, the seventh being, *Jaquelin Ambler*, b. Aug. 9, 1742; d. Feb. 10, 1798; m. May 24, 1764, Rebecca Burwell (b. May 29, 1746; daughter of Lewis Burwell and Mary Willis of Gloucester County) and had,—

1. Elizabeth Jaquelin Ambler, m. *1st*. William Brent; m. *2nd*. Col. Edward Carrington.
2. Mary Willis Ambler, m. John Marshall, Chief Justice of the United States.
3. Martha Burwell Ambler; d. young.
4. Rebecca Ambler; d. in infancy.
5. Rebecca Nelson Ambler; d. in infancy.
6. *Ann Ambler*, m. George Fisher, as above.
7. John Ambler; d. in infancy.
8. Lucy Nelson Ambler, m. Daniel Call.

Note 5. *Porterfield Family.*

§ 20. This family, which settled originally in Pennsylvania, is said to be of Scotch-Irish descent. Two brothers, Charles and William, removed to Frederick County, Virginia, at an early date, the latter being the ancestor of Col. G. A. Porterfield of Charlestown, W. Va., and of numerous other descendants living in the lower Valley. *Charles Porterfield* had at least four children:

1. Charles Porterfield, Jr., distinguished himself in the War of the Revolution, attaining the rank of Lieut-Colonel, and died from the effects of a wound received at the disastrous battle of Camden. He never married.
2. Eleanor Porterfield married William Heath, Attorney-General of Kentucky, but left no children.
3. Rebecca Porterfield lived with her brother Robert, and died at an old age unmarried.
4. *Robert Porterfield,* known as General Porterfield, was also highly distinguished in the Revolutionary Army. His military service, as recorded at the War Department and given in Heitman's "Historical Register" of the officers of the Continental Army, was as follows:—"2nd Lieut. 11th Va., 24th Dec, 1776; 1st Lieut, 1st June 1777; Adjutant, 19th Apr. 1778; transferred to 7th Va, 14th Sep. 1778; Capt. Lieut., 2d July 1779; Capt., 16th Aug. 1779; taken prisoner at Charleston, 12th May, 1780; transferred to 2d Va., 12 Feb, 1781, and served to close of War". He then settled in Augusta County, on Oct. 8th, 1784 purchasing a fine estate below Waynesboro on South River, which he called "Soldiers' Retreat". Here he died Feb. 13, 1843. There is in the possession of Dr. C. P. Kinney of Crossville, Ill., an old parchment signed by George Washington, being the certificate of membership of Capt. Robt. Porterfield in the Society of the Cincinnati, an organization instituted by the officers of the American Army at the close of the Revolution. He was at one time Colonel of the state militia, and during the War of 1812 was commissioned

Brigadier General of Virginia Volunteers; hence the title by which he was commonly known. He married Rebecca Farrar, daughter of Peter Farrar of Amelia County, by whom he had four children:

(1). Charles Porterfield; died unmarried.

(2). *Mary C.* (or *Polly*) *Porterfield*, b. June 10, 1789; d. April 16, 1852; m. June 18, 1818, Lewis Wayland of Augusta County (b. in 1787; d. Grant County, Ky., Feb. 4, 1857). They left a large family who have removed to Kentucky. Their daughter *Rebecca Wayland* married ROBERT H. KINNEY; see §8.

(3). John Porterfield married Betsy McCue, a sister of John and Col. Franklin McCue, and had only one child, Robert Porterfield, who married a daughter of John Wayt, and left one son, Robert Porterfield of Lewisburg, W. Va., who married a Miss McClung of Greenbrier County and had several children.

(4). *Rebecca Farrar Porterfield*, married WILLIAM KINNEY; see §10.

The line of descent of Rebecca Farrar, wife of General Robert Porterfield, has not been certainly established in every point, but the following is taken from the sketch of the family given in the "Virginia Magazine of History and Biography":

I. John Farrar of Hertford, England. His son,

II. Nicholas Farrar or Ferrar, merchant of London and member of the Virginia Company, m. Mary Woodnoth. Their son (?),

III. William Farrar or Ferrar, Member of the Council 1623 to 1633, m. Mrs. Cicely Jordan (?). His son,

IV. William Farrar, Burgess 1659-'60, '61-'76, m. Mary——. Their son,

V. Maj. William Farrar, Burgess 1700-'02, m. Priscilla Baugh. Their son,

VI. William Farrar, m. Judith Jefferson, first cousin of Thomas Jefferson. Their son, almost certainly, was—

VII. Peter Farrar, b. June 6, 1730; m. Jan. 17, 1754, Mary Magdalene Chastain (b. Aug. 23, 1827; widow of James Cocke of Malvern Hills, and daughter of Dr. Stephen

Chastain, one of the French Huguenots who settled Mannikin Town in Henrico County, who came over, we are told, "in the first ship", and whose name occurs on the records of Henrico in 1706; his wife's name was Martha, and she died it 1725, aged 52). Their sixth child was—

VIII. Rebecca Farrar, b. Dec. 28, 1764; m. Gen. Robert Porterfield, as above.

(See Peyton's "History of Augusta County", p. 317; "Va. Mag. of Hist. & Biog.", Vol. IV, pp. 431–439, Vol. V, p. 85, Vol. VII, pp. 320, 432, Vol. VIII, pp. 97, 206, 424, and Vol. IX, pp. 203, 322; and "Va. Hist. Col.", Vol. V, p. 79.)

Note 6. Stevenson Family.

§ 21. *William Stevenson*, who lived near Frederick, Md., was the father of *Levi Lamb Stevenson* of Augusta County, who married Elizabeth Dunlap, daughter of Robert Dunlap (whose father emigrated from Scotland and settled at Chambersburg, Pa., just before the Revolutionary War) and Margaret Kerr. Capt. L. L. Stevenson had the following children,—

1. *Margaret Ruth Stevenson*, m. CHESLEY KINNEY; see §13.
2. Robert W. Stevenson, m. Caroline Anderson.
3. John D. Stevenson, m. Hannah Letcher.
4. *Isabel Ann Stevenson*, m. ROBERT PORTERFIELD KINNEY; see §12.
5. Caroline V. Stevenson, m. Michael Harman.
6. Elizabeth G. Stevenson, m. Geo. W. Getty, U. S. A.

ERASMUS STRIBLING, AGED 62
25

THE STRIBLING FAMILY.

§22. There is a tradition preserved among some of the Striblings of Tennessee to the effect that this family is of Polish origin, the name having been originally spelled Striblinski, and that Thomas Stribling, the first of the name in this country, and said to have been closely related to one of the kings of Poland, was exiled from his native land because of his political or religious views or both. While I have been unable to find any historical basis for such a theory, the plausibility of the Polish origin of the name is borne out by the recurrence of the names Sigismund and Casimir in the different branches of the family. I am inclined to believe, however, that even if the name had such an origin, there must have been a sojourn of a generation or two in England before the emigration of the family to this country. There are Striblings residing in England today whose ancestors lived in Devonshire; and at the very time that Thomas Stribling settled in Virginia, one Benjamin Stribling with his family resided at Lavenham, Suffolk, England.

THOMAS STRIBLING probably came to America about the year 1710, and settled in Stafford County, Virginia. On July 11, 1727 there was granted to "Thomas Striblin of Stafford County" 1050 acres "on the middle grounds twixt Broad Run of Occaquan and Bull Run", which property was in that part of Stafford which shortly afterwards became Prince William County. Here he resided, in Dettinger Parish, about twenty years, when he removed to Frederick County. In 1752 "Thomas Stribling of Prince William, Gent." purchased 600 acres of land near Winchester. He died in 1755, his will being recorded March 25, 1755 in Prince William County, his sons Francis and Taliaferro qualifying as executors; but the will book was lost or destroyed during the Civil War. His estate in Frederick County was appraised May 3, 1755, and that in Prince William May 26, 1755. Shortly after 1715 he married *Elizabeth Taliaferro*, daughter of John Taliaferro of Essex, who represented that County in the House of Burgesses in 1699 (see §87). On account of the loss of his will, the names of all his children cannot be given with certainty. The three oldest are named in the will of Robert Taliaferro of Essex (dated Dec. 3, 1725; approved June 21, 1726), who mentions his sister Elizabeth, the wife of "Thomas Stripling", and her sons Francis, William, and Taliaferro "Stripling". Francis Stribling and Dorothy his wife were living in Prince William County in 1775. He inherited part of his father's estate in that County, but nothing further is known of him William Stribling moved to Frederick County, and died there unmarried(?) in 1748, his father qualifying as his executor Feb. 7, 1748-9. Taliaferro Stribling also settled in Frederick County, as shown below

That there were other children of Thomas and Elizabeth Stribling besides these three cannot be doubted. Thomas Stribling, the progenitor of the South Carolina branch of the family, was surely one of them (see §72). On July 23, 1754 one Colclough Stribling was paid for traveling 45 miles to and from the Prince William Court as a witness. On Feb 7, 1744 a tract of 119 acres was granted to Benjamin Stribling of Prince William County. A Samuel Stripling, aged thirty-three, enlisted in Caroline County in Capt. Mercer's Company on Dec 4, 1754, to fight the Indians. These must have been sons either of Thomas Stribling or of a brother who came to this country with him. That there was such a brother is indicated by the inventory of a William Stribling, deceased, recorded in Stafford County in 1765, the said William being either a brother or nephew of the first Thomas. I am convinced that Capt. Sigismund Stribling of the Revolutionary Army was a son of this Thomas. He is called "Uncle Sigismund" in several letters of the grand-children of Taliaferro Stribling, but could hardly have been the latter's son, as will be shown below. He was very old at the time of his death at "Hopewell" in 1816, having been born hardly later than 1740. He was a bachelor, and left his property to his name-sake, Sigismund Stribling, son of Francis Stribling, §45. Heitman's "Historical Register" of the Officers of the Continental Army gives the following record of his service: "2nd lieut 12th Va , Dec. 1776; 1st lieut, 10th May, 1777; regiment designated 8th Va., 14th Sep, 1778; Capt. —1781, and served to——". The Revolutionary Records in the State Land Office show that on June 21, 1783, 4666⅔ acres of land were granted to Capt. Sigismund Stribling for seven years service. On Oct. 23, 1807, 833 acres additional were granted to "Capt. Segismond Stribling as Captain of the Continental line for one year and three months service more than seven years". There is also a warrant for 400 acres, Oct 22, 1784, to William Stribling as Sergeant of the Continental Line, who enlisted for the war and served through. This was doubtless the same William Stribling who was pensioned in Fauquier County in 1818 for Revolutionary Service. There was a Benjamin Stribling, who, with his wife, Ann Vawters, and several children (Thomas T., George, Willis, and others), moved from Fauquier County, Va., to Scott County, Kentucky, about 1795, and who has left numerous descendants in Tennessee, Indiana and other western states. This Benjamin and the last mentioned William were evidently brothers, and perhaps sons of Francis or Benjamin Stribling, sons of the original Thomas Stribling.

§ 23. **Taliaferro Stribling,** son of Thomas and Elizabeth Taliaferro Stribling, was born in Stafford County about 1723. In early manhood he moved with his father to Frederick County, and at the latter's death inherited the 600 acre plantation referred to above. This he "and Elizabeth his wife" sold Nov. 7, 1771, the deed stating that the property had been willed to him by his father Thomas Stribling. On Oct. 16, 1771 he purchased the estate called "Hopewell", which descended to his son Francis. His will, made Oct. 4, 1774, was recorded in the Frederick court Dec. 7, 1774. His personal estate, including 30 negroes, was appraised April 24, 1775 at £1569. I have not been able to determine accurately the maiden name of his wife Elizabeth. The uniform tradition in the family has been that this Stribling, name unknown, married a Mary Taliaferro of Gloucester County, sister of the Elizabeth Taliaferro who married Edward Snickers of Frederick (see § 91). This could not have been the case. The fact that his own name was Taliaferro and that his mother was Elizabeth Taliaferro is sufficient ground for the tradition. And his wife was certainly named Elizabeth, as shown by the deed referred to above. I conjecture that her name was *Elizabeth Wright*, for the following reasons. Two of their grand-children, *Elizabeth* Stribling *Wright* Milton and Dr. Matthew *Wright* Stribling, bore that name, and I know of no other source from which it could have come. Then there is on record in Prince William County, dated March 29, 1742, the will of one Francis Wright, son of John Wright of that County, mentioning his wife *Anne*, and three young daughters, names not given. *Sigismund* Massey of Stafford County, probably a relative of the Striblings, was executor of the will. A short while after the death of Francis Wright, Thomas Stribling, Sr., was appointed guardian of these children. If Taliaferro Stribling had, about 1755, married one of these daughters, named Elizabeth, with whom he must have been well acquainted, all the facts in the case would be explained, as well as the origin of the name of his only daughter *Anne* Milton.

Taliaferro and Elizabeth Stribling had at least six children. In his will he leaves to his son Francis Stribling "the land whereon I live on condition he pay my son Taliaferro 100£ as soon as he become 21 years of age". After the payment of his just debts, the rest of his estate was to be divided equally among "my six children—Francis, Taliaferro, Ann, Thomas, William and John". From the wording of this will I conclude that Francis, at that time only eighteen years of age, was the oldest child; that Taliaferro was the second; that the other children are named in the order of their ages, this fact being supported by the dates of their marriages and other points to be mentioned later; that they were all, therefore, under age at the time; that those six were all of his children; and that his wife had died between the years 1771 and 1774, as she is not mentioned in the will. This of course excludes Capt. Sigismund Stribling (see §22) from the number of his children, and shows that they were brothers. He died Oct. 5, 1774, and was buried at "Hopewell". The following are his descendants:

§24 A. FRANCIS STRIBLING, b. Frederick County, in 1756; d. "Hopewell", Sep. 6, 1823, "aged 67"; m. "Belvidere", near Charlestown, W. Va., in 1783, *Nancy Tate* (b. ib. Feb. 15, 1763; d. "Hopewell", July 4, 1825; for her ancestry

ERASMUS STRIBLING, AGED 21
§ 25

see §88); they were both interred at "Hopewell". He inherited this estate from his father, and lived there all his life, by his industry and thrift accumulating a great amount of property. Here all of his ten children were born, and to them he gave the best education available. He was a man of lasting influence in the community, being especially interested in the public charities of the county. At the time of his death his personal property was valued at $8000.00, while his landed possessions were very large. In his will, made June 4, 1823 and approved Oct. 6, 1823, he mentions his children,—Erasmus, Taliaferro, Francis, Magnus T., Thomas, George W., Nancy Neill, and Margaret P. Pennybacker; the children of his daughter Mary T. Crawford, deceased; and the daughter and only child of his son Sigismund, deceased. The "Hopewell" estate he left to his wife Nancy, to be sold at her death and equally divided among his children. Accordingly in 1826 it was sold to Fayette Washington, and the name was changed to "Waverly". His son Dr. Taliaferro Stribling qualified as executor of his will on a bond of $70,000.00.

§25 I. ERASMUS STRIBLING, b. "Hopewell", June 1, 1784; d. at the residence of his son-in-law, John S Lewis, in Mason Co., W. Va., July 2, 1858; m. Staunton, April 23, 1807, *Matilda Kinney;* see KINNEY FAMILY, §3.

A notice written at the time of his death, says in part of Mr. Stribling,—"Endowed in a remarkable degree with all those mental and social qualities which fit a man for usefulness and endear him to society, it was his privilege during his long life to fill many honorable and important stations". He studied at Washington College, Lexington, Va., during the sessions of 1800–1803. While he was at an early date a merchant in Staunton, by profession he was a lawyer. The well known Stribling Springs property was owned and developed by him, from whom it derived its name. In early life he was for several years Clerk of the old District Court of the Sweet Springs. On Aug. 29, 1812 he was elected Clerk of the County Court of Augusta (to which county he had removed in 1805), and held that office till July, 1831. In 1846 he was appointed Clerk of the U. S. Court for the Western District of Virginia, which office he resigned in 1857, because of his advanced age and infirmity. Besides these positions he was, at different times, a Justice of the Peace for the County of Augusta, Clerk of the Corporation Court, Recorder of the town of Staunton in 1814, '15 and '17, and Mayor in 1816 and '18. On July 21, 1812 he was commissioned Captain of a company of Artillery of the Virginia militia, but was never called upon for active service. In 1816 he served with General Robert Porterfield and General John Brown as Commissioner of Elections for his district. "It may be said with perfect truth that all the trusts confided to him were discharged with fidelity, industry and unusual ability. His social qualities were of the very first order. Hospitable, sympathetic and well informed, it was impossible for any one to know him and not to love him. In the days of his prosperity his hospitable board was the great centre of attraction for all; and the charms of his conversation, the freedom of his entertainments, and his well known benevolence of disposition, made his house the resort of fashion as well as the shelter of the distressed. For many years before his death, the cloud of an adverse fortune and the death of a beloved wife, had closed his hospitable door, and dispersed his large and interesting family. But still he was cheerful—still beloved, and in his latter years he exhibited what he had no opportunity of exhibiting before: that noble, manly nature, which enabled him to withstand the shock of adversity." In the same strain Judge Sheffey writes in the "Memorials of Virginia Clerks": "He was a man of rare intelligence and geniality of nature, a fine talker, and warm hearted and devoted in his friendships. During the time, at least the earlier part of the time, he held the office of County Clerk, he was one of the foremost men of the county in wealth, prosperity, possessions and influence, and no one was more cordially beloved by all in the community than he. His heart was filled with gentle, almost womanly, affections, and he scattered his favors and kindnesses around him with a lavish hand."

When the Episcopal congregation was permanently organized at Staunton in 1820, Mr. Stribling was amongst the foremost with his efforts and with his purse, and was a member of the first vestry elected. While in early life he had been somewhat dissipated and careless concerning religion, for many years preceding his death he was a most worthy and exemplary member of the Church. When it was impossible for his family to attend worship Sunday mornings at the church in town, it was always his custom to have the service and a sermon read for them and their servants at "Oak Hill", their country home. Of his 140 descendants, only eleven living bear the name of Stribling.

Mrs. Stribling was a woman of unusual attractiveness. Several pictures are extant which were painted by her at the age of sixteen. She died in the very prime of life, leaving a family of eleven children, as follows:

§26   1. JACOB KINNEY STRIBLING, b. Staunton, Feb. 10, 1808; d. Parkersburg, W. Va., Sep. 10, 1854; m. Frederick City, Md., Aug. 21, 1840, *Harriett Engleman* (b. Augusta County, about 1822; d. Staunton, Nov. 4, 1886); he was at one time deputy clerk of the Augusta County Court.

    (1). PETER ENGLEMAN STRIBLING, b. Staunton, July 12, 1842; d. Giles Court House, Va., June 17, 1864, of a wound received in the War.

    (2). ERASMUS STRIBLING, b. Staunton, Jan. 10, 1844; d. Newport News, Feb. 1, 1898; m. Chesterfield County, Va., Dec. 19, 1872, *Mary Ann Talley* (b. ib. July 28, 1850; 1. Richmond).

        a. CHARLES ALFORD STRIBLING, b. Petersburg, Sep. 11, 1873; d. ib. Sep. 16, 1873.

        b. EVA STRIBLING, b. ib. Sep. 28, 1874; m. Washington, D. C., Aug. 10, 1891, *Charles Francis Hubbard* (b. Brooklyn, N. Y., April 17, 1871; he is a grocer); 1. Richmond.

           (a). ANNIE MARY HUBBARD, b. Richmond, Sep. 5, 1893; d. ib. Aug. 10, 1895.

           (b). THOMAS FRANCIS HUBBARD, b. ib. Jan. 22, 1898.

        c. ERASMUS STRIBLING, b. Norfolk, March 30, 1877; 1. Richmond.

        d. BETTIE ANN KINNEY STRIBLING, b. Tar-

boro, N. C., March 4, 1880; d. Richmond, June 18, 1881.
  e. CHESLEY KINNEY STRIBLING, b. ib June 30, 1882; 1. ib.
(3). SALLIE ANN STRIBLING, b. Staunton, July 29, 1845; m. Point Pleasant, W. Va., Nov. 5, 1867, *Andrew Joseph McMullin* (b. ib. Aug. 13, 1840; he is a tobacco manufacturer); 1. Sebree, Webster Co., Ky.
  a. HATTIE LEWIS MCMULLIN, b. McMullin's Landing, Ky., Aug. 27, 1869; m. Sebree, Ky., March 18, 1891, *Joseph Samuel Montague* (b. Cromwell, Ohio Co., Ky., Dec. 18, 1864; he is a merchant); 1. Delaware, Ky.
    (a). ETTA NORINE MONTAGUE, b. Sebree, Ky., Feb. 27, 1892.
    (b). SARAH MONTAGUE, b. ib. July 22, 1894.
    (c). MARY ELLEN MONTAGUE, b. ib. March 28, 1896; d. ib. Dec. 18, 1896.
    (d). JOSEPHINE MONTAGUE, b. ib. July 14, 1900.
  b. NORA ALLEN MCMULLIN, b. Delaware, Ky., March 23, 1871; m. Dixon, Ky., Sep. 7, 1893, *John Thornton Riddle* (b. Petersburg, Oct. 1871; d. Sebree, Ky., Sep 8, 1893); 1. ib.
    (a). MARY THORNTON RIDDLE, b. ib. June 4, 1894.
  c. FANNIE BURBANK MCMULLIN, b. Livermore, Ky., Feb. 4, 1874; d. Henderson, Ky., Sep. 6, 1888.
  d. SALLIE LYNN MCMULLIN, b. Livermore, Ky., Dec. 31, 1876; m. Sebree, Ky., Jan. 12, 1899, *Frank Marion Edwards* (b. ib. July 26, 1875; he is a farmer); 1. ib.
    (a). CHARLES LAMBERT EDWARDS, b. ib. Dec. 10, 1899.
    (b). JAMES MCMULLIN EDWARDS, b. ib. July 28, 1901.

DR. FRANCIS TALIAFERRO STRIBLING
¾ 27

e. JOSEPH MCMULLIN, b. Livermore, Ky., Dec. 25, 1878; d. ib. Jan. 14, 1879.
f. NANNIE BRANSON MCMULLIN, b. Henderson, Ky., Jan. 20, 1880; l. Sebree, Ky.
g. STEWART NELSON MCMULLIN, b. Henderson, Ky., Feb. 22, 1883; is in the U. S. Army in the Philippines.
h. KATIE HAYDEN MCMULLIN, b. Sebree, Ky., Jan. 8, 1885; d. ib. Nov. 20, 1885.
i. AGNES SEHON MCMULLIN, b. ib. June 29, 1886; l. ib.

§27 (4). ELIZABETH ANN KINNEY STRIBLING, b. Staunton, April 10, 1851; d. Richmond, April 11, 1895; m. McKinney, Tex., Dec. 3, 1872, *Richard Dangerfield Ryan*, her third cousin; see §100.

(5). JOHN WAYT STRIBLING, b. Staunton, July 2, 1854; l. Gypsum, Texas.

2. FRANCIS TALIAFERRO STRIBLING, b. Staunton, Jan. 20, 1810; d. ib. July 23, 1874; m. near Staunton, May 17, 1832, *Henrietta Frances Cuthbert* (b. Norfolk, July 3, 1813; d. Staunton, Feb. 28, 1889); he graduated at the University of Virginia in 1829; he was one of the most distinguished physicians of his time, and was for many years the Superintendent of the Western State Hospital at Staunton.

(1). ELLA MATILDA STRIBLING, b. Staunton, March 5, 1833; d. ib. June 28, 1885; m. ib. June 5, 1867, *Hugh Lee Powell* (b. Leesburg, July 20, 1839; he married a second time and is living at Leesburg).

a. LUCY LEE POWELL, b. Staunton, Feb. 5, 1868; l. ib.
b. LOUISE MATHILDE POWELL, b. ib. March 12, 1871; l. Richmond.
c. FRANCIS TALIAFERRO STRIBLING POWELL, b. Staunton, April 13, 1874; l. New York City.

(2). FANNIE CUTHBERT STRIBLING, b. Staunton, Dec. 8, 1836; m. ib. Feb. 8, 1860, *Richard Taylor Foster* (b. Petersburg, Sep. 14, 1830; d. Richmond, April 27, 1875); l. Staunton.

a. HENRIETTA CUTHBERT FOSTER, b. ib.; 1. Philadelphia.
b. MARY ENDERS FOSTER, b. Richmond; 1. Staunton.
c. RICHARD TAYLOR FOSTER (1st), b. Richmond, June 30, 1863; d. ib. July 14, 1863.
d. FRANK STRIBLING FOSTER, b. Goochland County, July 13, 1864; is connected with the First National Bank, Birmingham, Ala.
e. RICHARD TAYLOR FOSTER (2nd), b. Richmond, June 24, 1865; d. Staunton, Aug. 31, 1865.
f. ARTHUR PEGRAM FOSTER, b. ib. Oct. 27, 1866; d. ib. Sep. 28, 1891.
(3). FRANCIS TALIAFERRO STRIBLING, b. ib. Aug. 13, 1845; m. Norfolk, April 23, 1889, *Olive Caldwell Jackson* (b. Leesburg, July 22, 1857); 1. Staunton.
(4). HENRIETTA BERKELEY STRIBLING, b. Staunton, Sep. 17, 1852; d. ib. Aug. 6, 1893.

§28 3. NANCY STRIBLING, b. ib. Oct. 8, 1811; d. Washington, D. C., Jan. 4, 1882; m. Staunton, July 31, 1828, *John C. Bowyer* (b. ib. Oct. 4, 1803; d. ib. May 31, 1880; he studied law, but afterward turned his attention to journalism, editing papers in Winchester and Alexandria; after the War he held a government position in Washington.
(1). MATILDA KINNEY STRIBLING BOWYER, b. Staunton, June 8, 1829; d. Washington, D. C., Sep. 26, 1853; m. Staunton, Oct. 23, 1850, *Lieut. Pierce Crosby* (b. Chester, Pa., Jan. 16, 1824; d. Washington, D. C., June 16, 1899; he was married four times, and at the time of his death was Admiral in the U. S. Navy).
(2). ELIZABETH LEWIS BOWYER, b. Rockbridge County, June 2, 1831; d. Winchester, July 22, 1892; m. Washington, D. C., Oct. 5, 1854, *Dr. David Porter Heap* (b. Marseilles, France, in 1828; d. Germantown, Pa., Aug. 11, 1866; he was in the U. S. Diplomatic Service).

a. ANNIE ELLEN HEAP, b. Tunis, Africa,
June 19, 1855; d. Washington, D. C., Feb.
11, 1889; m. ib. July 5, 1877, *Reginald Fairfax Nicolson* (b. ib. Dec. 15, 1852; he is a
Lieutenant Commander in the U. S. Navy).
   (a). MARY JONES NICOLSON, b. Washington, D. C., June 13, 1878; l. ib.
   (b). REGINALD FAIRFAX NICOLSON, b.
ib. Dec. 18, 1879; d. Winchester, July
2, 1890.
b. SAMUEL LAWRENCE HEAP, b. Tunis,
Africa, Dec. 22, 1856; is a Paymaster in the
U. S. Navy.
c. MARGARET MATILDA HEAP, b. Tunis,
Africa, April 6, 1859; m. Washington, D. C.,
Jan. 20, 1892, *John Spotswood Garland* (b. ib.
Feb. 15, 1859; he is a civil engineer in the
office of the District Commissioners); l. ib.
   (a). ELIZABETH BOWYER GARLAND, b.
ib. Dec. 20, 1892.
   (b). JOHN SPOTSWOOD GARLAND, b.
Georgetown, D. C., Dec. 25, 1895.
   (c). MARY TRUXTUN GARLAND, b. Washington, D. C., June 19, 1897.
d. EVELINA MARY HEAP, b. Louisville, Ky.,
April 25, 1863; m. Washington, D. C., June
12, 1889, *Albert Gleaves* (b. Nashville, Tenn.,
Jan. 1, 1858; he is a Lieutenant Commander
in the U. S. Navy); l. Washington, D. C.
   (a). ANNIE HEAP GLEAVES, b. ib. July
15, 1890.
   (b). EVELINA PORTER GLEAVES, b. ib.
May 26, 1895.

(3). HENRY MORTON BOWYER, b. Rockbridge
County, April 28, 1833; d. ib. April 4, 1839.

(4). FANNIE MORTON BOWYER, b. ib. June 23,
1835; d. ib. Nov. 3, 1842.

(5). CHARLOTTE AUGUSTA BOWYER, b. ib. Oct.
27, 1838; d. Alexandria, June 5, 1853.

(6). Infant, b. and d. Rockbridge County, July 17, 1840.

(7) ALICE STUART BOWYER, b. Winchester, Dec. 23, 1845; d. Washington, D. C., May 13, 1859.

4. ERASMUS STRIBLING, b. Staunton, Aug. 4, 1813; d. ib. Sep. 20, 1828.

§29 5. MARY TATE STRIBLING, b. ib. Feb. 10, 1815; d. Mason County, W. Va , April 22, 1887; m. Staunton, Aug. 30, 1838, *John Stuart Lewis* (b. Mason Co. W. Va., June 21, 1813; d. Point Pleasant, W. Va., April 13, 1902; p. Col. Andrew Lewis and Margaret Stuart; gr. p. Col. Charles Lewis, killed at the battle of Point Pleasant, and Sarah Murray—Col. John Stuart and Agatha Lewis).

(1). FANNIE LEWIS, b. ib. Nov. 10, 1839; m. ib. May 5, 1862, *John Warth English* (b. Jackson County, W. Va., Jan. 31, 1831; he is a lawyer, and Judge of the Supreme Court of W. Va.); l. Point Pleasant, W. Va.

    a. LEWIS SEHON ENGLISH, b. ib. May 25, 1864; m. ib. June 5, 1887, *Virginia Hoover* (b. near ib. Feb. 14, 1865); he is a clerk with the Ohio River Ry., at Parkersburg, W. Va.

        (a). EUGENE ENGLISH, b. Point Pleasant, W. Va., Nov. 27, 1889.

    b. MARY STUART ENGLISH, b. ib. March 25, 1867; m. ib. April 26, 1887, *Edward Francis Recktenwald* (b. Logan, Ohio, Nov. 12, 1864; he is in the U. S. Postal Service); l. Charleston, W. Va.

        (a). FREDERICK LAWRENCE RECKTENWALD, b. Point Pleasant, W. Va., Jan. 26, 1888.

        (b). LEWIS RICHARD RECKTENWALD, b. ib. Oct. 11, 1890.

        (c). FRANCIS ENGLISH RECKTENWALD, b. Charleston, W. Va., Jan. 28, 1897.

        (d). MARY MARGUERITE RECKTENWALD, b. ib. Aug. 28, 1900.

c. MARGARET LYNN ENGLISH, b. Point
Pleasant, W. Va., April 28, 1869; m. ib.
June 15, 1889, *Dr. Lewis VanGilder Guthrie*
(b. ib. Jan. 8, 1868; he is the Physician in
charge of the Hospital for the Insane at
Spencer, W. Va).
   (a). KATHLEEN LEWIS GUTHRIE, b.
   Point Pleasant, W. Va., May 5, 1891.
d. JOHN WARTH ENGLISH, b. ib. Feb. 16,
1874; he is a physician at Bramwell, W. Va.
e. FANNIE ENGLISH, b. Point Pleasant, W.
Va., Dec. 23, 1874; d. ib. Sep. 23, 1881.
f. FREDERICK LEE ENGLISH, b. ib. April 17,
1876; d. ib. July 31, 1876.
g. JULIA WARTH ENGLISH, b. ib. July 31,
1878; d. ib. Oct. 7, 1881.
h. EUNICE ENGLISH, b. ib. May 4, 1881; m.
ib. Oct. 30, 1901, *Kossuth Tinker McKinstry*
(b. Albany, Ohio, July 8, 1878; he is a merchant); l. Point Pleasant, W. Va.
(2). SARAH ELIZABETH LEWIS, b. ib. Nov. 21,
1841; l. ib.
(3). MATILDA LEWIS, b. ib. April 7, 1844; d.
Staunton, Aug. 29, 1845.
(4). AGNES STUART LEWIS, b. Point Pleasant,
W. Va., June 13, 1846; m. ib. June 14, 1876,
Columbus Sehon (b. Mason County, W. Va., May
3, 1841); l. Huntington, W. Va.
   a. JOHN STUART SEHON, b. Point Pleasant,
   W. Va., Oct. 28, 1878; d. Columbus, Ohio,
   Jan. 21, 1897.
   b. ANNIE CAMDEN SEHON, b. Point Pleasant, W. Va., Feb. 28, 1882.
(5). MARGARET LYNN LEWIS, b. ib. July 18, 1850;
d. ib. Feb. 22, 1885.

§30 6. MATILDA KINNEY STRIBLING, b. Staunton, Nov.
28, 1816; d. ib. Nov. 2, 1892; m. ib. June 8, 1843,
Nicholas Kinney Trout, her second cousin; see TROUT
FAMILY, §101.

7. SARAH ANN STRIBLING, b. ib. Dec. 3, 1817; d. ib. April 8, 1841.

§31 8. MARGARET FRANCES STRIBLING, b. ib. Sep. 2, 1819; d. "Smithfield", Clarke County, Nov. 22, 1860; m. Staunton, Oct. 31, 1839, *William Dickerson Smith* (b. "Smithfield", June 21, 1815; d. ib. March 19, 1894; see §92).

9. HARRIOT MILTON STRIBLING, b. Staunton, April 20, 1821; d. ib. Nov. 27, 1870.

10. WILLIAM MAGNUS STRIBLING, b. ib. Dec. 7, 1822; d. Dayton, Ohio, April 24, 1902; m. Circleville, Ohio, Sep. 5, 1844, *Anna Maria Crouse* (b. ib. Jan 8, 1826; d. ib. Oct. 30, 1891); he was an M. D. graduate of the University of Pennsylvania in 1843, practiced medicine some years, and was afterwards a farmer.

(1) FANNIE MATILDA STRIBLING, b. Circleville, Ohio, Dec. 7, 1846; m. ib. Oct. 16, 1867, *Edward Doane Moore* (b. ib. Dec. 20, 1844; d. ib. May 30, 1885; he was a dentist by profession, but never practiced; was President of the City Gas Works); 1. Circleville, Ohio.

  a. ARCHIBALD STRIBLING MOORE, b. ib. Feb. 21, 1869; d. Eureka, Kansas, Oct. 30, 1872.

  b. MABEL MOORE, b. Circleville, Ohio, July 4, 1874; m. ib. Jan. 3, 1901, *Percy Ansell Walling* (b. ib. Feb. 14, 1870; he is a lawyer); 1. ib.

  c. HOWARD BENFORD MOORE, b. ib. Jan. 17, 1876; graduated at the Harvard Law School in June 1902.

(2). FLORA KINNEY STRIBLING, b. Circleville, Ohio, Sep. 17, 1848; d. ib. April 27, 1857.

(3). EVANS CROUSE STRIBLING, b. ib. June 19, 1850; d. Mason County, W. Va., Sep. 12, 1851.

(4). CHARLES ARTHUR STRIBLING, b. Circleville, Ohio, July 29, 1852; m. Columbus, Ohio, Oct. 18, 1876, *Harriette Margaret Williams* (b. ib. Feb. 14, 1856; d. ib. Nov. 7, 1901); he is an architect and a director in the City Deposit Bank); 1. ib.

a. ANNA NAOMI STRIBLING, b. ib. Nov. 5,
1877; m. ib. Feb. 2, 1898, *William Weston
Wood* (b. ib. May 3, 1875; he is in the coal
business); l. ib.
b. EDWARD WILLIAMS STRIBLING, b. ib.
Nov. 19, 1881; l. ib.
(5). ERASMUS GRANT STRIBLING, b. Circleville,
Ohio, July 29, 1852; d. ib. May 8, 1857.
(6). JOHN LEWIS STRIBLING, b. ib. July 12, 1857;
m. ib. June 21, 1894, *Emma Alice Hurdle* (b. ib.
Aug. 10, 1863; d. ib. Jan. 18, 1900); he is general manager of the light plant at Circleville, O.
(7). WILLIAM MAGNUS STRIBLING, b. ib. July
11, 1859; d. ib. June 5, 1895.
(8). ROBERT EVANS STRIBLING, b. ib. Jan. 25,
1862; d. ib. April 6, 1874.

§32   11. JOHN WAYT STRIBLING, b. Staunton, April 1–,
1824; d. Orange County, Va., Feb. 17, 1864; m.
Winchester, May 17, 1849, *Anne McCormick*; see
MILTON FAMILY, §179; he was a merchant in Baltimore, Md.
(1). BETTIE TAYLOR STRIBLING, b. Baltimore,
Md., Feb. 14, 1850; d. ib. Feb. 16, 1850.
(2). BUSHROD TAYLOR STRIBLING, b. ib. Sep. 5,
1851; m. Bell County, Texas, Dec. 18, 1890,
Margaret Anna Rich (b. ib. April 26, 1870);
l. Rogers, Bell Co., Texas; he is a farmer.
(3). ALICE MAUDE STRIBLING, b. Winchester,
July 17, 1854; m. Berryville, Sep. 23, 1873, *Randolph Kownslar* (b. ib. July 18, 1850; he is a farmer); l. Gindale P. O , Bell County, Texas.
a. ALICE MAUDE KOWNSLAR, b. Berryville,
Aug. 14, 1874; d. ib. Dec. 25, 1879.
b. RANDOLPH KOWNSLAR, b. ib. July 3, 1876;
l. Limestone County, Tex.; he is a farmer.
c. ELLEN JETT KOWNSLAR, b. Berryville,
Sep. 19, 1878; l. Gindale, Texas.
d. ELIZABETH SINCLAIR KOWNSLAR, b. Berryville, Dec. 5, 1879; d. ib. Feb. 10, 1884.
e. CONRAD KOWNSLAR, b. ib. Aug. 11, 1886.

  f. HARRIOT HAMMOND KOWNSLAR, b. Roanoke, Jan. 7, 1892; d. Gindale, Texas, March 31, 1900.
 (4). MARY LEWIS STRIBLING, b. Winchester, Aug. 25, 1856; d. ib. Sep. 23, 1856.
 (5). WILLIAM MCCORMICK STRIBLING, b. Staunton, Sep. 10, 1857; d. ib. Oct. 2, 1858.
 (6). EDWARD MCCORMICK STRIBLING, b. ib. June 1, 1859; d. Washington, D. C., March 25, 1892; m. Berryville, Jan. 11, 1883, *Lydia Kownslar* (b. ib. May 22, 1856; she is a sister of Randolph Kownslar mentioned above; 1. ib.); he was a farmer near Berryville.
  a. RANDOLPH KOWNSLAR STRIBLING, b. Berryville, Oct. 23, 1883; d. ib. July 4, 1884.
  b. EDWARD MCCORMICK STRIBLING, b. ib. June 4, 1885.
  c. JOHN WRIGHT STRIBLING, b. ib. April 5, 1887.
  d. ANNIE MAUDE STRIBLING, b. ib. April 5, 1887.

§33 II. TALIAFERRO STRIBLING, b."Hopewell", about 1785; d. Clarke County, May 4, 1850, "aged 65"; m near Martinsburg, W. Va., Jan. 18, 1814, *Mary Tate*, his first cousin, (b. ib. in 1792; d. Washington, D. C., July 31, 1885, "aged 93"; see Note 2, §89); he was a physician, and lived first at Charlestown, W. Va , and then at Berryville.
 1. MAGNUS TATE STRIBLING, b. Frederick County, Nov. 23, 1814; d. ib. Aug. 15, 1833.
 2. ANN TALIAFERRO STRIBLING, b. ib. Dec. 21, 1817; d. Washington, D. C , June 8, 1854; m. "Roselawn", Frederick County, Nov. 7, 1837, *James Jones Miller* (b. Leesburg, Oct. 18, 1812; d. Denton, Ky., Dec. 5, 1898; p. Samuel Miller and Hannah Potter. He was connected with the Indian and Post Office Departments of the Government, and was later an editor and publisher at Lexington, Ky.).

§34 (1). MARY TALIAFERRO MILLER, b. "Roselawn", Dec. 6, 1840; m. Frankfort, Ky., Nov. 7, 1865,

DR. TALIAFERRO STRIBLING
33

Magnus Stribling Thompson, her first cousin; see §36.

(2). ANNIE WALLACE MILLER, b. Charlestown, W. Va., July 30, 1842; m. Ashland, Ky., Oct. 17, 1861, *Charles Scott Dodge Jones* (b. Sinsinewa Mound, Wis., Sep. 23, 1832; d. Dubuque, Iowa, Jan. 1889; p. Senator George Wallace Jones of Iowa, and Mary Josephine Gregoire; gr. p. Judge John Rice Jones of the Supreme Court of Missouri. He was a lawyer by profession; served on the staff of General Bushrod Johnson in the Confederate Army); l. Washington, D. C.

   a. NANNIE STRIBLING JONES, b. and d. Richmond, in 1862.

   b. MARY JOSEPHINE JONES, b. near Richmond, in 1864; l. Washington, D. C.

   c. KATHARINE STRIBLING JONES, b. Dubuque, Iowa, Feb. 8, 1867; m. Washington, D. C., Nov. 1, 1892, *Clarence Edward Dawson* (b. "Kendal Green", Md., July 31, 1869; p. Edward Matthews Dawson and Clara Cox; gr. p. Edward Matthews Dawson and Susan Hambleton Parrott—Dr. Christopher Christian Cox and Amanda Northrup. He has been Private Secretary to the Post Master General of the United States); l. Chevy Chase, Md.

     (a). KATHARINE THELMA DAWSON, b. Washington, D. C., Nov. 22, 1895.

     (b). CLARENCE EDWARD DAWSON, b. ib. Jan. 18, 1899.

     (c). WALLACE STRIBLING DAWSON, b. Chevy Chase, Md., May 21, 1901.

   d. GEORGE WALLACE JONES, b. Sioux City, Iowa, in 1869; he is connected with the Post Office Department in Washington, D. C.

   e. MARY TALIAFERRO JONES, b. Dubuque, Iowa, Sep. 23, 1871; m. Washington, D. C., July 3, 1895, *John Josephus Lordan* (b. Galveston, Texas; he is a lawyer in New York City).

f. ELIZA BEN JONES, b. Dubuque, Iowa, May
31, 1876; m. Baltimore, Md., Aug. 28, 1895,
Willis Owen Hohenstein (b. in Missouri,
Sep. 9, 1872; he is manager for Armour's
establishment in Washington, D. C.).
  a. WILLIS OWEN HOHENSTEIN, b. ib.
   June 29, 1896.
  b. RALPH WALLACE HOHENSTEIN, b. ib.
   Jan. 16, 1900.
(3). CHARLES TALIAFERRO MILLER, b. Charlestown, W. Va., Nov. 16, 1846; m. Cincinnati, O.,
June 9, 1879, *Fannie Colden Moore* of Cincinnati
(p. Cadwallader Colden Moore and Mary Augusta
Farrell; gr. p. John Moore and Lydia Stevens).
He is a clerk in the Treasury Department at
Washington, D. C.
  a. CHARLES COLDEN MILLER, b. ib. April 7,
   1882; e. Georgetown College; 1. Washington,
   D. C.
(4). ELLWOOD STRIBLING MILLER, b. Charlestown,
W. Va., Oct. 8, 1848; m. Covington, Ky., Oct.
5, 1875, *Lollie Blanks Ward* (b. ib. June 27, 1856;
p. Robert D. and Margaret Blanks Ward). He
is a wholesale merchant at Covington, Ky.
  a. ROBERT WARD MILLER, b. ib. Dec. 30,
   1891.
  b. VIRGINIA STRIBLING MILLER, b. ib. Mch.
   3, 1895.

§35 3. CATHERINE MACKEY STRIBLING, b. Frederick Co.,
March 4, 1820; d. Sioux City, Iowa, May 14, 1874; m.
"Roselawn", Frederick Co., Nov. 7, 1837, *William
Broadus Thompson* (b. Culpeper Co., Aug. 8, 1816; d.
Purcellville, July 28, 1883; p. Capt. Meriweather
Thompson and Martha Broadus. He was a lawyer
in Frederick County).
 (1). WILLIAM TALIAFERRO THOMPSON, b. "Roselawn", Oct. 26, 1840; e. University of Virginia;
m. *1st*. Hancock, Md., Jan. 14, 1868, *Sarah
Bridges* of that place (d. ib. April 27, 1869); m.
2nd. Berryville, June 11, 1872, *Ann Eliza White*

(see McIlhany Family, §126); m. *3rd*. Mars Bluff, S. C., July 28, 1885, *Mrs. Julia Adams-Gregg* (b. Society Hill, S. C., Feb. 10, 1852; d. Columbia, S. C., Nov. 25, 1898); m. *4th*. Charleston, S. C., March 12, 1900, *Agnes Buist* (b. Cheraw, S. C., June 11, 1875). He was Captain of Co. D. 8th Missouri Cavalry, Army of Trans-Mississippi, C. S. A. He is now pastor of the Eckington Presbyterian Church in Washington, D. C. The degree of D. D. was conferred upon him by the University of Kansas in 1885. He had one child by the first marriage, one by the second, and two by the third.

 a. Henry Percival Parr Thompson, b. Hancock, Md., Oct. 21, 1868; e. Hampden-Sidney College and Charleston Medical College; m. Washington, D. C., Nov. 14, 1894, *Helen Grace Lowdermilk* (b. Cumberland, Md., Jan. 14, 1871); he is a physician at Washington, D. C.

  (a). William Percival Thompson, b. ib. Dec. 21, 1896.

 b. Mary Elzey Thompson, b. "Locust Thicket", Loudoun County, Aug. 28, 1873; l. Washington, D. C.

 c. William Taliaferro Thompson, b. Charleston, S. C., April 28, 1886; l. Washington, D. C.

 d. Magnus McKeever Thompson, b. Charleston, S. C., March 6, 1892; d. ib. July 3, 1892.

(2). Martha Lee Thompson, b. "Roselawn", Dec. 31, 1844; m. *1st*. Berryville, May 18, 1867, *Philip Roach* (b. Alexandria; d. in Texas in 1874); m. *2nd*. Sioux City, Iowa, Nov. 7, 1876, *John Wesley Young* (b. Boston, Mass., April 17, 1843; p. John Wesley Young and Annie Damon. He is a clerk at the Navy Yard in Washington).

 a. John Wesley Young, b. Sioux City, Iowa, Aug. 30, 1877; he is connected with

a wholesale stationery firm in New York City.
b. MAGNUS TALIAFERRO YOUNG, b. Sioux City, Iowa, Nov. 2, 1878; he is in business in New York City.
c. GEORGE HARRY DAMON YOUNG, b. Sioux City, Iowa, April 21, 1882; l. Washington, D. C.
d. GEORGE WILLIE YOUNG, b. Sioux City, Iowa, Sep. 22, 1887; l. Washington, D. C.

§36 (3). MAGNUS STRIBLING THOMPSON, b. "Roselawn", July 31, 1846; m. Frankfort, Ky., Nov. 7, 1865, *Mary Taliaferro Miller*, his first cousin; see §34. He served through the entire Civil War, first as a courier to "Stonewall" Jackson, and then in the 35th Va. Cavalry. He is a clerk in the Navy Department at Washington.

§37 4. MARY ELIZABETH STRIBLING, b. "Roselawn", in 1827; d. "Clerenront", near Berryville, July 14, 1853, "aged 26"; m. "Hopewell", Frederick County, Feb. 4, 1847, *Edward McCormick*, her second cousin; see MILTON FAMILY, §175.

§38 III. FRANCIS STRIBLING, b. "Hopewell", about 1787; d. "Montcalm", Loudoun Co., in 1828; m. *1st.* "Ithaca", Loudoun Co., Jan. 16, 1815, *Cecilia McIlhany* (see MCILHANY FAMILY, §132); m. *2nd.* "Kenilworth", Frederick Co., June 17, 1823, *Rebecca Littler* (d. about May 1, 1826; p. Samuel Littler and Ann Williams of Frederick County). He was at first a soldier, and afterwards a farmer at "Montcalm". About the time of his second marriage he was elected to the Virginia Legislature. The following record of his military service is found in the War Department at Washington: "Appointed Ensign, Rifle Regiment, 3 May, 1808; promoted second lieutenant 1 July, 1809; appointed first lieutenant, Light Artillery Regiment, 1 March, 1811; promoted Captain 1 November, 1813, and resigned May 1, 1816." He had five children by the first marriage and one by the second.

§39 1. MARGARET ANN STRIBLING, b. "Hopewell", Dec. 3, 1815; e. Woodstock and Leesburg; m. "Ithaca",

CAPT. FRANCIS STRIBLING
⁇ 38

Nov. 1, 1832, *Alexander Kilgour* (b. "Hollybush", St. Mary's Co., Md., Sep. 3, 1799; d. "The Pines", near Rockville, Md., Aug. 31, 1869; see §143); l. "The Pines".

(1). WILLIAM KILGOUR, b. Rockville, Md., July 24, 1833; e. Charlotte Hall, and St. John's College, Annapolis, Md.; m. Rockville, Md., Oct. 24, 1858, *Rose Ellen Queen* (b. ib. June 9, 1834; d. ib. Sep. 9, 1886; p. Charles Joningham Queen and Maria Purcell). He was at one time State's Attorney in Alexandria; is now an editor and lawyer at Rockville, Md. He has served three terms at different times in the state Legislature.

    a. ANNIE STRIBLING KILGOUR, b. ib. Sep. 4, 1859; d. Alexandria, June 20, 1877.

    b. MARY CARTER KILGOUR, b. Rockville, Md. Jan. 2, 1863; l. ib.

(2). CECILIA STRIBLING KILGOUR, b. ib. Jan. 8, 1835; d. "Clifton", Jan. 16, 1902; e. Brookeville Female Academy; m. "The Pines", Oct. 27, 1863, *Samuel Jones* (b. near Rockville, Md., July 31, 1820; d. "Clifton", near Rockville, Md., Sep. 14, 1891; p. John and Katherine Jones).

    a. FRANCIS KILGOUR JONES, b. ib. Nov. 7, 1864; d. ib. Jan. 10, 1898.

    b. SAMUEL MADDOX JONES, b. ib. Jan. 31, 1865; studied law at Columbian University, Washington, D. C., and is practicing in Baltimore, Md.

    c. MARGARET ALEXANDER JONES, b. "Clifton", Dec. 23, 1867; e. Academy of the Visitation, Frederick City, Md.; l. "Clifton".

    d. WILLIAM KILGOUR JONES, b. ib. Feb. 20, 1871; l. ib.

    e. CATHERINE JHON JONES, b. ib. June 18, 1873; e. Academy of the Visitation, Frederick City, Md.; m. Rockville, Md., March 8, 1899, *Albert J. Allder;* he is farming at Woodbridge, Prince William County; they have two children.

f. JAMES DECATUR JONES, b. "Clifton", June 22, 1878; d. ib. June 2, 1880.

§40   (3). FRANCIS STRIBLING KILGOUR, b. Rockville, Md., Oct. 10, 1836; e. ib.; m. Loudoun County, Nov. 22, 1870, *Margaret McIlhany Heaton*, his first cousin (see § 44). He served through the entire civil war in General Rosser's Brigade, 35th Va. Cavalry. He is farming at "The Pines", Montgomery County, Md.
    a. MATTIE CHILTON KILGOUR, b. ib. Sep. 7, 1871; d. ib. Jan. 31, 1896.
    b. CECILIA DECATUR KILGOUR, b. ib. Nov. 7, 1873; e. Wesleyan Female Institute, Staunton; l. "The Pines."
    c. JANE HAGUE KILGOUR, b. ib. Mch. 31, 1876; e. Rockville Seminary; l. "The Pines."
    d. ALEXANDER KILGOUR, b. ib. Nov. 9, 1878; d. ib. Oct. 27, 1900.
    e. LYDIA HEATON KILGOUR, b. ib. April 26, 1880; m. Potomac Church, Montgomery Co., Md., Aug. 7, 1901, *Dr. Ralph Francis Stribling Porter*, her second cousin (see § 42).
    f. ELLA NEWTON KILGOUR, b "The Pines", Feb. 28, 1885; l. ib.

(4). MARY LOUISA KILGOUR, b. Rockville, Md., July 21, 1838; d. ib. August 11, 1839.

(5). CHARLES JOURDAN KILGOUR, b. ib. March 30, 1840; d. Washington, D. C., Oct. 1, 1863.

(6). MARTHA MATILDA KILGOUR, b. "The Pines", May 14, 1842; d. Rockville, Md., Dec. 24, 1900; e. Rockville Seminary; m. "The Pines", Feb. 21, 1865, *Capt. Alexander Wheeler Chilton* (b. Kingston, Canada, Feb. 19, 1837; d. Alexandria, Jan. 8, 1882; p. Alexander Chilton of Canada. He was a Captain in the U. S. Army, and at the time of his death was city Judge of Alexandria).

(7). SARAH EDGERTON KILGOUR, b. "The Pines", Feb. 5, 1845; e. Rockville Seminary, and Maryland State Normal School in Baltimore; l. "The Pines".

(8). VIRGINIA KILGOUR, b. ib. Dec. 19, 1847; e. Washington, D. C.; d. Baltimore, Md., Oct. 27, 1878; m. "The Pines", Oct. 27, 1875, *Charles Oscar Vandeventer* (b. "Locust Grove", Loudoun Co., Oct. 10, 1849; p. Washington Vandeventer and Cecilia Braden of Loudoun Co.; gr. p. Joseph Vandeventer. He was a civil engineer with the Western Maryland R. R., and is now living at Hagerstown, Md.).

    a. BRADEN VANDEVENTER, b. "Locust Grove", May 5, 1878; e. Danville Military Institute and Washington and Lee University; is practicing law at Newport News.

(9). ALEXANDER KILGOUR, b. "The Pines", April 8, 1855; e. Washington, D. C. He was for some years State's Attorney of Montgomery County, Md.; is now practicing law at Rockville, Md.

§41   2. FRANCIS JAMES STRIBLING, b. "Hopewell", Feb. 3, 1817; e. Winchester; d. Parkersburg, W. Va., Nov. 19, 1889; m. "Wood Grove", Loudoun Co., in Nov. 1838, *Amanda Mary Ann Heaton* (b. ib. June 8, 1821; d. Parkersburg, W. Va., June 22, 1875; p. Dr. Jonathan Heaton and Patience Osborne; gr. p. Dr. James Heaton and Hannah Smith). In Loudoun County he was Captain of a militia company. He was a member of the city council in Parkersburg, W. Va., and was for more than fifty years connected with the B. & O. Railroad at different places.

(1). MARGARET ELIZABETH STRIBLING, b. "Wood Grove", Oct. 5, 1839; graduated at the Wheeling Female College; m. Parkersburg, W. Va., Feb. 29, 1876, *James Lafayette Hugh Longest* (b. Westmoreland Co., Oct. 28, 1824; p. Louis L'Ongest and Mary Pitts. He is farming at "Nauvoo", near Bon Air).

    a. AMA STRIBLING LONGEST, b. ib. March 26, 1877; graduated at the Richmond Female Seminary; m. Washington, D. C., Dec. 12, 1899, *Lynnwood Cheilds Moody* (b. Manchester, Jan. 12, 1875); 1. "Nauvoo".

(2). CECILIA MCILHANY STRIBLING, b. Loudoun Co.; e. Fetterman, W. Va.; l. Pittsburg, Penn.

(3). JONATHAN HEATON STRIBLING, b. "Wood Grove", March 7, 1846; e. Parkersburg, W. Va., and Cincinnati, O.; d. Parkersburg, W. Va., Mch. 17, 1885; m. ib. May 19, 1880, *Bettie Neal* (b. ib. Aug. 15, 1858; p. Geo. W. Neal and Carrie McKinley; gr. p. Capt. Jas. Neal. She has since married Mr. George Franklin Bowles of New Orleans, La.). He was a merchant in Parkersburg, W. Va.

    a. CARRIE HEATON STRIBLING, b. ib. Nov. 26, 1882; is a student at the Sophie Newcomb College, New Orleans, La.

(4). MARY JEANNETTE STRIBLING, b. Cumberland, Md.; e. Parkersburg and Point Pleasant, W. Va.; l. Pittsburg, Penn.

(5). ERASMUS MORTIMER STRIBLING, b. Fetterman, W. Va.; e. Parkersburg, W. Va.; m. ib. *Lottie Ingold* of that place. He is connected with the B. & O. Railroad at Philadelphia, Penn.

    a. PERCY STRIBLING, b. Parkersburg, W. Va., June 26, 1883; l. ib.

    b. FLORENCE STRIBLING, b. ib. March 19, 1886; l. Pittsburg, Penn.

    c. EDNA MAY STRIBLING, b. Parkersburg, W. Va., in May, 1888; d. ib. in 1890.

§42   3. ERASMUS MORTIMER STRIBLING, b. "Ithaca", Loudoun County, June 13, 1818; e. in Kentucky; d. Loudounville, O., Apr. 15, 1857; m. Springfield, O., Oct. 11, 1848, *Mrs. Caroline Mary Mott–Wilson* (b. Mt. Vernon, O., Nov. 19, 1821; p. Samuel Mott and Lurena Newell of Connecticut; gr. p. John Mott, of the Revolutionary War, and Mary Rowley of Connecticut —Riverius Newell, also of the Revolution, and Sarah Peek of Connecticut; l. Chicago, Ill.). He was chief civil engineer for the S. M. V. and P. R. R., with his home at Springfield, Ohio.

(1). ALBERT STRIBLING, b. ib. July 28, 1849; d. ib. Aug. 23, 1850.

(2). MARY FRY VIRGINIA STRIBLING, b. ib. Dec. 29, 1851; e. ib. and at the Mendota Lutheran College. She has been instructor in music at Cornell College, Mt. Vernon, Iowa.

(3). CAROLINE CECILIA STRIBLING, b. Springfield, O., Sep. 8, 1855; e. ib. and at the Mendota Lutheran College; m. Mendota, Ill., Oct. 21, 1873, *John Alexander Porter* (b. La Salle Co., Ill., Oct. 21, 1852; p. Peter Latchair Porter and Mary Smith; gr. p. John Porter and Ann Latchair—James Smith and Sarah Eaken); l. Chicago, Ill.

    a. RALPH FRANCIS STRIBLING PORTER, b. Fairfield, Ia., Nov 22, 1875; e. Chicago and Eureka, Kan., and took the degree of M. D. at Rush Medical College, Chicago, in 1897; m. Potomac Church, Montgomery Co., Md., Aug. 7, 1901, *Lydia Heaton Kilgour*, his second cousin (see § 40). He was Asst. Surgeon of the 2nd Illinois Infantry during the Spanish war, and is now stationed in the Philippines as a surgeon in the U. S. Army.

4. ELIZABETH STRIBLING, b. "Ithaca" about May 1, 1820; d. ib. in infancy.

§43   5. CECILIA MCILHANY STRIBLING, b. ib. Apr. 5, 1822; e. in Fairfax County; d. "Sunnyside", Loudoun Co., Aug. 8, 1862; m. "The Pines", Montgomery Co., Md., Jan. 21, 1842, *Dr. James Decatur Heaton* (b. "Exedra", Loudoun Co., April 25, 1816; d ib. Feb. 21, 1859; p. Dr. James Heaton and Lydia Osborne, a sister of Patience Osborne, § 41; gr. p. John Heaton —Abner and Patience Osborne).

    (1). ALBERT HEATON, b. "Exedra", Aug. 31, 1844; d. Washington, Va., Apr. 18, 1864, of sickness contracted during service in the 8th Va. Infantry, C. S. A.

    (2). TOWNSEND HEATON, b. "Exedra", Sept. 1, 1846; took the M. D. degree at the Univ. of Pa.; d. Hamilton, Dec. 16, 1883; m. Baltimore, Md., Oct. 30, 1873, *Florence Janney* (b. Hardy Co , W. Va., Aug. 30, 1848; p. Geo. W. Janney and

Mary Compher of Loudoun Co.; gr. p. John Janney and Susan Wells of Loudoun Co. She has since married a Mr. Mercer and lives near Hamilton). He was a courier to Gen. D. H. Hill in the early part of the Civil War, and was afterwards a member of Mosby's Command, 43rd Va. Cavalry. He practiced medicine in Michigan.
  a. FLORENCE JANNEY HEATON, b. Ishpeming, Mich., April 27, 1878; e. Baltimore Woman's College; l. near Hamilton.

§44 (3). MARGARET MCILHANY HEATON, b. "Exedra", Aug. 23, 1848; e. Leesburg; m. Loudoun County, Nov. 22, 1870, *Francis Stribling Kilgour*, her first cousin; see § 40.

  (4). FRANCIS ERASMUS STRIBLING HEATON, b. "Exedra", Sept. 8, 1850; d. Leesburg, Feb. 8, 1868.

  (5). LYDIA HEATON, b. "Exedra", June 5, 1853; e. Winchester; d. Pæonian Springs, Sept. 9, 1885.

  (6). CECILIA DECATUR HEATON, b. "Exedra", Nov. 29, 1857; e. Hamilton; m. ib. Dec. 23, 1880, *Rodney Walter Braden* (b. "Elmwood", Loudoun County, Sept. 12, 1858; p. Rodney C. Braden and Eliza Ann Vandeventer; gr. p. John Braden and Mary Stephens—Joseph Vandeventer and Mary Means. He is farming at "Elmwood".).

   a. TOWNSEND HEATON BRADEN, b. ib. April 26, 1884; d. ib. Nov. 12, 1885.

   b. OSCAR STEPHEN BRADEN, b. ib. April 21, 1886.

   c. ALBERT VANDEVENTER BRADEN, b. ib. February 19, 1888.

   d. WALTER DOUGLAS BRADEN, b. ib. Sept. 11, 1891.

 6. ANNE ELIZABETH STRIBLING, b. Frederick County, March 30, 1824; l. Mt. Jackson.

IV. MAGNUS TATE STRIBLING, b. "Hopewell", about 1789; he served in the war of 1812 in a troop of horse, then sailed for several years, and afterwards engaged in the flour business in Alexandria. He died unmarried about 1835.

§45 V. SIGISMUND STRIBLING, b. "Hopewell", about 1791; d. Frederick Co., now Clarke Co., in 1822; m. ib. Nov. 7, 1820, *Sarah Elizabeth Taliaferro Ware* (b. ib. about 1797; d. ib. April 16, 1878; see Note 3, § 91). He was a lawyer and lived in Frederick County. His only child was—
  1. SIGISMUNDA STRIBLING, b. ib. in Aug. 1821; d. Orkney Springs, Sept. 16, 1879; m. Clarke County, June 13, 1848, *Charles Edmund Kimball* (b. Baltimore, Md., Dec. 22, 1823; d. Macon, Ga., May 4, 1887; p. Leonard Kimball and Sarah Yates Smith; gr. p. Edmund and Rebecca Kimball of Bradford, Mass.,—Charles and Mary Yates Smith of Lancaster, Pa. He was a Major in the Confederate Army, and a farmer in Clarke county).
    (1). THEODORE HORATIO KIMBALL, b. Hardwicke, Clarke County, Nov. 8, 1854; d. Pensecola, Fla., Dec. 29, 1900; m. Independence, Kan., Feb. 16, 1886, *Mary Nolte* of that place. Their only child,
      a. WILLIE KIMBALL, died in infancy.
    (2). WILLIAM WARE KIMBALL, b. Hardwicke, August 3, 1857; e. Va. Theological Seminary; m. Macon, Ga., June 5, 1889, *Violet Wrigley* (b. ib. July 11, 1869). He is a minister of the Episcopal Church at Darlington, Md.
      a. ANNIE LUCY KIMBALL, b. Milledgeville, Ga., July 9, 1890.
      b. FLORETTA KIMBALL, b. Versailes, Ky., July 31, 1892.
      c. WILLIAM WARE KIMBALL, b. Waycross, Ga., Oct. 9, 1894; d. ib. Oct. 15, 1894.

§46 VI. MARY TATE STRIBLING, b. "Hopewell", about 1793; d. "Woodland", June 2, 1820; m. "Hopewell", Jan. 14, 1813, *Col. James Crawford* (b. Augusta Co., in 1787; d. "Woodland", May 11, 1855, "aged 68"; p. George Crawford; he was a lawyer and for a long time Presiding Justice of the County, and lived at "Woodland", near Staunton; he served in the war of 1812; he married secondly Mrs.

Margaret Allen Bell–Crawford, by whom he had ten children).
1. FRANCIS GEORGE CRAWFORD, b. "Woodland", Dec. 23, 1813; d. Greenwood, Miss., about 1856, unmarried.

§47 2. ERASMUS STRIBLING CRAWFORD, b. "Woodland," March 16, 1815; d. Memphis, Tenn., Feb. 7, 1865; m. Christian County, Ky., Sept. 4, 1840, *Elvira Ann West* (b. ib. Nov. 12, 1816; d. Memphis, Tenn., August 1, 1896); he was a wholesale grocer at Vicksburg, Miss., till 1859, when he removed to Memphis, Tenn.

(1). MARY STRIBLING CRAWFORD, b. Vicksburg, Miss., Nov. 15, 1842; d. St. Louis, Mo., March 11, 1891; m. Memphis, Tenn., June 29, 1868, *Captain Charles Tilghman Biser* (b. Burkitsville, Md., about 1837; d. St. Louis, Mo., March 13, 1896; he was a Captain in the Confederate Army, and afterwards engaged in the real estate business).

a. WEST CRAWFORD BISER, b. Memphis, Tenn., May 20, 1870; he is a lawyer in St. Louis, Mo.

(2). WEST JAMES CRAWFORD, b. Madison County, Miss., Nov. 1, 1844; m. Memphis, Tenn., Nov. 11, 1874, *Anna Louise Thompson* (b. Chickasaw County, Miss., May 20, 1850). He is President of the Commercial Appeal Publishing Company, Memphis, Tenn.

a. ERASMUS STRIBLING CRAWFORD, b. ib. August 13, 1875.

b. KATE THOMPSON CRAWFORD, b. ib. Dec. 4, 1877.

c. MARIANNE WEST CRAWFORD, b ib. June, 21, 1886.

(3). ERASMUS STRIBLING CRAWFORD, b. Vicksburg, Miss., in 1846; d. ib. in infancy.

(4). BETTIE ANN CRAWFORD, b. ib. May 15, 1849; m. Memphis, Tenn., Sep. 3, 1872, *Richard Dudley Jordan* (b. Hampton, Oct. 7, 1842; he is a lawyer); 1. Memphis, Tenn.

THE STRIBLING FAMILY. 61

  a. LOUISE CRAWFORD JORDAN, b. ib. June 7, 1873; m. ib. April 9, 1902, *William Louis Davis* (b. August 13, 1871; he is a wholesale dry goods merchant in Nashville, Tenn.).
  b. LAURA BANKS JORDAN, b. Memphis,Tenn., Feb. 3, 1875.
  c. ELVIRA JORDAN, b. ib. Jan. 22, 1879.
  d. RICHARD DUDLEY JORDAN, b. ib. April 27, 1887.
  e. WEST CRAWFORD JORDAN, b. ib. April 24, 1889.
 (5). VIRGINIA CRAWFORD, b. Vicksburg, Miss., in 1851; d. ib. in infancy.
 (6). IDA FLORENCE CRAWFORD, b. ib. May 1, 1853; d. Memphis, Tenn., Sept. 5, 1868.
 (7). ELVIRA LOUISE CRAWFORD, b. Vicksburg, Miss., March 23, 1856; m. Memphis, Tenn., Jan. 13, 1881, *Julius Alexander Taylor* (b. La Grange, Tenn., Feb. 6, 1840; d. Memphis, Tenn., August 1, 1895; he was a lawyer); l. ib.
  a. MARGARET TAYLOR, b. ib. March 14, 1882.
  b. WARREN CRAWFORD TAYLOR, b. ib. Sept. 23, 1885.
  c. LOUISE FOWLER TAYLOR, b. ib. August 15, 1889.

§48 3. MAGNUS WILLIAM CRAWFORD, b. "Woodland", April 18, 1817; d. Louisville, Ky., Nov. 12, 1896; m. *1st.* Seville, Madison Co., January 16, 1837, *Margaret Mildred Simms* (b. ib. March 5, 1818; d. Locust Grove, Greene County, Sept. 14, 1863; p. William and Eliza Simms); m. *2nd.* Stanardsville, Greene County, Jan. 10, 1867, *Mrs. Emily Amanda White* (b. Seville, Feb. 10, 1824; d. Locust Grove, in Aug. 1879; she was a sister of his first wife); he was a farmer, and lived in Madison and Greene counties; he had seven children by his first marriage, none by the second.
 (1). JAMES WILLIAM CRAWFORD, b. Augusta County, Dec. 28, 1838; m. Culpeper County, November 27, 1877, *Lucy Barbour Gaines* (b.

Locust Hill, Culpeper County, February 15, 1855); 1. Cincinnati, O ; he is a salesman.
- a. GEORGE LEE CRAWFORD, b. Culpeper, August 19, 1878.
- b. FRANCES KENNETH CRAWFORD, b. Hurricane, W. Va., November 30, 1883.
- c. FLORA VIRGINIA CRAWFORD, b. Richmond, Ky., Nov. 7, 1887.
- d. JAMES EDWIN CRAWFORD, b. Cincinnati, O., Sept. 1, 1892.

(2). MARY ELIZA CRAWFORD, b. Augusta County, Dec. 3, 1841; m. Charlottesville, March 15, 1882, *Joseph William May* (b. Amherst County, June 6, 1846; his first wife was her sister Margaret Flora; see below); 1. Indianapolis, Ind.

(3). FRANK HENRY CRAWFORD, b. near Staunton, April 3, 1843; d. Locust Grove, August 17, 1863.

(4). MARGARET FLORA CRAWFORD, b. near Staunton, June 11, 1845; d. Albemarle County, June 12, 1881; m. Greene County, May 7, 1878, *Joseph William May*, who afterwards married her sister Mary; see above.
- a. WILLIAM ALFRED MAY, b. Orange County, June 10, 1879; d. ib. June 11, 1879.
- b. CORA LEE MAY, b. Albemarle County, Dec. 25, 1880; d. Catlettsburg, Ky., Nov. 20, 1881.

(5). MAGNUS SIMMS CRAWFORD, b. near Staunton, in 1848; d. Richmond, Nov. 20, 1895; m. Greene County, Dec. 22, 1866, *Eliza Virenda Simms*, his first cousin (b. ib. March 21, 1844; d. ib. June 28, 1870); they had no children; he served with Col. Mosby in the Confederate Army.

(6). ERASMUS STRIBLING CRAWFORD, b. near Staunton, Feb. 1, 1852; m. Fairfield, Kanawha County, W. Va., Sep. 23, 1883, *Nancy Jane Porter* (b. ib. June 20, 1866); he is farming at Fairfield, W. Va.

THE STRIBLING FAMILY. 63

  a. ANNIE MILDRED CRAWFORD, b. ib. Aug. 5, 1884.
  b. WILLIAM HENRY CRAWFORD, b. ib. July 28, 1886.
  c. FRANK LEE CRAWFORD, b. ib. May 6, 1890; d. ib. August 22, 1890.
  d. KENNA CRAWFORD, b. ib. July 15, 1891.
  e. MARY MAY CRAWFORD, b. ib. March 22, 1894.
 (7). AMANDA MILDRED CRAWFORD, b. near Staunton, Feb. 24, 1855; d. ib. April 7, 1855.
4. JAMES SAMUEL CRAWFORD, b. "Woodland", Aug. 29, 1818; d. in Texas, in Dec. 1853, leaving a widow and one daughter, of whom nothing is known.

§49 5. MARY TATE CRAWFORD, b. "Woodland", Jan. 19, 1820; d. Washington, Rappahannock County, Va., April 16, 1860; m. near Staunton, Sept. 3, 1840, *Jechonias Yancy Menefee* (b. near Sperryville, April 15, 1815; d. Washington, Va., Nov. 9, 1888. He was a lawyer at Washington, being for some time Commonwealth's Attorney for the County).
 (1). MARY ELLA MENEFEE, b. Washington, Va., May 4, 1842; m. ib. Sept. 26, 1837, *William Franklin Anderson* (b. Rappahannock County, June 2, 1840. He served through the Civil War in the Confederate Army. He was formerly a merchant, and is now paymaster of the West Va. Pulp and Paper Company, at Covington, Va.).
  a. MARY STRIBLING ANDERSON, b. Washington, Va., July 27, 1868; m. ib. Nov. 24, 1897, *Rev. Joseph Howard Gibbons* (b. Washington D. C., Dec. 22, 1870; he is Rector of the Episcopal Church at Point Pleasant, W. Va.).
   (a). MARY ELLA GIBBONS, b. Stafford County, Dec. 19, 1898.
   (b). JOSEPH HOWARD GIBBONS, b. Covington, Feb. 20, 1901.
  b. SARAH JOSEPHINE ANDERSON, b. Washington, Va., April 30, 1870.

    c. BESSIE CARROLL ANDERSON, b. Washington, Va., Nov. 2, 1871; m. Winston, N. C., Dec. 18, 1895, *David Lincoln Luke* (b. Wilmington, Del., May 14, 1865); 1. Piedmont, W. Va.

        (a). JEAN ANDERSON LUKE, b. ib. Dec. 4, 1896.

        (b). DOROTHY LUKE, b. ib. Dec. 11, 1897.

        (c). DAVID LINCOLN LUKE, b. ib. Jan. 5, 1899.

        (d). MARY ANDERSON LUKE, b. ib. June 28, 1901.

    d. DORA MENEFEE ANDERSON, b. Washington, Va., March 27, 1875.

    e. WILLIAM FRANKLIN ANDERSON, b. Hawthorne, March 28, 1881.

    f. IDA MOFFETT ANDERSON, b. ib. Dec. 2, 1882.

(2). HENRY ST. CYR MENEFEE, b. Washington, Va., June 18, 1844. He served in the 6th Va. Cavalry and with Mosby's Men in the Civil War. He is now a lawyer at Washington, Va.

(3). JAMES CRAWFORD MENEFEE, b. ib. in 1846. He is farming at "Avondale", near Washington, Va.

(4). VIRGINIA FLORENCE MENEFEE, b. Washington, Va., July 8, 1848; 1. ib.

(5). FRANCIS GEORGE MENEFEE, b. ib. Dec. 25, 1850; graduated at the V. M. I.; m. *Mrs. Sarah Skinner* of Santa Cruz, Cal., where he is cashier of the Santa Cruz County Bank.

(6). ELVIRA MENEFEE, b. ib. in 1853; d. ib. in 1854.

(7). IDA STRIBLING MENEFEE, b. ib. March 12, 1854; m. ib. Oct. 1, 1878, *Horatio Gates Moffett* (b. "Glenwood", near ib., March 30, 1854; he is a lawyer; was at one time Commonwealth's Attorney for the County); 1. "Glenwood".

a. WILLIAM FRANKLIN MOFFETT, b. Hawthorne, Sep. 28, 1879.
b. MARY LOU MOFFETT, b. "Glenwood", Sept. 3, 1880.
c. HENRY ST. CYR MOFFETT, b. Washington, Va., Nov. 5, 1883.
d. NETTIE GATES MOFFETT, b. "Glenwood", July 15, 1892; d. ib. August 20, 1892.
e. HORATIO GATES MOFFETT, b. ib. March 21, 1894.
(8). DORA MENEFEE, b. Washington, Va., Aug. 19, 1858; l. ib.
(9). NITA McDONALD MENEFEE, b. ib. Nov. 10, 1860; d. ib. Dec. 16, 1898.

§50 VII. NANCY TATE STRIBLING, b. "Hopewell", June 30, 1795; d. "Norwood", Clarke County, Dec. 24, 1847; m. "Hopewell", Sept. 20, 1815, *Lewis Neill* (b. Frederick County, May 9, 1794; d. "Norwood", July 28, 1836; p. Joseph Neill and Rebecca McPherson; he was a merchant, and a farmer at "Norwood").

1. JOSEPH LEWIS NEILL, b. ib. Dec. 9, 1817; d. ib. Oct. 1, 1818.
2. WILLIAM HENRY NEILL, b. ib. Oct. 1, 1819; d. ib. July 24, 1820.
3. A daughter, b. and d. ib. August 15, 1821.
4. LEWIS NEILL, b. ib. May 13, 1823; e. West Point Military Academy; was a Lieutenant in the U. S. Army; d. in Mexico, Jan. 13, 1850, of a wound received in the Mexican War.

§51 5. SIGISMUND STRIBLING NEILL, b. "Norwood", Oct. 18, 1825; d. Berryville, Nov. 23, 1895; e. University of Va., and Medical Department of the University of Penn.; m. Winchester, June 11, 1850, *Catherine Snickers Baldwin* (b. Winchester, March 31, 1827; d. Berryville, Dec. 23, 1890; see Note 3, §93); he was a surgeon in the Confederate Army, and afterwards a physician at Berryville.

§52 (1). CATHERINE STUART NEILL, b. "Norwood", April 27, 1851; m. Berryville, Oct. 19, 1898, *William Hierome Thomas Lewis* (b. "The Rocks",

Jefferson County, W. Va., April 30, 1832; see §88); 1. Myerstown, Jefferson County, W. Va.
  (2). ANNIE REBECCA NEILL, b. "Norwood", August 20, 1853; d. Berryville, July 14, 1894.
  (3). LEWIS NEILL, b. ib. Jan. 16, 1858; d ib. March 26, 1863.
  (4). MARY BALDWIN NEILL, b. ib. April 5, 1860; d. ib. May 23, 1885.
  (5). JOHN MACKEY BALDWIN NEILL, b. ib. April 28, 1866; e. Roanoke College; m. Berryville, Dec. 19, 1895, *Ellen Douglas MacDonald* (b. Bullitt County, Ky., Oct. 3, 1870); he is deputy clerk of the county and circuit courts at Berryville
    a. JOHN BALDWIN NEILL, b ib. Oct 3, 1896.
    b. WILLIAM MACDONALD NEILL, b. ib. Sept. 28, 1901.

§53 6. ANN REBECCA NEILL, b. "Norwood", January 13, 1830; d. Clarke County, July 31, 1853; m. ib. in 1852, *Thomas McCormick* of "Elmington", as his second wife; see §200.
  7. MARY NEILL, b. "Norwood", Oct 2, 1831; d. Frederick County, Nov. 26, 1895; m. Clarke County, Feb. 17, 1857, *Joseph Marx Barton* (b. Richmond, March 26, 1835; p. Richard W. Barton and Caroline Marx of Frederick County; gr. p. Richard Peters Barton and Martha Walker; l. near Kernstown).
    (1). ANN NEILL BARTON, b. Frederick County, Nov. 22, 1857; d. ib. Jan. 8, 1879.
§54   (2). SAMUEL MARX BARTON, b. ib. May 9, 1859; graduated as A. B. and Ph. D. at the University of Va.; m. Winchester, Dec. 28, 1897, *Mary Millicent Tidball* (b. ib. March 18, 1866); he is Professor of Mathematics in the University of the South, Sewanee, Tenn.
      a. MARY NEILL BARTON, b. Winchester, March 20, 1899.
      b. HELEN THRUSTON BARTON, b. Sewanee, Tenn., July 2, 1900.

THE STRIBLING FAMILY. 67

 (3). LEWIS NEILL BARTON, b. Frederick County,
Dec. 15, 1860; m. Winchester, April 20, 1892,
Elizabeth Cover (b. Baltimore County, Md., Oct.
24, 1868; d. Winchester, Dec. 11, 1897); he is a
banker in Winchester.
  a. THOMAS COVER BARTON, b. ib. April 5,
1893.
  b. LEWIS NEILL BARTON, b. ib. Nov. 11,
1894.
  c. JOSEPH MARX BARTON, b. ib. March 14,
1896.
 (4). CAROLINE MARX BARTON, b. Frederick
County, Oct. 18, 1862; l. near Kernstown.
 (5). WILLIAM BARTON, b. ib. May 17, 1864; d.
ib. Feb. 3, 1865.
 (6). JOSEPH MARX BARTON, b. ib. Jan. 19, 1866;
d. ib. Nov. 11, 1881.
 (7). CHARLES MARX BARTON, b. ib. June 14,
1867; d. ib. Jan. 28, 1868.
 (8). FREDERICK MARX BARTON, b. ib. Nov. 28,
1868; m. Carlisle, Penn., Oct. 20, 1897, *Rose
Beula Getter* (b. "Maple Grove", Cumberland
County, Penn., Feb. 25, 1874); he is agent for the
Cumberland Valley R. R. at Carlisle, Penn.

§55 VIII. THOMAS STRIBLING, b. "Hopewell", about 1797; d.
New Orleans, La., in Nov. 1833; m. near Winchester,
June 17, 1823, *Rachel Ann Littler* (b. ib. in 1806; d. Springfield, Ill., June 5, 1868.) He was a merchant, but at
the time of his death was farming. He was murdered in
New Orleans while on his way to Texas to buy land.
 1. MARIA LOUISA STRIBLING, b. near Winchester, in
Feb. 1826; d. Winchester, Jan. 1, 1848.
 2. PORTIA HOPKINS STRIBLING, b. Winchester, Sept.
9, 1828; l. Springfield, Ill.; m. Lexington, Ky., Oct.
29, 1850, *Andrew Jackson Barry* (b. ib. June 6, 1825;
d. Columbus, Ky., in the summer of 1865, where he
was practicing law; his father, William T. Barry, was
Postmaster General under President Andrew Jackson).
  (1). WILLIAM TAYLOR BARRY, b. Woodford
County, Ky., Sept. 3, 1851; d. ib. Nov. 25, 1854.

(2). SIGISMUND STRIBLING BARRY, b. Lexington,
Ky., Dec. 28, 1852; d. Normal, Ill., Sept. 23,
1872.

(3). ARMISTEAD MASON BARRY, b. Woodford
County, Ky., June 16, 1854; m. Springfield, Ill.,
June 20, 1888, *Emily Gertrude Canfield* (b. Port
Elizabeth, N. J., Oct. 8, 1850); he is a retired
farmer, living at Columbus, Ky.
    a. EMILY GERTRUDE BARRY, b. Minneapolis,
Minn., April 15, 1889.
    b. ARMISTEAD MASON BARRY, b. ib. Oct. 7,
1890.
    c. MARY VREDENBURGH BARRY, b. ib. Sept.
6, 1892.

(4). LOUISA STRIBLING BARRY, b. Newport, Ky.,
March 31, 1856; d. Springfield, Ill., July 9, 1902;
m. ib. April 30, 1884, *Augustus Louis Ulrich* (b.
ib. August 2, 1854; he is a grain dealer at Springfield, Ill.).
    a. BARRY STRIBLING ULRICH, b. Chicago,
Ill., July 6, 1888.
    b. PORTIA MARGARET ULRICH, b. ib. Sept. 9,
1889.
    c. EDWRAD VON REISENCAMP ULRICH, b. ib.
Sept. 29, 1893.

(5). WILLIAM TAYLOR BARRY, b. Columbus, Ky.,
Nov. 26, 1858; m. *1st*. Chicago, Ill., March 30,
1891, *Lillian Morse* (b. Mobile, Ala., Jan. 5,
1866; d. Florence, Ariz., Feb. 4, 1894); m. *2nd*.
San Francisco, Cal., May 28, 1901, *Julia Victoria
Morse*, a sister of his first wife (b. Mobile, Ala.,
Sept. 16, 1873); he is a physician at Salinas,
California.
    a. WILLIAM TAYLOR BARRY, b. San Bernadino, Cal., Jan. 15, 1892.
    b. DAVID MORSE BARRY, b. Florence, Arizona, Jan. 12, 1894.

(6). CATHARINE MASON BARRY, b. Columbus,
Ky., Dec. 22, 1861; m. Chicago, Ill., Oct. 17,
1893, *Alfred Charles Le Baron*; l. Springfield, Ill.

a. MASON ETHELBERT LE BARON, b. San
Bernardino, Cal., April 28, 1895.
b. LOUIS ULRICH LE BARON, b. San Jose,
Cal., Dec. 27, 1897.
3. SIGISMUND TAYLOR STRIBLING, b. near Huntington, W. Va., Nov. 22, 1830; d. Point Lookout, Aug. 22, 1864.
4. MARGARET ANN STRIBLING, b. near Huntington, W. Va., July 20, 1834; d. Richmond, Va., Jan. 21, 1884; m. *1st*. Lexington, Ky., Oct. 29, 1850, *Samuel Preston Humphreys* (b. in Kentucky, June 28, 1828; d. in New Mexico, about 1856); m. *2nd*. Springfield, Ill., August 28, 1876, *Henry Emery Coleman Baskerville* (b. Lombardy Grove, Va., Oct. 14, 1817; d. Richmond, Jan. 14, 1900; he was a merchant in early life, but retired from active business about the time of his marriage).
(1). DAVID CARLYSLE HUMPHREYS, b. Woodford County, Ky., January 13, 1852; d. Santa Barbara, Cal., July 6, 1893.
(2). THOMAS STRIBLING HUMPHREYS, b. Woodford County, Ky., Oct. 31, 1853; d. Jacksonville, Fla., Nov. 28, 1893.

§56 IX. MARGARET PERRY STRIBLING, b. "Hopewell", April 11, 1800; d. Mt. Jackson, July 18, 1861; m. "Hopewell", May 28, 1823, *Joel Pennybacker* (b. Shenandoah County, August 9, 1793; d. Mt. Jackson, April 5, 1862; he was a lawyer and served several terms as State Senator. His house, called "The White House", was situated at Pine Forge, four miles south of Mt. Jackson).
1. MARY CRAWFORD STRIBLING PENNYBACKER, b. Woodstock, March 22, 1824; d. Lebanon, Pa., Oct. 20, 1900; m. Pine Forge, Oct. 24, 1844, *Lemuel Allen* (b. near Mt. Jackson, June 6, 1820; d. Mt. Jackson, Dec. 16, 1900; p. Rhesa Allen and Catharine Kingree; he was a farmer at "Greenwood", near Mt. Jackson, and at San Angelo, Tex.).
(1). FRANCIS TALIAFERRO ALLEN, b. "Greenwood", July 29, 1848; d. Mt. Jackson, Oct. 24, 1872.

(2). JOSEPH RHESA ALLEN, b. "Greenwood", Jan. 26, 1850; d. Ft. Worth, Tex., Dec. 15, 1895; e. Roanoke College; m. Tom Green County, Tex., Nov. 2, 1882, *Martha Frances Grooms* (b. Key West, Fla., July 19, 1861; 1. Ft. Worth, Texas).
    a. RHESA ALLEN, b. San Angelo, Tex., Dec. 31, 1883; d. ib. Jan. 2, 1884.
    b. IDA FRANCES ALLEN, b. ib. Jan. 18, 1885.
    c. JOSEPH STRIBLING ALLEN, b. ib. March 23, 1887.
    d. ELIZABETH JOSEPHINE ALLEN, b. ib. March 9, 1890.
    e. ANNIE REBECCA ALLEN, b. Itaska, Tex., Sept. 21, 1894.

(3). LEMUEL ETHAN ALLEN, b. "Greenwood", Oct. 10, 1852; e. Roanoke College; m. San Angelo, Tex., Dec. 8, 1880, *Minnie Annie Fisher* (b. in Germany, Aug. 21, 1865); 1. San Angelo, Texas.
    a. FRANK PENNYBACKER ALLEN, b. ib. April 26, 1882.
    b. GEORGE FISHER ALLEN, b. ib. Oct. 21, 1883; d. Mansfield, Ark., Nov. 21, 1887.
    c. LEMUEL ETHAN ALLEN, b. San Angelo, Tex., July 18, 1886.
    d. EDNA MATILDA ALLEN, b. ib. Dec. 2, 1888.
    e. RUDOLPH ROBERT ALLEN, b. ib. Nov. 28, 1891.

(4). FLORENCE WILLELMA ALLEN, b. "Greenwood", Shenandoah County, August 17, 1858; m. Mt. Jackson, Oct. 20, 1887, *Rev. William Elias Stahler* (b. Norristown, Pa., July 3, 1858; he is a Lutheran minister at Lebanon, Pa.).
    a. ALAN DONALD STAHLER, b. ib. Oct. 12, 1897.

2. SARAH ANN PENNYBACKER, b. Woodstock, in 1826; d. "The White House", in May 1842.

3. CAROLINE PENNYBACKER, b. ib. in 1828; d. ib. at eighteen months of age.

§57   4. GEORGE MAYBERRY PENNYBACKER, b. ib. Feb. 2, 1830; d. Mt. Jackson, Dec. 14, 1893; m. *1st.* Richmond, July 11, 1854, *Julia Egbertine Wortham* (b. near Richmond, Oct. 31, 1834; d. Paris, Tex., Sept. 1, 1873); m. *2nd.* Baltimore, Md., Dec. 3, 1878, *Rebecca Jane Oliver* (b. ib. in 1834; l. Baltimore, Md.); he was a physician, and lived for many years at Paris and at Honey Grove, Texas, but returned to Virginia before his death.

    (1). PERCY VIVIAN PENNYBACKER, b. Paris, Tex., Feb. 17, 1856; d. Nevada, Mo., May 15, 1899; m. Tyler, Tex., Oct. 31, 1884, *Anna J. Hardwicke* (b. Petersburg, Va., May 7, 1861; l. Austin, Tex.; she is the author of a History of Texas used extensively in the schools of the State); he was Superintendent of Public Schools in Palestine, Tex.

        a. LORINE PENNYBACKER, b. Tyler, Texas, August 18, 1885; d. ib. Jan. 6, 1886.

        b. PAUL BONNER PENNYBACKER, b. Jefferson, Texas, April 10, 1888.

        c. PERCY VIVIAN PENNYBACKER, b. Palestine, Texas, Jan. 7, 1895.

        d. RUTH PENNYBACKER, b. ib. Feb. 24, 1897.

    (2). MAUD PENNYBACKER, b. Paris, Tex., Aug. 19, 1857; d. Delta County, Tex., Oct. 28, 1878.

    (3). JULIAN PENNYBACKER, b. Lamar County, Tex., March 28, 1862; m. Honey Grove, Tex., April 20, 1887, *Jennie Stephens* (b. West Station, Miss., Sept. 30, 1866); he is a wholesale book dealer at Palestine, Tex.

        a. MAURINE EMILY PENNYBACKER, b. Honey Grove, Tex., Feb. 16, 1889; d. ib. Sept. 20, 1890.

        b. GEORGE OLIVER PENNYBACKER, b. ib. July 15, 1892.

        c. JULIAN WORTHAM PENNYBACKER, b. Palestine, Tex., August 16, 1895.

  d. Joe Pennybacker, b. ib. August 16, 1895;
d. ib. August 20, 1895.
  e. Charles Dana Pennybacker, b. ib.
June 19, 1897.
  f. Nina Pennybacker, b. ib. June 5, 1899.
 (4). Nina Pennybacker, b. Paris, Tex., Jan.
27, 1864; d. Bonham, Tex., Jan. 12, 1897; m.
Honey Grove, Tex., Nov. 4, 1884, *Leslie Curtis
White* (b. Russellville, Ala., Feb. 23, 1861; l.
Bonham, Tex.; he is a traveling salesman).
  a. Bertine White, b. Honey Grove, Tex.,
Oct. 16, 1885.
  b. Doris White, b. Bonham, Tex., July
22, 1889; d. ib. Feb. 8, 1896.
  c. Leslie Gordon White, b. ib. Feb. 29,
1892.
  d. Kennon Pennybacker White, b. ib.
July 20, 1893.
 (5). Adele Pennybacker, b. Paris, Tex., Dec.
2, 1866; m. Bonham, Tex., Oct. 10, 1888, *Benjamin Curtice Epperson* (b. New Iberia, La., Aug.
25, 1861; he is a lumber merchant at Pittsburg,
Texas).
  a. Adele Epperson, b. Jefferson, Tex., Oct.
6, 1889.

§58 5. Willelma Tate Pennybacker, b. "The White
House", April 28, 1832; d. Mt. Jackson, Feb. 6, 1861;
m. ib. Nov. 25, 1852, *Solomon Kingree Moore* (b.
Moore's Store, Shenandoah County, April 30, 1827;
d. Mt. Jackson, July 4, 1896; he lived at Mt. Jackson).
 (1). Magnus Stribling Moore, b. ib. Feb. 21,
1855; m. *1st.* San Angelo, Tex., May 13, 1878,
Fannie Groomes of Key West, Fla.; m. *2nd.* Mt.
Jackson, May 2, 1883, *Cora Alice Ritenour* (b.
Buck Hill, Nov. 29, 1864); he is a jeweler at
Mt. Jackson; he had one child by the first marriage and two by the second.
  a. Florence Willelma Moore, b. San Angelo, Tex., Feb. 24, 1879; m. Ft. Worth,

Tex., June 24, 1897, *Samuel McHam* (b. Lamar County, Tex., Feb. 6, 1872); l. Ft. Worth, Tex.
    (a). IRENE MCHAM, b. ib. May 14, 1898.
  b. WILLELMA GOLDIE MOORE, b. Mt. Jackson, March 24, 1885.
  c. CLARENCE ROBERT MOORE, b. ib. Sept. 16, 1888.
 (2). ARTHUR LEWIS MOORE, b. ib. Nov. 8, 1855; he is a stock dealer at Onawa, Iowa.
 (3). MARY EGBERTINE MOORE, b. Mt. Jackson, Jan. 21, 1859; d ib. March 12, 1861.
6. REBECCA JANE PENNYBACKER, b. "The White House", April 12, 1834; d. Mt. Jackson, March 21, 1881.
7. MARGARET MUSE PENNYBACKER, b. "The White House", June 12, 1836; l. New York City.
8. JOEL PENNYBACKER, b. "The White House", Sept. 7, 1838; e. Roanoke College; d. Sioux City, Iowa, about 1876; m. St. Louis, Mo., August 8, 1866, *Eliza Marie Power* (b. Calonmel, Ireland, August 19, 1846; d. St. Louis, Mo., Feb. 6, 1900); he was a salesman.
 (1). EDWARD FRANCIS PENNYBACKER, b. ib. March 17, 1867; m. ib. Oct. 31, 1900, *Elizabeth Loretta O'Rourke* (b. ib. July 6, 1878); l. ib.; he is chief clerk for a railroad.
  a. EDWARD RAYMOND PENNYBACKER, b. ib. Dec 8, 1901.
 (2). MADELINE PENNYBACKER, b. ib. Sept. 22, 1869; m. ib. August 1, 1896, *William Edwin Matthews* (b. Biglyville. Tenn., Jan. 31, 1870; he is a traveling salesman); l. Memphis, Tenn.
  a. WILLIAM EDWARD MATTHEWS, b. ib. Feb. 14, 1901.

§59 9. FRANCIS STRIBLING PENNYBACKER, b. "The White House", Sept. 26, 1840; e. Roanoke College; m. "Locust Thicket", Loudoun County, Dec. 4, 1867, *Lucy Ellzey White* (b. ib. Feb. 6, 1846; see MCILHANY FAMILY, §126); he served through the Civil War in the

6th Va. Cavalry; he is now in the insurance business at Mt. Jackson.

§60 X. GEORGE WILLIAM STRIBLING, b. "Hopewell", April 9, 1802; d. Point Pleasant, W. Va., Oct. 29, 1851; m. *1st.* Mason County, W. Va., April 10, 1828, *Mary Nelson Neale* (b. Loudoun County, Sept. 10, 1802; d. Point Pleasant, W. Va., April 15, 1843; p. William Presley Neale and Nancy Maria Smith); m. *2nd.* Staunton, Dec. 8, 1845, *Mary King* (b. Norfolk, in 1812; d. Point Pleasant, W. Va., May 11, 1849); he was a lawyer, and for a number of years clerk of the circuit court of Mason County. He had four children by his first marriage and one by the second.

1. NANNIE TATE STRIBLING, b. Point Pleasant, W. Va., March 17, 1829; d. ib. Sept. 5, 1867; m. ib. April 20, 1853, *William Smith* (b. Jan. 6, 1823; d. April 1, 1890; he was a merchant at Point Pleasant).
    (1). FRANCIS STRIBLING SMITH, b. ib. in May, 1854; l. in Connecticut; m. *Kittie Lane*, a Presbyterian minister's daughter, and had two daughters,
        a. BESSIE SMITH.
        b. NELLIE SMITH.
    (2). OLIVIA SMITH, b. Point Pleasant, W. Va., March 1, 1856; d ib. June 20, 1856.
    (3). MARY SMITH, b. ib. March 16, 1858; d. ib. March 18, 1858.
    (4). LEWIS NELSON SMITH, b. ib. April 5, 1859; d. ib. May 18, 1859.
    (5). EDGAR GARRISON SMITH, b. ib. Jan. 11, 1861; is living in Minnesota.
2. FRANCIS STRIBLING, b. Point Pleasant, W. Va., Sept. 5, 1831; d. Staunton, Sept. 27, 1850.
3. TALIAFERRO STRIBLING, b. Point Pleasant, W.Va , Feb. 17, 1834; d. ib. April 7, 1893; m. Hancock, Md., Dec. 4, 1862, *Mary Louise Byers* (b. Sharpsburg, Md., Jan. 9, 1835; d. Point Pleasant, W. Va., August 23, 1891; p. John A. and Charlotte M. W. Byers); he studied law at Washington College in 1853–'54; was

THE STRIBLING FAMILY. 75

Cashier of the Merchants' National Bank of Point
Pleasant, W. Va.
  (1). A daughter, b. and d. ib. Sept. 23, 1863.
  (2). GEORGE WILLIAM STRIBLING, b. ib. Sept 2,
    1864; e. West Va. University; m Elm Grove,
    W. Va., June 17, 1896, *Annette Katherine Long*
    (b. Mason County, W. Va., Nov. 26, 1870; p.
    James W. Long and Katherine Hannan); he is
    Secretary and Treasurer of the Municipal Engin-
    eering and Construction Company of Baltimore.
  (3). KATE BYERS STRIBLING, b. Point Pleasant,
    W. Va., July 16, 1866; l. ib.
  (4). NANNIE TATE STRIBLING, b. ib. Feb. 6,
    1868; d. ib. Sept. 15, 1868.
  (5). TALIAFERRO STRIBLING, b. ib. July 16, 1869;
    e. West Va. University; he is Assistant Cashier
    of the Merchants' National Bank at Point Pleas-
    ant, W. Va.
4. MATILDA JANE STRIBLING, b. ib. August 1, 1836;
  d. Pleasant Flats, W. Va., July 27, 1892; m. Point
  Pleasant, W. Va., April 29, 1862, *Andrew Chapman
  Waggener* (b. Edgehill, W. Va., Jan. 24, 1837; p.
  Col. C. B. Waggener and Margaret Lewis; gr. p. Maj.
  Andrew C. Waggener and Attarah Beall—Thomas W.
  Lewis and Eliza A. Beall); he is a farmer in Mason
  County, W. Va.
  (1). CHARLES BEALL WAGGENER, b. Point Pleas-
    ant, W. Va., March 2, 1863; d. ib. July 5, 1863.
  (2). GEORGE STRIBLING WAGGENER, b. ib. July
    17, 1864; d. ib. Jan. 23, 1867.
  (3). LEWIS STUART WAGGENER, b. ib. Feb. 3,
    1866; d. ib. Jan. 17, 1867.
  (4). ANDREW CHAPMAN WAGGENER, b. ib. April
    25, 1868; d. ib. Nov. 22, 1868.
  (5). GRAHAM BEALL WAGGENER, b. Pleasant
    Flats, W. Va., May 29, 1870; m. ib. Sept. 27,
    1893, *Clara Estelle Windon* (b. Mason County,
    W. Va., August 20, 1872); he is a farmer in
    Mason County, W. Va.

a. GRAHAM WINDON WAGGENER, b. Kanawha County, W. Va., May 15, 1895.
b. ERNEST CHAPMAN WAGGENER, b. ib. March 2, 1898.
c. JAMES SAMUEL WAGGENER, b. ib. Sept. 18, 1900.
(6). MARY SUSAN WAGGENER, b. Pleasant Flats, W. Va., Feb. 19, 1872; 1. Maggie, Mason County, W. Va.
5. WILLIAM STARK STRIBLING, b. Point Pleasant, W. Va., June 8, 1847; d. ib. July 27, 1847.

§61 B. TALIAFERRO STRIBLING, b. Frederick County, about 1758; was living there in 1784, but probably died shortly afterwards unmarried, as nothing further is known of him.

§62 C. ANN STRIBLING, b. Frederick County, about 1760; d. "Milton Valley", near Berryville, Jan. 15, 1811; m. "Hopewell", July 20, 1782, *John Milton*. For their more than two hundred descendants see MILTON FAMILY, §§160–179.

§63 D. THOMAS STRIBLING, b. Frederick County, about 1761; d. Red House, Putnam County. W. Va., in 1821; m. Frederick County, Dec. 4, 1788, *Elizabeth Snickers* (b. ib. Nov. 11, 1761; d. ib. April 19, 1819; for her ancestry see §§ 91–93). He was a merchant at Battletown, now Berryville, and owned a great deal of property in that neighborhood, being one of the trustees of the town when it was established in 1798. About 1786 he made a very perilous journey to Boonsborough, Ky., by way of the Kanawha River and down the Ohio in a canoe, intending to establish a trading post with the Indians, but afterwards returned to Berryville; and about 1810 he removed to Kanawha, West Virginia.
I. WILLIAM S. STRIBLING, b. Berryville, in 1790; d. Malden, W. Va., in 1834; he never married.
§64 II. ROBERT MACKEY STRIBLING, b. Berryville, Feb. 14, 1793; d. "Mountain View", Aug. 24, 1862; graduated at the Philadelphia Medical College; m. Fauquier County,

THE STRIBLING FAMILY. 77

Jan. 29, 1818, *Caroline Matilda Clarkson* (b. ib. Feb. 8, 1800; d. "Mountain View", May 2, 1887; p. William Clarkson and Mildred Pickett); he was a physician, universally admired and beloved, and lived at "Mountain View", at Markham, Fauquier County, Va. Several of his children married descendants of Chief Justice John Marshall. See Paxton's "Marshall Family", pp. 54, 55, 99, 100, etc.

1. WILLIAM CLARKSON STRIBLING, b. "Mountain View", June 22, 1819; d. "Hartlands", in Jan. 1868; m. Columbia, Mo., *Mildred Pickett Clarkson*, his first cousin (b. "Belleview", near Warrenton; d. "Hartlands", Sept. 2, 1890; p. Henry M. Clarkson and Marion Morson Payne); he was a physician and lived at "Hartlands".
    (1). HENRY CLARKSON STRIBLING, b. ib. about 1848; d. ib. about 1851.
    (2). ROBERT MACKEY STRIBLING, b. ib. August 27, 1850; d. ib. Dec. 29, 1883.
    (3). MARION MORSON STRIBLING, b. ib. Jan. 15, 1852; m. Markham, *Dr. Walter Bruce*, who has since died; 1. Fredericksburg.
    (4). WILLIAM CLARKSON STRIBLING, b. "Hartlands", Oct. 13, 1853; m. St. Louis, Mo., Nov. 6, 1889, *Martha McKittrick* (b. ib. Jan. 12, 1866; d. ib. Nov. 5, 1892); he has recently retired from the wholesale shoe business in St. Louis, Mo.
        a. MILDRED CLARKSON STRIBLING, b. ib. August 23, 1890.
        b. WILLIAM CLARKSON STRIBLING, b. ib. Jan. 27, 1892.
    (5). ELIZABETH STRIBLING, b. "Hartlands", Feb. 14, 1855; m. ib. June 22, 1881, *John Hunton Foster* (b. The Plains, June 18, 1848; d. Marshall, Jan. 31, 1898; he was a merchant at Marshall); 1. Alexandria.
        a. THOMAS REDMON FOSTER, b. Marshall, Sept. 7, 1882.
        b. MILDRED CLARKSON FOSTER, b. ib. Oct. 11, 1886.

(6). THOMAS EDWARD STRIBLING, b. "Hartlands",July 13, 1857; m. Jacksonville, Fla., *Mary Hart* of that place; 1. Markham.
    a. MILDRED CLARKSON STRIBLING, b. Jacksonville, Fla., in August, 1880; d. ib. in May, 1881.
    b. WILLIAM CLARKSON STRIBLING, b. ib. in the winter of 1881; d. "Hartlands", June 19, 1882.

(7). JOHN SCOTT STRIBLING, b. ib. in 1860; d. ib. Feb. 27, 1862.

(8). CAROLINE MATILDA STRIBLING, b. ib. Feb. 27, 1862; 1. Alexandria.

(9). ANNE SCOTT STRIBLING, b. "Hartlands", March 3, 1864; d. Columbia, Mo., Feb. 28, 1887.

2. ELIZABETH SNICKERS STRIBLING, b. "Mountain View", May 20, 1821; d. ib. in June, 1846.

§65   3. MILDRED PICKETT STRIBLING, b. "Mountain View", Feb. 22, 1823; d. Culpeper, Dec. 1, 1898; m. "Mountain View", Sept. 17, 1861, *John Marshall* (b. "Leeds", Fauquier County, Oct. 9, 1822; d. "Glendale", near Markham, Feb. 1, 1877; he was a graduate of Princeton, practiced law in Alexandria and Warrenton, and after the Civil War lived at "Glendale").

    (1). ROBERT STRIBLING MARSHALL, b. Fauquier County, July 23, 1862; d. ib. April 2, 1864.

    (2). JAMES KEITH MARSHALL, b. ib. July 3, 1864; d. ib. Dec. 16, 1880.

    (3). CAROLINE STRIBLING MARSHALL, b. "Mountain View", July 30, 1866; m. ib. June 27, 1894, *Frederick Goodwin Ribble* (b. Nelson County, April 15, 1867; he is Rector of St. Stephens Episcopal Church at Culpeper).
        a. MILDRED STRIBLING MARSHALL RIBBLE, b. Lawrenceville, April 25, 1895.
        b. FRANCES LE BARON RIBBLE, b. Wytheville, August 13, 1896.
        c. FREDERICK DEANE GOODWIN RIBBLE, b. Culpeper, Jan. 14, 1898.

d. JOHN MARSHALL RIBBLE, b. ib. May 9, 1900.
4. THOMAS STRIBLING, b. "Mountain View", Oct. 24, 1825; d. "Oakwood", in June, 1846.
5. LUCY MARSHALL STRIBLING, b. "Mountain View", Oct. 17, 1827; d. ib. in Jan. 1828.
6. ROBERT MACKEY STRIBLING (1st), b. and d. ib. March 19, 1830.
7. CAROLINE STRIBLING, b. and d. ib. March 19, 1830.

§66 8. ANNE ELIZA STRIBLING, b. ib. Jan. 14, 1832; m. ib. Feb. 28, 1855, *Withers Waller* (b. "Clifton", Stafford County, April 28, 1825; d. ib. Jan. 14, 1900; he was a farmer at "Clifton", and conducted a large herring fishery; p. Withers Waller and Katherine Conway; gr. p. William Waller and Ursula Withers); l. "Clifton".

(1). KATHERINE HARWOOD WALLER, b. "Clifton", Jan. 24, 1857; l. Alexandria; m. Wytheville, July 19, 1876, *Rev. Robert South Barrett* (b. Milton, N. C., June 9, 1851; d. Wytheville, Sept. 12, 1896; he was an Episcopal minister and for two years General Missioner of the Church; he had the degree of D. D.).

a. ROBERT SOUTH BARRETT, b. Richmond, March 30, 1877; m. Atlanta, Ga., Nov. 17, 1898, *Annie Viola Tupper* (b. Leavenworth, Kan., Jan. 25, 1877); he is the general representative of the Southern Railway in the City of Mexico.

(a). ROBERT TUPPER BARRETT, b. Atlanta, Ga., Jan. 8, 1900.
(b). CLIFTON WALLER BARRETT, b. Alexandria, June 1, 1901.

b. WITHERS WALLER BARRETT, b. Richmond, July 2, 1878; d. Wytheville, August 30, 1878.
c. JOHN BARKER BARRETT, b. Richmond, August 30, 1879.
d. LILA WALLER BARRETT, b. Henderson, Ky., May 10, 1881.

The Stribling Family.

e. REBECCA HARVEY BARRETT, b. ib. Oct. 7, 1883.
f. CHARLES DODSON BARRETT, b. ib. Aug. 30, 1885.
g. KATHERINE STEEL BARRETT, b. Atlanta, Ga., Sept. 5, 1888.

(2). CAROLINE STRIBLING WALLER, b. Falmouth, Oct. 6, 1858; d. "Mountain View", in Aug. 1859.
(3). WILLIAM CLARKSON WALLER, b. Falmouth, July 3, 1860; d. Garrisonville, in March, 1862.
(4). NANNIE WITHERS WALLER, b. "Clifton", Feb. 28, 1862; m. Clifton Chapel, Dec. 7, 1887, *Richard Cassius Lee Moncure* (b. Glencairn, near Fredericksburg, Jan. 16, 1855; he is farming near Wide Water).
   a. WITHERS WALLER MONCURE, b. ib. Sept. 25, 1889; d. Garrisonville, July 16, 1891.
   b. RICHARD CASSIUS LEE MONCURE, b. Wide Water, May 20, 1892.
   c. LOUIS AVERY MONCURE, b. ib. Feb. 12, 1894.
   d. CAROLINE CLARKSON MONCURE, b. Garrisonville, Sept. 1, 1895.
   e. VIRGINIA ANDREWS MONCURE, b. Wide Water, March 12, 1899.

(5). AGNES WALLER, b. "Clifton", Jan. 25, 1864; m. Clifton Chapel, Dec. 7, 1887, *Robert Ambler Moncure* (b. Windsor Forest, July 12, 1864; he is farming near Stafford Court House).
   a. HENRY MONCURE, b. "Fleurrys", Stafford County, March 21, 1889.
   b. JULIA WARWICK MONCURE, b. ib. May 31, 1892.
   c. ANNE ELIZA STRIBLING MONCURE, b. ib. Feb. 4, 1895.
   d. ELIZABETH ELLEN ADIE MONCURE, b. ib. Nov. 1, 1897.
   e. ROBERTA AMBLER MONCURE, b. ib. May 31, 1899.

(6). MILDRED PICKETT WALLER, b. "Clifton", Jan. 5, 1866; 1. ib.
(7). CAROLINE STRIBLING WALLER, b. "Clifton", Aug. 17, 1867; m. Wide Water, April 27, 1887, *John North Caldwell* (b. Caldwell, W. Va., July 17, 1858; he is a farmer at Lewisburg, W. Va.).
    a. ANNE ELIZA WALLER CALDWELL, b. Caldwell, W. Va., Jan. 18, 1888.
    b. ISABEL EAKLE CALDWELL, b. ib. March 13, 1889.
    c. JAMES ROBERTSON CALDWELL, b. ib. July 3, 1892.
    d. ROBERT DENNIS CALDWELL, b. ib. Feb. 7, 1894.
    e. CAROLINE WALLER CALDWELL, b. ib. April 1, 1897.
    f. JOHN NORTH CALDWELL, b. ib. Feb. 24, 1899.
    g. MARTHA CALDWELL, b. Lewisburg, W. Va., Sept. 21, 1900.
(8). MARY CARY WALLER, b. "Clifton", July 30, 1869; m. Clifton Chapel, April 27, 1893, *Alfred Joseph Pyke* (b. Preston. England, August 23, 1865; he is farming at Wide Water).
    a. HANNAH CARR PYKE, b. "Richland", near Wide Water, Oct. 23, 1895.
    b. ANNE STRIBLING PYKE, b. ib. Oct. 15, 1897.
    c. MARY CARY PYKE, b. "Red Top", Stafford County, August 13, 1901.
(9). MARION STRIBLING WALLER, b. "Clifton", Sept. 27, 1871; 1. ib.
(10). NELLIE LEE WALLER, b. "Clifton", Feb. 27, 1876; 1. ib.

§67   9. ROBERT MACKEY STRIBLING, b. "Mountain View", Dec. 3, 1833; m. *1st.* "Morven", near Markham, August 19, 1857, *Mary Cary Ambler* (b. ib. Sept. 9, 1835; d. "Mountain View", Feb. 9, 1868); m. *2nd.* "Weyanoke", Charles City County, July 28, 1870, *Agnes Harwood Douthat* (b. ib. Dec. 28, 1849); 1.

"Mountain View". He studied at the University of Virginia and at a Medical College in Philadelphia; was Colonel of a regiment of artillery during the Civil War; and has served several terms in the Virginia Legislature. He had four children by his first marriage and three by the second.

(1). LETITIA AMBLER STRIBLING, b. near Markham, May 22, 1861; d. ib. Oct. 4, 1861.

(2). CAROLINE STRIBLING, b. "Morven", June 17, 1863; l. "Mountain View".

(3). THOMAS AMBLER STRIBLING, b. ib. Feb. 6, 1866; d. ib. Feb. 8, 1866.

(4). ROBERT CARY STRIBLING, b. ib. Oct. 5, 1867; d. Newport News, April 4, 1901; he was a lawyer.

(5). MARY DOUTHAT STRIBLING, b. "Mountain View", August 22, 1871; m. Markham, June 24, 1897, *George Howard Ford* (b. Memphis, Tenn., Oct. 25, 1871; he is teaching at the University School); l. Memphis, Tenn.

    a. AGNES HARWOOD FORD, b. ib. Jan. 14, 1899.

(6). AGNES HARWOOD STRIBLING, b. "Mountain View", Nov. 10, 1878; d. Wide Water, in April, 1884.

(7). WILLIAM CLARKSON STRIBLING, b. "Mountain View", April 18, 1885; l. ib.

§68   10. HENRY CLARKSON STRIBLING, b. "Mountain View", Oct. 4, 1836; m. "Leeds", June 16, 1869, *Rebecca Peyton Marshall* (b. ib. Nov. 5, 1847; d. "Clermont", Dec. 26, 1898); he is a farmer at "Clermont", near Hume, Fauquier County. He was a Lieutenant of Artillery during the Civil War.

(1). CLAUDIA BURWELL STRIBLING, b. "Ashley", June 11, 1870; l. "Clermont".

(2). ROBERT MACKEY STRIBLING, b. "Buck Farm", Jan. 1, 1872; d. Williamsburg, Sept. 2, 1897.

(3). HENRY CLARKSON STRIBLING, b. "Leeds", August 20, 1874; m. Kirkwood, Mo., June 28,

1900, *Susan Amelia Lawton* of St. Louis; 1. ib., where he is connected with the Tennent Shoe Co.

(4). JAMES KEITH MARSHALL STRIBLING, b. "Leeds", March 20, 1877; he is a salesman in St. Louis, Mo.

(5). GRAY CARROLL STRIBLING, b. "Leeds", May 20, 1879; he is a salesman in St. Louis, Mo.

(6). ELIZA JAQUELIN STRIBLING, b. "Clermont", Jan. 1, 1882; 1. ib.

III. EDWARD SNICKERS STRIBLING, b. Berryville, in 1794; d. Clarksburg, W. Va., March 9, 1818.

§69 IV. MATTHEW WRIGHT STRIBLING, b. Berryville, Oct. 16, 1796; d. Fauquier County, Sept. 25, 1845; graduated at the Philadelphia Medical College; m. Mercer's Bottom, Mason County, W. Va., Jan. 23, 1828, *Elizabeth Page Hereford* (b. Fauquier County, Jan. 29, 1800; d. Atchison, Kan., Dec. 29, 1872; p. Robert Hereford and Mary Mason Bronaugh); he lived and practiced medicine at Point Pleasant and Charleston, W. Va.; he was in the Virginia Legislature in 1828.

1. MARY CAROLINE STRIBLING, b. Fauquier County, March 20, 1829; d. Atchison, Kan., Dec. 15, 1872; e. Steubenville, Ohio; m. Marshall, Mo., March 3, 1858, *Junius Temple Hereford* (b. Charleston, W. Va., in 1830; d. Atchison, Kan., Nov. 17, 1872; he was a lawyer at Atchison).

    (1). FREDERICK STRIBLING HEREFORD, b. Atchison, Kan., August 1, 1860; d. Mercer's Bottom, W. Va., July 20, 1880.

2. MARGARET MASON STRIBLING (1st), b. Point Pleasant, W. Va., July 10, 1830; d. Putnam County, W. Va., Nov. 5, 1830.

3. MARGARET MASON STRIBLING (2nd), b. Charleston, W. Va., Dec. 31, 1831; d. Mercer's Bottom, W. Va., August 23, 1833.

4. ROBERT MACKEY STRIBLING, b. Charleston, W. Va., Jan. 30, 1834; d. St. Louis, Mo., Jan. 30, 1888; e. Drenen College, Ky., and graduated at the Ohio Medical College, Cincinnati. He was a surgeon

in the Confederate Army, and after the War practiced in St. Louis. He never married.

5. OTIS FRANCIS STRIBLING, b. Point Pleasant, W. Va., Sept. 13, 1836; e. Gallipolis, Ohio, and at the Lexington Law School, Va., now the Law Department of Washington & Lee University; m. Ben Lomond, W. Va., Nov. 9, 1869, *Virginia Caroline Neale* (b. ib. Nov. 24, 1839; p. Wm. P. Neale and Catherine Steenbergen; gr. p. Wm. Neale and Ann Smith, of Loudoun County.—Peter H. Steenbergen and Maria Jourdan); he is a farmer at Mercer's Bottom, Mason County, W. Va.

    (1). MATTHEW WEIGHTMAN STRIBLING, b. ib. Jan. 13, 1871; m. Point Pleasant, W. Va., Dec. 29, 1897, *Mary Margaret Hunter* (b. Ironton, Ohio, Oct. 3, 1873); he is a farmer at Mercer's Bottom, W. Va.

    (2). CATHERINE BEALE STRIBLING, b. ib. March 13, 1873; m. Huntington, W. Va., Dec. 26, 1899, *James Albert Young* (b. Magnolia, Ark., April 5, 1870; he is an insurance agent at Nashville, Tenn.).

    (3). ELIZABETH VIRGINIA CAROLINE STRIBLING, b. Mercer's Bottom, W. Va., August 18, 1875; d. ib. March 26, 1902.

    (4). WILLIAM NEALE STRIBLING, b. ib. Dec. 13, 1877; l. ib.

---

§70 E. WILLIAM STRIBLING, b. Frederick County, about 1763; d. ib. in the early part of 1793; m. ib. April 23, 1789, *Mrs. Sarah Berry-Humphreys*, widow of John Humphreys (who in his will, made July 8, 1775, approved March 4, 1777, mentions his wife, Sarah Humphreys, and her father Benjamin Berry, but no children), and daughter of Benjamin Berry of Berryville (who in deeds mentions his daughter Sarah Stribling and his grand-daughter Elizabeth T. Stribling). It is recorded in April, 1783, that William Stribling, orphan of Taliaferro Stribling, dec'd, chose Francis Stribling as his guardian. He was a merchant in Winchester, and at his early death left property valued at more than $8000.00. His wife must have been several years his senior, and she lived to an old age, dying in Butler County, Ky., in 1827. It was partly on her land that Berryville was established Jan. 15, 1798. In her will, a copy of which is on record in the Frederick court house, she mentions her two daughters.

 I. ELIZABETH T. STRIBLING, b. Winchester, about 1790; m. June 14, 1810, *George Steptoe Lane.* They had four children.

  1. MARY LANE, m. *Marshall Nicklin.* She left no children.

  2. ELIZABETH LANE, m. *Fisher Ames Lewis* of "The Rocks"; see §88. She lived only two years after marriage, and left no children.

  3. JOSEPH LANE, died unmarried.

  4. BENJAMIN LANE, died unmarried.

 II. DULCIBELLA W. STRIBLING, b Winchester about 1792; m. after 1815, *Edward Beeson*, and moved to Texas, leaving several children at her death.

§71 F. JOHN STRIBLING, b. Frederick County, about 1765; d. ib. about 1797; m. ib. January 20, 1792, *Sarah Drummond*, an only child of one John Drummond. After his death she married July 8, 1802, Alexander Ross Milton (see MILTON FAMILY, §146). He had two children.

 I. BUSHROD STRIBLING, b. Frederick County, Sept. 16, 1794; d. ib. unmarried August 18, 1824.

 II. JOHN STRIBLING, b. ib Oct. 11, 1796; d. ib. May 5, 1806.

§72. **Thomas Stribling,** the progenitor of the South Carolina branch of the family, was undoubtedly the son of Thomas and Elizabeth Taliaferro Stribling (see §22). While I have no positive proof of this connection. the following facts seem to indicate its certainty. Mr. J. W. Stribling of Seneca, S. C., writes that he has been unable to trace his ancestors further back than to Thomas Stribling who emigrated from Berryville, Va., to Union County, S. C. The uniform tradition among the family of Rear Admiral Cornelius Stribling has been that this Thomas Stribling, said to have been of Swedish and Welsh descent (?), "left Berryville, then Battletown, when quite young, his father giving him a horse, gun and colored man, with which to seek his fortune in the world"; and that he finally settled in South Carolina. Dr. S. S. Neill (§ 51), who was always considered an authority in such matters, wrote some years before his death that Taliaferro Stribling (§23), though he did not know that this was his name, had a brother who came with him and his father from Prince William County to Frederick County, and who afterwards removed to South Carolina and became the ancestor of the Striblings of that State. One thing is certain, that the members of the two branches who have been acquainted have always claimed a close kinship with one another.

§73. It can be safely said, therefore, that Thomas Stribling, born in Prince William County about 1730, moved first to Frederick County and thence, shortly after 1750, to South Carolina, where he settled on Seneca River in what is now Anderson County. He afterwards married *Nancy Kincheloe,* said to have been of English and Irish parentage. She may have been a sister or a daughter of Cornelius Kincheloe (son of John Kincheloe), who was Surveyor of Prince William County in 1768; for his name occurs frequently among her descendants. They had a family of at least four children,—Thomas, Jesse, Lucy (m. ——— Trimmier), and Nancy (m. ——— Tate). There was perhaps a fifth child, Sigismund, whose son John B. Stribling moved from South Carolina to Tennessee in 1834, and was the ancestor of Striblings now living at Clifton, Lawrenceburg and other places in that State. A history of Tennessee published in 1886 states that this

THE STRIBLING FAMILY. 87

John B. Stribling was "an own cousin of Commodore Cornelius K. Stribling". The names Sigismund, Casimir and Kincheloe occur in this branch of the family, indicating the connection with the other branches.

Because of lack of time I have not attempted to trace the descendants of Thomas and Nancy Stribling in detail, and for the following outline of the families of their two sons Thomas and Jesse I am indebted almost entirely to Mr. C. K. Stribling (§75) of Fort Griffin, Texas, and to Miss Mary Stribling (§82) of Walhalla, S. C. These facts are given without verification on my part with the hope that they may some time be used as the basis of a more extended history of that branch of the family.

§74. A. THOMAS STRIBLING married *Elizabeth Haile* of South Carolina, daughter of John Haile and Ruth Mitchell. They had seven children.
    I. ROBERT STRIBLING, m. *Sabra Clark*. He moved with his family from Georgia to Arkansas.
    II. MARK MITCHELL STRIBLING, married and had five sons (Flavius Josephus, Harrison, Oliver, Matthew and Robert) and several daughters, with whom he moved from Pickens County, Ala., to Mississippi about 1836.
    III. BENJAMIN HAILE STRIBLING, m. Nov. 21, 1820, *Ruth Bradley Greenwood*: issue,—
        1. JAMES HARRISON STRIBLING, D. D., for fifty years a prominent Baptist minister in Texas. He married *Jane Cleveland*, a grand-daughter of Nancy Stribling-Tate (§73): issue,—Kate (m. Ad. Gentry), Ruth (m. Hugh Witcher), Fannie (m. —— Morrison), Cleveland, and Cornelius K. Some of them are living at Rockdale, Tex.
        2. MARIA ELIZABETH STRIBLING, m. *William Mills Tandy:* issue,—James A., Ben, Frank, Mary Josephine, Cordelia, Ruth, Kate and William.
        3. THOMAS H. STRIBLING, a lawyer and for many years District Judge; m. *Eleanor Alexander:* issue,—Lola, Elizabeth (m. Price Maury of Charlottesville, Va.; five children), and Ben (l. San Antonio, Texas).
        4. BENJAMIN F. STRIBLING, m. *Effie McNeal:* issue,—Cornelius K., Frank, Clem, Kitty and Benjamin.

§75   5. CORNELIUS KINCHELOE STRIBLING, b. Feb. 28,
        1833; m. *Nancy C. Stribling* (see §82). He is county
        surveyor at Fort Griffin, Texas.
            (1). CALLIE RUTH STRIBLING, m. *John Bennett:*
                issue,—Merle, Neil Clinton, Stephen, Omie,
                Callie, John.
            (2). OLLIE PICKENS STRIBLING, m. *Woodson Coffee:*
                issue,—Ben Stribling, Woodson, Oran, Roy
                Coburn, Ollie.
            (3). BEN DAVID STRIBLING, m. *Sue Graham:*
                issue,—David, Albert, Susie.
            (4). JOE NAN STRIBLING, m. *Samuel Stewart:*
                issue,—Ida, Charles, C. K.
            (5). MARY ELIZABETH STRIBLING, m. *Robert B.
                Robertson:* issue,—George.
            (6). IDA ELLEN STRIBLING.
            (7). FRANK BENNETT STRIBLING.
            (8). FREDERICK HODGES STRIBLING.
        6. MOLLIE FRANCIS STRIBLING, m. *F. C. Kelly:* issue,
        —Bird and Cora.
        7. NANCY A. STRIBLING, m. *William H. Gentry:* issue,
        —George, Henry and Bruce.
        8. EMILY STRIBLING, m. *Maj. L. M. Rogers:* issue,—
        Willie, Gentry and Nettie.
        9. WILLIAM H. C. STRIBLING, m. *Allie Kesee:* issue,—
        Frank, Nannie and Emily.

§76 IV. CORNELIUS KINCHELOE STRIBLING, b. in 1796; m. in
    1820, *Helen Maria Payne* (p. Benjamin Payne and Mary
    Maxwell; gr. p. Capt. Maxwell and Helen Calvert; gr. gr.
    p. Maximilian Calvert; gr. gr. gr. p. Cornelius Calvert and
    Mary Saunders; gr. gr. gr. gr. p. Rev. Jonathan and Mary
    Saunders). He was appointed a midshipman in the U. S.
    Navy June 18, 1812; promoted to Lieutenant April 1,
    1818; Commander March 11, 1840; Captain August 1,
    1853; appointed to command East India Squadron April
    29, 1859; Commodore August 2, 1862; Rear Admiral on
    the Retired List, August 6, 1866; d. Martinsburg, W. Va.,
    Jan. 17, 1880.
        1. ELIZABETH STRIBLING, d. unmarried.
        2. LOUISA STRIBLING, d. unmarried.

REAR-ADMIRAL CORNELIUS K. STRIBLING
§ 76

THE STRIBLING FAMILY. 89

3. MARY STRIBLING, d. unmarried.
4. CORNELIUS KINCHELOE STRIBLING, b in 1831; m. 1st. in 1852, *Emma J. Nourse*; m. 2nd. in 1863, *Ann Elizabeth Riddle*. He had two children by the first marriage and five by the second.
    (1). CORNELIUS K. STRIBLING, m. *Mamie McDanald;* issue,—Mamie, Helen and Cornelius.
    (2). LOUISA PAYNE STRIBLING, m. *William H. Criswell:* issue,—Emma Nourse and William H.
    (3). CHARLES RIDDLE STRIBLING, m. *Janie B. Armstrong:* issue,—A. Elizabeth, Agnes Brown, Charles R., and Janie B. He is pastor of the Presbyterian Church at Waynesboro, Va.
    (4). JOHN M. STRIBLING, d. in 1866.
    (5). JAMES MAXWELL STRIBLING.
    (6). MARY CALVERT STRIBLING.
    (7). SUE BROWN STRIBLING, m. *Magnus A. Snodgrass*: issue,—Ann Porterfield and Cornelius Stribling.
5. JOHN MAXWELL STRIBLING. He was a Lieutenant in the U. S. Navy; resigned in Feb. 1861 to serve in the C. S. Navy with Admiral Semmes. He ran the blockade at Mobile, Sept. 10, 1862, and died of yellow fever a few days later, aged 27.

V. MARY STRIBLING, m. *Richard Roseman* or *Rosamond*. They had a large family and moved to Mississippi.

VI. FRANCES STRIBLING, m. *I. J. Foster;* moved from Union District, S. C., in 1847, to Lavacca, Texas: issue,— A. K., Thompson, Haile, Benton, Clem, Sarah and Frances.

VII. MARIA STRIBLING, m——— *Moreland;* moved to Arkansas.

---

§77 B. JESSE STRIBLING, b. April 9, 1775; d. Nov. 30, 1841; m. April 29, 1805, *Elizabeth Sloan*, daughter of David Sloan (b. in 1751; d. Oct. 9, 1826) and Susan Majors (b. July 29, 1763; d. Sept. 5, 1854).
    I. THOMAS M. STRIBLING, b. Jan. 25, 1806; d. Dec. 31, 1879; m. *Mary Jones* (b. May 3, 1813; d. Nov. 9, 1867).

THE STRIBLING FAMILY.

1. JONES H. STRIBLING, b. June 23, 1834; d. July 7, 1862, in the Confederate Army.
2. WILLIAM E. STRIBLING, b. July 6, 1837; d. July 6, 1862, in the Confederate Army.
3. THOMAS JABES STRIBLING, b. July 13, 1839; killed in the Confederate Army, April 25, 1865.
4. MARTHA HANNAH STRIBLING, b. July 1, 1841; m. *Alexander Ramsey;* 1. Seneca, S. C.
    (1). ELIZABETH RAMSEY, b. in May, 1864; 1. Seneca, S. C.; m. *Yancey Sligh:* issue,—Harry Kuthman, b. in April, 1892, and Edgar Yancey, b. in Dec. 1896.
    (2). SALLIE R. RAMSEY, b. June 1866; 1. Anderson, S. C.; m. *Townes Holleman:* issue,—J. Ramsey, b. August 1889; Frank A., b. Nov. 1891; Whitfield, b. June 1894; Julian Bruce, b. June 1897, and Sarah Lee, b. May 1899.
    (3). W. ALEXANDER RAMSEY, b. August 1869; m. *Clelia Lowery:* issue,—Gladys, b. April 1893; 1. Ellesville, Miss.
    (4). EUGENE BASKIN RAMSEY, b. Oct. 1873; m. *Lula Lawrence*: issue,—Lilian, b. Nov. 1898; Mattie E , b. Feb. 1901; 1. Seneca, S. C.
    (5). THOMAS R. RAMSEY, b. May 1880; m. *Susan Kennimore:* issue,—Martha E., b. Dec. 1900; Linda K., b. July 1902.
5. JESSE CORNELIUS STRIBLING, b. Sept. 27, 1844; m. June 5, 1867, *Virginia Hunter;* 1. Pendleton, S. C.
    (1). HARRY LEE STRIBLING, b. Nov. 20, 1869; m. May 4, 1892, *Ella Osborne:* issue,—Augustus Lee, b. Jan. 30, 1893; Raymond Wilson, b. Jan. 23, 1895; Robert, b. Sept. 13, 1899.
    (2). JESSE CORNELIUS STRIBLING, b. Oct. 25, 1876; m. Feb. 18, 1902, *Meta Henshael.*
    (3). JAMES HUNTER STRIBLING, b. Dec. 19, 1878.
    (4). MARY ELIZA STRIBLING, b. May 19, 1881.
    (5). THOMAS EUGENE STRIBLING, b. August 23, 1883; d. August 4, 1894.
    (6). ELIZABETH STRIBLING, b. August 14, 1885.
    (7). ROXIE ALICE STRIBLING, b. March 14, 1887.

THE STRIBLING FAMILY. 91

§78   6. MARY E. STRIBLING, b. July 31, 1846; m. Jan. 20, 1870, *Clayton Lytle Reid* (b. Sept. 25, 1838). He first married her sister; see below.
   (1). CHARLES SLOAN REID, b. April 30, 1871; m. Dec. 4, 1897, *Louise Strother:* issue,—Frances Elizabeth, b. Sept. 24, 1898; Roxie Louise, b. Sept. 28, 1901; l. Walhalla, S. C.
   (2). ROXIE ELIZABETH REID, b. Dec. 15, 1872; l. Walhalla, S. C.
   (3). CLAYTON JONES REID, b. Feb. 10, 1874; d. July 7, 1874.
   (4). J. B. SITTON REID, b. Oct. 8, 1876.
   (5). MARY ANNIE REID, b. Dec. 17, 1878.
   (6). SARAH ELLA REID, b. July 8, 1881.
7. SLOAN Y. STRIBLING, b. Dec. 18, 1848; m. Dec. 1, 1871, *Ida Sligh* (b. Oct. 12, 1853); l. Roswell, Ga.; is president of a cotton mill.
   (1). THOMAS SLIGH STRIBLING, b. Oct. 31, 1872; m. Nov. 29, 1899, *Julia Maude Verner:* issue,—Mary Ida, b. Nov. 16, 1900; Robert Sloan, b. Nov. 10, 1901.
   (2). PAUL ORLANDO STRIBLING, b. June 18, 1874; m. Nov. 30, 1899, *Yancy Jane Bush:* issue,—Paul Orlando, b. Oct. 11, 1900; Dorothy, b. Dec. 24, 1901.
   (3). MARY KATHERINE STRIBLING, b. Dec. 25, 1876; l. Roswell, Ga.
   (4). JONES HOUCK STRIBLING, b. August 18, 1879.
   (5). EARLE STRIBLING, b. July 29, 1882.
   (6). NINA SLOAN STRIBLING, b. June 10, 1885.
   (7). MARTHA NEEL STRIBLING, b. July 12, 1888.
   (8). SUMMER YOWELL STRIBLING, b. Feb. 16, 1891.
   (9). HUGH YANCY STRIBLING, b. Oct. 10, 1893.
8. ROXIE A. STRIBLING, b. May 27, 1850; d. April 24, 1869; m. March 12, 1868, *Clayton Lytle Reid* (b. Sept. 25, 1838). He afterwards married her sister; see above.
   (1). THOMAS CLAYTON REID, b. March 8, 1869; d. July 15, 1869.

The Stribling Family.

9. LLEWELLEN STRIBLING, b. Oct. 25, 1853; d. Jan. 25, 1902; m. *Mrs. Ida D. Fincannon*.
    (1). CLIFTON EARLE STRIBLING, b. July, 1877.
    (2). MARY E. STRIBLING, b. Oct., 1879.
    (3). STELLA AMELIA STRIBLING, b. Sep. 23, 1881.
    (4). ELIZABETH ETHEL STRIBLING, b. March, 1885.

II. MARY S. STRIBLING, b. June 4, 1807; m. *Hartwell Jones*. They had thirteen children.

§79 III. WILLIAM HARRISON STRIBLING, b. Feb. 9, 1809; d. Nov. 23, 1889; m. Sept. 27, 1832, *Jane B. McKindly* (b. Dec. 23, 1815; d. Oct. 3, 1855).
   1. JESSE SLOAN STRIBLING, b. August 5, 1833; d. June 27, 1856.
   2. ELIZABETH CAROLINE STRIBLING, b. Dec. 18, 1835; l. Seneca, S. C.; m. Jan. 4, 1866, *James T. Reid*.
        (1). ELIZABETH REID, b. Nov. 24, 1866; l. Washington, D. C.; m. Dec. 6, 1887, *James M. Webb:* issue,—James R., b. Nov. 9, 1889; William C., b. May 5, 1892.
        (2). SAMUEL REID, b. July 19, 1869; m. Feb. 2, 1898, *Myra Lay:* issue,—James S., b. Nov. 2, 1898; Mamie J., b. June 28, 1900.
        (3). GEORGE T. REID, b. March 13, 1871; m. March 10, 1892, *Jane Fisher:* issue,—Ludie C., b. May 21, 1893; William R., b. Nov. 15, 1894; E. Caroline, b. July 2, 1896; George Braxton, b. April 7, 1898; Frank, b. Jan. 3, 1900; Samuel, b. Oct. 27, 1901.
        (4). MAMIE REID, b. Sept. 26, 1874; m. July 20, 1898, *Dr. W. Frank Ashmore:* issue,—Elizabeth C., b. March 30, 1901; l. Newry, S. C.
   3. THOMAS H. STRIBLING, b. May 23, 1838, m. Sept. 3, 1867, *Josie Reeder* (b. January 14, 1846); is farming in Oconee County, S. C.
        (1). ESSIE S. STRIBLING, b. Jan. 26, 1870; d. Oct. 2, 1870.
        (2). SUE ALICE STRIBLING, b. in 1871; m. Feb. 8, 1893, *John Lawrence:* issue,—Thomas Charles, b. Feb. 1, 1894; Mattie Louise, b. Feb. 17, 1896;

THE STRIBLING FAMILY. 93

Jesse Stribling, b. Sept. 30, 1897; John, b. Sept. 8, 1899; Joe, b. April 29, 1902; d. July 31, 1902; l. Seneca, S. C.

(3). WILLIAM H. STRIBLING, b. May 19, 1874.

(4). JESSIE S. STRIBLING, b. Jan. 1, 1878.

4. MARY ELIZA STRIBLING, b. Dec. 23, 1840; d. May 1, 1889; m. Dec. 6, 1860, *William A. Barron* (d. March 30, 1887).

   (1). IDA BARRON, b. Sept. 11, 1861; l. Seneca, S. C.; m. Oct. 16, 1883, *Lawrence McMahan*.

   (2.) WILLIE BARRON, b. in 1866; d August 17, 1901; m. August 15, 1889, *Nan Bibbs*.

   (3.) SALLIE BARRON, b. in 1868; d. March 7, 1895; m. Dec. 22, 1891, —— *McMahan*.

   (4). ROSA BARRON, b. Jan. 8, 1871.

   (5). ELIJAH MACK BARRON, b. July 1, 1873; m. Dec. 26, 1897, *Belle Biggerstaff;* l. Seneca, S. C.

   (6). MAMIE BARRON, b. Dec. 12, 1875.

   (7). E. STOKES BARRON, b. May 5, 1878; m. Dec. 22, 1896, *J. F. Alexander*.

§80   5. JAMES McB. STRIBLING, b. July 13, 1843; killed at the battle of Fredericksburg, Dec. 13, 1862.

6. WILLIAM DAVID STRIBLING, b. Nov. 10, 1845; m. *Louise Harbin:* issue,—Ora Jane, Samuel S., Carrie May, Hattie K., Robert Warren; l. Richland, S. C.

7. ELIJAH S. STRIBLING, b. April 25, 1848; d. June 4, 1865.

8. ROBERT W. STRIBLING, b. April 9, 1851; d. July 7, 1869.

9. SUSAN J. STRIBLING, b. Sept. 5, 1854; l. Richland, S. C.; m. Dec. 22, 1869, *Orwed Sligh*.

   (1). ROBERT CLARENCE SLIGH, b. Oct. 10, 1870; m. June 30, 1893, *Daisy A. Bobbitt:* issue,—Roy Clair, b. August 1894; d. August 1895; Glenn Orr, b. Feb. 23, 1896.

   (2). SARAH KATE SLIGH, b. Sept. 2, 1872; d. Oct. 8, 1896; m. August 31, 1894, *E. B. Smith*.

   (3). ROWENNE FAY SLIGH, b. Oct. 19, 1874; d. Jan. 31, 1893.

The Stribling Family.

(4). NEEL SLIGH, b. Oct. 2, 1876; m. June 30, 1901, *Emma C. Gaines*.

(5). SUE SLIGH, b. Oct. 12, 1878; m. Dec. 10, 1899, *Frank Patterson:* issue,—Neel, b. April 20, 1901.

IV. REBECCA C. STRIBLING, b. Sept. 10, 1810, m. *B. F. Kilpatrick;* they lived in Mississippi.

V. ROBERT STRIBLING, b. March 12, 1812; d May 11, 1877; m.Jan. 30, 1834, *Ruth P. Bruce:* issue,—Susan E., b. 1834; d. 1837; Mary C., b. 1836; d. 1844; Susan Annie, b. 1839; d. 1843; Robert, b. 1841; died during the War; Thomas W., b. 1844; d. 1852.

§81 VI. DAVID SLOAN STRIBLING, b. July 3, 1814; d. Sept. 13, 1883; m. Oct. 16, 1834, *Jo Anna C. Hodges* (b. Nov. 18, 1814; p. James and Elizabeth Brown Hodges).

    1. MARY E. STRIBLING, b. Dec. 23, 1835; 1. Acton, Tex.; m. *Larkin C. Cleveland*.

        (1). LOU BERRY CLEVELAND.

        (2). ESSIE W. CLEVELAND, m. *Edward Clifton:* issue,—Claude, Joseph Earle.

        (3). ANNIE J. CLEVELAND, m. *Clifton Davis:* issue,—Trenholm.

        (4). HASKELL O. CLEVELAND.

        (5). CARLTON CLEVELAND.

    2. JESSE WALES STRIBLING, b. April 28, 1838; m. *1st.* Nov. 9, 1859, *Sarah Shelor* (b. Sept. 18, 1837; she was his first cousin; see §83); m. *2nd.* Sept. 1889, *Mrs. Sallie C. Cherry;* 1. Seneca, S. C.; he is cashier of a bank.

        (1). THOMAS EDWARD STRIBLING, b. August 27, 1860; m. *Mattie Verner:* issue,—Thomas Edward, Verner, Jesse W., Charles; 1. Seneca, S. C.

        (2). EMMA P. STRIBLING, b. July 17, 1863.

        (3). JO ANNA STRIBLING, b. Oct. 17, 1867; d. July 29, 1900; m. Dec. 28, 1887, *Thomas M. Lowery:* issue,—Wales, b. Feb. 17, 1889; Thomas M., Sarah, Louise Emma.

    3. LUCINDA W. STRIBLING, b. Oct. 4, 1840; d. Aug. 6, 1887; m. *Dr. John N. Doyle;* 1. Granbury, Tex.

        (1). MAMIE B. DOYLE.

(2). ROBERT EDWARD DOYLE, m. Dec. 25, 1900, *Bessie* ———: issue,—Robert Edward; 1. Granbury, Tex.

(3). HATTIE B. DOYLE.

4. RUTH P. STRIBLING, b. Jan. 14, 1843; d. Dec. 2, 1867.

§82 5. NANCY C. STRIBLING, b. July 10, 1845; m. *Cornelius K. Stribling;* see §75.

6. REBECCA C. STRIBLING, b. June 10, 1847; d. Sept. 12, 1875; m. *James A. Tandy.*

(1). EMMET TANDY.

(2). JOHN CLARK TANDY, m. *Josie Kerr:* issue,—Madeline; 1. Granbury, Tex.

(3). DAVID SLOAN TANDY, m. *Maud Donathan:* issue,—Fay, Flo.

7. JAMES HODGES STRIBLING, b. April 4, 1849; m. *Zena Taylor:* issue,—Lillie Maude (m. *Ben Clifton:* issue,—Kathleen), Jesse, Bessie Lee, Ethel, Fred H., Myrtle, Warren, James Oran; 1. Acton, Tex.

8. WILLIAM JOHN STRIBLING, b. May 12, 1851; m. Dec. 15, 1880, *Lizzie Norton* (b. Feb. 15, 1861; p. Joseph J. Norton and Tabitha A. Campbell); issue,—Mary, b. March 6, 1882; Sallie, b. July 9, 1886; Anna, b. June 26, 1888; Frances, b. Dec. 15, 1890; Norton, b. Sept. 6, 1892; Elizabeth, b. Nov. 26, 1894; Tabitha Atkinson, b. Oct. 30, 1898; William John, b. Aug. 12, 1901; 1. Walhalla, S. C.; he is a lawyer.

9. LUCY C. STRIBLING, b. June 21, 1853; m. *James A. Tandy:* issue,—Burt E. (1. Blanket, Texas), Mary Viola (m. Dec. 1900, ——— *Jarrett*), Albert, Elizabeth, Lou, Lucy; 1. Acton, Tex.

§83 VII. SUSAN A. STRIBLING, b. Jan. 22, 1817; m. *Thomas R. Shelor.*

1. MARY SHELOR, m. *Dr. Harbin:* issue,—Thomas (m. *Ida Harland:* issue,—Maxwell, Milda; 1. Calhoun, Ga.); Dr. Robert M. (m. *Jane Acker;* 1. Rome, Ga.); Dr. William (1. Rome, Ga.); Nina.

2. SARAH E. SHELOR, m. *Jesse W. Stribling;* see §81. She was his first cousin.

3. REBECCA SHELOR, 1. Calhoun, Ga.; m. *William Steele:* issue,—Annie (m. William Swain; four children); Virginia (m.———Garet; issue,—Robert, Bertha); Thomas; Henry; Sadah (m. Dr. Franklin: issue, Minerva); Robert.
4. VIRGINIA SHELOR, 1. Calhoun, Ga.; m. *Calvin Wright:* issue,—Sunie, C. Shelor, Jesse, Frederick.
5. JESSE R. SHELOR, m. *Emma Bruce:* issue,—J. Wales, Mamie, Ryland, Clarence, Floy, Varina.
6. JOSEPH W. SHELOR, m. *1st.* Nov. 7, 1878, *Lou Neville*; m. *2nd.* Feb. 27, 1883, *Lizzie Hix:* issue,—Sallie, b. May 12, 1880; Hattie, b. August 11, 1884; T. B., b. Dec. 7, 1890; 1. Calhoun, Ga.
7. WILLIAM SHELOR, m. *Ada Swain:* issue,—Mary, Sudie, Louise, Swain, Ellen, Ethel, Joe, William C.; 1. Calhoun, Ga.
8. SUSAN SHELOR, m. *Dr. G. W. Gardner;* 1. Greenwood, S. C.

§84 VIII. M. STOKES STRIBLING, b. May 2, 1819; d. 1890; m. May 2, 1843, *Anna M. Verner* (d. March 4, 1901).
1. REBECCA E. STRIBLING, b. Dec. 16, 1843; d. Sept. 6, 1877; m. June 10, 1867, *Warren Shelor:* issue,—Toccoa, Stokes W. (m. Dec. 27, 1901, *Mrs. A. Duckett*); 1. Seneca, S. C.
2. LEMUEL DAVID STRIBLING, b. March 1, 1845; m. Nov. 26, 1867, *Martha Jane Brownlee:* issue,—Annie, Talula Kate, Clinton, Mary, Rebecca, George Brownlee, Joseph Clark, Jesse D., Maria Perry, Montford, Mattie E.; 1. Helena, Ga.
3. JOHN VERNER STRIBLING, b. Jan. 30, 1847; m. Dec. 23, 1875, *Susan Willard*: issue,—Annie Verner (m. in 1900, *Joe Jenings:* issue,—Willard; 1. Anderson, S. C.), Samuel, William George, James Wyatt, John Carl, Carrie; 1. Anderson, S. C.; he is a civil engineer.
4. WILLIAM JESSE STRIBLING, b. May 25, 1848; m. Nov. 26, 1873, *Augusta Jamison:* issue,—Effie Young, Jessie Rebecca, Leo, Maude, Allie Marie, Roy, Jamison, Grace Augusta, Frank; 1. Westminster, S. C.; he is a merchant.

THE STRIBLING FAMILY. 97

5. SAMUEL PETTIGREW STRIBLING, b. Feb. 11, 1850; m. Nov. 27, 1875, *Jane Sheldon:* issue,—Margaret Hampton, Leslie, Mark; l. Fair Play, S. C.
6. GEORGE THOMAS STRIBLING, b. July 9, 1851; m. *Hattie West.* issue,—Garnet, B. B., Eugene, Myrtle, Lillian; l. Atlanta, Ga.; he is a travelling salesman.
7. MARY JANE STRIBLING, b. Dec. 31, 1852; m. May 7, 1874, *John W. Shelor:* issue,—Marye, Rebecca, Annie, Wayne, Ryland, Gama, Jane, George; l. Tugaloo, S. C.
8. SUSAN M. STRIBLING, b. Sept 18, 1854.
9. ANNIE MARIA STRIBLING, b. Oct. 5, 1856; l. Richland, S. C.; m. June 11, 1878, *Thomas B. Wyly:* issue,—Byrd Samuel, Stokes Oliver, Anna Adaline, David Lemuel, Jamie D., Cora R., Clark J., Hugh Strong, Lola, Lula, Wayne.
10. M. STOKES STRIBLING, b. April 19, 1859; m. in 1880, *Elizabeth Brown:* issue,—Elizabeth, Mary; l. Seneca, S. C.; is a commission merchant.
11. WARREN D. STRIBLING, b. Nov. 16, 1860; m. in 1888, *Alice Butler:* issue,—Mayfield, Samuel, Eliza, Edwin Warren, Faith; l. Eatonton, Ga.
12. EBENEZER SLOAN STRIBLING, b. April 7, 1862; l. Eatonton, Ga.
13. JOSEPH SHELOR STRIBLING, b. Jan. 10, 1864; is a physician at Seneca, S. C.

§85 IX. NANCY TRIMMIER STRIBLING, b. August 7, 1821; d. Feb. 20, 1887; m. Oct. 11, 1838, *Henry N. White* (b. Sept. 2, 1812; d. Jan. 13, 1884).

1. B. FRANK WHITE, b. March 31, 1849; married three times; issue,—Monroe, William, Birdie, and others; l. Greenville, S. C.
2. D. SLOAN WHITE, b. Nov. 3, 1852; m. Oct. 30, 1872, *Virginia Cox:* issue,—Iola Pearl, b. August 11, 1873 (m. W. E. Ledbetter); Kiturah Gertrude, b. Nov. 21, 1875 (m. E. M. Sturges); Latula Trimmier, b. March 22, 1878 (m. Fred. R. Young); Bonner Sloan, b. July 22, 1880; Clarence Stokes, b. March 6, 1883; Henry Lucius, b. August 13, 1885; Allie Mira, b. Sept. 25, 1888; Horace Hodges, b. June 27, 1893; d. March 26, 1894; l. Sherman, Tex.

3. SALLIE E. WHITE, b. Jan. 21, 1855.
X. ELIZABETH KATHERINE STRIBLING, b. Nov. 27, 1823; d. July 26, 1860; m. Nov. 14, 1852, *Josiah Harkey* (b. in April 1818; d. March 2, 1863): issue,—Joseph F., Mary E., Susan E., Henry Bass, William C.; (1. Atlanta, Ga.).

§86 XI. WARREN WEBB STRIBLING, b. April 18, 1826; d. Dec. 14, 1872; m. Dec. 11, 1850, *Emily Rebecca Dendy* (b. June 5, 1831).

    1. ELIZABETH CATHERINE STRIBLING, b. Oct. 26, 1851; m. Oct. 14, 1874, *Sloan Bruce:* issue,—Minerva Emily, b. June 29, 1875; d. Oct. 4, 1885; 1. Richland, S. C.

    2. MARSHALL STOKES STRIBLING, b. Jan. 24, 1854; m. Dec. 22, 1886, *Martha Helen Sheldon:* issue,—Margie, b. August 29, 1887; Lee Webb, b. June 24, 1890; Alice, b. August 6, 1894; Emily, b. August 29, 1897; 1. Seneca, S. C.

    3. ROBERT STILES STRIBLING, b. Nov. 2, 1856; d. June 29, 1879.

    4. LOU ALICE STRIBLING, b. Oct. 22, 1859; m. Aug. 28, 1889, *John Newton Doyle:* issue,—Lucy Stribling, b. June 22, 1890; d. Dec. 28, 1894; Emily, b. June 5, 1894.

    5. JAMES PAUL STRIBLING, b. July 19, 1862; m. Dec. 10, 1891, *Bessie May Conger:* issue,—Edna, b. Sept. 4, 1892; d. Sept. 7, 1896; Stiles Conger, b. May 21, 1894; Bruce Hodgson, b. Jan. 16, 1896; Belle Bernice, b. Dec. 16, 1897; Charles Lane, b. March 10, 1899; d. June 29, 1901; James Paul, b. April 30, 1902; 1. Richland, S. C.

    6. THOMAS MCKNIGHT STRIBLING, b. Nov. 30, 1865; 1. Princeton College.

    7. LUCY TRIMMIER STRIBLING, b. April 6, 1868; 1. Greenville, S. C.; m. Oct. 17, 1894, *Green Berry Jordan:* issue,—Emily, b. June 5, 1894; Sloan Bruce, b. Dec. 17, 1897.

    8. JESSE DENDY STRIBLING, b. March 24, 1871; d. June 9, 1898; m. Jan. 31, 1894, *Sudie A. Buchannan:* issue,—Fred Dendy, b. Nov. 17, 1894; Neta, b. Oct. 19, 1897; d. April 27, 1898.

Note 1. Taliaferro and Smith Families.

§87. *Robert Taliaferro, Gent.*, the founder of this family in Virginia, and undoubtedly of English parentage, settled in Gloucester county in 1636 where he received a large grant of land. He also owned extensive possessions in what is now Essex County. He married a daughter of the Reverend Charles Grymes of Middlesex County, and had at least five sons,—Francis (m. Elizabeth Catlett), John (m. Sarah Smith), Richard, Charles, and Robert (m. Sarah Catlett).

John Taliaferro was born about 1660 and died in 1720, his will (made June 1, 1715) being probated in the Essex Court June 21, 1720. About 1682 he married Sarah Smith, daughter of Col. Lawrence Smith of Gloucester county (see below). On June 19, 1699 he gave bond as sheriff of Essex County, and in the same year represented his county in the House of Burgesses. That he was prominent in the early Colonial Wars with the Indians is shown by the record of Oct. 31, 1692, in the Calendar of Virginia State Papers, that "Lieut John Taliaferro gives return of his expenses in Tobacco, as Ranger with eleven men & two Indians", etc. The records of York and Essex Counties show that his children were,—Lawrence, John, Charles, Robert, Zachariah, Richard, William, Mary, *Elizabeth* (who married THOMAS STRIBLING, §22), Sarah and Catherine. It is this last named Robert Taliaferro of St. Paul's Parish, Stafford County, who, in his will dated Dec. 3, 1725 and recorded in the Essex Court June 21, 1726, mentions his sister Elizabeth, the wife of "Thomas Stripling", and her sons Francis, William and Taliaferro "Stripling".

Col. Lawrence Smith, of Abingdon Parish, Gloucester County, was a man of great influence and wealth in his day. He bore the coat-of-arms of the Smiths of Tottne, County Devonshire, England, from which place he had perhaps emigrated to the Colony. His wife's name was Mary ...., and his will was dated Aug. 8, 1700, but no copy of it has been preserved. He was surveyor for the counties of Gloucester and York in 1686, and in 1691 laid out the town of Yorktown. In 1699 he was recommended by the Governor among the "gentlemen of estate and standing" suitable for appointment to the Council, but his

THE TATE FAMILY. 100

death the following lyear 'prevented the bestowal of this honor upon him. He was conspicuous also as a leader in the early Colonial Wars. In 1676 he commanded "111 men out of Gloucester Co." at a fort near the falls of the Rappahannock River, and the same year he led the "trained bands" of Gloucester against the rebels under Bacon. The following were his children, as far as is known:—

1. John, of Gloucester County; member of the Council and county lieutenant.
2. Lawrence, of York County; Colonel, Justice, Sheriff of the County, and member of the House of Burgesses.
3. William.
4. Augustine, of St. Mary's Parish, Essex; one of the first bench of justices for Spotsylvania County in 1722.
5. Charles, of Essex County; died in 1710.
6. Elizabeth, m. Capt. John Battaile of St. Mary's Parish, Essex, and had issue: John, Lawrence, Hay, Nicholas, and others.
7. *Sarah Smith*, m. John Taliaferro, as above.

(See "Old King William Homes & Families", p. 101; Calendar of Virginia State Papers, Vol. I, p. 44; Stanard's "Colonial Virginia Register", p. 92; "William & Mary Quarterly", Vol. II, p. 5 and Vol. IX, p. 42.

Note 2. Tate Family.

§88 *Magnus Tate*, the first of the name in this country, emigrated from the Orkney Islands, north of Scotland, and landed at Philadelphia May 20, 1696, eventually locating in that part of Frederick County, Virginia, which finally became Jefferson County, West Virginia. He is said to have died in Sept. 1747. On May 2, 1749, Honour Tate, evidently his wife, qualified in the Frederick Court as administratrix of his estate. The inventory of his property was filed May 8, 1749. She must have died shortly afterwards, since it is recorded that on August 16, 1750 Magnus Tate qualified as administrator of Honour Tate, dec'd., and the inventory of her estate was filed Oct. 29, 1750. Their home was near Charlestown, now in Jefferson County, W. Va. As far as is known, they had only one child.

Magnus Tate, b. April 5, 1732; d. "Belvidere", in March 1808; m. Frederick County, Sept. 26, 1759. Mary Riley McCormick (b. in 1736; d. in 1810; see §193). They lived at "Belvidere", near Charlestown, which estate was perhaps the home of his father also. Their seven children were,—

A. Mary Tate, b. Feb 2, 1761; m. Joseph Daugherty: issue,— Ennis (d. in California), William (m. a Miss Henderson, but left no children), and Mary (never married).

B. *Ann* (usually called *Nancy*) *Tate*, b. Feb. 15, 1763; m. FRANCIS STRIBLING; see §24.

C. *Margaret* (usually called *Peggy*) *Tate*, b. in 1765; d in 1830; m. May 12, 1785, Battaile Muse (b. April 30, 1751; d. March 29, 1803; p. Col. George Muse and Elizabeth Battaile. Col. Muse was born in England in 1720 and was a Major in the English Army. He left the army about the same time as Lawrence Washington, and settled in Virginia. He achieved some distinction as Adjutant in the Spanish Wars, and wrote a book on military discipline. He is said to have instructed Washington in the evolution and movement of troops. In 1754 he was engaged in an expedition against the French and Indians, and also rendered conspicuous service in the Revolutionary War, for which he received a large grant of land in Kentucky, where he died in 1790. See Washington's "Life" by Weems, Irving, and Schroder. Battaile Muse was the attorney for General Washington in the management of his estate.)

  I. George Augustine Muse, d. early unmarried.
  II. Battaile Muse, d. early unmarried.
  III. *Mary* (or *Polly*) *Muse*, m. Dr. John H. Lewis of Loudoun County.

   1. James B. Lewis, m. Ann Hume: issue,—Mary (d. unmarried), Robert (m. Cary Jones of Winchester: issue,—Rebecca, m. Rev. Charles N. Tyndall, and Annie),Virginia (m. John H. Kemp of Rockville, Md.; one son, James), Bettie (m. Charles H. Lewis: issue,— Virginia and Ann; see below), and Kate (unmarried).
   2. *Fisher Ames Lewis*, m. ELIZABETH LANE: no children; see §70.
   3. Charles H. Lewis, m. Estelle Green: issue,—Charles H. (m. his cousin Bettie Lewis; see above), John (m. Jessie Camden; several children), James (married and

THE TATE FAMILY.   102

lives in the West), Magnus M. (m. Susie Rose; three children; 1. Fredericksburg), Arthur (unmarried; is a minister in West Virginia), Gertrude (m. Minteo Ralston of Clarksburg, W. Va.; two children), Aldridge and George.

4. John H. Lewis, m. a Miss Kennedy of Maryland: issue,—Fisher Ames (l. Philadelphia, Pa.), Henry St. Pierre, and Ellen.

5. Mary Jane Lewis.

6. Dr. Magnus M. Lewis, m. Evelyn Brent of Alexandria; no children.

7. Joseph Newton Lewis, died in California, unmarried.

8. Robert Vincent Lewis, m. Belle Boyd of Kentucky; three sons.

9. *William Hierome Thomas Lewis*, m. *1st*. Belle S. Green of Falmouth; m. *2nd*. CATHERINE STUART NEILL; see §52. He had five children by the first marriage:—William Green (d. Nov. 7, 1900; m. Mary M. Beardsley of Kentucky; one daughter, Annabelle), Joseph Newton (m. Lyle O. Davidson of Selma, Ala.; no children), Duff Green (m. Agnes M. Proctor of England; no children), Alexander M. (m. Sallye Stone of Texas; one son, William Stone), and Ann Payne (unmarried).

IV. Elizabeth Battaile Muse, m. Jan. 4, 1810, Joseph Smith of Staunton. One child,

1. Elizabeth Smith, m. Robert S. Brooke: issue,—
   (1). Margaret Brooke, m. Thomas P. Eskridge: issue,—Elizabeth (m. M. Filmore Gilkerson; three children, Janie, Eskridge and Maslin), Brooke (m. Nellie Garber; two sons), Meta (m. R. Spottswood Payne; two sons, Edwin and Robert), and Mary (m. James Anderson; one child).
   (2). Virginia Brooke, m. Dr. Briscoe Baldwin Donaghe: issue,—Mary Berkeley (m. .... Mauzey; two children,—Catherine and Richard), Florence (m. Charles Hutcheson), Virginia (m. Matthew Fletcher; five children; 1. San Francisco) and George Price.

THE TATE FAMILY. 103

(3.) Elizabeth Brooke, m. Col. James C. Cochran of "Folly": —issue, John, James, Anne Elizabeth (m. L. Seymour Rawlinson, son of the late Canon George Rawlinson of Canterbury Cathedral; one daughter, Elizabeth Seymour), Joseph Smith (l. Staunton).

V. Margaret Muse, m. in May 1811, Major Hierome Lindsay Opie.
   1. Hierome Lindsay Opie, m. Annie Locke of Martinsburg: issue,—Hierome Lindsay, Dr. Thomas of Baltimore, May (m. Dr. Basil Meade), and Hon. John N. Opie of Staunton (m. Ida Fletcher; see below).
   2. Juliet Opie, m. *1st.* Maj. Gordon; m. *2nd.* a Mr. Hopkins, Member of Congress from Alabama. She left no children.
   3. Mary Opie, m. William Norris: issue,— William and Wormley.
   4. Virginia Opie, m. Robert Hume Butcher of Baltimore: issue,—Hume, Charles, Jennie, Juliet (m. Gen. Ayres), Margaret and others.
   5. Margaret Opie, m. Hon. George Reed Riddle, Senator from Delaware; she left no children.

VI. Magnus Tate Muse, died in August 1811, unmarried.

VII. Lucinda Muse, b. August 17, 1797; d. in Feb. 1859; m. in 1816, Rev. William Claiborne Walton (d. Feb. 18, 1834).
   1. Margaret Ann Walton, d. in 1825.
   2. William Claiborne Walton, d. in 1837.
   3. Lucy Muse Walton, b. May 3, 1822; m. in 1847, Rev. Patterson Fletcher (d. in 1891).
      (1). Lucinda Fletcher, d. in infancy.
      (2). William Walton Fletcher, d. unmarried in 1895.
      (3). Nannie Fletcher, m. in 1885, John W. Basore of Broadway.
      (4). Minnie Fletcher, m. Rev. William A. Mackey, D. D., now of Whatcom, Washington State.
      (5). Ida Fletcher, m. Hon. John N. Opie of Staunton: see above.

THE TATE FAMILY. 104

(6). Lucy Fletcher, m. Mortimer Wilson Smith of Clarksburg, W. Va.

4. Eliza Walton, b. August 8, 1824; d. May 21, 1877; m. Alexandria, June 3, 1843, Rev. Rufus Wheelwright Clark of the Dutch Reformed Church, brother of Bishop Clark of the Episcopal Church.

(1). Rev. Rufus Wheelwright Clark, b. Portsmouth, N. H., May 29, 1844; m. April 9, 1874, Lucy Dennison, daughter of William Dennison, War-Governor of Ohio, and Postmaster General under President Lincoln: issue,—Helen (b. Jan. 18, 1875); Rufus Wheelwright (b. Dec. 20, 1876); Elizabeth (b. Feb. 27, 1879; m. Sept. 24,1901, Harry W. Leonard; one son, Raymond Clark, b. June 23,. 1902); William Dennison (b. Oct. 21, 1885); Jane Dennison (b. June 7, 1889). He is Rector of an Episcopal Church in Detroit, Mich.

(2). Rev. William Walton Clark, b. Portsmouth, N. H., May 8, 1846; m. March 4, 1868, Elizabeth M. Wyckoff of Brooklyn: issue,—Elizabeth Morris (b. December 8, 1869; now in Wellington, South Africa); Marion (b. May 15, 1875); Alice Webster (b. Nov. 11, 1877); l. Brooklyn, N. Y.

(3). Edward Warren Clark, b. Portsmouth, N.H., Jan. 27, 1849; m. Sept. 10, 1879, Louisa McCulloch: issue,—Edith Louisa (b. Sept. 2, 1880); Edward Warren (b. Feb. 17, 1882); Robert Stanton (b. March 16, 1884; d. Nov. 17, 1892); Henry McCulloch (b. Feb. 26, 1887); Robert Ernest (b. Jan. 10, 1889); Lucius Lehman (b. Jan. 26, 1891); Margery Williston (b. July 1, 1896); l. Tallahassee, Fla.

(4). Rev. Fletcher Clark, b. Boston, Mass., Nov. 23, 1852; m. Nov. 7, 1881, Elizabeth Matson Nyce; one daughter, Lillian Matson (b. Nov. 26, 1884); l. Philadelphia, Penn.

(5). Francke Lucien Clark, b. Brooklyn, N. Y., April 15, 1859; l. Philadelphia, Penn., unmarried.

(6). Eliza Walton Clark, b. Albany, N. Y., Aug. 27, 1865; m. Sept. 19, 1888, Theodore H. Ea-

THE TATE FAMILY. 105

ton: issue,—Theodore Horatio (b. June 23, 1889; d. in 1891); Margaret Montgomery (b. May 9, 1892); Berrien Clark (b. August 3, 1893); l. Detroit, Mich.
5. Henry Martyn Walton, d. in 1877; m. Magdalene Neill of Jefferson County, W. Va.; one child, Lily, widow of Ruthven Morrow of Charlestown, W. Va.
6. Rev. Edward Payson Walton, m. Janet Skinker of Richmond: issue,—Rev. William (Archdeacon of Georgia), May and Edward.
7. Rev. Jeremiah Evarts Walton, b. March 27, 1831; m. Helen Mar Randal of Massachusetts: issue,— William, Helen (m. her cousin, Rev. W. W. Walton), Lucy (m. Hyde Marshall Mich), Jeremiah, Florence (m. Charles Gorham), Marshall Mich.
8. Rev. Robert Hall Walton, m. Annie Lewis of Harrisonburg: issue,—Maude (m............ Mays of Birmingham, Ala.), Minnie, Rev. Fletcher (a minister of the Methodist Church in Georgia), William, Robert (of Atlanta, Ga.), Francke.

§89 D. *Magnus Tate*, b. "Belvidere", Sept. 1, 1767; d. March 30,1823; m. Mrs. Elizabeth Tryatt–Shrodes (p. John Tryatt and Elizabeth Tillottson, great-grand-daughter of the Archbishop of Canterbury; they were very wealthy, and came to America about 1770). He was elected to the Virginia House of Representatives in 1797, '98, '99, 1802, '03, '09, and '10. He was commissioned Magistrate in 1799, and was twice commissioned Sheriff of the County, in 1819 and 1820. In 1815 he was elected to the United States Congress. He was a Trustee of Charlestown at its establishment in 1786. His home was about three miles from Martinsburg.

 I. Erasmus Tate, m. Ann Packett of Charlestown. He died at the age of seventy-five, leaving no children.
 II. John Tate.
 III. *Mary Tate*, m. DR. TALIAFERRO STRIBLING; see §33.
 IV. Lucinda Tate, m. George Thomas of Hancock, Md.; two sons, Erasmus of Springfield, Ohio, and James.
 V. Amanda (?) Tate, perhaps married a Mr. Goode.
E. John Tate, died unmarried.
F. George Tate, died unmarried.

THE TATE FAMILY.

§90 G. William Tate, b. "Belvidere", Jan. 20, 1776; d. in 1818; m. Feb. 5, 1807, Abigail North Humphreys (b. July 4, 1787; d. Nov. 15, 1862; p. David Humphreys, immigrant from Wales, and Ann North, daughter of Roger North and Ann Rambo, and grand-daughter of Caleb North, who landed in Philadelphia, from Cork, Ireland, July 20, 1729).

I. Mary Ann Tate, b. in 1808; d. Jan. 22, 1832; m. a Mr. Daugherty: issue,—Mary A. (d. unmarried in 1888), W. T., and others.

II. Dr. Magnus W. Tate of Lexington, Mo., married twice: issue, by second marriage,—Gay, John, William, a daughter who married George Crawford of Louisville, Ky., and others.

III. Willelma Tate, b. in 1813; d. Sept. 20, 1853; m. a Mr. Aisquith of Baltimore, Md.; issue,—Mary V., Lyttleton, William, and others.

IV. George H. Tate, d. unmarried in Cincinnati, Ohio, April 25, 1890.

V. John Humphreys Tate, b. "Belvidere", Dec. 26, 1816; d. Feb. 7, 1891; m. Cincinnati, O., May 11, 1853, Margaret Kincaid Chenoweth (b. Harrodsburg, Ky., Jan. 8, 1832; d. Feb. 2, 1889).

1. John Chenoweth Tate, b. Cincinnati, O., March 11, 1854; m. in Oct. 1876, Fanny Casey: issue,—James Casey, Margaret Chenoweth, and John H.; l. Kansas City, Mo.

2. Abbie Humphreys Tate, b. Cincinnati, O., Feb. 8, 1856; m. Perrin G. March; l. Fernbank, O.: issue,—Margaret Churchward (b. April 2, 1882); Janet Louise (b. August 10, 1886); Perrin Flack (b. July 26, 1888).

3. William Ross Tate, b. Cincinnati, O., Feb. 14, 1858; l. Chicago, Ill.

4. Lizzie Polk Tate, b. Cincinnati, O., Dec. 14, 1860; d. ib. Sept. 2, 1867.

5. George North Tate, b. ib. March 22, 1863; l. Chicago, Ill.

6. Thomas Orkney Tate, b. Cincinnati, O., June 17, 1865; l. ib.

7. Dr. Magnus Alfred Tate, b. ib. Nov. 12, 1867; m. Nov. 25, 1896, Katherine Welch Donnally; l. ib.

(1). Miriam Welch Tate, b. May 1, 1898.
8. Frank McCormick Tate, b. ib. Dec. 18, 1869; d. ib. Jan. 30, 1871.
9. Ralph Booth Tate, b. ib. Oct. 10, 1872; l. ib.

Note 3. Snickers Family.

§91. *Edward Snickers* was a wealthy planter and large land owner of Frederick County. A town in Loudoun County, a gap in the Blue Ridge, and a ferry on the Shenandoah all took their name from him. He died late in 1790. About 1755 he is said to have married Elizabeth Taliaferro, perhaps a niece of the Elizabeth Taliaferro who married the first Thomas Stribling (see §§22 and 23), and had four children. No descendants by the name of Snickers remain today.

A. *Sarah Snickers*, b. June 18, 1756; m. Feb. 12, 1773, Morgan Alexander (b. Jan. 10, 1746); she had one child,
    I. *Elizabeth Alexander*, m. Nov. 10, 1796, James Ware (b. July 13, 1771; p. James Ware and Catherine Todd). Three children,—
        1. *Sarah Elizabeth Taliaferro Ware*, m. SIGISMUND STRIBLING; see §45.
        2. Charles Alexander Ware.
        3. Josiah William Ware, b. August 7, 1802; d. August 13, 1883; m. *1st*. Feb. 22, 1827, Frances Toy Glassell; m. *2nd*. Edmonia Jaquelin Smith (see below, §92). There were six children by the first marriage and four by the second.
          (1). James Ware.
          (2). Hon. James Alexander Ware, m. Jane Morton Smith: issue,—Fannie (m. ....Elliott), Summerville, Eudora (m. ....Deane).
          (3). John Glassell Ware.
          (4). Elizabeth Alexander Ware, m. *1st*. Dr. Edward Wharton Britton, and had one son, Josiah Ware Britton; m. *2nd*. Dr. James Mercer Garnet McGuire; l. Berryville.
          (5). Lucy Balmain Ware, m. Edward Parke Custis Lewis: issue,—Eleanor Angela, Lawrence

THE WARE FAMILY. 108

Fielding, John Glassell, Edward Parke Custis, Lucy Ware (m. Charles McCormick of Chicago).
(6). Charles Alexander Ware; 1. St. Louis, Mo.
(7). Jaquelin Smith Ware, m. Helen Grinnan; 1. Clarke County.
(8). Rev. Sigismund Stribling Ware, m. Elizabeth Walker: issue,—Cornelia, Edmonia Jaquelin, Edward Jaquelin; he is Rector of the Episcopal Church at Port Royal.
(9). Rev. Josiah William Ware, m. Annie Nottingham: issue,—Helen, John Nottingham, Jaquelin, Josiah William, Kennard; he is Rector of the Episcopal Church at Ashland.
(10). Robert Mackey Ware, m. Caroline Waughop: issue,—Ellen, Josiah William, Harry, Alice Wilson; 1. Chicago, Ill.

B. *Catherine Snickers*, b. August 20, 1757, m. Dr Robert Mackey of Winchester.
  I. Mary Mackey, m. Samuel Taylor.
    1. Mary Taylor, m. Dr. R. McKim Holliday.
      (1). Mary Holliday, m. Thomas McCormick of "Elmington", as his third wife; see §200.
      (2). Col. Frederick William Mackey Holliday, m. *1st*. Hannah McCormick (see §200); m. *2nd*. Caroline Stuart. He was elected Governor of Virginia in 1877.
      (3). Margaret Holliday, m. Dr. G. F. Mason: issue,—Mary Herbert Mason; 1. Charlestown, W. Va.
      (4). Dr. Samuel Taylor Holliday.
    2. Robert Mackey Taylor.
    3. Charles Taylor.
    4. Elizabeth Taylor.
§92 II. Betsy Mackey, m. Edward Jaquelin Smith of "Smithfield", Clarke County.
    1. Catharine V. Smith, m. Edward Hall: issue,—Emily, Virginia, Betty Mackey, Adelaide (m. Roger Annan).
    2. *William Dickerson Smith*, m. *1st*. MARGARET FRANCES STRIBLING (see §31); m. *2nd*. Agnes Williams: issue by second marriage.

(1). Rev. William Dickerson Smith, m. Lucy Harrison Powers: issue,—Agnes Pickett, Annie Jaquelin, William Dickerson, Mary Bryson; he is Rector of St. George's Episcopal Church at Fredericksburg.

(2). Edward Jaquelin Smith, m. Mary Thompson: issue,– Lucile Pickett, Mary Jaquelin; 1. Wickliffe.

(3). Annie Williams Smith, m. Richard Buckner Smith; 1. Wickliffe.

(4). Elizabeth Mackey Smith, m. Robert Randolph Smith: issue,—Elizabeth Mackey, Agnes Williams, Susie Wellford; 1. Wickliffe.

3. Edmonia J. Smith, m. Josiah William Ware; see above, §91.
4. Edward Smith.
5. Elizabeth Bush Smith, m. *1st.* John Bush; m. *2nd.* Oliver Tousey. There were three children by the first marriage and four by the second.

(1). Catherine Bush.
(2). Mary Bush.
(3). Betty Bush.
(4). Olive Tousey, m. F. A. Fletcher: issue,—Bessie, Frank, Roberta, Catherine; 1. Evanston, Ill.
(5). Emily Tousey, m. Truston B. Boyd: issue,— David, Ingram; 1. St. Louis, Mo.
(6). Lydia Paxton Tousey, m. George W. Boyd, Asst. Genl. Pass. Agent of the Pennsylvania R. R.: issue,—Oliver, Lydia Paxton, Anna; 1. Philadelphia, Penn.
(7). Roberta Tousey, m. Stanley Grepe: issue,— John Stanley, Lydia Jaquelin; 1. Evanston, Ill.

6. Emily Smith.
7. Roberta Mackey Smith, m. Philip Powers; 1. Wickliffe.

(1). Alice Burnett Powers.
(2). Elizabeth Mackey Powers.
(3). Jaquelin Smith Powers, m. Estelle Castleman: issue,—Roberta, Mary, Estelle, Emily, Henry, Fannie Catherine, Sophie.

THE MACKEY FAMILY.

    (4). William Smith Powers, m. Jeanette Brown: issue,—Jeanette; 1. Chicago, Ill.
    (5). Fannie Ballard Powers, m. Rev. T. Carter Page: issue,—Philip Powers, Virginia Newton, Roberta Mackey; 1. Cambridge, Md.
    (6). Kate Stuart Powers.
    (7). Philip H. Powers, m. Mary Grove: issue,—Philip H., Louise Berry; 1. Clarke County.
    (8). Mary H. Powers.
    (9). Edmonia Ware Powers.
III. Frederick Mackey.
IV. John Mackey, m. Rebecca McGuire.
  1. Frederika Mackey, m. Nathan S. White of Jefferson County.
    (1). Benjamin White.
    (2). Rebecca White, m. Joseph Trapnell: issue,—Benjamin, Emily, Joseph, Frederika, Ellen, William, White, Rebecca, Thomas, Richard, John Mackey; 1. Charlestown, W. Va.
  2. Elizabeth Mackey, m. John Meade.
    (1). Catherine Meade, m. James William Fletcher: issue,—William Meade, James; 1. Rappahannock County.
    (2). Louise Meade, m..........Richie.
    (3). Mary Meade.
    (4). John Meade.
  3. Catherine Mackey, m. Scott Tidball.
    (1). Nannie Tidball, m..........Dickinson: issue,—Warren, Catherine.
    (2). Rev. Thomas A. Tidball, D. D., m. Josephine Brown; 1. Philadelphia, Pa.
V. Sally Mackey, m. Dr. Robert T. Baldwin; no issue.
§93 VI. *Kitty Mackey*, m. Dr. Archibald Stuart Baldwin.
  1. Mary Mackey Baldwin, m. Joseph Tidball, a lawyer.
    (1). Stuart Baldwin Tidball.
    (2). William Hill Tidball, m. Mary Swartzwelder: issue,—Leonard; 1. Fort Worth, Texas.
    (3). Susan Watkins Tidball, m. E. M. Tidball; 1. Winchester.

The following was omitted by mistake from the opposite page.

4½. Dr. Robert Frederick Baldwin, m. Caroline Marx Barton. He was a Colonel and Surgeon in the Confederate Army, and Superintendent of the Western State Hospital for the Insane at Staunton.

    (1). Caroline Marx Baldwin, m. Hugh Caperton Preston: issue,—James Francis, Robert Baldwin, Caroline Marx, Sarah Caperton, William Ballard and Katherine Stuart.

    (2). Katherine Mackey Baldwin, m. Barton Myers of Norfolk: issue,—Robert Baldwin, Julia Barton, Katherine Barton, Louisa Barton, Caroline Barton, Barton, and Frances Stuart.

    (3). Archibald Stuart Baldwin, m. Martha Frazier; issue,—Robert Frederick, Martha Frazier, Archibald Stuart, William Frazier, Caroline Barton, Howard Frazier and Katherine Mackey.

    (4). Robert Frederick Baldwin, m. Elizabeth Deans Boykin: issue,—Robert Frederick, Elizabeth Irwin and William Boykin.

    (5). William Barton Baldwin, m. Bessie Saunders Taylor: no issue.

    (6). John Mackey Baldwin, unmarried.

THE BALDWIN FAMILY. 111

    (4). Robert Baldwin Tidball.
    (5). Catherine Stuart Tidball.
  2. Margaret Daniel Baldwin, m. Robert Whitehead, a lawyer.
    (1). Stuart Baldwin Whitehead, m. Susan Massay: issue,—John, Stuart Baldwin, Robert, Katherine; 1. Lovingston, Nelson County.
    (2). Kittie Mackey Whitehead, m. Frederick Moss: issue,—Kimbrough, Jean Irwin, Margaret, Archibald Stuart Baldwin; 1. Markham.
    (3). Mary Briscoe Whitehead.
    (4). Samuel Whitehead.
    (5). Sarah Whitehead.
    (6). Robert Frederick Whitehead.
  3. *Catherine Snickers Baldwin*, m. DR. SIGISMUND STRIBLING NEILL; see §51.
  4. Sarah Elizabeth Taliaferro Baldwin.
  5. *Dr. John Mackey Baldwin*, m. Martha W. Barton.
    (1). Archibald Stuart Baldwin, m. Emma Clark: issue,—Laura, Mildred.
    (2). *Maria Marshall Baldwin*, m. JAMES RICHARDS TAYLOR; see §11.
  6. Dr. Cornelius Baldwin, m. Anna Marshall Jones:
    (1). Charles Marshall Baldwin, m. Belle Hammat.
  7. Fannie Ware Baldwin.
C. William Snickers, b. in July, 1759; m. May 30, 1793, Frances Washington, daughter of Warner and Mary (Whiting) Washington.
  I. Mary Snickers, m. Moses Hunter: issue,—Frances Washington, Nancy (m. William Weeks; issue,—Mary, Fannie, William, Brooke, Hunter; 1. Washington, D. C.), Moses, Henry St. George, Beverley, and Brooke.
  II. Emily Snickers.
  III. Betty Snickers, m. Henry Brown: issue,—Frederick, William, Frank, Fannie, and others.
  IV. William Snickers.
  V. Beverley Snickers.
  VI. Edward Snickers.
D. *Elizabeth Snickers*, m. THOMAS STRIBLING, see §63.

THE TROUT FAMILY.

§94. From the traditions preserved in several branches of the Trout family today, it would seem that many years before the Revolutionary War three brothers, Lutherans, fleeing from religious persecution in Germany, emigrated from the neighborhood of Frankfort-on-the-Main and settled at Germantown, Pennsylvania. One of them, Nathaniel (?), remained in Pennsylvania; the second, Daniel (?), removed to Frederick County, Virginia; and the third, Jeremiah (?), who never married. was a Lutheran minister and a chaplain in the Army during the Revolution. A sermon preached by him the evening before the battle of the Brandywine was published in Harper's Magazine many years ago, but was there attributed to a Joab or Jacob Trout. His Bible, in which all his texts were marked with red ink, was preserved until about fifty years ago, when it was lost. Several heir-looms still remain, including an old hundred-year almanac, bound in leather and preserved in a leather case, printed in German in the year 1699, and illustrated with curious woodcuts. The name was originally spelled Traut, meaning in German, "lovely" or "dear". One thing is uniformly said,—that these ancestors for many generations have been a God-fearing, honest and industrious people. An examination of the court and other records of Philadelphia County, Pa., and Frederick County, Va., shows that this tradition is in the main correct, though the names of the original immigrants have been handed down inaccurately. The following account of the family is based upon these records.

About 1740, there were three brothers, John Balthazar (generally called Baltzer). George and Jeremias Trout, residing at Germantown, Pa., their names being spelled indiscriminately Trout and Traut. They were among the earliest settlers at Ger-

MRS. JOSEPH TROUT
Æ 99

mantown, George Trout owning 28 acres and Baltzer Trout 25 acres of land there. I am not at all sure that they emigrated from Germany about that time, but am inclined to believe that they were sons of one "John Trout of Upper Dublin Township in Philadelphia County, yeomen", who in his will, made April, 3, 1728, and approved May 7, 1728, mentions his wife Catharine, his eldest son John as his executor, and his youngest son Philip, but does not give the names of his other children. This oldest son may have been the John Baltzer Trout mentioned above; and all the names occur frequently in the Trout family. Though I could find no proof of this connection, there was nothing to disprove it.

George Trout died in July, 1745. In his will, made July 17, 1745 and approved August 3, 1745, in which he calls himself "George Troud of Germantown, yeoman", he mentions his wife Cassie, his daughters Leaney (?) and Catherine, his son Henry, and five other children not named. John Baltzer Trout was one of the witnesses to the will. Jeremias Trout may have been the minister referred to in the tradition above. Nothing further is known of him.

§95. **JOHN BALTZER TROUT,** perhaps the oldest of the three brothers, died in the year 1750. There is no will of his on record, and the name of his wife is not known; but on May, 26, 1747, he made a will respecting certain property jointly with his brother Jeremias Trout, in which are mentioned "our beloved sons and cousins Jacob, Balthazer and Jeremias Trout (the three sons of John Balthazar Trout)". It would appear that his wife had died and that these were his only sons. The will was probated June 21, 1750, John B. Trout having died shortly before that date, Jeremias Trout surviving him. His son Baltzer Trout died in Nov. 1762, his will mentioning his wife Barbara Trout, his daughter Mary, and his brother-in-law Nicholas Rittenhouse. His other son Jeremias Trout died in 1789, his will naming his wife Hannah, and his five children, Margaret, Bottes (?), Hannah, William and John. One striking feature of nearly all these early wills is the fact that special provision is made for the thorough education of the children of the testators.

§96. **Jacob Trout,** son of John B. Trout, removed about 1760 from Germantown to Frederick County, Va., and settled at Newtown (also called Stephensburg, but now Stephens City).

There was a Nicholas Trout living in that county in 1752, but whether he was related to the family or not, is not known Jacob Trout died shortly before April 5, 1774, for on that date Barbara Trout and Jacob Trout, Jr., are mentioned as administrators of Jacob Trout, deceased. His wife was *Barbara Klein*, who came to this country from Germany about 1750. She lived to an old age, dying at Newtown after 1812. Her grandchildren used to love to visit her and hear the stories she would relate to them about her childhood in the Fatherland. She was perhaps a sister of Adam Klein, who in his will, made December 9, 1799 and approved Dec. 1, 1800, named among others, his son-in-law Daniel Trout (see §97), his daughter Barbara Grapes, his brother Jacob and his sons Michael and John. Jacob and Barbara Trout had at least six children,—Jacob, Baltzer, Daniel, Philip, Henry and Catherine. It is said that there were one or two other sons who moved to Tennessee or Georgia.

A. JACOB TROUT, lived at Newtown, and died there unmarried in 1790. In his will, made Feb. 1, 1790 and approved April 8, 1790, he mentions his mother Barbara Trout, his sister Catherine Boyers and her son, Henry Trout the son of his brother Baltzer Trout, and his brothers Philip, Daniel and Henry. His brother Baltzer was his executor.

B. BALTZER TROUT had at least three sons,—Henry, John and William. He is said to have moved with his family to Sandusky County, Ohio, between the years 1790 and 1810.

§97. C. DANIEL TROUT married *Anne Maria Klein*, daughter of Adam Klein of Frederick County; see §96. He moved with his family to Kentucky in 1811, one of his sons having preceded him to that State. His eight children were: Anne Mary, Jacob, Daniel, Rachel, Jeremiah, Sarah (m. Jacob Overpeck), Isaac, and Catherine Trout (m. William Buchanan). Daniel Trout, Jr., married Anne Bradley Moreland and had thirteen children: Mary (m. Isaac Coleman), Catherine, William, Priscilla (m. .... Walton), Elkanah, Louisa (m. William Duncan), Jeremiah, Daniel B., Lucetta (m. J. S.

Maddox), Eliza Ellen (m. W. G. Luckett),John A. (married and had two sons, James V. and Albert E), Albert A., and Andrew J. Trout.

§98. D. PHILIP TROUT, b. Newtown (?), August 11, 1759; d. ib. August 21, 1812; m. Strasburg, in 1786, *Mary Magdalene Lambert* (b. ib. Feb. 22, 1758; d. Newtown, Feb. 12, 1826; see §111); he lived at Newtown, and reared all his family there. In his will, made August 21, 1812 and approved March 2, 1813, he mentions his wife Mollie, and his mother, and names his wife, his brother Henry and Jacob Boyers as executors. He had nine children, as follows:

§99 I. JOSEPH TROUT, b. Newtown, Oct. 16, 1787; d. Port Republic, March 26, 1850; m. Augusta County, December 24, 1812, *Sarah Whitesides;* see KINNEY FAMILY, §5. He lived at Greenville, Augusta County, till about 1818, when he removed to Port Republic, where he resided until his death. For a number of years he was practically an invalid, having suffered a stroke of paralysis. The records of the War Department show that he served for a short while in the War of 1812 as a private in Capt. John C. Sowers's Company of Virginia Artillery from Augusta County. His name appears on the rolls of that organization with remarks: "Com. of service, Jan. 4, 1814; Ex. of service, April 13, 1814; Term charged 3 mos. 8 da." He had eleven children, as follows:

    1. WILLIAM HENRY HARRISON TROUT, b. Greenville, Oct. 14, 1813; d. ib. Dec. 14, 1814.

    2. MARY ANN TROUT, b. ib. Nov. 27, 1815; d. Port Republic, Nov. 22, 1860; m. ib. August 14, 1839, *Thomas William Ryan* (b. Baltimore, Md., March 29, 1813; d. Mt. Jackson, August 12, 1883; he was a farmer in Rockingham County).

        (1). JOSEPH NICHOLAS RYAN, b. Port Republic, June 27, 1840; d. Staunton, Nov. 30, 1892; m. Augusta County, May 14, 1867, *Martha Eliza Francisco* (b. Warm Springs, Dec. 16, 1845; l. Staunton); he was Clerk of the Circuit Court of Augusta County from 1864 till his death.

a. MARY CARRINGTON RYAN, b. Staunton, April 2, 1868; m. ib. Oct. 5, 1892, *Schuyler Bradley Lyle* (b. Rockbridge County, August 21, 1866; he is a farmer); l. near Staunton.
- (a). HUGH FRANKLIN LYLE, b. Staunton, July 11, 1893.
- (b). JOSEPH RYAN LYLE, b. near Staunton, Dec. 11, 1895.
- (c). HARVEY FRANCISCO LYLE, b. ib. Nov. 29, 1901.

b. JOSEPHINE CAMERON RYAN, b. ib. Oct. 26, 1872; l. Staunton.

c. MARGARET HYDE RYAN, b. ib. Jan. 15, 1876; l. ib.

d. WILLIE FRANCISCO RYAN, b. ib. March 27, 1877; l. ib.

(2). JEFFERSON KINNEY RYAN, b. Port Republic, Sept. 20, 1841; was killed at the Battle of Cedar Mountain, August 9, 1862.

(3). ANNA LEE RYAN, b. Port Republic, Sept. 20, 1843; m. ib. Nov. 23, 1870, *Dr. William Harvey Byerly* (b. Rockingham County, Jan. 29, 1845; he is a physician); l. Franklin, Nebraska.

a. MARY KINNEY BYERLY, b. McGaheysville, Rockingham County, July 1, 1872; m. Franklin, Neb., Sept. 20, 1893, *Frederick Otto Miller* (b. Lawrence, Mass., June 10, 1869; he is a merchant); l. Franklin, Neb.
- (a). JOSEPH CHESTER MILLER, b. ib. August 11, 1894.
- (b). ANNA LEE MILLER, b. ib. April 18, 1897.
- (c). GRACE ELLEN MILLER, b. ib. May 5, 1899.

b. WILLIAM YANCEY BYERLY, b. McGaheysville, Jan. 7, 1874; d. ib. July 13, 1874.

c. ANNA LEE BYERLY, b. ib. Jan. 7, 1875; d. ib. July 24, 1875.

d. AUGUSTA STUART BYERLY, b. Staunton, Oct. 17, 1876; l. Franklin, Neb.

NICHOLAS KINNEY TROUT
⅛ 101

THE TROUT FAMILY. 117

      e. MATILDA TROUT BYERLY, b. Staunton, Nov. 7, 1877; m. Franklin, Neb., May 21, 1901, *Rev. Oran Rishel Bowen* (b. Ulah, Ill., Sept. 12, 1875; he is Pastor of the Methodist Church at Meadow Grove, Neb.).
          (a). VIRGINIA EARL BOWEN, b. ib. Aug. 4, 1902.
      f. MARTHA ELIZA BYERLY, b. Staunton, Apr. 16, 1879; m. Franklin, Neb., Nov. 20, 1901, *Clement Leach Wilson* (b. Johnson, Neb., April 24, 1874; he is a lawyer at Colby, Kan.).
      g. VIRGINIA LEE BYERLY, b. Franklin, Neb., Dec. 12, 1880; 1. ib.
      h. LUCILE HUBER BYERLY, b. ib. Dec. 27, 1882; m. ib. April 16, 1902, *Harry Hector Miller* (b. Cheyenne, Wyo., Feb. 18, 1873; he is a pharmacist at Lincoln, Neb.).
      i. JOSEPH RYAN BYERLY, b. Franklin, Neb., Oct. 31, 1885.

§100   (4). RICHARD DANGERFIELD RYAN, b. Port Republic, Oct. 2, 1845; d. Staunton, Nov. 28, 1876; m. McKinney, Tex., Dec. 3, 1872, *Elizabeth Ann Kinney Stribling*, his third cousin; see §27.
      a. THOMAS RANSON RYAN, b. Staunton, July 20, 1873; 1. in Texas.
      b. RICHARD CRAIG RYAN, b. Staunton, June 9, 1876; d. San Antonio, Tex., Apr. 7, 1896.
(5). JOHN CHESLEY RYAN, b. Port Republic, Oct. 26, 1847; d. Staunton, July 21, 1891.
(6). SARAH MATILDA RYAN, b. Port Republic, August 12, 1849; d. Grottoes, Sept. 8, 1898.
(7). JAMES WILLIAM RYAN, b. Port Republic, Oct. 17, 1851; 1. Grottoes.
(8). LLEWELLYN KEMPER RYAN, b. Port Republic, Oct. 31, 1854; m. Mt. Jackson, May 7, 1882, *Mary Catherine Myers* (b. Hamburg, Va., Dec. 25, 1858); 1. Mt. Jackson.
      a. THOMAS ISAAC RYAN, b. ib. Oct. 13, 1883.
      b. MARY ELIZABETH RYAN, b. ib. Sept. 10, 1894.

(9). MARY ARCHER RYAN, b. Port Republic, Oct. 30, 1857; m. Mt. Jackson, Dec. 22, 1882, *Robert Tunstall Miller* (b. Rockingham County, May 28, 1857); 1. Grottoes.
    a. NANNIE STRIBLING MILLER, b. Mt. Crawford, Sept. 23, 1883.

§101   3. NICHOLAS KINNEY TROUT, b. Greenville, Dec. 12, 1817; d. Staunton, Sept. 3, 1875; m. ib. June 8, 1843, *Matilda Kinney Stribling*, his second cousin; see STRIBLING FAMILY, §30. He was without doubt the most widely known member of the Trout family, being in his day one of the most distinguished chancery lawyers of his section of the State. He filled numerous positions of trust and honor in his community. At various times he was by appointment of the Governor a visitor to the two State Institutions in Staunton. He was a director in several of the banks of the city, and after the death of William Kinney, Esq., was elected President of the Old Central Bank of Virginia. In 1852 he was elected Mayor of Staunton, and for twenty-three years, with the exception of the year 1869, he discharged the duties of that office with singular fidelity and acceptability till the day of his death. He was elected without opposition to the State Senate in 1865 to represent his County in the Legislature, and served in that body with marked ability for three years, resigning the position the fourth year of his term.

(1). ERASMUS STRIBLING TROUT, b. Staunton, April 15, 1844; d. ib. Oct. 20, 1866; he was educated at the V. M. I., and was a Captain at the close of the War, though only twenty-one years old.

(2). SARAH ANN TROUT, b. ib Dec. 15, 1845; 1.ib.

(3). MARY LEWIS TROUT, b. ib. June 20, 1847; m ib. April 16, 1873, *Charles Lyttleton Cooke* (b. Raleigh, N. C, Sept. 26, 1848; he is connected with the Realty Bond and Trust Company); 1. Richmond.

a. MATILDA STRIBLING COOKE, b. Staunton, February 27, 1874; 1. Richmond.
b. CHARLES LYTTLETON COOKE, b. Staunton, July 6, 1875; m. Bristol, Tenn., March 13, 1901, *Sarah Horton Elliott* (b. Bedford County, April 17, 1880); he is a Clerk in the C. & O. offices at Richmond.
    (a). MAUDE STRIBLING COOKE, b. Roanoke, Jan. 18, 1902.
c. NICHOLAS TROUT COOKE, b. Staunton, Sept. 17, 1876; m. ib. Jan. 15, 1902, *Pattie Woodward Burnett* (b. ib. Aug. 3, 1882); 1. Richmond; he is a book-keeper.
d. LUCY WADDELL COOKE, b. Staunton, Jan. 28, 1878; 1. Philadelphia, Pa.
e. WILLIAM DEWEY COOKE, b. Staunton, March 18, 1883; he is clerking at Lynchburg.

(4). MATILDA CRAIG TROUT, b. Staunton, July 25, 1850; d. ib. Dec. 4, 1881; m. ib. Feb. 1, 1872, *Hugh Milton McIlhany*, her third cousin; see MCILHANY FAMILY, §131.

(5). FANNIE SMITH TROUT, b. ib. Feb. 28, 1853; d. ib. April 29, 1889.

(6). LOUISE SHEFFEY TROUT, b. ib. June 15, 1854; 1. ib.

(7). MARGARET GAY TROUT, b. ib. March 22, 1856; 1. ib.

(8). EVA LYLE TROUT, b. ib. June 28, 1857; d. ib. March 12, 1858.

(9). HARRIOT STRIBLING TROUT, b. ib. Jan. 15, 1859; 1. ib.

(10). NICHOLAS KINNEY TROUT, b. ib. Nov. 11, 1860; 1. Telluride, Col.; he has served two terms as County Assessor.

§102   4. ELIZABETH REBECCA TROUT, b. Port Republic, August 3, 1821; d. Milnesville, Augusta County, Sept. 11, 1888; m. Port Republic, July 21, 1842, *Peachy Harrison Wheeler* (b. Harrisonburg, March 21, 1816;

d. Milnesville, Dec. 25, 1890; he was a merchant and a farmer).
- (1). JOSEPH MCKENDREE WHEELER, b. Mt. Meridian, April 20, 1843; 1. Murphrysboro, Ill.; is a salesman.
- (2). LUCRETIA CLAY WHEELER, b. Mt. Meridian, Sept. 8, 1844; d. Milnesville, Nov. 2, 1895; m. ib. Nov. 18, 1868; *John Wise Arey* (b. ib. Feb. 11, 1846; 1. ib).
    - a. ELLANORA ZAIN AREY, b. ib. Sept. 14, 1869; m. ib. Dec. 25, 1893, *Charles Edward Wine* (b. Lilly, Rockingham County, April 8, 1871); 1. Milnesville.
        - (a). RUTH PAULINE WINE, b. ib. Feb. 19, 1896.
        - (b). AUBREY GLENN WINE, b. ib. Oct. 6, 1898.
    - b. LOUISE VICTORIA AREY, b. ib. Nov. 30, 1870; m. ib. Oct. 21, 1897, *Marcus Lee Cupp* (b. Rockingham County, Dec. 15, 1873); 1. Milnesville.
        - (a). ALFRED LESTER CUPP, b. ib. April 28, 1899.
        - (b). MARGARET LUCRETIA CUPP, b. ib. Aug. 9, 1900.
    - c. GEORGE WILLIAM AREY, b. ib. Jan. 10, 1873; m. ib. Dec. 27, 1898, *Bettie Belle Meyerhoeffer* (b. ib. Sept. 21, 1876); 1. Mt. Solon; he is a farmer.
        - (a). CHARLES GOLDEN AREY, b. Dayton, Rockingham County, Sept. 20, 1899.
    - d. ARTHUR HARRISON WHEELER AREY, b. Milnesville, August 20, 1874; m. Mt. Crawford, Sept. 27, 1895, *Cora Virginia Huffman* (b. Milnesville, May 21, 1875); 1. ib.; he is a farmer.
        - (a). CLARENCE MARION AREY, b. ib. Feb. 15, 1897.
        - (b). MARY CLAY AREY, b. ib. May 27, 1899.

The Trout Family.

(c). WARREN WASHINGTON AREY, b. near Bridgewater, Feb. 22, 1901.
e. SAMUEL WISE AREY, b. Milnesville, April 24, 1876; 1. Keota, Keokuk County, Iowa; he is a farmer.
f. JOHN HARVEY AREY, b. Milnesville, March 12, 1878; m. Augusta County, March 26, 1902, *Iva Jessamine Crosby;* 1. "Valley View", Augusta County.
g. HUBERT IRVING AREY, b. Milnesville, Nov. 22, 1879; 1. Bridgewater.

(3). JACOB WIRT WHEELER, b. Mt. Meridian, Dec. 21, 1845; d. ib. July 15, 1849.

(4). THOMAS BUSEY WHEELER, b. ib. Dec. 1, 1847; d. ib. July 31, 1849.

(5). NICHOLAS ZACCHEUS WHEELER, b. ib. Nov. 19, 1849; m. near Staunton, Nov. 15, 1881, *Lizzie Kate Hepler* (b. Goshen, March 31, 1857); 1. Milnesville; he is a teacher.

a. INA ESTHER WHEELER, b. Long Glade, May 26, 1883.
b. ROSCOE NICHOLAS WHEELER, b. ib. Sept. 17, 1885.
c. ELIZABETH KATE WHEELER, b. ib. May 19, 1887.
d. EMMA BROWNE WHEELER, b. ib. Oct. 15, 1894.

(6). SARAH CHESTINE WHEELER, b. Mt. Meridian, Nov. 7, 1851; m. Milnesville, May 24, 1888, *John Allison Brown* (b. New Paris, Ohio, May 16, 1838; he is a farmer); 1. Mt. Sidney.

(7). JAMES DAVID WHEELER, b. Mt. Meridian, Jan. 19, 1854; d. ib. April 24, 1856.

(8). SAMUEL KENNERLY WHEELER, b. ib. Nov. 20, 1855; m. Dayton, June 11, 1888, *Sallie Annie Snell* (b. Bridgewater, July 10, 1873); he is a merchant; 1. Churchville.

a. CHARLES RUFUS WHEELER, b. Milnesville, Jan. 3, 1891.

THE TROUT FAMILY. 122

b. LENA LUCRETIA WHEELER, b. ib. Sept. 24, 1894.
c. OLIVIA TROUT WHEELER, b. ib. Sept. 9, 1896.

(9). PHILIP EMBRY WHEELER, b. Mt. Meridian, May 31, 1858; d. Milnesville, March 27, 1863.

§103   5. MARTHA SELINA TROUT, b. Port Republic, Jan. 12, 1824; d. ib. July 9, 1892; m. ib. May 18, 1842, *John William Lee* (b. near Front Royal, March 13, 1820; 1. New Hope).

(1). SARAH ELIZABETH LEE, b. Port Republic, July 17, 1844; d. ib. Sept. 16, 1894.

(2). JOSEPH WILLIAM LEE, b. Port Republic, March 13, 1846; d. "Engleside", Monroe County, W. Va., Jan. 15, 1901; m. Nickell's Mill, Monroe County, W. Va., Oct. 17, 1872, *Sarah Rebecca Nickell* (b. ib. August 22, 1848; 1. "Engleside").

a. ERNEST NICKELL LEE, b. Nickell's Mill, W. Va., July 11, 1873.
b. MATTIE TROUT LEE, b. ib. August 30, 1875.
c. SARAH ANN LEE, b. ib. Feb. 11, 1877.
d. LAURA GERTRUDE LEE, b. ib. Feb. 20, 1879.
e. WILLIAM GORDON LEE, b. "Engleside", Oct. 14, 1880.
f. JAMES ASHBY LEE, b. ib. Nov. 12, 1883.
g. LYLE LACY LEE, b. ib. Nov. 8, 1889.

(3). ARAMINTA MARTHA LEE, b. Port Republic, May 25, 1849; m. ib. Dec. 23, 1881, *John Coffman Scott* (b. New Hope, Oct. 3, 1847); 1. ib.

(4). JULIA THORNTON LEE, b. Port Republic, March 1, 1850; d. ib. Feb. 11, 1882.

(5). JOHN NICHOLAS LEE, b. ib. Jan. 9, 1851; d. ib. Feb. 20, 1851.

(6). CHARLES KELLEY LEE, b. ib. Jan. 1, 1852; m. Charleston, W. Va., June 15, 1876, *Hester Ann Morgan* (b. ib. Oct. 10, 1857); 1. ib.

a. DORA VIRGINIA LEE, b. ib. August 7, 1877.

The Trout Family. 123

    b. John William Lee, b. ib. Feb. 9, 1879.
    c. Alfred Ose Lee, b. ib. July 16, 1881.
    d. Julia Thornton Lee, b. ib. Nov. 1, 1883.
    e. Philip Olen Lee, b. ib. August 21, 1886.
    f. Lucy Scott Lee, b. ib. March 3, 1890.
    g. Martha Adlai Lee, b. ib. Oct. 31, 1892.
    h. Lona Elizabeth Lee, b. ib. Sept. 1, 1895.
    i. Ruth Lee, b. ib. Nov. 29, 1897.
    j. Edith May Lee, b. ib. Oct. 13, 1900.

(7). Mary Craig Lee, b. Port Republic, April 1, 1855; m. ib. Feb. 7, 1878, *William Henry Harnsberger* (b. near ib. Oct. 14, 1854; he is in the cotton mill industry at Alberton, Md.).

    a. Virginia Harnsberger, b. Port Republic, Feb. 23, 1879; d. ib. March 22, 1882.
    b. Sallie Fauntleroy Harnsberger, b. ib. Feb. 1, 1881; d. ib. August 10, 1882.
    c. Wilbur Trout Harnsberger, b. ib. August 26, 1882.
    d. Lucy Lee Harnsberger, b. ib. June 15, 1884.
    e. John Scott Harnsberger, b. ib. July 13, 1886; d. ib. July 5, 1888.
    f. Stephen Fauntleroy Harnsberger, b. ib. Oct. 22, 1888.
    g. Raymond Magruder Harnsberger, b. ib. July 13, 1891.
    h. Annette Lorelle Harnsberger, b. ib. March 15, 1894.
    i. Lillian Archer Harnsberger, b. ib. March 25, 1896.
    j. William Henry Harnsberger, b. ib. August 22, 1898.

(8). Angeline Kemper Lee, b. ib. July 9, 1857; d. ib. in June, 1858.

(9). Stephen Archer Lee, b. ib. April 1, 1859; m. Pittsylvania County, Feb. 10, 1892, *Lillian Ainsly Graves* (b. Toshes, Pittsylvania County, June 13, 1871); 1. ib.

THE TROUT FAMILY. 124

(10). DORA VIRGINIA LEE, b. Port Republic,
Jan. 4, 1861; m. ib. Feb. 27, 1879, *Henry Dice
Robey* (b. Union, Loudoun County, Nov. 13, 1858;
he is in the cotton mill industry at Alberton, Md.).
    a. ARCHA LEE ROBEY, b. Port Republic, Sept.
7, 1880.
    b. JOHN ANDREW ROBEY, b. Frederick County, August 31, 1882.
    c. HARRY TALMAGE ROBEY, b. ib. August 16, 1884.
    d. NELLIE VIRGINIA ROBEY, b. Edinburgh, Jan. 22, 1886.
    e. CHARLES LEWIS ROBEY, b. Warren County, Feb. 13, 1888.
    f. FRANK COON ROBEY, b. ib. Sept. 27, 1890.
    g. PHILIP TROUT ROBEY, b. ib. Sept. 4, 1892.
    h. ARAMINTA MARTHA ROBEY, b. ib. August 18, 1894; d. Alberton, Md., Dec. 6, 1895.
    i. NINA ELIZABETH ROBEY, b. ib. Oct. 25, 1896.
    j. ARNOLD ABBOTT ROBEY, b. ib. Sept. 2, 1898.
    k. DORA VIVIAN ROBEY, b. ib. Nov. 24, 1900.
(11). HARRIETTE SELINA LEE, b. Port Republic, March 24, 1864; d. ib. June 9, 1869.
(12). LUCY FLYNN LEE, b. ib. May 21, 1868; m. ib. Dec. 31, 1890, *Harry Lightner Morrison* (b. Oakdale, Rockbridge County, July 16, 1863; he is a merchant at Marmion, Rockbridge County).
    a. HARRY LEE MORRISON, b. ib. June 6, 1894.
    b. WILLIAM DAVIDSON MORRISON, b. ib. Feb. 13, 1898.

§104 6. SARAH JANE TROUT, b. Port Republic, April 30, 1826; m. ib. Oct. 11, 1846, *John Harper* (b. ib. April 1, 1806; d. ib. August 25, 1889; he was a farmer at Port Republic); 1. ib.
    (1). WILLIAM JOSEPH HARPER, b. ib. June 24, 1848; 1. ib.; he is a farmer.

THE TROUT FAMILY. 125

(2). WILSON CHESLEY HARPER, b. ib. March 24, 1850; 1. ib.; he is a farmer.
(3). SAMUEL NICHOLAS HARPER, b. ib. Feb. 15, 1852; m. ib. Oct. 12, 1882, *Hannah Elizabeth Snapp* (b. Hampshire County, W. Va., April 1, 1863); l. Port Republic.
    a. LOTTIE VIRGINIA HARPER, b. ib. August 22, 1883.
    b. JOHN ROBERT HARPER, b.ib. June 1, 1885.
    c. HELEN VICTORIA HARPER, b. ib. Oct. 25, 1887.
    d. IRMA GRACE HARPER, b. ib. August 27, 1890.
(4). JENNIE BELL HARPER, b. ib. Nov. 27, 1853; 1. ib.
(5). MARY HARPER, b. ib. July 16, 1856; d. ib. Dec. 3, 1856.
(6). MARTHA HARPER, b. ib. July 16, 1856; d. ib. July 19, 1858.
(7). CHARLES ADDISON HARPER, b. ib. Oct. 20, 1858; d. ib. June 15, 1896.
(8). ANNIE ARCHIA HARPER, b. ib. Feb. 22, 1861; m. ib. August 27, 1881, *Charles Edward Snapp* (b. Romney, W. Va., June 23, 1857; he is a brother of Mrs. Samuel Harper); l. Portsmouth.
    a. WILLIAM ALVIN SNAPP, b. Port Republic, Jan. 31, 1883.
    b. JENNIE BELL SNAPP, b. Stanleyton, Page County, Feb. 23, 1885; d. Grottoes, Feb. 17, 1899.
    c. BESSIE EDNA SNAPP, b. Stanleyton, April 24, 1888.
    d. CHARLES HARPER SNAPP, b. ib. Oct. 28, 1889.
    e. RUBY ETHEL SNAPP, b. Grottoes, March 28, 1892.
    f. LEON LESLIE SNAPP, b. ib. Feb. 13, 1899.
(9). ELIZABETH REBECCA HARPER, b. Port Republic, April 5, 1864; m. ib. Nov. 24, 1887,

William Stuart Nicholas (b. near ib. Dec. 16, 1861; he is a farmer); l. ib.
  a. JOHN JACOB NICHOLAS, b. ib. June 11, 1889.
  b. LUCILE NICHOLAS, b. ib. March 11, 1894; d.ib. April 24, 1894.
  c. JENNIE STUART NICHOLAS, b. ib. Feb. 25, 1900.
(10). ARRIE OLIVIA HARPER, b. Port Republic, July 16, 1867; d. ib. Dec. 29, 1867.
(11). JOHN HARRY HARPER, b. ib. April 5, 1870; l. New York City; he is a buyer for C. B. Rouse, Clothing Department.

7. WILLIAM DAVID TROUT, b. Port Republic, Sept. 5, 1828; d. Harrisonburg, June 25, 1869.

§105   8. JOSEPH CHESLEY TROUT, b. Port Republic, Oct. 16, 1829; m. *1st*. Nelson County, Oct. 16, 1855, *Matilda Craig Vaughan* (b. ib. March 23, 1837; d. ib. Oct. 22, 1871); m. *2nd*. Amherst County, August 4, 1875, *Elizabeth White* (b. Nelson County, August 11, 1825); l. New Glasgow, Amherst County; he had seven children by the first marriage.
  (1). JAMES EDMONDS TROUT, b. Port Republic, Jan. 5, 1857: m. *1st*. Clifford, Amherst County, June 7, 1882, *Anna Laura Hudson* (b. ib. Aug. 27, 1855; d. Lynchburg, Nov. 6, 1888); m. *2nd*. ib. July 3, 1889, *Fannie Beatrice Hudson* (sister of his first wife; b. Clifford, Dec. 26, 1869); l. Newport News; he has two children by his first marriage and one by the second.
    a. EWELL VAUGHAN TROUT, b. Clifford, March 22, 1884.
    b. EMMA MERLE TROUT, b. Lynchburg, Nov. 24, 1885.
    c. ANNIE LAURA TROUT, b. Roanoke, Nov. 5, 1890.
  (2). GEORGE VAUGHAN TROUT, b. Washington County, March 30, 1859; d. Nelson County, Oct. 26, 1862.

(3). WILLIAM JACKSON TROUT, b. ib. August 20, 1861; d. ib. Oct. 25, 1862.

(4). JOSEPH CHESLEY TROUT, b. Arrington, Nelson County, May 27, 1863; m. Buena Vista, June 14, 1891, *Bettie Ann Ballard* (b. Fluvanna County, May 17, 1859); 1. Scottsville, Va.

    a. ROLAND ODELL TROUT, b. near ib. June 9, 1892.

(5). SADA INEZ TROUT, b. Nelson County, April 19, 18:6; d. Amherst, Oct. 25, 1889; m. Lynchburg, Feb. 12, 1889, *William Nicholas Bryant* (b. Amherst, April 20, 1863; 1. New Glasgow).

    a. WILLIAM CHESLEY BRYANT, b. Amherst County, Oct. 20, 1889; 1. New Glasgow.

(6). PHILIP HENRY TROUT, b. Arrington, Jan. 11, 1869; m. Nelson County, Sept. 9, 1890, *Minnie Dazzle Vaughan* (b. Paris, Texas, Sept. 9, 1865); 1. Newport News.

    a. MARY MATILDA TROUT, b. Roanoke, July 8, 1891.

    b. INEZ BETTIE TROUT, b. ib. Oct. 14, 1893; d. ib. Oct. 15, 1893.

    c. MINNIE DAZZLE TROUT, b. Charlottesville, July 28, 1897.

    d. VIRGINIA PEARL TROUT, b. Newport News, Oct. 30, 1899.

(7). A son, b. and d. Nelson County, Oct. 22, 1871.

§106   9. JAMES RUSSEL TROUT, b. Port Republic, April 23, 1832; d. Spring Hill, Augusta County, May 26, 1900; m. near Milnesville, April 13, 1865, *Amanda Jane Arey* (b. ib. Nov. 9, 1838; 1. Spring Hill).

(1). GEORGE ANNA TROUT, b. New Hope, March 7, 1866; m. Spring Hill, Sept. 11, 1890, *Sumpter Brock Hill* (b. Clayton, Ala., May 18, 1857; he is a merchant and orange grower at Maitland, Florida).

    a. MARGUERITE AGNES HILL, b. ib. Oct. 14, 1891.

    b. KATHLEEN LOUISE HILL, b. ib. Aug. 2, 1893.

The Trout Family.

c. George Willis Hill, b. ib. Nov. 21, 1895; d. ib. Nov. 10, 1896.
d. James Harold Hill, b. ib. August 29, 1897.
e. Sumpter Brock Hill, b. ib. Dec. 9, 1899.

(2). William Edgar Trout, b. Milnesville, Aug. 24, 1867; m. Fauquier County, June 30, 1902, *Nora Lightner* of that County; l. Clifton Forge.

(3). Olivia Virginia Trout, b. Milnesville, Feb. 11, 1869; d. near Laurel Hill, Augusta County, June 16, 1894; m. Spring Hill, Sept. 10, 1891, *Charles James Myers* (b. near Annex, Augusta County, Dec. 2, 1869; d. ib. April 18, 1893).

(4). Louella Whisner Trout, b. Spring Hill, Oct. 11, 1870; l. ib.

(5). Joseph Oscar Trout, b. ib. Nov. 24, 1872; m. ib. Jan. 10, 1900, *Jannette Elizabeth Coyner* of Augusta County; l. near Spring Hill.

   a. Olivia Virginia Trout, b. ib. June 4, 1901.

(6). Nicholas Kemper Trout, b. Spring Hill, July 6, 1875; l. ib.

(7). Mary Elizabeth Trout, b. ib. Sept. 29, 1877; m. ib. April 28, 1897, *Cameron Haughton Vint* (b. Sangersville, Augusta County, Feb. 9, 1870; he is in the U. S. Postal Service at Staunton).

   a. Lillian Olivia Vint, b. Spring Creek, Rockingham County, March 7, 1898.

   b. Russell Vint, b. Spring Hill, July 17, 1901.

(8). Martha Viola Trout, b. Spring Hill, Sept. 29, 1877; m. Staunton, Oct. 30, 1901, *Welton Switzer Vint* (b. Sangersville, Nov. 29, 1871); l. ib.

   a. Mary Whisner Vint, b. ib. August 15, 1902.

(9). James Chesley Trout, b. Spring Hill, Aug. 19, 1880; l. Maitland, Fla.

THE TROUT FAMILY. 129

  10. JACOB ARCHIBALD TROUT, b. Port Republic, Nov. 9, 1834; d. Staunton, Sept. 12, 1879.

§107 11. PHILIP HENRY TROUT, b. Port Republic, August 29, 1837; m. Baltimore, Md., May 15, 1867, *Olivia Benson* (b. Montgomery, Alabama, July 28, 1842); he is a broker at Staunton; he has been a City Councilman, Bank Director, and member of the Western State Hospital Board, and for thirty-five consecutive years has been treasurer of the Masonic Lodge.

   (1). PHILIP HENRY TROUT, b. ib. March 24, 1873; he is a graduate of Lehigh University and an Electrical Engineer; l. Atlanta, Ga.

   (2). WILLIAM BENSON TROUT, b. Staunton, Sept. 15, 1875; l. ib.; is in the insurance business.

   (3). CATHERINE GOLDTHWAIT TROUT, b. ib. Feb. 8, 1877; m. ib. April 17, 1900, *William Abbott Pratt* (b. near Waynesboro, Nov. 2, 1871; he is a lawyer at Staunton).

   (4). HUGH HENRY TROUT, b. ib. June 8, 1878; is an M. D. graduate of the University of Virginia; l. Baltimore, Md.

   (5). OLIVIA BENSON TROUT, b. Staunton, Oct. 25, 1879; m. ib. Jan. 21, 1902, *Waller Redd Staples* of Lynchburg; he is a lawyer at Sistersville, W. Va.

§108 II. REBECCA TROUT (1st), b. July 1, 1789; d. in infancy.

  III. ISAAC TROUT, b. Dec. 17, 1790; d. March 29, 1873; m. April 9, 1830, *Araminta Donner Pagett* (b. Jan. 19, 1807; d. Dec. 19, 1886). Besides the following two children, four died in infancy.

   1. MARY JANE TROUT, b. March 8, 1831; d. March 16, 1864; m. in 1854, *Dr. Thomas Daugherty*. Only two children survived, several others dying young.

    (1). CARRIE PAGETT DAUGHERTY, d. Jan. 1901.

    (2). MINNIE DAUGHERTY.

   2. WILBUR ASBURY TROUT, b. Oct. 21, 1849; m. March 5, 1878, *Mary Richardson Hall*; l. Front Royal.

    (1). MARVIN ASBURY TROUT, b. Jan. 23, 1879.

    (2). WILBUR FITZGERALD TROUT, b. Oct. 16, 1882.

    (3). CHARLES HALL TROUT, b. June 4, 1887.

  IV. JACOB TROUT, b. July 24, 1792; d. May 22, 1853.

V. MARY MAGDALENE TROUT, b. Jan. 13, 1794; d. Jan. 22, 1865.
VI. DAVID TROUT, b. Newtown, Dec. 25, 1795; d. Front Royal, Dec. 6, 1869; m. Augusta Co., Jan. 14, 1841, *Rebecca Blair* (b. ib. March 14, 1816; d. Front Royal, July 2, 1881).
  1. WILLIAM JACOB TROUT, b. Dec. 12, 1841; d. July 5, 1842.
  2. JACOB BLAIR TROUT, b. Apr. 5, 1843; d. Aug. 9, 1844.
  3. MARY ELIZABETH TROUT, b. Oct. 29, 1844; d. Apr. 7, 1845.
  4. CATHERINE BRUCE CALMES TROUT, b. Nov. 28, 1848; l. Front Royal.
  5. ANN REBECCA TROUT, b. July 28, 1850; l. ib.
  6. MARGARET CULLUM TROUT, b. July 29, 1853; d. August 12, 1853.
  7. ELLEN JANE PACELEY TROUT, b. May 5, 1855; l. ib.
VII. ELIZABETH TROUT, b. Dec. 10, 1797; d. young unmarried.
VIII. REBECCA TROUT (2nd), b. Nov. 23, 1799; d. Staunton, Nov. 3, 1855.
IX. ABRAHAM TROUT, b. Apr. 9, 1801; drowned in childhood.

§109 E. HENRY TROUT, lived at Front Royal, and owned some of the land on which the town was established in 1788. He died about 1817. His wife was *Susana Lambert*, sister of his brother Philip's wife; see §111. Their six children were:
I. Elizabeth Trout.
II. Isaac Trout, m. Elizabeth Donaldson, and lived at Woodstock: issue,—
  1. William Trout.
  2. James Samuel Trout.
  3. Mary Trout, m. James Norris: issue,—William, James and Elizabeth Norris.
III. Rebecca Trout, m. John Thomas Hickman: issue,—
  1. Susan Mary Hickman, m. William Edward Donaldson; they lived at Woodstock; issue,—Elizabeth Rebecca, Mary Lou (m. John William Magruder, and had—William, Edward, Dunbar, Thomas Hickman, May Susan, Frank, Lulu Massie, John and Robert), Caroline Graybill, William and Minnie.

2. Elizabeth Hickman, m Benjamin Pennybacker Newman: issue,—Walter Hickman Newman (m. Byrd Stephenson, and had—Mary Elizabeth and Walter Stephenson), Judge Edgar Douglas Newman of Woodstock (m. Mary Walton, and had—Wilbur, Edgar, Helen, Houston, and Harold), and Caroline Mary Newman (m. Mark Wunder, and had—Charles, Walter, Mary Elizabeth and Edgar).
3. Catherine Rebecca Hickman.
4. Emma Hickman.
5. Maggie Hickman, m. Rev. James Edward Armstrong, a Presiding Elder of the Methodist Church: issue,— Joseph Lamb (m. Katie Watts), Charles Martin (m. Mrs. Magruder, née, Hallie Cassard Sisson), Thomas Hickman, Emma Kate, William Trout, Fannie Stuart, and Edward Cooke Armstrong, Ph.D.
6. Dr. Joseph Thomas Hickman of Mt. Jackson, m. Alice Moore: issue,—John Thomas, Mary Elizabeth, Caroline (m. Frank Whistler), Edward, Lucy, Emma Kate, Winifred and Nannie Chalmers Hickman.

IV. Mary Trout, m. Samuel Myers of Front Royal: issue,—
1. Jacob Henry Myers, m. Rebecca Hendren: issue,— Edmund Howard Myers, m. Mrs. Virginia Caldwell-Trout.
2. Judge William Myers of Highland County.
3. Mary Catherine Myers.
4. Margaret E. Myers.
5. Julia E. Myers.

V. Joseph Trout, lived at Front Royal, and died at over ninety years of age.

VI. Henry Trout, of Hampshire County, W. Va., m. Susan Myers: issue,—
1. James Trout, m. Susan Caldwell, and had several children.
2. William Trout.
3. John Trout, m. Alberta Esten: issue,—Mattie C. Trout (m. Harper Dovell, and had—Alberta Dovell).
4. Isaac Trout, m. Virginia Caldwell: issue,—Susie Trout (m. Dr. David Kipps, and had Edwin Kipps), and Henry Trout.

§110 F. CATHERINE TROUT, m. *1st. Jacob Boyers*, and had one son, Jacob Boyers of Morgantown, W.Va,; m. *2nd. Henry Ritenour*, and had seven children: David (m. Fannie Rudacil, and had five children), Daniel (m. Louisa Newlon, and had several children), Joseph (m. Elizabeth Clendenning, and had—John Henry, Mandeville, Virginia, Emily, and Eliza), Henry (m. Elizabeth Fletcher, and had—Milton, Virginius and Henrietta), Elizabeth (m. Lewis Rudacil, and had—William, Joseph, Catherine, Elizabeth and Susan), William (m.......... Browning, and had several children), and Sarah (m. William McCord, and had—Henry, who married Hannah J. Minor, Kate Louise, and Sarah William, who married Edward Zea of Strasburg and had nine children).

Note 1. Lambert Family.

§111. *Christopher Lambert* emigrated to this country from Germany about the year 1750. A letter is extant, written to him by a relative from Frankfort-on-the-Main, May 20, 1787, in which full information is given about the families of his two brothers and three sisters who lived in Germany, particular mention being made of the fact that his brother John Nicholas was then residing at Jugenheim "in his father's and grandfather's house". This shows that the ancestral seat was at Jugenheim. It is not known who Christopher Lambert's wife was. He owned property in Winchester, granted him by Lord Thomas Fairfax Nov. 15, 1753, which he sold May 7, 1762. His home thereafter was at Strasburg in Shenandoah County. The names and dates of birth of his ten children are preserved in an old book, written in German.

1. Jacob Lambert, b. Nov. 6, 1755.
2. *Maria Magdalena Lambert*, b. Feb. 22, 1758; m. PHILIP TROUT; see §98.
3. Roberta Lambert, b. Nov. 29, 1759; d. August 3, 1767.
4. Tobias Lambert, b. Nov. 26, 1761.
5. *Susana Lambert*, b. Nov. 1, 1763; m. HENRY TROUT; see §109.
6. Abraham Lambert, b. Dec. 24, 1765.
7. Eva Lambert, b. Feb. 25, 1768; she never married.
8. Sara Lambert, b. June 24, 1771; married a Mr. Anspach, but left no children.
9. Daniel Lambert, b. June 19, 1773.
10. Elizabeth Lambert, b. April 6, 1775; married a Mr. Yager, and moved to Missouri.

THE McILHANY FAMILY.

§112. **John McIlhany** of Scotland was the founder of this family in America. I have not attempted to trace his home or ancestors prior to the time of his coming to this country. He was an ardent supporter of Charles Edward, the "Young Pretender", grandson of James II of England, and followed him faithfully from the time that he landed in Scotland, July 25, 1745, till his final defeat at Culloden Moor, April 16, 1746. With many of the survivors of this unfortunate struggle he was compelled to leave the country immediately. He was at the time about to be married to *Rosannah Stuart*, who her daughter Hannah Parker and other immediate descendants always said was a near relative of the Young Pretender, and thus a member of the Royal Stuart family. They were hurriedly married and sailed for America, landing at Yorktown, Virginia. They soon made their way to that portion of Fairfax County which in 1757 became Loudoun County. A deed in the Fairfax court records dated Feb. 16, 1756, speaks of him as John McIlhany, Farmer, and mentions Rosannah his wife and Thomas McIlhany his son. He seems to have acquired quite a good deal of property in Loudoun County and some in Botetourt County. On July 12, 1757, he was appointed by the Governor as a member of the first bench of County Justices, and in that capacity he served almost continuously till the time of his death. On Nov. 5, 1768 he was commissioned by Lord Botetourt, the Governor of the Colony, as High Sheriff of the County. The original commission is now hanging in the Chairman's office at the University of Virginia. In Nov. 1769 he is spoken of in the Order Book as "John McIlhany of the Parish of Cameron in the County of Loudoun, Gent. Sheriff." It may not be out of place to say that in those days "the Sheriff was the Executive officer of the County Court, which was composed of a body of gentlemen selected and appointed by the Governor for their standing and intelligence, who served without salary or fees, and were entitled in rotation to the post of High Sheriff, to which a good salary was attached. This office they usually farmed out to a deputy, and thus avoided the disagreeable duties it entailed. Then to be High Sheriff was to be high born".

John McIlhany's will was made March 27, 1773, and approved in court May 10, 1773. In signing it he spelled his name "McIlhaney", but the "e" has since been dropped. He mentions as legatees his wife Rosannah, his sons Thomas, James and John, and daughters Rachael, Mary and Hannah. His wife and son James were the executors of his will. I have not attempted to trace accurately the descendants of any of these children except James.

§113. Mr. J. Mortimer Kilgour is authority for the statement that the McIlhanys were originally Scottish Episcopalians. When they settled in upper Loudoun County, there was no church nearer to them than Leesburg, and hence there were really no church privileges for them to enjoy. When the Wesleyan movement began to spread in this country, the Rev. Robert Strawbridge (?), an Episcopal clergyman from Frederick, Md , joined in the movement and held revival services in an old brick school house at the place where Rehoboth Church now stands. Nearly all the McIlhany family, especially the girls, became interested in his preaching, and were really the organizers and builders of the Rehoboth church. It is not certain whether Mr. Strawbridge ever separated from the Church or not. Loudoun became the great stronghold of Methodism in Virginia. The best preachers came there, and the country was in a continual state of revival. While nearly all the family became Methodists, many have since returned to the Episcopal Church. None of the name remain in Loudoun County today.

A. THOMAS McILHANY was perhaps the oldest child. He is referred to as a witness in the Loudoun court on Oct. 15, 1766. He inherited from his father some property in Botetourt County; but as nothing further is known of him, he must have died young and unmarried.

B. JAMES McILHANY; see below, §114.

C. RACHAEL McILHANY, m. *James White* of Loudoun County, who died in 1797. Her estate was appraised in 1820, mention being made of her children Thomas, James, Rachael (Janney), Robert and Beneah White. There were at least eight children. The following outline was gotten several years ago from Mr. Josiah T. White, and I have not verified it in any particular:
  I. John White.
  II. Robert White; m. 1st .... Hardy; m. 2nd. .... Hunter.
  III. Thomas White, m. Jane Nixon: issue,—
    1. James White, m. Elizabeth Best: issue,—Thomas William and Mary Jane (m. her cousin Josiah T. White; see below).
    2. Thomas White, m. Mahala Householder: issue,— Thomas, Sciota, Flavias and Fletcher.
    3. William White.
  IV. James White, m. Mary Vernanda: issue,—
    1. John H. White, m. Melinda George: issue,—Mary Elizabeth, James George (m. Julia Brown), Thomas Mortimer, Anne Eliza, Robert (m. Laura Chamberlain), Joshua, William and John.
    2. Joshua White, m. Ann Brown: issue,—Frederick, Julia (m. Martin Wheeler), Edwin (m. Minnie Helm), Elizabeth (m. ...... Brown), George (m. Emma John), James Day, Frank and William.
    3. Rosannah White, m. John George: issue,—Cecilia (m. Ebenezer Grubb: issue,—Laban, Anna [m. James White, and had—James Mortimer, Anna Louise, John Wallace and Augusta Cecilia], Wallace, Roberta, Esther, John, Walter and Harry), John, Lydia, Mary Louisa, Roberta, Wallace, James, Edgar and Robert.
    4. Mary White, m. .... Roberts.
    5. Louisa White, m. .... Smith.
    6. James White.
    7. Robert White.

V. Rachael White, m. Nov. 11, 1805, Mahlon Janney: issue,—
  1. Josiah Janney, m. Orra Campbell: issue,—Belle (m. Dr. Turner), Walter and Campbell.
  2. Rosannah Janney, m. James Best; issue,—Dr. William Janney (m. Fannie Jefferson: issue,—Dr. Janney, Carl, May, Frank, and Gertrude), Rachael, Amanda, Mary Elizabeth, Josiah Albert, Charles, Orra Jane (m. .... Jefferson) and Thomas.

VI. Josiah White.

VII. Mary White. m. John Jones: issue,—Rachael.

VIII. Beneah White, m. Frances Saunders: issue,—
  1. Mary Elizabeth, m. *1st*. Henry St. George Tucker Strother: issue,—Kate and Willis; m. *2nd*. Charles Strother.
  2. Aaron R. White.
  3. Josiah T. White. m. his cousin Mary Jane White: see above: issue,—Frances Elizabeth, James Beneah, Thomas William, Annie Allen (m. James Manor: issue,—Virginius, Everett and Jeanette), Sue Carson, Leigh Richmond, Jeanette Ross, Catherine Duncan, William Respass and Mary Best.
  4. George White.
  5. Alfred White.
  6. Franklin White.

D. MARY McILHANY is mentioned in her father's will as Mary McCamey (?); but nothing further is known of her.

E. JOHN McILHANY, b. Jan. 15, 1756; d. Sept. 20, 1809. He is given in Heitman's Historical Register as a Captain in a Virginia State regiment in the Revolutionary War from April 1777 to May 1781. In the Revolutionary Records of the State Land Office there is a warrant, dated May 13, 1783, for 4000 acres of land to "Capt. John McIlhany for service rendered from April 1777 to May 1780". He never married. In his will made Sept. 18, 1809, and approved Oct. 9, 1809, he leaves almost his entire estate to his sister Hannah.

F. HANNAH McILHANY, b. in 1760; d. Dec. 14, 1839; m. June 16, 1812, *William H. Parker* (b. Jan. 12, 1759; d. Dec. 2, 1815). She had no children. She was a remarkable woman in many ways, and was always considered an authority in matters relating to the history of the family.

§114. JAMES McILHANY, son of John and Rosannah Stuart McIlhany, was born Sept. 22, 1749; d. "Ithaca", Sept. 17, 1804; m. in 1778, *Mrs. Margaret Tribbey-Williams* (b. Mar. 2, 1760; d. March 11, 1837). An obituary written at the time of his death says of him, that "the early part of his life was devoted to the pursuits of husbandry, and (after the death of his father) to the protection and support of his mother and her orphan children. At the age of twenty-five he joined the American Army, and assisted in avenging his country's wrongs. In the beginning his advantages of fortune and education were few, but nature had given him a mind of the first order, and formed in her finest mould, which afforded a wonderful instance of the power of native genius in rising to the highest degree of respectability when aided by unremitting perseverance and inflexible integrity. He lived as he died in peace with all his neighbors, beloved and respected by all who knew him".

His landed possessions were enormous. It is said that he owned 9000 acres of land in one body around the Short Hill, near Hillsboro, and extending as far as Lovettsville, and 4000 acres in another body on Goose Creek near Lincoln. He was a great business man, and would doubtless have been very wealthy, had he not died when still comparatively young. Each of his children is said to have received property valued at $50,000.00. Shortly after his death his personal property alone was appraised at $19,010.00.

His home near Hillsboro was called "Ithaca". The old mansion was long since destroyed by fire, and nearly all of his extensive possessions have passed out of the hands of the family. The household furnishings were massive and antique. The silver service was superb, some of it being still in the possession of his descendants. He spent a great deal of money on the education of his children. The best teachers available were employed at his home continuously, and two of his three sons completed their education at Princeton.

In the burying ground at "Ithaca" at least twenty-two members of the family are interred. Not having been attended to for many years, the plot is now in wretched condition, and some of the inscriptions are almost illegible. But many of the dates given herewith were taken from these stones.

James McIlhany was prominent in many ways, his influence extending far beyond his own community. He sat on the bench of County Justices along with James Monroe and others, and later became High Sheriff of the County. In the Order Book under date of April 11, 1781 it was "ordered that James McIlhany, Gent., be paid Two Hundred Pounds of Tobacco according to Law for attending Court Eight Days as a Witness against the several non-conformists in his District".

§115. The Records in the War Department state that "James McIlhany served as 1st lieutenant and captain, in the 5th, known also as the 9th Virginia Regiment, commanded by Col. Josiah Parker, Revolutionary War. His name appears on the rolls for the period from November 28, 1776, to May, 1778, on which he is reported as having been commissioned 1st lieutenant March 25, 1776, and he is reported on the muster and pay rolls of Capt. John Anderson's Company, same regiment, for June, 1778, with rank given as Captain, which roll shows that he resigned June 18. This roll is dated at Brunswick, July 5, 1778." See also Heitman's "Historical Register", and the "Virginia Magazine of History and Biography", Vol. II, p. 250. In the Revolutionary Records in the State Land Office, Book 3, p. 345, under date of May 24, 1834, there is a warrant for 4000 acres of land issued to the heirs of James McIlhany, deceased, on account of his services as Captain in the Continental Line for three years. It has always been said that he was a Major in Morgan's rifle brigade, but I have been able to find no authority for this, except the mention of "Majr. McIlhaney" among the officers of Virginia troops listed in the "Virginia Magazine of History and Biography", Vol. VII, p. 27.

The wife of James McIlhany, Margaret Tribbey-Williams, was a daughter of John and Elizabeth Fabian Tribbey, who were living in Loudoun County as late as 1793. It is said that her parents immigrated to this country from Wales. They

THE MCILHANY FAMILY.

were Quakers, but the family separated from that church on account of the Revolutionary War, several of the brothers being in the Continental Army. Her first husband was a Mr. Thomas Williams, by whom she had one son Uriah Williams, who died unmarried Sept. 25, 1804, aged 27 years. She was an elegant woman, tall and queenly looking, almost masculine in her strength of character and very pronounced in her religious views. She was remarkably intelligent and especially fond of history. It is related of her that she would often have some of her orphan grand-children roused at 4 o'clock in the morning to read Roman history to her. So advanced were her ideas that she became convinced very early that slavery was an evil, and accordingly freed all her slaves, sending them over the border to Pennsylvania.

They had at least nine children, as follows:

§116 I. NANCY MCILHANY, b. "Ithaca", Oct. 2, 1779; d. "Stony Point", Oct. 24, 1842; m. *1st*. "Ithaca" in 1799, *Nathaniel Davisson* (his will made April 28, 1806, was approved Oct. 13, 1806 in the Loudoun County Court; he was a lawyer; p. Maj. Daniel Davisson, an early pioneer and Indian fighter, and Prudence Izzard, a niece of Aaron Burr); m. *2nd*. Loudoun County, Feb. 6, 1808, *John White* of that County (b. Dec. 16, 1774; d. April 24, 1835); they lived at "Stony Point" which was her share of her father's estate. She had three children by her first marriage, and six by the second.

    1. MARGARET ROSANNAH DAVISSON, b. Loudoun County, August 14, 1800; e. Winchester; d. Council Bluffs, Ia., July 22, 1862; m. Winchester, Nov. 11, 1817, *Richard Milton*. For their descendants see MILTON FAMILY, §§165-170.

    2. FREDERICK AUGUSTUS DAVISSON, b. Clarksburg, W. Va., March 25, 1803; d. "Stony Point", May 30, 1869; m. Leesburg, May 29, 1832, *Elizabeth Derrickson Wickes* (b. "Snow Hill", Md., Dec. 24, 1812; d. Hillsboro, August 31, 1881; p. Rev. William Wickes and Sophia Pryse). He was educated at Transylvania University, Lexington, Ky., and studied law with Judge Tucker in Winchester. Later he studied medicine, and practiced in Hillsboro the remainder of his life.

§117 (1). SOPHIA ANNE DAVISSON, b. ib. March 8, 1833; m. ib. April 9, 1861, *Dr. James William Taylor* (b. Hillsboro, Sept. 13, 1832; see §188). They lived until recently at Hillsboro, but now reside at Leesburg. Dr. Taylor is a retired physician.
 a. FREDERICK WILLIAM TAYLOR, b. Hillsboro, Jan. 21, 1862; studied at the University of Virginia, and took the M. D. degree at the University of Maryland. He is practicing in Baltimore, Md.
 b. NELSON WEST TAYLOR, b. Hillsboro, Oct. 27, 1863; d. ib. June 21, 1866.
 c. ANN ELIZA TAYLOR, b. ib. Jan. 4, 18_7; d. ib. May 30, 1869.
 d. ELIZABETH DAVISSON TAYLOR, b. ib. Jan. 26, 1869; m. Hamilton, June 24, 1896, *Dr. Henry Randall Elliott* (b. Washington, D.C., July 14, 1874; p. Henry Randall Elliott and Helen Thompkins of Washington. He took the degree of M. D. at the University of Va. in 1895); l. Leesburg, where he is a physician.
  (a). RANDALL DAVISSON TAYLOR ELLIOTT, b. Hillsboro, August 31, 1897.
 e. JAMES BRATTON WHITE TAYLOR, b. ib. Sept. 12, 1870; d. ib. Sept. 4, 1871.
 f. VIRGINIA TAYLOR, b. ib. July 27, 1872; m. *1st*. Washington, D. C., April 25, 1892, *George Addison Fowle* (b. "Franconia", Fairfax County, July 20, 1867); m. *2nd*. Leesburg, Jan. 21, 1899, *Frederick Philip Metzger;* l. Washington, D. C., where he is in the government service.

(2). ROSANNAH DAVISSON, b. Hillsboro, Oct. 15, 1835; d. Warrenton, Dec. 13, 1869; m. Hillsboro, June 2, 1858, *Rev. John Francis Poulton* (b. Loudoun County, Feb. 22, 1831; d. Richmond, March 11, 1901. He was a Methodist minister).
 a. EDGAR DAVISSON POULTON, b. Suffolk,

THE MCILHANY FAMILY.

April 7, 1859; e. Bethel Military Academy; keeps a book store at Front Royal.
- b. ARTHUR WESTWOOD POULTON, b. Culpeper C. H., April 21, 1861; e. Bethel Academy; is in business at Augusta, Ga.
- c. ELIZABETH DAVISSON POULTON, b. Charlotte County, Oct. 8, 1863; e. Fauquier Female Institute; l. Kyle, Tex.
- d. JOHN CLARKSON POULTON, b. Charlotte County, July 16, 1865; e. Warrenton; m. Kyle, Hays County, Tex., June 25, 1896, *Nellie May Mitchell* (b. San Marcos, Texas, August 7, 1874; p. Christopher Columbus Mitchell and Julia Nance); l. Kyle, Texas, where he is ranching.
  - (a). JOHN COLUMBUS POULTON, b. ib. Sept. 26, 1897.
  - (b). CHARLES HILLIARD POULTON, b. ib. Sept. 8, 1901.
- e. ROSE DAVISSON POULTON, b. Alexandria, Aug. 11, 1867; e. Winchester; l. Warrenton.
- f. HUGH TAYLOR POULTON, b. ib. Dec. 5, 1869; l. Washington, D. C.

(3). AGNES DAVISSON, b. Hillsboro, Jan. 13, 1838; d. ib. Feb. 7, 1856.

(4). ELIZABETH DAVISSON, b. ib. Oct. 14, 1839; d. ib. Sept. 13, 1847.

(5). JOHN WILLIAM DAVISSON, b. ib. May 26, 1841; m. Atlanta, Ga., Nov. 23, 1886, *Nettie Petronia Hendrix* (b. ib. July 31, 1867; p. John C. and Mary E. Hendrix of Atlanta). During the Civil War he served in the 8th Va. Regiment of Infantry and 38th Bat. of Cavalry, two years in each. He is in the real estate business in Atlanta, Ga.
  - a. MARY ELIZABETH DAVISSON, b. ib. April 20, 1889.

(6). ETTA DAVISSON, b. Hillsboro, about 1850; l. Herndon, Va.

(7). AUGUSTUS DAVISSON, b. Hillsboro, July 25, 1857. He attended Vanderbilt and Johns-Hopkins Universities, at the former place winning a medal and the scholarship in Philosophy. He has been pastor of several Methodist and two Congregational Churches, and is now pastor of a Presbyterian Church in Charleston, S. C.

§118.   3. THEODORE NATHANIEL DAVISSON, b. "Long Wood", Loudoun County, Jan. 30, 1806; d. Jeffersonton, Culpeper County, August 4, 1890; m. "Stone Hill", Loudoun County, March 22, 1830, *Sarah Rogers*; see ROGERS FAMILY, §227. He was at one time Adjutant of a Militia Regiment. He lived for five years at "Liberty Hall" in Culpeper County, and the latter part of his life he spent at Jeffersonton.

(1). ANN CORNELIA DAVISSON, b. "Long Wood", July 27, 1832; d. Alexandria, Jan. 31, 1858; m. "Liberty Hall", June 19, 1851, *James Luther Chamberlain* (b. Alexandria, April 12, 1826; p. Luther Chamberlain and Jane Selina Adam of Alexandria. He married 2nd. Miss Helen Holmes, and lives at Warrenton).

a. ELLA JANE CHAMBERLAIN, b. Alexandria, March 16, 1852; d. Powhatan County, August 22, 1854.

b. JAMES DAVISSON CHAMBERLAIN, b. Alexandria. Sept. 26, 1854; m. Richmond, Oct. 14, 1885, *Helen Pendleton Wortham* (b. ib. April 24, 1867; p. Samuel Wortham and Edmonia Foushee); 1. Baltimore, Md.; he is a traveling salesman.

(2). MARY ROSANNA DAVISSON, b. "Milton Hall", Loudoun County, August 15, 1834; m. Jeffersonton, August 9, 1860, *Dr. John La Fayette Read* (b. ib. April 22, 1825; d. Warrenton, Dec. 1, 1895. He was a physician and surgeon); 1. Warrenton.

(3). JULIA ELLEN DAVISSON, b. "Long Wood", Dec. 29, 1836; d. Jeffersonton, April 15, 1859; m. Mt. Pleasant, Powhatan County, January 11, 1855, *Dr. William Henry Hening* (b. Powhatan

County, Jan. 17, 1831. He has married again, and is living at Jefferson P. O., Powhatan County).
- (4). JAMES McILHANY DAVISSON, b. "Long Wood", May 7, 1839; d. ib. Jan. 19, 1840.
- (5). HUGH NATHANIEL DAVISSON, b. ib. Nov. 25, 1841; d. Jeffersonton, Feb. 10, 1868. He served the first three years of the Civil War with the Warrenton Rifles, 17th Va. Inf., and afterwards served in the commissary department on account of ill health.
- (6). SARAH ELIZABETH DAVISSON, b. "Liberty Hall", Oct. 25, 1851; d. Jeffersonton, Sept. 25, 1862.

§119   4. AGNES BRATTON WHITE, b. "Stony Point", Feb. 25, 1809; e. Leesburg; d. "Salentum", Loudoun County, in Nov. 1875; m. "Stony Point", April 17, 1834, *James Bratton White* (b. Hillsboro; d. Hamilton, about 1884; p. Josiah White and Sarah Roach; gr. p. Josiah White—James and Elizabeth Roach). They lived at "Salentum".
- (1). ANN AUGUSTA WHITE, b. "Salentum", Feb. 23, 1835; d. ib. April 8, 1842.
- (2). JOHN JOSIAH WHITE, b. ib. about 1837; graduated at Dickinson College, Penn.; d. Atlanta, Ga., March 12, 1894; m. *1st.* Carlisle, Penn., June 17, 1859, *Mary Campbell Piper* (b. Harrisburg, Pa., Feb. 25, 1836; d. "Salentum", in May 1875; p. Alexander Moore Piper and Ann Espy Elder; gr. p. Samuel Elder and Margaret Espy); m. *2nd.* "Long Wood", March 6, 1876, *Mary Elizabeth White* (b. ib. Oct. 28, 1853; p. Joshua White and Mary Johnston; gr. p. Robert and Polly White—Reuben Johnston and Elizabeth Dawe); m. *3rd.* Atlanta, Ga., *Mrs. Almeda McConnell-Carlton* (d. ib. Dec. 22, 1893). During the Civil War he was a Major on General Ewell's staff, C. S. A. He moved to Atlanta in 1876, after which time he was a commercial traveller. He had six children by his first marriage and one by the second.

THE MCILHANY FAMILY.

    a. HARRY DORSEY WHITE, b. "Salentum", about 1863; d. Atlanta, Ga., Jan 2, 1893.
    b. JAMES ALEXANDER WHITE, b. "Salentum", June 24, 1865; m. Atlanta, Ga , Jan. 2, 1895, *Bertha Weinmeister* (b. ib. Feb. 16, 1875); l. Atlanta, Ga. He is assistant chief clerk in the U. S. Railway Mail Service.
        (a). MARGARITE AMELIA WHITE, b. ib. Nov. 16, 1895.
    c. ANN AUGUSTA WHITE, b. "Salentum", about 1867; d. Atlanta, Ga., May 28, 1888.
    d. AGNES DAVISSON WHITE, b. "Salentum", about 1870; d. Atlanta, Ga., Feb. 17, 1886.
    e. JOHN MORTIMER WHITE, b. "Salentum", Oct. 25, 1872; d. Atlanta, Ga., Sept. 2, 1897.
    f. ROBERT CAMPBELL WHITE, b. "Salentum", in May, 1875; d. ib. in August, 1875.
    g. FRANK DEVNEAUX WHITE, b. "Salentum", April 8, 1876; l. Washington, D. C.
  (3). MARGARET MCILHANY WHITE, b. "Salentum", Oct. 13, 1839; d. ib. May 1, 1842.
  (4). WILLIAM WICKES WHITE, b. ib. about 1841; d. "Locust Thicket", August 10, 1843.

5. JAMES MCILHANY WHITE, b. "Stony Point", June 5, 1811; d. ib. Sept. 10, 1831.
6. JOHN MORTIMER WHITE, b. ib. Aug. 27, 1813; d. ib. young and unmarried.

§120 7. MARY ELIZABETH WHITE, b. ib. March 9, 1816; d. Hamilton, Jan. 22, 1891; m. "Stony Point", Dec. 28, 1833, *Hiram McVeigh* (b. Middleburg, Sept. 3, 1798; d. Hannibal, Mo., Nov. 25, 1865; p. Jesse McVeigh and Ann Rogers of Loudoun County; see ROGERS FAMILY, §233. He was a successful merchant at Middleburg, Va., and Hannibal, Mo.).
  (1). AGNES WHITE MCVEIGH, b. "Retirement", Fauquier County, about 1835; d. ib. about 1837.
  (2). JOHN WHITE MCVEIGH, b. "Retirement", about 1837; d. Hannibal, Mo., August 25, 1864. He was in the banking business.

(3). HIRAM MCVEIGH, b. "Retirement", Nov. 29, 1839; e. U. S. Naval Academy at Annapolis, Md.; d. Jonesboro, Ark., Dec. 30, 1894; m. Mississippi County, Ark , Nov. 1, 1863, *Susan Hickman Fletcher* (b. Osceola, Ark., May 31, 1843; p. Elliot Hackey Fletcher and Frances Hickman; gr. p. Elliot Hickman and Julia Anna Dudley; l. with her children) He was a Captain in the Confederate Army. He was twice a member of the House of Representatives, and once Commonwealth's Attorney in his State. He was a lawyer at Osceola, Ark.

    a. FRANCES FLETCHER MCVEIGH, b. ib. Oct. 17, 1865; m. ib. June 25, 1889, *George William Smith* of Kentucky. He is pastor of the Parkview Baptist Church at Shreveport, La.

        (a). HIRAM MCVEIGH SMITH, b. Walnut Ridge, Ark., March 23, 1890.

        (b). SUSIE MARIE SMITH, b. Auvergne, Ark., Nov. 14, 1892; d. Detroit, Tex., April 12, 1900.

        (c). GEORGE WINSTON SMITH. b. Jonesboro, Ark., Dec. 12, 1894.

        (d). JESSE SMITH, b. ib. Sept. 23, 1896.

        (e). ELLIOT FLETCHER SMITH, b. Detroit, Tex , August 23, 1899.

    b. ELLIOT FLETCHER MCVEIGH, b. Osceola, Ark., March 25, 1867; m. St. Louis, Mo., April 5, 1899, *Mary Caroline Patterson* (b. Grand Junction, Tenn., June 25, 1875; p. Nathan Smith Patterson and Virginia Caroline Bowers); he is in business in Memphis, Tenn.

    c. MARY ELIZABETH MCVEIGH, b. Osceola, Ark., Feb. 20, 1869; d. ib. Oct. 9, 1869.

    d. JESSE MCVEIGH, b. ib. Jan. 29, 1871; d. Bald Knob, Ark., June 4, 1897; m. Jonesboro, Ark., Feb. 9, 1896, *Maybell Westbrooke* (b. Trenton, Tenn., July 28, 1872; l. Jonesboro, Ark.).

e. ANNA BLAND MCVEIGH, b. Osceola, Ark.,
Jan. 24, 1873; m. Jonesboro, Ark., Jan. 3,
1898, *Dr. John Gillam Clay* (b. Madison,
Ala.; he is a physician and surgeon at Dallas,
Texas).
    (a). ROSE CAROLYNE CLAY, b. ib. July
29, 1901.
f. AGNES WHITE MCVEIGH, b.Osceola, Ark.,
August 21, 1875; m. Denton, Tex., Nov. 15,
1900, *James Knox Sartain* (b. Aug. 8, 1872);
1. Bolivar, Tex.
g. SARAH HICKMAN MCVEIGH, b. Osceola,
Ark., April 3, 1877; d. ib. August 10, 1884.
h. ROSE MATHEWS MCVEIGH, b. ib. Dec.
30, 1879; m. Memphis, Tenn., Oct. 16, 1901,
Jose Maria Ramirez (b. Colzingo, Peru, Oct.
13, 1871); 1. Memphis, Tenn.
i. SUSIE FLETCHER MCVEIGH, b. Osceola,
Ark., Jan. 4, 1883; 1. Dallas, Texas.

(4). JAMES MORTIMER MCVEIGH, b. "Retirement", about 1842; d. Baltimore, Md., Feb. 12, 1881, where he was in the mercantile business.

(5). NANCY WHITE MCVEIGH, b. Hillsboro, about 1845; e. Hannibal, Mo., and Baltimore, Md. She has been a most successful teacher, and is now Principal of Bellewood Seminary at Anchorage, Ky.

(6). ELIZABETH HUMPHREY MCVEIGH, b. Hillsboro, about 1847; d. Baltimore, Md., May 10, 1879.

(7). JESSE MCVEIGH, b. Middleburg, about 1849; d. Hannibal, Mo., Nov. 15, 1863, having been accidently shot.

§121   (8). ROSE MCVEIGH, b. ib. July 30, 1852; e. Baltimore, Md.; m. ib. Oct. 8, 1872, *Joseph William Mathews* (b. Lewisburg, W. Va., Sept. 17, 1841; d. ib. Sept. 27, 1897; p. Mason Mathews and Eliza Reynolds of Lewisburg; gr. p. Joseph Mathews and Polly Edgar—Thomas Reynolds and Sally Ann McDowell. He was a soldier in th

THE MCILHANY FAMILY.

Confederate Army and a member of General Stevenson's staff. He was a banker in Lewisburg, W. Va.); l. ib.
- a. MARY ELIZA MATHEWS, b. ib. Sept.30, 1873; e. New Windsor College, Md.; l. Lewisburg, W. Va.
- b. JOHN WHITE MATHEWS, b. ib. May 29, 1876; is connected with the Rapanno Chemical Company, Wilmington, Del.
- c. HENRY MASON MATHEWS, b. Lewisburg, W. Va., May 5, 1878; l. ib.
- d. WILLIAM PATTON MATHEWS, b. ib. May 28, 1880; was drowned at Memphis, Tenn., May 5, 1901.
- e. HUGH MCVEIGH MATHEWS, b. Lewisburg, W. Va., Oct. 8, 1886.
- f. ALFRED VIRGINIUS MATHEWS, b. ib. May 24, 1893.

(9). HUGH ROGERS MCVEIGH, b Hannibal, Mo., May 7, 1854; e. Baltimore, Md.; m. Memphis, Tenn., Oct. 24, 1899, *Florence Rogers* (b. ib. Sept. 29, 1872; p. Arthur C. and Emma Rogers); l. ib. He is Secretary of the St. Francis Levee Board.
- a. HUGH ROGERS MCVEIGH, b. ib. Nov. 25, 1900.

(10). KATHLEEN STUART MCVEIGH, b. Hannibal, Mo., May 29, 1859; e. Baltimore, Md., and the Maryland State Normal School; m. Baltimore, Md., Feb. 6, 1884, *Dr. Thomas Farrow Keen* (b. Union, Loudoun County, July 29, 1855; p. John Keen and Amanda F. Broadus); l. Hamilton, where Dr. Keen is a practicing physician.
- a. HAZEL KEEN, b. ib. Jan. 5, 1882; d. ib. March 11, 1894.
- b. HUGH BROADUS KEEN, b. ib. Sept. 13, 1888.

§122 8. ANN CECILIA WHITE, b. "Stony Point", May 17, 1819; d. Alexandria, Feb. 23, 1892; m. "Stony Point", May 16, 1839, *Alexander Ross Milton;* see MILTON FAMILY §146).

(1). JOHN MILTON, b. ib. Feb. 21, 1840. He served part of the Civil War in the 8th Va. Infantry, Pickett's Division. He is President of the American Locomotive Appliance Company at Washington, D. C.

(2). ALEXANDER ROBERT MILTON, b. "Stony Point", Feb. 10, 1842; d near Wheatland, Sept. 2. 1857.

(3). NANCY McILHANY MILTON, b. "Stony Point", Dec. 1, 1843; d. ib. Dec 11, 1849.

(4). MORTIMER MILTON, b. ib. Nov. 26, 1845; d. Richmond, June 15, 1862. He was a courier in D. H. Hill's Division, C. S. A.

(5). THEODORE DAVISSON MILTON, b. "Stony Point", Jan. 24, 1848; m. "Valley View", near Hamilton, Oct. 2, 1873, *Lydia Cecilia Vandeventer* (b. ib. Nov. 28, 1851; p. Gabriel Vandeventer and Cecilia Heaton; gr. p. Joseph and Elizabeth Vandeventer—James Heaton and Lydia Osborne); l. Washington, D. C. For a short while at the close of the Civil War he was a member of Co. H., Mosby's Command, 43d Va. Cavalry.

 a. NANCY McILHANY MILTON, b. Hamilton, August 22, 1874; e. Millwood; l. Washington, D. C.

 b. JOSEPH VANDEVENTER MILTON, b. Hamilton, Nov. 30, 1876; e. Danville Military Institute; took the M. D. degree at the University of Maryland; l. Washington, D. C.

 c. ALEXANDER MORTIMER MILTON, b. Hamilton, March 30, 1879; e. Danville Military Institute; is now a cadet at the U. S. Military Academy at West Point, N. Y.

 d. KATHERINE BRADEN MILTON, b. near Round Hill, Sept. 23, 1881; l. Washington, D. C.

 e. LYDIA HEATON MILTON, b. Pæonian Springs, August 5, 1885.

 f. MARY STUART MILTON, b. ib. Jan. 31, 1888.

g. LOUISE NORTON MILTON, b. ib. Dec. 15, 1896.

§123   9. ROBERT JOSIAH THOMAS WHITE, b. "Stony Point", Feb. 27, 1822; e. Alexandria and at Dickinson College, Penn.; d. Hamilton, May 18, 1889; m. Hillsboro, about 1859, *Mary Louisa Taylor* (b. Hillsboro; d. Little Rock, Ark., March 13, 1869; see §188). He was a lawyer by profession. For eight years he was a member of the Virginia Legislature, holding a seat in both houses at different times. He was also a member of the Constitutional Convention of 1850. During the fifteen years of his residence in Arkansas, he was at one time Secretary of State for the State.

  (1). JOHN KILGOUR WHITE, b. Detroit, Mich., May 1, 1860; took the degree of M. D. at the University of Maryland; is now resident physician at Ocean Mines, Alleghany County, Md.

  (2). ROBERT ALEXANDER WHITE, b. Van Buren, Ark., Jan. 1, 1862; l. Washington, D. C.

  (3). VIRGINIA WHITE, b. Little Rock, Ark., Sept. 3, 1863; d. ib. July 3, 1864.

  (4). GEORGE ANNA TAYLOR WHITE, b. ib. Sept. 10, 1867; e. New Windsor College, Md.; l. Washington, D. C.

  (5). MARY LOUISA WHITE, b. Little Rock, Ark., March 10, 1870; e. Hamilton; m. ib. April 13, 1891, *Prof. Emil Ludwig Scharf* (b. Metz, Germany, August 3, 1856; p. Theodore Scharf, Principal of the University of Metz, and Bertha Binz; gr.p. Dr. Pantaleon Binz and Anna Galura); l. Washington, D. C.

    a. EDWARD GALURA SCHARF, b. Alexandria, Feb. 7, 1892.

§124 II. ROSANNAH MCILHANY, b. "Ithaca", in 1781; d. "Locust Thicket", Nov. 16, 1821; m. "Ithaca", in Aug. 1801, *Lewis Ellzey*, (b. Mt. Middleton, Loudoun County, in April 1780; d. Aldie, in August 1841; p. William Ellzey and Alice Blackburn. He was a lawyer and a very highly educated man, and taught a boys' school for a number of years. He served in the war of 1812). They lived at "Locust Thicket" in Loudoun County.

1. MARGARET TRIBBEY ELLZEY, b. ib. June 8, 1802; d. ib. Nov. 4, 1804.
2. ALICE BLACKBURN ELLZEY, b. ib. Jan. 7, 1809; d.ib. March 15, 1810.
3. ANNE ELIZABETH ELLZEY, b. ib. Sept. 18, 1811; d. near Williamsburg, Callaway County, Mo., Sept. 12, 1865; m. "Locust Thicket", April 14, 1829, *Edward Sanford Washington* (b. near Fairfax C. H., April 14, 1808; d. Callaway County, Mo., April 22, 1885; p. Edward Washington and Betsy Sanford. He was a farmer and stock-raiser). From Loudoun County they moved to Scott and Fayette Counties, Ky., and thence in 1849 to Callaway County, Mo.

　(1). GEORGE WILLIAM WASHINGTON, b. Scott County, Ky., Feb. 12, 1832; e. Fulton, Mo.; m. Callaway County, Mo , Sept. 27, 1866, *Elizabeth McClanathan Tate* (b. ib. Nov. 9, 1831; p. Isaac Tate and Jane W. Henderson; gr. p. Daniel Henderson and Martha Steele). He is farming and stock-raising near Fulton, Mo.

　　a. ANNE ELLZEY WASHINGTON, b. Callaway County, Mo., Jan. 23, 1870; e. Synodical College, Fulton, Mo.; d. ib. Dec. 3, 1892.

　　b. JANE MILTON WASHINGTON, b. Callaway County, Mo., Dec. 22, 1872; graduated with honors at the Synodical College in 1894; l. at home.

　　c. EDNA SANFORD WASHINGTON, b. Callaway County, Mo., Oct. 7, 1875; graduated with honors at the Synodical College in 1896; is clerking at Fulton, Mo.

　(2). LEWIS ELLZEY WASHINGTON, b. near Lexington, Ky., August 12, 1835; e. Central College, Howard County, Mo.; m. Callaway County, Mo., Dec. 27, 1874, *Marion Bryan* (b. ib. Dec. 10, 1855; p. John Bryan and Charlotte Windsor of Virginia; gr. p. Burton and Elizabeth Windsor). He is farming near Portland, Mo.

THE McILHANY FAMILY.

a. EDWARD MILTON WASHINGTON, b. Callaway County, Mo., Oct. 5, 1875; e. Westminster College, Fulton, Mo.; m. Eufaula, Ind. Ter., Oct. 19, 1898, *Sarah Kathryn Simpson* (b. ib. August 3, 1878). He is a book-keeper in the Eufaula National Bank.
    (a). MARION MORRIS WASHINGTON, b. ib. May 14, 1900.

b. BETTIE MARION WASHINGTON, b. Callaway County, Mo., March 20, 1878; d. Montgomery County, Mo., May 12, 1879.

c. LOTTIE LEWIS WASHINGTON, b. ib. Sept. 5, 1880; e. Synodical Female College, Fulton, Mo.

d. WILLIE DOUGLAS WASHINGTON, b. Montgomery County, Mo., March 27, 1883; is a salesman at Eufaula, Ind. Ter.

e. VERA ALICE WASHINGTON, b. Montgomery County, Mo., Oct. 23, 1886.

f. LEWIS ELLZEY WASHINGTON, b. Callaway County, Mo, Nov. 23, 1894.

(3). ROSANNAH McILHANY WASHINGTON, b. near Lexington, Ky., August 2, 1837; e. Fulton, Mo.; 1. ib.

(4). MARSHALL WASHINGTON, b. near Lexington, Ky., May 10, 1839; e. Central College, Fayette, Mo.; m. Wellsville, Mo , Sept. 10, 1879, *Elizabeth Arnold* (b. St. Charles, Mo., Oct. 29, 1856; p. W. H. Arnold of Danville, Mo.). He served in Price's Army during the Civil War. He is a livestock dealer at Montgomery City and St. Louis, Mo.

    a. VIRGINIA WASHINGTON, b. Wellsville, Mo., June 21, 1880; d. ib. June 20, 1881.

    b. MARSHALL WASHINGTON, b. ib. March 11, 1882.

    c. LUCILE WASHINGTON, b. ib. July 31, 1884.

    d. JOSEPH WASHINGTON, b. Montgomery City, Mo., Oct. 21, 1887.

THE MCILHANY FAMILY. 152

  e. MARGARET WASHINGTON, b ib. Dec. 11, 1896; d. ib. Dec. 17, 1896.

 (5). JOSEPH HOUGH WASHINGTON, b. near Lexington, Ky., June 29, 1841. He was a soldier in the Civil War, and died at St. Louis, Mo., Jan. 29, 1862, from disease contracted in prison.

 (6). EDWARD SANFORD WASHINGTON, b. near Lexington, Ky., August 26, 1843; d. near Williamsburg, Mo., July 21, 1860.

 (7). ALFRED OFFUTT WASHINGTON, b. near Lexington, Ky., Oct. 5, 1845; e. Williamsburg and High Hill, Mo ; m. near Williamsburg, Mo., Dec. 5, 1876, *Mary Jane Langtry* (b. Callaway County, Mo., Oct. 18, 1850; p. William Langtry and Sarah Hamilton; gr. p. William and Kitty Arbuckle Langtry—John and Sarah Hamilton). He is farming and stock-raising near Williamsburg, Callaway County, Mo.

  a. JOSIE LEWIS WASHINGTON, b. ib. Oct. 16, 1877.

  b. SARAH ELLZEY WASHINGTON, b. ib. Dec. 29, 1878.

  c. LUTIE SANFORD WASHINGTON, b. ib. Apr. 14, 1880.

  d. JOHN LANGTRY WASHINGTON, b. ib. Sept. 10, 1882.

§125 4. MARY CECILIA ELLZEY, b. "Locust Thicket", May 4, 1814; d. ib. Sept. 15, 1860; m "Ithaca", Jan. 10, 1832, *John Richard White* (b. Hillsboro, Oct. 7, 1810; d. ib. March 5, 1886. He was a merchant and farmer, and a brother of James Bratton White, §119).

 (1). ROSANNAH MCILHANY WHITE, b. ib. Oct. 2, 1833; d. ib. Dec. 25, 1833.

 (2). SARAH LOUISA WHITE, b. ib. March 6, 1836; d. ib. April 25, 1838.

 (3). ELIZABETH VIRGINIA WHITE, b. ib. July 11, 1839; d. ib. Feb. 25, 1840.

 (4). JOHN RICHARD WHITE, b. ib. March 4, 1842; m. Berryville, June 12, 1872, *Margaretta Holmes McGuire* (b. "Norwood", Clarke County, June

12, 1845; d. Sioux City, Ia., Jan. 21, 1891; p. William David McGuire and Nancy Boyd Moss; gr. p. Edward McGuire and Gertrude Holmes); l. Sioux City, Ia.

 a. NANNIE MOSS WHITE, b ib. May 30, 1873; m. Berryville, May 30, 1901, *Francis Beverley Whiting;* l. near Millwood; he is a lawyer.

 b. MARY ELLZEY WHITE, b. Sioux City, Ia., Nov. 11, 1874; l. Berryville.

 c. WILLIAM MCGUIRE WHITE, b. Sioux City, Ia., Feb. 24, 1878; d. ib. July 4, 1878.

§126   (5). LUCY ELLZEY WHITE, b. "Locust Thicket", Feb. 6, 1846; m. ib. Dec. 4, 1867, *Francis Stribling Pennybacker;* see STRIBLING FAMILY, §59.

(6). ANN ELIZA WHITE, b. ib. Sept. 29, 1848; d. Charleston, S. C., May 28, 1884; m. Berryville, June 11, 1872, *Rev. William Taliaferro Thompson;* see STRIBLING FAMILY, §35.

 a. MARY ELLZEY THOMPSON, b. "Locust Thicket", August 27, 1873; l. Washington, D. C.

(7). AGNES BRATTON WHITE, b. "Locust Thicket", Oct. 26, 1850; e. Berryville; m. Frederick City, Md., April 12, 1875, *Thomas Edwin Hough* (b. Old Town, Md., August 8, 1843; d. near Hillsboro, July 16, 1902; p. William Hough and Louisa Offutt); l. "Mountain Glen", near Hillsboro.

 a. FRANK PENNYBACKER WHITE HOUGH, b. Hillsboro, July 11, 1884.

 b. LEWIS ELLZEY HOUGH, b. ib. Jan. 9, 1887.

5. CATHERINE LEWIS ELLZEY, b. "Locust Thicket", June 15, 1816; d. ib. July 7, 1820.

§127   6. ROSE MORTIMER ELLZEY, b. ib. Oct. 18, 1818; m. Hillsboro, Dec. 10, 1839, *Col. Francis McCormick* (b. "Weehaw", Clarke County, Oct. 20, 1801; d. "Frankford", near Berryville, April 16, 1872; see §199); l. ib.

 (1). MARY ELIZA MCCORMICK, b. "Weehaw", Oct. 18, 1840; e. Richmond Seminary; m. "Frankford", Dec. 17, 1867, *Col. Marshall McDonald* (b.

Romney, W. Va., Oct. 18, 1836; d. Washington, D. C., Sept. 1, 1895; p. Angus William McDonald and Lucy Ann Naylor; gr. p. Angus William McDonald and Mary McGuire—William Naylor and Ann Sanford. He was a Colonel in the Confederate Army, a professor at the Virginia Military Institute, and later Commissioner of Fisheries for the United States); 1. "Frankford". She has been twice elected Treasurer General of the Daughters of the American Revolution and was one of the first invited to organize that Society.

    a. MARY MCDONALD, b. and d. Lexington, in March 1869; lived only six days.

    b. ROSE MORTIMER ELLZEY MCDONALD, b. Lexington, Nov. 23, 1871; e. Norwood Institute, Washington, D. C.; is principal of a school at Berryville.

    c. ANGUS MCDONALD, b. Lexington, May 28, 1873; e. University of Virginia, and took the LL B. degree at the National University in Washington. He served in the 3rd Va. Inft. during the Spanish War, and also with the English Army in South Africa. He is in business in Idaho.

    d. NANNIE FRANK MCDONALD, b. Washington, D. C., Jan. 17, 1883; d. ib. April 10, 1886.

(2). MARGARETTA MCCORMICK, b. "Frankford", April 9, 1843; d. ib. May 4, 1885.

(3). CYRUS MCCORMICK, b. ib. April 27, 1845; e. V. M. I. and University of Virginia, and graduated in medicine at the University of Maryland; m. Alexandria, Sept. 28, 1869, *Anne Elizabeth Taylor* (b. Alexandria, July 12, 1847; p. Lawrence Berry Taylor and Catherine Virginia Powell; gr. p. Robert I. Taylor and Mollie Elizabeth Berry —Dr William L. Powell and Ann Maria Powell, both grand-children of Col. William Levin Powell, a member of the first Philadelphia Congress and Colonel of the 16th Va. Volunteers in the

Revolutionary War. In 1863 he joined the 6th Va. Cavalry, and in the latter part of the War was a prisoner at Camp Chase, Ohio. He is a physician at Berryville.)
    a. FRANK MCCORMICK, b. "Cool Spring", Clarke County, July 9, 1870; d. Berryville, August 9, 1892.
    b. NANNIE POWELL MCCORMICK, b. Theological Seminary, near Alexandria, April 12, 1872; e. Berryville; m. ib June 14, 1899, *Maj. Charles Ellet Cabell* (b. Nelson County, Nov. 22, 1871; he is a lawyer at Big Stone Gap; he served with distinction in the U. S. Army during the War with Spain).
        (a). ANNE ELIZABETH CABELL, b. Berryville, May 20, 1900.
        (b). MARY VIRGINIA ELLET CABELL, b. ib. May 3, 1902.
    c. LAWRENCE BERRY TAYLOR MCCORMICK, b. Theological Seminary, July 12, 1874; took the degree of B. L. at Columbian University, Washington, in 1895; is practicing law in Temple, Tex.

§128   (4). NANNIE FRANK MCCORMICK, b. "Frankford", Feb. 16, 1847; e. Piedmont Institute, Charlottesville; m. "Frankford", Dec. 19, 1871, *Thomas McCormick*, her first cousin (b. "Elmington", August 4, 1848; d. "Frankford", July 10, 1901; see §201); 1. ib.
    a. ROSE ELLZEY MCCORMICK, b. ib. July 19, 1873; e. Edgehill; l. "Frankford".
    b. ELIZA MCCORMICK, b. ib. Sept, 28, 1874; d. ib. July 28, 1875.
    c. FRANK MCCORMICK, b. ib. May 17, 1877; e. University of Va.; is farming at "Frankford".
    d. HANNAH HOLLIDAY MCCORMICK, b. "Frankford", May 13, 1881; d. ib. August 4, 1881.

(5). SAMUEL MCCORMICK, b. ib. July 5, 1849; e. Washington College, now Washington and Lee University, where he took the B. L. degree in 1871; m. Berryville, Dec. 7, 1882, *Esther Maria Lewis* (b. "Monterey", Clarke County, August 6, 1856; p. George Washington Lewis and Emily Contee Johnson; gr. p. Lorenzo Lewis and Esther Maria Coxe—Reverdy Johnson, once Minister to England); l. Berryville.
 a. EMILY CONTEE MCCORMICK, b. "Monterey", Sept. 15, 1885.
 b. MARY LEWIS MCCORMICK, b "Norwood", Oct. 11, 1887; d. ib. July 17, 1888.
 c. EDWARD LEWIS MCCORMICK, b. Berryville, May 22, 1895.
(6). FRANCIS MCCORMICK, b. "Frankford", Oct. 15, 1851; d. ib. Nov. 20, 1862.
(7). ROSE ELLZEY MCCORMICK, b. ib. July 21, 1855; e. Virginia Female Institute, Staunton; m. "Frankford", April 28, 1885, *Lorenzo Lewis* (b. Baltimore, Md., March 11, 1853; d. "Fielding", Clarke County, Feb. 27, 1887. He was a brother of Esther Maria Lewis, above, and lived at "Fielding"); l. "Frankford".
 a. GEORGE WASHINGTON LEWIS, b. "Fielding", July 22, 1886; l. "Frankford."
(8). HANNAH TAYLOR MCCORMICK, b. ib. June 16, 1858; d. ib. August 8, 1881.

III. ELIZABETH MCILHANY, b. "Ithaca", in 1783; d. ib. Jan. 7, 1811. "She was in every way a very superior woman."

§129 IV. JOHN MCILHANY, b. "Ithaca", in 1785; d. "Milton Hall", Loudoun County, April 7, 1808; m. "Milton Valley", Frederick County, March 13, 1806, *Harriot Milton;* for her ancestry, see MILTON FAMILY, §161. He was educated under a private tutor, and entered the Junior Class at Princeton College in November, 1803; but a year later he had to discontinue his studies and return home on account of his father's death. His home, "Milton Hall", adjoined "Ithaca". He died suddenly at the very beginning of a most promising life, leaving an infant son.

1. TALIAFERRO MILTON MCILHANY, b. "Milton Valley", May 24, 1807; e. at a military school; d. "Cherry Hill", Charles County, Md., Sept. 11, 1850; m. "Stone Hill", Loudoun County, Nov. 20, 1827, *Ann Rogers;* see ROGERS FAMILY, §228. He was an ardent Whig, and represented his party in the Virginia Legislature in 1841. He lived at "Milton Hall" till about 1849, when he removed to Washington City. Shortly before his death he received an appointment to a prominent government office there.

 (1). HARRIOT ANN MCILHANY, b. "Stone Hill", August 6, 1828; m. Warrenton. April 26, 1855, *William Perry Hilleary* (b. "Mt. Pleasant", Md., Oct. 17, 1825; d. Warrenton, August 2, 1890; p. Tilghman Hilleary and Ann Worthington; gr. p. John Hilleary and Ann Perry—William Worthington and a Miss Granby; all of Maryland. He went to California in 1849 and remained there for several years. The latter part of his life he lived at Warrenton, engaged in the real estate business); 1. Staunton.

  a. RICHARD WASHINGTON HILLEARY, b. Mt. Pleasant, Md., Feb. 20, 1856; e. Bethel Military Academy; m. Cumberland, Md., Nov. 8, 1882, *Heriot Jane Annan* (b. ib. Feb. 11, 1859; d. Washington, D. C., July 8, 1901; p. James R. Annan and Priscilla I. Perry; gr. p. Dr. Daniel Annan and Jane Roberdeau). He is a merchant in Warrenton. For a number of years he has been a member of the town council and a vestryman in the Episcopal Church.

   (a). RICHARD PERRY HILLEARY, b. ib. May 15, 1884.

   (b). WILLIAM BENT HILLEARY, b. ib. March 1, 1886.

   (c). VIRGINIA MILTON HILLEARY, b. ib. July 10, 1888.

b. HUGH WORTHINGTON HILLEARY, b. "Conway Grove", Warrenton, Oct. 13, 1857; e. Bethel Military Academy, and studied law at the University of Va.; l. Staunton; in the real estate business. He is a vestryman in the Emmanuel Episcopal Church.

c. ANNIE MILTON HILLEARY, b. Hastings, Minn., July 31, 1859; e. Fauquier Female Institute; l. Staunton.

d. WILLIAM MURRAY HILLEARY, b. "Dakota", near Warrenton, Dec. 1, 1867; e. Bethel Military Academy and Brooklyn Polytechnic Institute; m. Staunton, Oct. 4, 1899, *Susan Baldwin Cochran* (b. ib. July 17, 1867; p. George Moffett Cochran and Margaret Lynn Peyton; gr. p. George Moffett Cochran and Maria Teresa Boys—John Howe Peyton and Ann Montgomery Lewis). He is head book-keeper in the Augusta National Bank at Staunton.

  (a). MARGARET PEYTON HILLEARY, b. ib. Sept. 28, 1900.

(2). MARY LOUISA MCILHANY, b. "Stonehill", Oct. 5, 1829; m. Washington, D. C., Sept. 5, 1848, *William Winter Rennoe* (b. "Littleton", Charles County, Md., Sept. 25, 1822; d. Nanjemoy, Md., Sept. 14, 1850; p. William Rennoe and Catherine Adams); l. Staunton.

§130 (3). JOHN WILLIAM MCILHANY, b. "Milton Hall", July 25, 1835; d. Staunton, August 16, 1891; e. Episcopal High School, Alexandria, and studied medicine at the Jefferson Medical College in Philadelphia, whence he seceded with a number of students in 1860 to the Richmond Medical College, where he took his M.D. degree; m. "Huntley", near Warrenton, Feb. 5, 1861, *Margaret Bispham Skinker* (b. ib. Dec. 26, 1837; d. Warrenton, Feb. 22, 1896; p. James Keith Skinker and Elizabeth Eyre Chambers; gr. p. William and Harriet Skinker—Richard and Ann

THE MCILHANY FAMILY.

Chambers). He was a surgeon in the Confederate Army, and also saw active service as a private in Company D. of Mosby's Command. After|the War he practiced in Warrenton.

 a. ROSE LAMAR MCILHANY, b. "Huntley", Jan. 31, 1862; e. Fauquier Female Institute; l. Marion, Va.

 b. JOHN MILTON MCILHANY, b. "Huntley", August 25, 1863; e. Bethel Military Academy; m. "Forest Home", near Christiansburg, Sept. 16, 1885, *Elizabeth Deskins Wygal* (b. Floyd C. H., Nov. 15, 1862; p. Sebastian Wygal and Mary Wilson; gr. p. James Wygal and Mary Cecil—Samuel Wilson and Catherine Byrnes). He has been connected almost continuously with the Norfolk and Western Road, and is now chief train dispatcher of the Radford Division; 1. Roanoke.

  (a). ROBERT MILTON MCILHANY, b. New River Depot, Jan. 23, 1887.

  (b). NELLIE KEITH MCILHANY, b. Radford, May 1, 1888.

  (c). WILLIAM HERBERT MCILHANY, b. ib. Feb. 12, 1892.

  (d). PAUL SEBASTIAN MCILHANY, b. ib. Jan. 15, 1894.

  (e). BERNARD ASHBY MCILHANY, b. ib. Nov. 4, 1895.

  (f). ELIZABETH VIRGINIA MCILHANY, b. Roanoke, May 30, 1898.

  (g). MARGARET LUCILE MCILHANY, b. ib. Nov. 4, 1900.

 c. LILLIE MCILHANY, b. "Huntley", March 26, 1865; d. Houston, Texas, Feb. 10, 1867.

 d. MARGARET SKINKER MCILHANY, b. ib. Feb. 4, 1867; e. Fauquier Female Institute; m. Warrenton, Oct. 3, 1894, *William Harrison Bolen* (b. Culpeper County, March 26, 1865; p. Sanford W. and Sarah C. Bolen); 1.

Washington, D. C.
- (a). MARGARET MCILHANY BOLEN, b. Roanoke, July 19, 1895.
- (b). AMELIE SANFORD BOLEN, b. ib. Dec. 30, 1897.

e. JAMES KEITH MCILHANY, b. "Huntley", March 10, 1870; d. Warrenton, June 25, 1874.

f. ANNETTE HAMILTON MCILHANY, b. ib. Dec. 23, 1872; e. Fauquier Female Institute; d. Roanoke, Jan. 6, 1900.

g. MARY STUART MCILHANY. b. Warrenton, Jan. 10, 1877; e. Fauquier Female Institute; l. Washington, D. C.

§131 (4). HUGH MILTON MCILHANY, b. "Milton Hall", Nov. 25, 1840; e. Hallowell's School, Alexandria; m. *1st.* Staunton, Feb. 1, 1872, *Matilda Craig Trout* (see TROUT FAMILY, §101); m. *2nd.* Emmanuel Church, Fauquier County, April 30, 1884, *Fannie Barton Jones* (b. "Woodside", Fauquier County, Sept. 25, 1850; p. James Fitzgerald Jones and Anne Lewis Marshall; gr.p. William Strother Jones and Anna Maria Marshall—Thomas Marshall, son of Chief Justice John Marshall, and Margaret W. Lewis). He entered the Confederate Army with the Warrenton Rifles, 17th Va. Inft., was promoted to Longstreet's headquarters as Quartermaster Sergeant, but became Asst. Quartermaster, with rank of Captain, in 1864. Having resigned on account of ill health, he accepted the position of 1st. Sergeant of Company F., 43d Va. Battalion of Cavalry (Mosby's Rangers), where he served until captured Dec. 21, 1864. He was imprisoned at the Old Capitol Prison, Washington, and in Fort Warren, Boston Harbor, till June 15, 1865. He is engaged in the real estate business in Staunton. For nearly twenty-five years he has been a vestryman in the Episcopal Church, and at six different times has

CAPT. HUGH MILTON McILHANY
131

been President of the Staunton Young Men's Christian Association.
    a. A son, b. and d. Staunton, Oct. 6, 1872.
    b. HUGH MILTON MCILHANY, b. ib. April 25, 1874; e. Washington and Lee University, where he took the degrees of A.B. in 1895, M.A. in 1896, and Ph.D. in 1899, having been four years Instructor in German in the University; m. Staunton, June 28, 1900, *Calvert Walke* (b. Powhatan County, Jan. 28, 1872; p. Rev. Lewis Walke and Mary Tabb Atkinson; gr. p. William Walke and Elizabeth Nash of Norfolk—Roger B. Atkinson and Mary Timberlake Withers of "Sherwood", Lunenburg County). He has for three years been Southern College Secretary of the International Committee of Young Men's Christian Associations, with headquarters at Staunton, and is now General Secretary of the Association Work at the University of Virginia.
        (a). MARY ATKINSON MCILHANY, b. Staunton, April 1, 1901.
        (b). MATILDA FRANCES MCILHANY, b.ib. June 13, 1902.
    c. NICHOLAS TROUT MCILHANY, b. ib. Aug. 6, 1875; d. ib. Dec. 11, 1875.
    d. STRIBLING MCILHANY, b.ib. Oct. 11, 1876; d. ib. Apr. 15, 1877.
    e. A son, b. and d. ib. July 11, 1877.
    f. A son, b. and d. ib. Sept. 26, 1878.
    g. JOHN ROGERS MCILHANY, b. ib. Oct. 2, 1880; d. ib. May 5, 1881.
  (5). BUSHROD TAYLOR MCILHANY, b. "Milton Hall", August 25, 1845; d. ib. August 31, 1845.
V. MARY MCILHANY, b. "Ithaca", about 1787; m. *1st*. ib. in the early part of 1806, *Solomon Davis*. Some years after his death she married *2nd. Rev. George M. Fry*, a Methodist minister of Montgomery County, Md., who did

not live many years afterward. She had no children, and died at "Milton Hall" about 1840.

§132 VI.- CECILIA MCILHANY, b. "Ithaca" about 1795; d. "Montcalm", April 5, 1822; m. "Ithaca", Jan. 16, 1815, *Capt. Francis Stribling*. For their descendants see STRIBLING FAMILY, §§ 38-44. Her share of her father's estate was on Goose Creek, at a place now in the hands of some Quakers.

§133 VII. JAMES MCILHANY, b. "Ithaca", March 2, 1797; d. Houston, Texas, Nov. 1, 1867; graduated at Princeton with third honors, taking the M. A. degree in 1819; afterwards studied law; m. *1st.* Leesburg, May 5, 1825, *Margaret Henderson* (b. ib. May 5, 1806; d. "Montcalm", Loudoun County, Nov. 18, 1844; p. Richard Henry Henderson and Orra Moore of Leesburg; gr. p. Alexander and Sallie Henderson); m. *2nd.* Alexandria, Oct. 22, 1850, *Elizabeth Johnston* (b. ib. June 30, 1814; d. Summit Point, W. Va., Jan. 23, 1901; p. Reuben Johnston and Elizabeth Dawe of Alexandria). He was a member of the Virginia Senate from 1837 to 1841. Up to this time he practiced law, but the latter part of his life he was a farmer, and lived at "Montcalm" and "Meadow Hill". He had seven children by his first marriage and two by his second.

   1. LOUISA MCILHANY, b Leesburg, Dec. 23, 1826; m. "Montcalm", Nov. 30, 1843, *James McIlhany Kilgour*, her first cousin; see below, §135, for their descendants.

   2. ORRA MOORE MCILHANY, b. near Hillsboro, Aug. 14, 1828; d. Washington, D. C., May 6, 1890; m. near Hillsboro, Nov. 12, 1850, *Rev. George Washington Carter* (b. near Middleburg, in 1826; p. John Carter and Elizabeth Rust; gr. p. Richard Carter and Agnes Rutledge. He was a Methodist minister).

      (1). JAMES MCILHANY CARTER, b. "Meadow Hill", Nov. 9, 1852; m. *1st.* Mexico City, June 12, 1886, *Juana Ramirez* (b. Guana Juato, Mex., May 4, 1870; d. Acambaro, Mex., August 5, 1888); m. *2nd.* San Juan Bautista, Tobasco, Mex., Nov. 24, 1889, *Teutila de Correa* (b. Merida, Yucatan, Nov. 10, 1866); he is general land agent at San Juan Bautista, Tobasco, Mex.

a. SANTIAGO CARTER, b. ib. Oct. 26, 1892.
b. GRACIELLA CARTER, b. ib. Nov. 11, 1894.
c. GEORGE CARTER, b. ib. Nov. 13, 1896; d. ib. Feb. 4, 1902.
d. PABLO CARTER, b. ib. Oct. 26, 1899.

(2). GEORGE RUTLEDGE CARTER, b. in Virginia in the autumn of 1853; d.ib. in the spring of 1854.

(3). MARY DAVISSON CARTER, b. in Virginia, August 1, 1855; e. Wesleyan Female Institute, Staunton; l. Washington, D. C.

(4). MARGARET HENDERSON CARTER, b. Lynchburg, in the spring of 1857; d. ib. in fall of 1859.

(5). PAUL EDGAR BRANCH CARTER, b. Chapel Hill, Washington County, Texas, July 30, 1860; m. Berryville, Sept. 29, 1884, *Orra Lee Milbourne* (b. Hamilton, Jan. 23, 1865); he is a physician at Guadalupe, Santa Barbara County, Cal.

    a. PAUL IRVING CARTER, b. Hamilton, Aug. 28, 1885.

    b. LEE JEFFERSON CARTER, b. ib. June 11, 1889.

(6). FRANK RUST CARTER, b. in Texas, in the spring of 1862; d. Houston, Texas, of yellow fever in the autumn of 1866.

(7). GEORGE ORRA CARTER, b Plantersville, Texas, Sept. 18, 1865; m. Hamilton, Feb. 15, 1883, *Dr. William Phillips Carr*, (b. Boydton, May 10, 1858; p. William Brown Carr and Laura Phillips; gr. p. David Carr and Susan Brown— William F. Phillips and Sarah Edith Ashmore Cannon. He studied at Randolph-Macon College and took his M. D. degree at Columbia Medical College, Washington, D.C. He is now professor of Physiology at Columbia Medical College and Surgeon-in-chief of the Emergency Hospital in Washington, D. C.).

    a. DAISY PHILLIPS CARR, b. near Hamilton, Nov. 29, 1883; d. Washington, D.C., March 10, 1893.

THE MCILHANY FAMILY. 164

  b. WILLIAM BROWN CARR, b. near Hamilton, Oct. 23, 1884.
  c. EDWARD RAVENEL CARR, b. Washington, D. C., July 23, 1897.
 3. MARGARET MCILHANY, b. "Montcalm", Nov. 26, 1831; d. ib. Jan. 31, 1836.
 4. SARAH ANNE MCILHANY, b. ib. March 20, 1833; d. "Meadow Hill", Jan. 17, 1853.
 5. MARY MCILHANY, b. "Montcalm", Nov. 5, 1834; d. ib. Oct. 10, 1855.
 6. JAMES MORTIMER MCILHANY, b. ib. Oct. 12, 1837; d. ib. Nov. 30, 1841.
 7. ALEXANDER HENDERSON MCILHANY, b. ib. May 30, 1839; e. Randolph–Macon College; d. Richmond, July 21, 1862, as the result of a wound received in the Seven Days' Fight.

§134 8. JAMES STUART MCILHANY, b."Meadow Hill", Aug. 7, 1851; took the degree of M. D. at the University of Maryland in 1884; m. Frostburg, Md., Dec. 15, 1886, Georgiana De Vecmon (b. Cumberland, Md., Feb. 25, 1856; p. Thomas De Vecmon and Althea Margaret Coombs). He is a physician and Surgeon at Everett, Washington State.

 9. ELIZABETH MCILHANY, b. "Meadow Hill", Sept. 26, 1854; m. ib. Oct. 20, 1874, *Dr. Augustus Pembroke Thomson* (b. "Hawthorne", Summit Point, W. Va., Jan. 11, 1847; p. John Augustus Thomson and Mary Scott; gr. p. Dr. John Thomson and Lucy Roots Throckmorton of Berryville—Beverly Scott and Elmira Anderson of Bedford County); l. "Hawthorne".

  (1). JOHN AUGUSTUS THOMSON, b. ib. Jan. 4, 1876; took the degree of Mining Engineer at Lehigh University in 1896; l. in Mexico.

  (2). JAMES MCILHANY THOMSON, b. "Hawthorne", Feb. 13, 1878; graduated at the Johns-Hopkins University in 1897; is editor of a daily paper in Norfolk.

  (3). MARY SCOTT THOMSON, b. "Hawthorne", March 2, 1880; e. Virginia Female Institute, Staunton; l. "Hawthorne".

(4). ELIZABETH PASCOE THOMSON, b. ib. June 14, 1882; e. Virginia Female Institute, Staunton; l. "Hawthorne".

(5). PAUL JONES THOMSON, b. ib. May 20, 1884; is a cadet at the Virginia Military Institute.

(6). OCTAVIA HAXALL THOMSON, b. "Hawthorne", August 23, 1886.

(7). DOROTHY THOMSON, b. ib. Sept. 20, 1891.

(8). IMOGEN STEPTOE THOMSON, b. ib. Apr. 2, 1894.

§135 VIII. LOUISA MCILHANY, b. "Ithaca", Jan. 29, 1799; d. Montgomery County, Md., May 20, 1822; m. "Ithaca", June 16, 1818, *Charles Jourdan Kilgour* (b. St. Mary's County, Md., in 1790; d. Montgomery County, Md., August 22, 1837, by being thrown from a carriage. He was a Judge of the fifth Circuit Court of Maryland, and served in the Maryland Legislature about 1815. See §143).

1. JAMES MCILHANY KILGOUR, b. "Ithaca", April 28, 1819; e. Princeton College from 1834-1837; m. "Montcalm", Nov. 30, 1843, *Louisa McIlhany*, his first cousin (see above, §133); they lived at "Montcalm" and Meadow Hill", and reside now at "The Willows", Loudoun County.

(1). ELSPETH KILGOUR, b. "Montcalm", May 29, 1849; d. "Cedar Ridge", Montgomery County, Md., August 21, 1901; m. "Meadow Hill", Oct. 20, 1874, *Henry Bradley* (b. "Cedar Ridge", August 22, 1846; p. Henry Bradley and Mary Prout; l. "Cedar Ridge").

(2). ROBERT WHITE KILGOUR, b. "Montcalm", March 15, 1854; he has traveled abroad for seven years; l. "The Willows".

(3). JOHN MORTIMER KILGOUR, b. "Montcalm", Jan. 31, 1857; l. Williams, Arizona.

(4). HENRY JOURDAN KILGOUR, b. "Meadow Hill", Sept. 4, 1859; m. Hillsboro, April 19, 1883, *Florence Isabella Leslie* (b. ib. Sept. 9, 1859; p. Benjamin F. Leslie and Elizabeth Martain; gr. p. Benjamin Leslie and Rebecca Kinsey—Thomas Martain and Mary Mann). He has been living in the West a number of years as an industrial teacher

among the Indians; is now at "The Willows."
   a. ROBERT MORTIMER KILGOUR, b. near "The Willows", June 6, 1884.
   b. MARY ELIZABETH KILGOUR, b. Hillsboro, Dec. 24, 1885.
   c. LOUISA JOURDAN KILGOUR, b. Fort Simcoe, Wash., Dec. 14, 1887.
   d. HENRY BRADLEY KILGOUR, b. Stevens County, Washington, June 11, 1891.
   e. GEORGE SHOWER KILGOUR, b. Hillsboro, August 1, 1893.
   f. FRANK LESLIE KILGOUR, b. ib. August 1, 1893.
(5). CHARLOTTE KILGOUR, b. "Meadow Hill", Dec. 8, 1861; 1. "The Willows".
(6). ALICE WILLIAMS KILGOUR, b. "Meadow Hill", Dec. 15, 1865; 1. "The Willows".
(7). ANN CECILIA KILGOUR, b. "Meadow Hill", Jan. 4, 1869; 1. Washington, D. C.

2. JOHN MORTIMER KILGOUR, b. "Rosemont", Rockville, Md., May 19, 1822; studied law at Harvard College; m. Washington, D. C., May 5, 1847, *Martha Wilson Wootton* (b. "Mount Hope", near Rockville, Md., Feb. 25, 1827; p. John Wootton and Elizabeth Lynn Magruder; gr. p. Richard Wootton and Martha Perry). He was a member of the Constitutional Convention of Maryland in 1852. During the Civil War he served in the 35th Virginia Cavalry, Rosser's Brigade, and also as a Captain in the quartermaster department. He has been Commonwealth's Attorney for Loudoun County, and was for several years State Lecturer for the Good Templars. He lives at "Wakefield", near Round Hill.

  (1). CHARLES JOURDAN KILGOUR, b. Rockville, Md., Feb. 18, 1849; e. Washington College, now Washington and Lee University, and at Nashotah Theological Seminary, Wisconsin; m. Baltimore, Md., Oct. 26, 1875, *Fannie Claiborne Beaufort* (b. New Orleans, La., March 9, 1845; p. Charles Bertram Beaufort and Sarah Jane Betts;

gr. p. Robert and Ephemia Beaufort—Stephen and Mary King Betts). He is Rector of the Episcopal Church at Lykens, Penn.
    a. ELIZABETH CORNELIA KILGOUR, b. Baltimore, Md., April 11, 1877; l. Lykens, Penn.
  (2). ELIZABETH CORNELIA WOOTTON KILGOUR, b. "Rosemont", April 13, 1852; l. "Wakefield".
  (3). JAMES MCILHANY KILGOUR, b. "Rosemont", March 23, 1855; l. "Wakefield".
  (4). MARY ADELAIDE WOOTTON KILGOUR, b. "Rosemont", Jan. 26, 1858; l. "Wakefield".

§136 IX. MORTIMER MCILHANY, b. "Ithaca", Jan. 30, 1801; d. New Florence, Mo., Dec. 20, 1860; e. Bruce's Academy, Winchester; m. Loudoun County, Nov. 7, 1820, *Mary Ann Washington* (b. Fairfax County, Feb. 28, 1801; d. Palmyra, Mo., in April 1869; p. Edward and Betsy Hugh Washington of Fairfax County). He was a farmer and lived at "Rosewood", near Hillsboro, Loudoun County, till 1840; at "Oakland", "Bannockburn" and "Buena Vista", Frederick County, Md., till 1849; and thereafter in Montgomery County, Mo.

  1. MARGARET ELIZABETH MCILHANY, b. "Rosewood", Jan. 1, 1822; d. near Lexington, Ky., Sept. 9, 1839.

  2. JOHN MCILHANY, b. "Rosewood", Nov. 23, 1823; e. Dickinson College, Penn.; m. *1st*. "Woodlawn", Callaway County, Mo., Jan. 8, 1858, *Mary Jane Offutt*, (b. Fairfax County, in May 1824; d. St. Louis, Mo., Dec. 12, 1882. She was a sister of Eli Rezin Offutt, §141); m. *2nd*. Hannibal, Mo., June 4, 1888, *Margaret Ann Washington* (b. Loudoun County, August 19, 1820; d. Lampassas, Texas, in March 1898; p. John A. and Amelia Washington); m. *3rd*. Lampassas County, Texas, Dec. 13, 1900, *Harriet E. Dorsey* (b. Jefferson County, W. Va., about 1838; d. Lampassas County, Texas, May 16, 1902); l. near Lampassas, Texas. At one time he was County Judge in Texas; has been farming and teaching for many years.

  3. HANNAH ANN MCILHANY, b. "Rosewood", March 1, 1825; m. Williamsburg, Mo., Feb. 21, 1867, *Rich-*

ard Thompson Bond (b. Chambersburg, Penn., Sept. 25, 1838; p. Rev. Richard Bond and Eliza Ann Thompson of Danville, Mo.; gr. p. Richard Thompson and Sallie Yeatman. He is a minister of the Methodist Church, and for many years has been Professor of Mathematis and Astronomy in Central College, Fayette, Mo.); 1. ib.

 (1). MORTIMER McILHANY BOND, b. Glasgow, Mo., Nov. 27, 1867; d. Danville, Mo., July 2, 1868.

4. JAMES McILHANY, b. "Rosewood", in June 1826; d. Frederick County, Md., Feb. 2, 1842.

§137 5. EDWARD WASHINGTON McILHANY, b. "Rosewood", June 20, 1828; m. *1st.* Loutre Island, Mo., Nov. 4, 1863, *Henrietta Virginia Bascom* (b. St. Louis, Mo., Sept. 28, 1840; d. Sedalia, Mo., Dec. 15, 1881; p. Hiram Bascom and Catherine Jane Hersey); m. *2nd.* Sedalia, Mo., Sept. 1, 1891, *Mrs. Mary Wooldrife–Emack* (b. Verseilles, Kentucky, Nov. 4, 1849). He is a live stock dealer at Kansas City, Mo. He had six children by the first marriage and one by the second.

 (1). WILLIAM TALBOT McILHANY, b. Loutre Island, Mo., Oct. 4, 1864; d. Sedalia, Mo., July 9, 1874.

 (2). JOSIE DOUGLAS McILHANY, b. Loutre Island, Mo., April 2, 1867; m. Boonsville, Mo., June 24, 1890, *Rev. Frederick Fuller Wyatt* (b. Lincoln, Ill., July 30, 1865; p. John and Sarah Wyatt. He is pastor of the First Christian Church at Mena, Ark.)

 (3). MAGGIE BASCOM McILHANY, b. Loutre Island, Mo., July 24, 1870; e. Pritchett College, Glasgow, Mo.; m. Westport, Mo., Oct. 9, 1888, *William Wallace McIlhany*, her first cousin; for their three children see below, §138; 1. Fayette, Mo.

 (4). EDWARD MORTIMER McILHANY, b. Sedalia, Mo., August, 27, 1873; d. ib. Dec. 10, 1874.

 (5). CATHERINE HERSEY McILHANY, b. ib. Feb. 15, 1879; e. Central College, Fayette, Mo.; 1. Fayette, Mo.

THE MCILHANY FAMILY. 169

(6). BRUCE BASCOM MCILHANY, b. Sedalia, Mo.,
Dec. 5, 1881; d. Glasgow, Mo., in March 1884.
(7). CHARLES STEVENSON MCILHANY, b. Sedalia,
Mo., July 11, 1892.
6. MARY RECECCA MCILHANY, b. "Rosewood", in
1829; d. Frederick County, Md., in 1848.
7. MORTIMER MCILHANY, b. "Rosewood", Feb. 27,
1831; studied law at New London, Mo.; m. St. Charles,
Mo., Dec. 17, 1857, *Mary-Elizabeth Daugherty* (b. in
Ohio about 1831; p. Samuel Daugherty and a Miss
Parks of Ky.) While living in Missouri he served as
City Attorney, was several times a member of the
Legislature, being twice elected Speaker of the House
of Representatives, and was President of the State
Board of R. R. Commissioners. He was a Colonel in
the Confederate Army, serving also as Judge Advocate
in the 2nd. Div. of Price's Army, on the staff of Gen'l.
Harris. After practicing law for many years, he retired,
and is now ranching and gold-mining, San Diego, Cal.

§138   8. ROBERT BRUCE MCILHANY, b. "Rosewood", April
14, 1832; d. Nevada, Mo., March 23, 1899; e. Central
College, Fayette, Mo., and studied law; m. Danville,
Mo., July 3, 1860, *Missouri Anna Bond* (b. Boonville,
Mo., April 26, 1841; 1. Nevada, Mo.; she is a sister
of Richard Thompson Bond, §136). He was a minister of the M. E. Church, South; was at one time Professor of Law and Literature in Pritchett Institute,
Glasgow, Mo., and President and Professor of Metaphysics of Shelbina Institute, Shelbina, Mo.
(1). MARY MORTIMER MCILHANY, b. Danville,
Mo , April 5, 1861; e. Pritchett Institute, Glasgow, Mo.; m. Salisbury, Mo., August 1, 1878,
Almond Boswell Cockerill (b. Platte City, Mo., July
11, 1860; p. Henry Clay Cockerill and Lalla Esther
Almond. He is Vice-President of the Cherokee-
Lanyon Spelter Company at Nevada, Mo.).
a. MISSOURI MCILHANY COCKERILL, b. Schell
City, Mo., Dec. 30, 1879;
b. MARY MORTIMER COCKERILL, b. ib. Feb.
7, 1882; d. ib. July 2, 1882.

c. NELLIE WOODSON COCKERILL, b. ib. July 25, 1883.
d. HARRY WIRT COCKERILL, b. Glasgow, Mo., Sept. 2, 1886.
e. MAGGIE MCILHANY COCKERILL, b. Weir City, Kan., Dec. 5, 1889.
f. FLORENCE EMMA COCKERILL, b. ib. May 14, 1891.
g. LALLA ESTHER COCKERILL, b. ib. Feb. 16, 1897.

(2). JOHN MCILHANY, b. High Hill, Mo., Feb. 16, 1863; d. ib. June 23, 1863.

(3). RICHARD BOND MCILHANY, b. ib. April 30, 1864; e. Washington University, St. Louis, Mo., m. Columbus, Kan., Dec. 18, 1887, *Sadie Davis* (b. Scranton, Penn., Nov. 19, 1870; p. W. H. and Sarah Davis); 1. Gas, Kan.

    a. ROBERT BRUCE MCILHANY, b. Jonesboro, Ark., July 4, 1888.
    b. WILLIAM DAVIS MCILHANY, b. Weir City, Kan., Dec. 9, 1892; d. ib. Dec. 13, 1892.
    c. ZOULA MCILHANY, b. ib. July 10, 1894; d. ib. July 26, 1894.
    d. MARY MORTIMER MCILHANY, b. Nevada, Mo., July 7, 1896.

(4). WILLIAM WALLACE MCILHANY, b. Danville, Mo., June 6, 1866; d. Galena, Kan., April 8, 1898; graduated at Pritchett Institute, Glasgow, Mo.; m. Westport, Mo., Oct. 9, 1888, *Maggie Bascom McIlhany*, his first cousin. See above, §137. He was a book-keeper and stenographer.

    a. MARY MORTIMER MCILHANY, b. Weir City, Kan., August 30, 1889; d. ib. March 14, 1896.
    b. THOMPSON BOND MCILHANY, b. ib. Aug. 30, 1891; d. Galena, Kan., Dec. 13, 1897.
    c. WILLIAM WALLACE MCILHANY, b. Nevada, Mo., July 23, 1898; 1. Fayette, Mo.

(5). HENRY POPE MCILHANY, b. Danville, Mo., Sept. 26, 1867; d. ib. Nov. 14, 1867.

§139   9. WILLIAM WALLACE MCILHANY, b. "Rosewood", Nov. 30, 1833; d. Chicago, Ill., March 12, 1897; m. Macon County, Ill., Jan. 1, 1867, *Sophia Florence Marlow* (b. Petersville, Md., June 27, 1847; l. Chicago, Ill.; p. Zuisco Marlow and Violetta Claggett; gr. p. Dr. Thomas and Mary Marlow—Thomas and Sophia Claggett). He was a live stock merchant in Chicago.

    (1). ELLEN DOUGLAS MCILHANY, b. New Berlin, Ill., Feb. 6, 1868; m. Chicago, Ill., June 30, 1891, *Charles Wright Lynn* (b. Amboy, Ill., May 5, 1862; p. Charles Franklin Lynn); l. Chicago, Ill.

       a. FLORENCE MARY LYNN, b. ib. Feb. 11, 1894.

       b. FRANKLIN WRIGHT LYNN, b. ib. Feb. 18, 1896.

    (2). HERBERT WARREN MCILHANY, b. New Berlin, Ill., May 1, 1869; l. Chicago, Ill.

    (3). RAND MCILHANY, b. ib. July 23, 1882; l. ib.

    (4). MORTIMER MARLOW MCILHANY, b. ib. Apr. 19, 1884; e. Central College, Fayette, Mo.; l. Chicago, Ill.

   10. DOUGLAS MCILHANY, b. "Rosewood", Sept. 17, 1835; m. Monroe County, Mo., Sept. 25, 1877, *Louisa Eleanor Houston* (b. ib. Jan. 23, 1854; p. Dr. William M. Houston and Marie Frances Davis; gr. p. David and Margaret Houston—Capt. B. T. and Eleanor B. Davis). He is farming near Santa Fe, Monroe Co., Mo.

    (1). SIDNEY MCILHANY, b. Audrain County, Mo., Jan. 27, 1880; e. Mexico, Mo.; l. Monroe County, Mo.

§140   11. MARSHALL MCILHANY, b. "Rosewood", Jan. 4, 1837; e. Centenary College, Fayette, Mo.; m. *1st*. Glasgow, Mo., Nov. 22, 1860, *Anna Mary Blackwell* (b. ib. Sept. 18, 1840; d. St. Paul, Minn., Oct. 2, 1865; p. Joseph and Eliza Blackwell of Glasgow, Mo.); m. *2nd*. St. Charles, Mo., March 6, 1867, *Virginia Catherine Johnston* (b. Romney, W. Va., March 8, 1846; d. Palmyra, Mo., March 3, 1870; p. Henry and Mary A. Johnston of Va.); m. *3rd*. Monticello, Mo., June 9,

1874, *Lucy Turner Plant* (b. ib. May 15, 1856; p. Massanello and Elizabeth Plant). He is a minister of the Methodist Episcopal Church, South, but has been engaged very successfully in educational work all his life. He is now President of Goodnight College, Goodnight, Armstrong County, Tex. He had one child by the first marriage, two by the second, and twelve by the third

(1). ELI OFFUTT MCILHANY, b. near Hannibal, Mo., May 1, 1863; e. Stephenville, Tex.; m. ib. Dec. 21, 1892, *Mary Emma Cage* (b. ib. Feb. 23, 1875; p. James House and Sarah J. Cage); l. ib., where he is a successful dry goods merchant.

(2). HENRY JOHNSTON MCILHANY, b. Palmyra, Mo., Jan. 6, 1868; graduated with the degree of M. A. at Centenary College, Lampassas, Tex., in 1893; is Professor of Mathematics at John Tarlton College, Stephenville, Tex.

(3). ANNA MARY MCILHANY, b. Palmyra, Mo., Oct. 31, 1869; graduated at Centenary College, Lampassas, Tex., in 1892; m Vernon, Tex., June 19, 1899, *Walter Flynt* (b. Madison County, Ala., Aug. 26, 1862. He is a farmer and travelling adjuster and collector); l. Vernon, Tex.

    a. ANNA MARY FLYNT, b. ib. Apr. 26, 1900; d. ib. Feb. 8, 1901.

    b. STELLA FLYNT, b. ib. March 4, 1902.

(4). MORTIMER MCILHANY, b. Monticello, Mo., March 17, 1875; e. John Tarlton College, Stephenville, Tex.; l. ib.; clerking.

(5). MASSANELLO PLANT MCILHANY, b. Monticello, Mo., June 14, 1876; e. John Tarlton College, Stephenville, Texas; l. Goodnight, Texas.

(6). VIRGINIA MCILHANY, b. Lexington, Mo., March 17, 1878; d. Dallas, Tex., July 26, 1879.

(7). ELIZABETH MCILHANY, b. ib. Sept. 23, 1879; d. ib. June 21, 1881.

(8). MARSHALL MCILHANY, b. Stephenville, Tex., August 29, 1882; d. Lampassas, Tex., Jan. 26, 1885.

THE MCILHANY FAMILY. 173

(9). JOHN EDWARD MCILHANY, b. Stephenville, Tex., April 28, 1884.
(10). LILY PLANT MCILHANY, b. Lampassas, Tex., May 26, 1886.
(11). ROBERT MCILHANY, b. Lampassas, Tex., August 5, 1888; d. ib. Jan. 9, 1889.
(12). LOU-LU MCILHANY, b. ib. Nov. 9, 1889.
(13). VICTORIA VANDIVER MCILHANY, b. ib. Nov. 14, 1891.
(14). MARCIA MCILHANY, b. Stephenville, Tex., Dec. 6, 1893; d. ib. June 27, 1894.
(15). DOUGLAS FRANK MCILHANY, b. ib. July 28, 1895.

§141 12. BETTIE WASHINGTON MCILHANY, b. "Rosewood", Jan. 10, 1839; e. Fulton Female Seminary, Fulton, Mo.; m. *1st.* New Florence, Mo., Nov. 25, 1856, *Dr. George Robert Milton*, her cousin (for their four children, see MILTON FAMILY §169); m. *2nd.* St. Louis, Mo., Dec. 20, 1883, *Ripley Warren Sparr* (b. Rush County, Ind., July 6, 1832; p. John and Mary Guthery Sparr; he is a banker at Lawrence, Kan.).

13. ANNE LOUISA MCILHANY, b. Berlin, Md., Feb. 16, 1841; e. Danville, Mo.; m. New Florence, Mo., March 14, 1861, *Eli Rezin Offutt* (b. Fairfax County, Feb. 20, 1835; p. Eli Offutt and Margaret Sanford Washington, a sister of Edward Sanford Washington. §124. For eighteen years he was Professor of Mathematics in Washington University, St. Louis, Mo. He is stock farming now near Cleburn, Tex.).

(1). MARSHALL MCILHANY OFFUTT, b. "Woodlawn", Callaway County, Mo., May 7, 1862; e. Washington University, St. Louis, Mo.; m. Camden, Ontario, Canada, July 4, 1889, *Emma Catherine Moyer* (b. ib. July 6, 1863; p. Jacob S. and Elizabeth Moyer). He is stock farming near Cleburn, Tex.

a. ALLEN DOUGLAS OFFUTT, b. Wichita Falls, Tex., July 27, 1893.
b. EDGAR LYLE OFFUTT, b. Iowa Park, Tex., Jan. 31, 1895.

c. EARL OFFUTT, b. Gainesville, Tex., Nov. 5, 1896; d. ib. May 11, 1897.

(2). MARGARET CHASE OFFUTT, b. "Woodlawn", Feb. 8, 1864; e. Pritchett Institute, Glasgow, Mo., and Mary Institute, St. Louis, Mo.; m. St. Louis, Mo., May 29, 1884, *William Conway* (b. ib. Feb. 22, 1857; p. Joseph and Virginia Lanham Conway); 1. Kirkwood, Mo.

   a. ROY DOUGLAS CONWAY, b. Lamonte, Mo., March 7, 1885.

   b. HAROLD LANHAM CONWAY, b. ib. April 27, 1886.

   c. LOUTIE OFFUTT CONWAY, b. St. Louis, Mo., June 18, 1890.

   d. EDGAR FINDLEY CONWAY, b. ib. Dec. 18, 1892.

   e. ROBERT MILTON CONWAY, b. ib. Aug. 13, 1894.

   f. WILLIAM GORDON CONWAY, b. ib. June 9, 1897.

   g. VIRGINIA LEE CONWAY, b. ib. Feb. 24, 1900.

(3). MARY WASHINGTON OFFUTT, b. "Woodlawn", May 24, 1865; d St. Louis, Mo., Dec. 26, 1873.

(4). DOUGLAS OFFUTT, b. "Bleak House", Williamsburg, Mo., Nov. 24, 1866; e. Washington University, St. Louis, Mo.; m. Los Angeles, Cal., June 1, 1892, *May Cordelia Holland* (b. St. Louis, Mo., Jan. 1, 1871; p. Joseph Holland and Virginia Matthews; gr. p. Stephen and Elizabeth Holland —John and Mary Matthews). He is a merchant at Los Angeles, Cal.

   a. BERENICE OFFUTT, b. St. Louis, Mo., June 20, 1893; d. ib. July 7, 1893.

   b. BEULAH MAY OFFUTT, b. ib. Jan. 21, 1895.

(5). ELIZABETH OFFUTT, b. Audrain County, Mo., Nov. 7, 1869; e. Mary Institute, St. Louis, Mo.; m. Kirkwood, Mo., July 10, 1901, *Bertram Brown* (b. ib. April 6, 1873); 1. St. Louis, Mo., where he is a salesman.

14. HERBERT MCILHANY, b. Frederick County, Md., in Nov. 1842; d. near Florence, Mo., in April 1853.

§142 15. JOSEPH WASHINGTON MCILHANY, b. Frederick County, Md., Feb. 22, 1844; m. *1st.* in Arkansas, Jan. 13, 1874, *Mary Elizabeth Coker* (b. ib. about 1856; d. Dublin, Tex., Feb. 16, 1884); m. *2nd.* Sipe Springs, Tex., Feb. 25, 1886, *Mrs. Lydia Frances Doty-Elliot* (b. in Alabama, Nov. 29, 1859); he is farming and teaching school near Lockhart, Tex. He had five children by his first marriage and seven by the second.

(1). BEULAH BENTON MCILHANY, b. Lead Hill, Ark., Sept. 30, 1875; m. Lockhart, Tex., July 30, 1899, *Benjamin Averite Laurie* (b. Milam County, Tex., Sept. 10, 1877); l. Kerrville, Tex., where he is book-keeping.

    a. EARL RUSSELL LAURIE, b. Tilman, Tex., June 8, 1900.

(2). WARNER MCILHANY, b. Lead Hill, Ark., Oct. 27, 1877; is clerking at Smithville, Tex.

(3). JOHN MARSHALL MCILHANY, b. Denton, Tex., August 15, 1880; d. ib. Oct. 5, 1881.

(4). LOUTIE MCILHANY, b. Denton, Tex., July 17, 1882; m. Big Foot, Frio County, Tex., Aug. 10, 1901, *Samuel Massengale* (b. Helena, Tex., Dec. 25, 1876); l. Fentress, Tex.

    a. ROBERT RUSSELL MASSENGALE, b. ib. May 9, 1902.

(5). MARY ELIZABETH MCILHANY, b. Dublin, Tex. Feb. 16, 1884; d. Comanche, Tex., in June 1886.

(6). ALBERT MARVIN MCILHANY, b. ib. April 27, 1887.

(7). BESSIE MCILHANY, b. ib. May 1, 1889.

(8). WANDA LEE MCILHANY, b. Longview, Tex., Dec. 29, 1890.

(9). LYDIA MCILHANY, b. Lockhart, Tex., April 18, 1893.

(10). RUTH MCILHANY, b. ib. June 4, 1895.

(11). JOSEPH WASHINGTON MCILHANY, b. Harwood, Tex., April 8, 1897; d. ib. Oct. 20, 1897.

(12). ERNEST LINWOOD MCILHANY, b. Big Foot, Tex., Jan. 30, 1901.

Kilgour Family.

§143. The following facts were gotten several years ago from Mr. J. Mortimer Ki gour. *William Kilgour* of Aberdeen, Scotland, a merchant, settled near Benedict, Charles County, Md., about 1740. He married Eliza Keech: issue,—

1. *James Kilgour*, m. Margaret Jourdan: issue,—
    (1). *Charles Jourdan Kilgour*, m. LOUISA MCILHANY; see §135.
    (2). John A. T. Kilgour, m. Ann Shelmerdine: issue,— John A. T., m. Harriet Jones: issue,—Flavel, Clarence, Annie and Charlotte.
    (3). Elizabeth Kilgour.
    (4). Charlotte Kilgour.
2. Robert Kilgour.
3. *William Kilgour*, m. Sallie Edgerton: issue,—
    (1). *Alexander Kilgour*, m. MARGARET ANN STRIBLING; see §39.
    (2). James Kilgour.
    (3). Ann Kilgour.
    (4). Mary Kilgour; m. .... Stephens: issue,—John and Ann.
    (5). Rosetta Kilgour, m. Louis Shotts: issue,—John Louis.
4. John Kilgour, m. Jane Hague Gouldy: issue,—
    (1). Jane Hague Kilgour, m. Maj. .... Collins, U.S.A.
5. Elspeth Kilgour.
6. Elizabeth Kilgour.
7. Amy Kilgour.
8. Martha Kilgour.
9. Nancy Kilgour, m. James Miltimore: issue,—
    (1). James Miltimore.
    (2). Mary Ann Miltimore, m. Dr. Beand: issue,—Harry, etc.

THE MILTON FAMILY.

§144. On account of my inability to make the necessary researches, it has been impossible for me to trace accurately the early history of the Milton Family in this country. Tradition says that Richard Milton, who came from England, was married in Pennsylvania to a Miss Ross of Scotland; that later he settled in Virginia on the Potomac River; and that afterwards he removed to Prince William County, taking up lands on Bull Run. It is also said that his brother John, who came from England with him, removed about the same time to South Carolina. I find, however, that the county records, so far as examined, take the family back in Virginia at least one generation further than this. I am certain that they came at first from England, but when they came and where they first settled I have not been able to determine. Among the early land grants recorded in the State Land Office are several in 1636 and 1638 to Richard Milton at Westover in Charles City County, on the James River. While I have no proof of any connection, it is possible and even probable that he was the grandfather of the first Richard Milton mentioned below. In the half century following the time of these grants, a large number of persons removed from that section to the more newly opened lands in the central and northern parts of the State.

RICHARD MILTON and Eliza, his wife, were living in Richmond County about the year 1720. The Parish Register contains the birth dates of at least three of their children:—Anne, b. August 31, 1720; Eliza, b. March 26, 1723; and Sarah, b. May 18, 1728. Their son Richard was born before these entries were made. On August 10, 1725 (Northern Neck Grants, Book A, p. 165) a tract of 454 acres in "Stafford County on

Buck Hall branch of Occaquan" was granted to "R'chard Melton of Richm⁴ County". This part of Stafford County soon afterward became Prince William County. Here he died about the year 1733, his will of that date being mentioned in a deed; but the will-book containing it has been destroyed. From deeds recorded in the Prince William courthouse, it is seen that, besides his son Richard mentioned below, he had a son William, who also had a son William who died in 1777, leaving a wife named Fanny. I have not been able to discover the maiden name of Richard Milton's wife Eliza. It may be mentioned that in the early court records the name is spelled Melton as frequently as Milton.

§145. **Richard Milton,** son of Richard and Eliza Milton, was born about 1715. He inherited from his father a tract of land "adjoining Coupers Cabin Branch" in Prince William County, where he lived and reared a family of nine children. His wife, whose name is mentioned in deeds along with his, was *Margaret Ross*. It is said that she came of a Scotch family of that name in Pennsylvania. Her grand-children remembered her as being tall, spare, and very neat in dress and appearance. She lived to be about ninety-five years of age, and when a very old lady she was still able to ride on horseback to the home of her son Elijah, making the distance of forty miles in one day. She was born about 1716 and died in 1811. Shortly after the Revolutionary War Richard Milton removed to Kentucky with his wife, his son Moses, and his married daughters, and settled on the Chaplin Fork of Salt River in Nelson County. Here he died about the year 1800. His nine children were,—

§146 A. MOSES MILTON must have been born as early as 1740. His wife's name was Mary, as is shown by a deed of 1787 at the time of his removal to Kentucky. He lived to be a very old man. His numerous posterity are scattered throughout the States of the Middle West. The following outline, with the exception of the descendants of Alexander Ross Milton, was compiled by Rev. Charles L. Milton of Fort Scott, Kan., and I have not attempted to verify it in any particular.

THE MILTON FAMILY.

I. JAMES MILTON did not move to Kentucky with his parents, but lived near the Shenandale Sp ings in Virginia. He was probably born about 1760. He never married.

II. ROBERT MILTON, probably born about 1762, also lived in Virginia.

III. ALEXANDER ROSS MILTON, born about 1764, remained in Virginia, and lived near Berryville. He is said to have been quite a wealthy man. He married July 8, 1802, *Sarah Drummond-Stribling*, widow of John Stribling; see §71. He died August 23, 1824, leaving five children. An extant letter written August 27, 1824 states that Harriot Taylor (§161) and Ross Milton died "on Sunday", August 23rd, and that within a few days Bushrod Stribling (§71) and Susan Milton, his sister, had died. I mention this as contemporary evidence of these dates.

    1. CHARLES WILT MILTON, b. April 8, 1805. He left Virginia when a young man, and settled either in South Carolina or Georgia.

    2. MARGARET LUCINDA MILTON, b. Dec. 23, 1808; d. Nov. 10, 1864; m. Sept. 29, 1825, *Alfred Castleman:* issue,—Osborn, Nathaniel, William, Mann Page (m. Nov. 22, 1866, Maria Ashton Milton, his first cousin: issue,—Clarane Milton, May Willington, Ada Page and Charles Randolph), Mary, Portia, Edward, Fremont, and John R.

    3. ALEXANDER ROSS MILTON, b. Frederick County, Sept. 7, 1810; d. "Stony Point", Loudoun County, July 12, 1847; m. ib. May 16, 1839, *Ann Cecilia White;* for their descendants see §122. He lived first at Winchester, and then at "Stony Point".

    4. JAMES FOSTER BARNET MILTON, b. May 28, 1812; m. in 1831, *Susan Chinn:* issue,—Sarah Ann, Hugh Alexander, Louise Littleton, Susan Peyton, Maria Ashton (m. Mann Page Castleman, her first cousin; see above), Charles Alfred, Henry Clay and James Foster.

    5. SUSAN A. MILTON, b. July 26, 1813; d. August 12, 1824.

§147 IV. MOSES MILTON, born about 1766; lived and died in Southern Kentucky: issue,—

1. JOHN MILTON, lived in Oldham County, Ky.: issue,—William, Isaac. John M. (issue,—William T., James Merritt, John and L. R), Fannie, (m. ....; Huffaker) and Mollie (m. .... Tuttle).
2. WILLIAM MILTON.
3. JAMES MILTON.
4. ROBERT MILTON, lived in Oldham County, Ky.: issue,—Lizzie, James T., Eliza and Sallie.

V. RICHARD MILTON, born about 1768; d. Shelby County, Ky., in 1843; m. *Sarah Williams* of Virginia: issue,—
   1. WILLIAM MILTON, lived in Nelson County, Ky.: issue,—Napoleon and Elizabeth.
   2. JAMES MILTON, lived in Davis County, Ky.: issue,— Richard (1. Carthage, Mo.), James, John, Bushrod, Sarah (m. Dr. Knox), and others.
   3. THOMAS MILTON, b. May 16, 1811; m. in 1831, *Mildred Green* of Bloomfield, Ky.; lived in Spencer County, Ky.: issue,—
       (1). ZACK GREEN MILTON, b. Nelson County, Ky., in 1834; m. in 1854, *Malissa Davis* of Van Buren, Ky.; 1. ib.: issue,—Zack Green (d. young), William Bell (b. in 1859; m. in 1887, Hallie Newman of Spencer County, Ky.: issue,—Ollie J., Henry E., Millie A., Wilbert G., and Edward L.), Anna (b. in 1860; m. in 1881, Musker Sullivan of Spencer County, Ky.: issue,—Bettie M., Malissa G., and Frank Allen), James C. (b. in 1862; m. in 1885, Susie Tombs of Mt. Eden, Ky.: issue,—Annie May, Malissa, Thomas G., Owen Davis, Joe Lewis, Mildred Duncan and Ruby Jane), Dr. Richard L. (b. in 1864; m. in 1892, Alice Elliston of Anderson County, Ky.: issue,— William Bryan, John T. and Claude E ; 1. Fox Creek, Ky.), Dr. Ellis H. (b. in 1866; 1. Louisville, Ky.), Ida M. (b. in 1869; m. William Mason: issue,—Luther B., Guy, Harry F. and William P.; 1. Alton, Ky.), Riley D. (b. in 1871; m. in 1899, Myrtle Goodnight of Van Buren, Ky.: issue,—Burton), Leven G. (b. in 1874) and Edward Evert (b. in 1877).

(?). William Morton Milton, lived in Anderson County, Ky.

§148   4. RICHARD MILTON, b. Nelson County, Ky., in 1815; m. April 7, 1853, *Jane Davis* of Van Buren, Ky.; they lived in Shelby County, Ky. She died in May, 1899; issue,—
   (1). John T. Milton, b. June 21, 1854; m. *1st.* Mary Davis of Gun City, Mo.; m. *2nd.* Mrs. Emma Henderson of Colorado; 1. Salida, Col.
   (2). William H. Milton, b. May 12, 1855; m. Relta Vincent of Floydsburg, Ky.; no issue; 1. Stafford, Kan.
   (3). Bettie E. Milton, b. Feb. 28, 1857; m. W. E. Wright of Simpsonville, Ky.: issue,—Milton, Roy, Ada, Jane, Malissa and Richard; 1. Veechdale, Ky.
   (4). Rev. Charles Louis Milton, b. Dec. 5, 1859; m. Dec. 14, 1881, Suna Callaway of Smithfield, Ky.: issue,—Margaret Virginia (b. Lexington, Ky., Dec. 23, 1882), Sidney McG. (b. Chestnut Grove, Ky., Oct. 24, 1884), Richard Roy (b. Stafford, Kan., June 18, 1887), Willis Garth (b. ib. Nov. 25, 1889), Charles Louis (b. McPherson, Kan., Nov. 21, 1891), Everest Kirkbride (b. Ft. Scott, Kan., Oct. 12, 1894) and John William (b. ib. Nov. 9, 1898); 1. ib.
   (5). Miles H. Milton, b. Oct. 9, 1862; m. Lena Coots of Davis County, Ky.: issue,—Mildred; 1. Lagrange, Ky.
   (6). Robert L. Milton, b. Sept. 13, 1864; m. May 4, 1887, Ida Minor of Missouri; 1. Stafford, Kan.: issue,—Inza, Ruth, Pearl, Minor, and William Arthur.
   (7). Nancy M. Milton, b. Sept. 16, 1866; m. Prof. John C. Willis; 1. Lexington, Ky.

§149   5. CHARLES MILTON, lived in Texas: issue,—Grigsby (1. Midlothian, Tex.), Robert, Benjamin, Nancy, Richard, Sallie and Mary.
   6. RACHEL MILTON, m. *Benjamin Mugg* of Indiana.
   7. PRISCILLA MILTON, m. *William Crawford* of Ill.

THE MILTON FAMILY.

8. MILLIE MILTON, m. *John Mugg*, of Indiana.
9. HENRIETTA MILTON, m. *Leven Green* of Nelson County, Ky.
10. ELIZABETH MILTON, m. *James Green*, of Nelson County, Ky.
11. SARAH MILTON, m. *Henry White*.
12. NANNIE MILTON, m. *Thomas McCemmie* (?) of Shelby County, Ky.: issue,—Lizzie, Nannie, Sue and John T.

VI. JOHN MILTON lived in Nelson County, Ky.: issue,— Joseph (m. Sue Heady), William (l. in Kansas), Doc and John (lived near Bloomfield, Ky.).

VII. WILLIAM MILTON lived in Kentucky; had two daughters.

VIII. ELIJAH MILTON lived in Nelson County, Ky.; had three daughters.

IX. PRESLEY MILTON lived in Kentucky; he never married.

§150 B. WILLIAM MILTON lived and died in Prince William County, Virginia. It is known that he had at least one daughter. He was, perhaps, the Milton who married a Miss Foster in Prince William County, and had issue,—

I. William Milton, m. Mary Robinson (or Robertson): issue,—Harrison, James, Wesley Alexander, Anna (m. .... Elwell of Illinois), Mary (m. James Doughty), Elizabeth (m. Thomas McCune: issue,—Rev. Thomas McCune), and Turner Ashby (b. Dec. 27, 1814; m. Sarah Warden Beeler, of Jefferson County: issue,—Sarah Cornelia, Mary Adaline, Anna Gertrude [m. Thomas H. Miller of Roanoke], Dr. James Ransom, Benjamin Franklin, and Turner Ashby [m. Alberta Gilbert: issue,—Gilbert]).

II. Harry Milton of Kentucky.
III. Elijah Milton of Kentucky.
IV. Alexander Ross Milton; d. unmarried.
V. Mildred Milton, m. *1st.* .... Lattimore; m. *2nd.* Judge McClain (?) of Hannibal, Mo.

§151 C. ELIJAH MILTON, b. Prince William County, Dec. 23, 1755; d. Fayette County, Ky., Nov. 10, 1833; m. "Green Hill", Frederick County, Jan. 28, 1794, *Catherine Taylor* (b. ib. June 9, 1776; d. Fayette County, Ky., July 29, 1828; see §192). He is said to have served as Master of the Army Wagons during the Revolutionary War, being closely associated with General Rochambeau during the latter part of the war. When he removed to Kentucky about 1792, he took up lands on Elk Horn Creek in Fayette County, about eight miles west of Lexington. The house which he built in 1807, is owned and occupied today by his grandson, Elijah Watkins.

 I. CAROLINE TAYLOR MILTON, b. Nelson County, Ky., Dec. 2, 1794; d. Lexington, Ky., June 8, 1868; m. Fayette County, Ky., Jan. 12, 1811, *John Hancock Watkins* (b. Hanover County, Va., Oct. 1, 1785; d. Scott County, Mo., Sept. 3, 1845; he was a son of Henry Watkins, and a half brother of Henry Clay; he was a farmer, and lived in Woodford County, Ky. In 1842 he moved to Missouri).

  1. HENRY WATKINS, b. Woodford County, Ky., Jan. 14, 1813; d. Auburndale, Fla., June 23, 1888; m. *1st. Sarah Ashford;* m. *2nd. Mrs. Sarah Brodie* (b. Montgomery County, Tenn., May 28, 1823; d. Auburndale, Fla., in July 1885); he was a fruitgrower and lived at Bartow, Fla.; he had two children by each marriage.

   (1). EDWARD WATKINS, d. aged twenty-one.
   (2). EMILY WATKINS, d. aged fourteen.
   (3). THOMAS BODLEY WATKINS, b. Island No. 10, Tenn., April 5, 1858; m. Auburndale, Fla., June 10, 1886, *Rachel Beaton* (b. Prince Edward Island, N. S., Jan. 14, 1868); 1. Laredo, Tex.

    a. GEORGE HUDSON WATKINS, b. Auburndale, Fla., April 7, 1887.

   (4). EMILY ELIZABETH WATKINS, b. Grimes County, Texas, July 10, 1860; d. Bartow, Fla., August 23, 1894; m. ib. Sept. 7, 1876, *Reading Jehu Blount* (b. ib. Oct. 21, 1855; he is farming at Bartow, Fla.).

    a. ELIJAH BLOUNT, b. and d. ib. Oct. 10, 1878.
    b. AUDREY JANIE BLOUNT, b. ib. June 14, 1880; 1. ib.

c. FRANCES MARION BLOUNT, b. ib. June 3, 1886; d. ib. March 10, 1887.
2. A daughter, b. about 1814; died in infancy.
3. THOMAS BODLEY WATKINS (1st), b. about 1816; d. aged one year.
4. CATHERINE MILTON WATKINS, b. about 1818; d. July 16, 1886; m. *Richard C. Woolfolk*, a commission merchant of Lexington, Ky. They had no children.
5. EMILY MILTON WATKINS, b. about 1820; d. aged nineteen; m. *James Hawkins*, a farmer and merchant in Woodford County, Ky. They had no children.

§152
6. ELIJAH MILTON WATKINS, b. ib. Oct. 25, 1822; l. Fort Spring, Fayette County, Ky.
7. JOHN MILTON WATKINS, b. about 1825; d. aged eighteen.
8. MAY LOUISA WATKINS, b. Woodford County, Ky., Dec. 14, 1828; d. Cincinnati, Ohio, Sept. 24, 1895; m. Lexington, Ky., in Nov. 1855, *Maj. Thomas Lewinski* (b. London, England, Jan. 12, 1800; d. Lexington, Ky., Sept. 18, 1882; he was an architect).
    (1). CAROLINE LEWINSKI, b. Lexington, Ky., August 10, 1856; m. Aberdeen, Ohio, Sept. 1, 1890, *John Henry Johnson* (b. in Virginia, Nov. 20, 1845; d. in Colorado, August 28, 1892; he was a commercial traveler).
        a. KATHERINE FORD JOHNSON, b. Cincinnati, O., June 17, 1891.
9. EBEN MILTON WATKINS, b. Woodford County, Ky., in 1831; l. Fort Spring, Fayette County, Ky.
10. ELIZABETH JENINGS WATKINS, b. Woodford County, Ky., about 1833; l. Lakeport, Ark.
11. THOMAS BODLEY WATKINS (2nd), b. Woodford County, Ky., Nov. 11, 1835; m. *1st.* ib. Nov. 24, 1868, *Marion Walker* (b. Fayette County, Ky., in 1838; d. Lexington, Ky., July 16, 1871); m. *2nd.* ib. Sept. 26, 1876, *Annie Bell McMurtry* (b. Fayette County, Ky., Oct. 15, 1855); he is a merchant in Lexington, Ky.
    (1). SAMUEL WALKER WATKINS, b. ib. March 4, 1871; d. Fayette County, Ky., July 15, 1871.

THE MILTON FAMILY. 185

(2). THOMAS BODLEY WATKINS, b. ib. Oct. 9, 1877.
(3). JOHN WATKINS b. ib June 14, 1879.
(4). BESSIE CLARK WATKINS, b. ib. Sept. 6, 1883.
(5). JENNIE WALKER WATKINS, b. ib. Sept. 8, 1885.
(6). GEORGE ROGERS CLARK WATKINS, b. ib. Sept. 29, 1887.
(7). CAROLINE TAYLOR WATKINS, b. ib. May 4, 1890.
(8). HARVEY WORLEY WATKINS, b. ib. Sept 4, 1892.

12. BUSHROD PORTER WATKINS, b. Woodford County, Ky., Sept. 17, 1838; m. Lexington, Ky., Dec. 25, 1874, *Martha Richardson Jones* (b. ib. in May 1848); 1. Lexington, Ky.
  (1). PAULINE WATKINS, b. ib. m. a Mr. Mitchell, who died soon afterwards; 1. ib.

§153 II. EBEN TAYLOR MILTON, b. Fayette County, Ky., May 8, 1796; d. Somerset, Ky., May 21, 1880; m. *1st.* "Morgan Spring", Frederick County, Feb. 14, 1820, *Emily Bushrod Taylor*, his first cousin (b. ib. Feb. 11, 1804; d. Jeffersonville, Indiana, Aug. 2, 1857; see §189); m. *2nd.* in 1861, *Mrs. Jane Fox Caldwell*, widow of John A. Caldwell. Until 1830 he lived at Winchester, Va., during which time he was sheriff of the County; then until 1857 in Fayette County, Ky , where he conducted a hemp farm and factory; and thereafter at Somerset, Ky., where he was cashier of the Farmers' Bank and the Somerset Deposit Bank. About 1857 he was Secretary of the Louisville and Indianapolis Railroad. He was for many years Superintendent of the Kentucky pikes. He was a Presbyterian, and a man of generous, manly and gentle disposition, and of great executive ability. By his first wife he had fourteen children,—none by the second.
  1. ELIJAH BUSHROD MILTON, b. Winchester, May 25, 1821; d. Pulaski County, Ky., in 1892; he was a bookkeeper.

2. MARTHA CATHERINE MILTON, b. Winchester, Feb. 20, 1823; d. in Kentucky at fourteen years of age.
3. CAROLINE LOUISA MILTON, b. Winchester, Oct. 24, 1824; d. Harford County, Md., in 1883.
4. JOHN MILTON, b. Winchester, March 20, 1826; d. Fayette County, Ky., in 1856.
5. EMILY ELIZABETH MILTON, b. Winchester, Jan. 18, 1828; m. Fayette County, Ky., in May 1849, *Rev. Samuel Bayless* (d. Harford County, Md., March 18, 1873; he was a Presbyterian minister); l. Louisville, Ky.
6. ADDISON MILTON, b. Fayette County, Ky., in 1830; d. Pratt County, Ill., in Aug., 1857; he was a farmer.
7. MARY BERRYMAN MILTON, b. Fayette County, Ky., April 14, 1832; m. Somerset, Ky., Nov. 10, 1870, *Judge William H. Pettus* (b. Gerrard County, Ky., Sept. 9, 1827; d. Somerset, Ky., June 24, 1902; he was a lawyer, judge of Pulaski County, Ky., and a member of the State Legislature); l. ib.
    (1). EBEN MILTON PETTUS, b. ib. Dec. 22, 1871; is a lawyer; l. ib. His twin brother died at birth.
8. SALLIE RAINE MILTON, b. Fayette County, Ky., about 1835; l. Louisville, Ky.

§154
9. THOMAS TIDBALL MILTON, b. Fayette County, Ky., about 1837; d. Louisville, Ky., Sept. 9, 1890; e. Centre College, Danville, Ky.; m. Harrodsburg, Ky., Nov. 10, 1880, *Mrs Sarah E. Moore* (b. Shelbyville, Ky., May 24, 1846; l. Louisville, Ky.); for twenty-seven consecutive years he was chief deputy of the Circuit Court at Louisville, Ky.
    (1). HENRY STITES MILTON, b. ib. May 31, 1883; l. ib.
10. EBEN OMEGA MILTON, b. Fayette County, Ky., Jan. 30, 1840; d. New Market, Ky., Sept. 18, 1896; m. Bardstown, Ky., Feb. 27, 1866, *Margaret Ellen Kirtley* (b. Bardstown, Ky., Jan. 26, 1845; l. New Market, Ky.). He was a member of General John H. Morgan's brigade during the Civil War, and afterwards engaged in the lumber business in Memphis, Tenn.

THE MILTON FAMILY. 187

 (1). EDWIN KIRTLEY MILTON, b. Bardstown, Ky., July 12, 1867; l. Louisville, Ky.; he is a travelling salesman.
 (2). BENJAMIN TAYLOR MILTON, b. Memphis, Tenn., April 1, 1869; m. Lebanon, Tenn., August ι. ѕ95, *Harriet Hilliard Blanton* of that place; l. Memphis, Tenn.; he is a travelling salesman.
  a. MARGARET KIRTLEY MILTON, b. New Market, Ky., May 13, 1897.
 11. BENJAMIN HARLAND MILTON, b. Fayette County, Ky., in 1841; d. Louisville, Ky., Nov. 6, 1867; was Captain of Co. K., 1st. Ky. Cavalry, in the Civil War.
 12. JAMES BERRYMAN MILTON, b. Fayette Co. Ky., in 1843; d. Louisville, Ky., Jan. 23, 1871; e. Centre College, Ky.; m. April 22, 1868, *Ellen ¦Courtney* (b. Independence, Mo., Dec. 8, 1844; l. Louisville, Ky.); he was a bookkeeper at Louisville.
  (1). MAY NAOMI MILTON, b. ib. March 17, 1869; d. ib. March 17, 1870.
 13. A son, b. and d. Fayette County, Ky., in 1845.
 14. GRIFFIN TAYLOR MILTON, b. ib. March 24, 1847; m. Nov. 12, 1878, *Isabelle Silver* of Maryland; he lived in Louisville, Ky., till 1874, and since that time has been farming in Harford Co., Md., near Darlington.

§155 III. JOHN MILTON, b. Fayette County, Ky., March 24, 1802; d. Baltimore, Md., Nov. 18, 1860; m. Frederick Co., Sept. 7, 1826, *Louisa Ann Taylor*, his first cousin (b. Loudoun County, Va., Sept. 5, 1807; d. Louisville, Ky., Apr. 6, 1869; see §189). He was an Elder in the Presbyterian Church, and Cashier of the Northern Bank of Kentucky.
 1. ELIJAH NEWTON MILTON, b. Winchester, Va., July 10, 1827; d Memphis, Tenn., August 30, 1898; m. Louisville, Ky., May 12, 1853, *Ellen Temple Clark* (b. Lexington, Ky., Sept. 13, 1832; l. Louisville, Ky.); he was a commission merchant in Louisville.
  (1). MARY LOUISA MILTON, b. ib. March 7, 1854; d. ib. Oct. 14, 1877; m. ib. Oct. 6, 1875, *Karl Jungbluth* (b. Arolsen, Germany; he is an importer at Louisville).

a. KARL JUNGBLUTH, b. ib. July 20, 1876; 1. Cincinnati, O.
b. MARION JUNGBLUTH, b. Louisville, Ky., Oct. 5, 1877; l. ib.
(2). CHARLES JOHNSON MILTON, b. ib. Jan. 31, 1857; m. Wheeling, W. Va., Jan. 14, 1892, *Lucy Seville Loring* of Wheeling; he is President of the Smokeless Fuel Company at Cincinnati, O.
 a. ALONZO LORING MILTON, b. Wheeling, W. Va., December 16, 1893.
 b. CHARLES JOHNSON MILTON, b. ib. August 20, 1899.
 c. MARY CHAPLANE MILTON, b. ib. August 29, 1900.
(3). FRANCIS CLARK MILTON, b. Louisville, Ky., July 12, 1866; is a commission merchant at Memphis, Tenn.
2. WILLIAM MILTON, b. Lexington, Ky., August 22, 1829; d. Louisville, Ky., about 1880; m. Louisville, Ky., June 6, 1861, *Sarah Elizabeth Adams* (b. Corydon, Ind., May 3, 1833; she married afterwards Capt. Price Curd Newman, who is dead; 1. Berkeley Springs, W. Va); he was a commission merchant in Louisville, Ky.
(1). KATE ADAMS MILTON, b. near Louisville, Ky., April 3, 1862; m. Louisville, Ky., June 1, 1885, *William Milo Locke*, a dealer in powder and dynamite at Pittsburg, Penn.
 a. PRICE NEWMAN LOCKE, b. Louisville, Ky., May 21, 1886.
(2). MARY MILDRED MILTON, b. near Louisville, Ky., Oct. 23, 1863; l. Berkeley Springs, W. Va.
(3). LOUISA RAINE MILTON, b. Louisville, Ky., August 2, 1871; d. ib. Feb. 27, 1878.
3. ANNIE ELIZABETH MILTON, b. Lexington, Ky., Jan. 15, 1832; d. Louisville, Ky., Feb. 22, 1895; m. ib. Nov. 7, 1854, *Robert Morrison Cunningham* (b. Green County, Ala., March 13, 1829; d. Louisville, Ky., Nov. 25, 1878; p. Joseph Parks Cunningham

THE MILTON FAMILY. 189

and Elizabeth F. Webb; he was Cashier of the First
National Bank of Louisville.
,(1). BETTIE SCOTT CUNNINGHAM, b. ib. Dec. 27,
1855; d. ib. Sept. 18, 1890.
(2). JOHN MILTON CUNNINGHAM, b. ib. Nov. 10,
1857; m. Independence, Kan., Feb. 18, 1886,
Rose Ione Brown (b. Carey, O., August 22, 1865);
he owns a large cattle ranch near Caney, Kan.,
and is Asst. Cashier of the Home National Bank.
    a. WILLIAM BROWN CUNNINGHAM, b. Independence, Kan., Dec. 21, 1886; d. Caney, Kan., June 13, 1887.
    b. JOHN MILTON CUNNINGHAM, b. Independence, Kan., August 19, 1888.
    c. ROBERT BROWN CUNNINGHAM, b. Caney, Kan., April 6, 1899.
    d. ROBERT MILTON CUNNINGHAM, b. ib. Nov. 3, 1900; d. ib. Jan 13, 1901.
(3). ROBERT MORRISON CUNNINGHAM, b. Louisville, Ky., Sept. 11, 1859; m. ib. Oct. 19, 1886, *Frances Marmaduke Barnett* (b. Jefferson County, Ky., July 5, 1862; she is a daughter of Judge Andrew Barnett); he is a wholesale lumber merchant in Louisville, Ky.
    a. KATHLEEN CUNNINGHAM, b. ib. August 2, 1887.
    b. ROBERT MORRISON CUNNINGHAM, b. ib. June 24, 1890.
    c. ANNIE MILTON CUNNINGHAM, b. ib. Feb. 27, 1894.
    d. ANDREW BARNETT CUNNINGHAM, b. ib. Sept. 3, 1896.

§156   4. EBEN MILTON, b. Lexington, Ky., June 11, 1834;
d. Louisville, Ky., Sept. 10, 1888; m. ib. in Dec.
1863, *Emma Meriwether* (b. ib. August 3, 1839; d.
New York City, Jan. 16, 1895); he was in the real estate business in Louisville, Ky.
(1). DAVID MERIWETHER MILTON, b. ib. Nov.
20, 1864; m. Dilston Hall, Jefferson County, Ky.,
Nov. 25, 1896, *Ellen Hunt Fink* (b. Louisville,

Ky., March 4, 1870); he is a lawyer in New York City.
- a. ALBERT FINK MILTON, b. Westchester County, N. Y., Sept. 11, 1897.
- b. DAVID MERIWETHER MILTON, b. New York City, Feb. 22, 1900.

(2). THOMAS SMITH MILTON, b. Louisville, Ky., in 1866; d. ib. aged nine months.

5. MARY LOUISA MILTON, b. Lexington, Ky., Dec. 25, 1836; d. ib. March 13, 1837.
6. JOHN BUSHROD MILTON, b. ib. Oct. 20, 1838; d. ib. Oct. 10, 1839.
7. JOHN MILTON, b. Lexington, Ky., Nov. 20, 1840; d. Louisville, Ky., Dec. 4, 1897; m. ib. Dec. 17, 1863, *Laura Smyser* (b. Bullitt County, Ky., Oct. 17, 1842; d. Louisville, Ky., Dec. 2, 1891); he was a merchant in Louisville.

(1). LEWIS SMYSER MILTON, b. ib. Dec. 2, 1864; d. ib. Nov. 14, 1867.

(2). NOLAND SMYSER MILTON, b. ib. Aug. 14, 1869; m. ib. April 5, 1899, *Amelia Neville Pearce* (b. ib. May 31, 1878); he is discount clerk of the National Bank of Kentucky; l. ib.

(3). LAURA MILTON, b ib. April 5, 1873; m.ib. Feb. 27, 1899, *James Florian Browinski*, Supt. of the Chicago & Eastern Illinois Railroad; l. Joppa, Ill.
- a. BEVERLY BROWINSKI, b. Cincinnati, O., Dec. 11, 1899.

(4). JOHN LEWIS MILTON, b. Louisville, Ky., July 14, 1875; he is president of the Sterling Electric Motor Co., at Dayton, Ohio.

(5). ANNA CORA MILTON, b. Louisville, Ky., March 7, 1884; l. ib.

8. MATTHEW SCOTT MILTON, b. Lexington, Ky., June 21, 1843; d. Louisville, Ky., June 6, 1887; m. ib. Dec. 6, 1870, *Jennie Logan Smith* (b. ib. Sept. 5, 1848; l. ib.); he was in the insurance business in Louisville.

(1). CORNELIA SMITH MILTON, b. ib. Feb. 4, 1874; d. ib. Feb. 29, 1876.

THE MILTON FAMILY. 191

  (2). THOMAS SMITH MILTON, b. ib. Oct. 6, 1879;
  l. ib.; is in the lumber business.
 9. ELIZABETH CASTLEMAN MILTON, b. ib. August 23,
 1846; m. ib. Oct. 4, 1870, *Philip Slaughter Campbell*
 (b. Middleburg, Va., June 19, 1844; he is in the insurance business); l. Jackson, Miss.
  (1). LOUISE MILTON CAMPBELL, b. Louisville,
  Ky., Sept. 20, 1871; d. ib. July 17, 1894.
  (2). PHILIP SLAUGHTER CAMPBELL, b. ib. Sept.
  1, 1875; l. ib.; he is connected with the California
  Fig Syrup Company.
  (3). ROBERT CUNNINGHAM CAMPBELL, b. ib. Jan.
  17, 1878; d. ib. Dec. 14, 1880.
 10. EMMA MILTON, b. ib. March 5, 1849; d. ib. June
 12, 1850.
 11. LOUISA MILTON, b. ib. March 5, 1849; d. ib. Feb.
 20, 1850.
§157 IV. BUSHROD TAYLOR MILTON, b. Fayette Co., Ky., Nov.
10, 1807; d. Henderson, Ky., March 19, 1899; m. near
Versailes, Ky., Dec. 5, 1833, *Mary Anne Claypool* (b. Vincennes, Ind., Nov. 29, 1813; d. Lexington, Ky., Sept. 20,
1890; she was a descendant of Oliver Cromwell); he was
for twenty-six years Treasurer of Lexington, Ky., and for
fifty-two years an Elder in the Presbyterian Church; he
was in the clothing business; he was a man of sterling
worth and integrity, was well versed in the Bible, and had
a fine figure and a keen mind.
 1. CATHERINE MILTON, b. Versailes, Ky., Nov. 7,
 1835; m. Lexington, Ky., Oct. 6, 1859, *Wyatt Hawkins Ingram* (b. Henderson, Ky., March 20, 1832; he
 is a farmer); l. Henderson, Ky.
  (1). LOUISA CUMMINGS INGRAM, b. ib. Aug. 17,
  1860; m. Henderson County, Ky., Feb. 24, 1880,
  James Avasco Priest, a farmer at Hebardsville,
  Henderson County, Ky.
  (2) JOHN MILTON INGRAM, b. Coahoma County,
  Miss., July 10, 1862; m. San Francisco, Cal.,
  July 22, 1893, *Elizabeth Keaton* (of San Jose,
  Cal.; d. May 8, 1896); l. Nome, Alaska.

THE MILTON FAMILY.

   a. WYATT HAWKINS INGRAM, b. Palo Alto, Cal., May 1, 1894.
   b. BRUCE KEATON INGRAM, b. ib. April 14, 1895.
(3). MARY ANNIE INGRAM, b. Henderson Co., Ky., April 4, 1865; m. ib. June 14, 1894, *Dr. Charles Bruce Walls* of Aberdeen, Scotland; 1. Chicago, Illinois.
   a. CATHERINE JEAN WALLS, b. ib. May 13, 1897.
(4). MARIE LETITIA INGRAM, b. Henderson County, Ky., June 9, 1867.
(5). WYATT HAWKINS INGRAM, b. ib. Sept. 21, 1869; is trust officer of the Farmers' Bank and Trust Company at Henderson, Ky.
(6). MATILDA FORD INGRAM, b. Henderson County, Ky., May 30, 1872.
(7). BUSHROD TAYLOR INGRAM, b. ib. Nov. 18, 1875; 1. San Diego, Cal.

2. ANN MARGARET MILTON, b. Versailes, Ky., Jan. 19, 1839; m. Lexington, Ky., Dec., 14, 1869, *William Warfield Ford* (b. Paris, Ky., Sept. 8, 1838; he is a cotton planter at Lakeport, Ark.).
   (1). MARY MILTON FORD, b. Lexington, Ky., Aug 17, 1872; d. Lakeport, Ark., Oct. 28, 1881.
   (2). PATTIE PAGE FORD, b. Lexington, Ky., Sept. 18, 1874; m. Lakeport, Ark., July 14, 1896, *William Furguson Fenton*, a civil engineer of Orlando, Fla.
      a. CATHERINE FENTON, b. Lakeport, Ark., May 14, 1897.
      b. MILTON FORD FENTON, b. ib. Sept. 2, 1900.
   (3). KATHERINE INGRAM FORD, b. Lexington, Ky., Nov. 23, 1879; m. Lakeport, Ark., Feb. 7, 1899, *Ellis McKeen Chamberlin*, a merchant of that place.
      a. WILLIAM FORD CHAMBERLIN, b. ib. April 11, 1902.

§158   3. WILLIAM AGUN MILTON, b. Versailes, Ky., May
22, 1844; m. Henderson, Ky., Oct. 13, 1869, *Florence
Maria Clark* (b. Washington, D. C., August 4, 1848);
he served in John Morgan's brigade in the Civil War;
he is Secretary and Treasurer of the Courier-Journal
Job Printing Company, Louisville, Ky.
> (1). FLORENCE CLARK MILTON, b. Lexington,
> Ky., April 26, 1872; d. ib. July 13, 1873.
>
> (2). SUSAN BARRETT MILTON, b. Lexington, Ky.,
> Nov. 6, 1870; m. Louisville, Ky., Oct. 6, 1897,
> *Edward Jefferson Watkins*, Southern Manager of
> the "Insurance Field"; l. ib.
>> a. BARBARA WATKINS, b. ib. July 8, 1898.
>
> (3). ANNIE FORD MILTON, b. Lexington, Ky.,
> Dec. 24, 1873; m. Louisville, Ky., Jan. 20, 1892,
> *Bruce Haldeman* (b. Knoxville, Tenn., Nov. 7,
> 1864; he is President of the Louisville Courier-
> Journal Company and of the Louisville Times
> Company); l. Louisville, Ky.
>> a. FLORENCE MILTON HALDEMAN, b. ib.
>> Jan. 24, 1893.
>>
>> b. ELIZABETH ANN HALDEMAN, b. ib. June
>> 8, 1896.
>>
>> c. WALTER NEWMAN HALDEMAN, b. ib. Jan.
>> 14, 1901.

   4. JOHN BROWN MILTON, b. Lexington, Ky., April
25, 1847; m. San Francisco, Cal., Oct. 20, 1880,
Harriet Buchanan Steele (b. Washington, D. C., Dec.
27, 1858); he is a Commander in the U. S. Navy; l.
San Francisco, Cal.
> (1). MAXWELL CLAYPOOL MILTON, b. ib. July
> 16, 1881.
>
> (2). MATTIE STEELE MILTON, b. ib. May 3, 1883.

§159 V. WILLIAM MILTON, b. Fayette County, Ky., July 21,
1811; d. Memphis, Tenn., Dec. 18, 1868; m. *1st.* Fayette
County, Ky., Nov. 19, 1833, *Elizabeth Simpson* (b. ib.
August 10, 1813; d. Lexington, Ky., about 1847); m.
2nd. Frankfort, Ky., Feb. 6, 1849, *Louisa Rennick* (b. ib.
July 10, 1828; d. Memphis, Tenn., June 4, 1901); he was

THE MILTON FAMILY.

a commission merchant in Memphis, Tenn.; he had five children by his first marriage and three by the second.
1. ELIJAH MILTON, b. Fayette County, Ky., Sept. 8, 1834; d. ib. June 27, 1836.
2. JOSHUA WORLEY MILTON, b. Lexington, Ky., July 8, 1839; d. Memphis, Tenn., Oct. 21, 1860.
3. WILLIAM SIMPSON MILTON, b. Fayette County, Ky., June 3, 1841; d. ib. April 14, 1846.
4. MARTHA JANE MILTON, b. Lexington, Ky., Feb. 10, 1845; m. Newport, Ky., May 25, 1866, *Bushrod Taylor Castleman* (b. ib. May 26, 1838; he was her second cousin; see §190; he is in the clothing business in Louisville, Ky.; he served in the 8th Ky. Cavalry in the Civil War, General John Morgan's command).
    (1). WILLIAM WORLEY CASTLEMAN, b. Lexington, Ky., May 22, 1871; 1. New York City, connected with a large dry goods house.
    (2). ELIZABETH MILTON CASTLEMAN, b. Lexington, Ky., May 22, 1873; d. ib. in infancy.
5. ELIZABETH SIMPSON MILTON, b. Lexington, Ky., Sept. 8, 1847; m. Memphis, Tenn., Sept. 18, 1871, *James Oscar Cox* of that place; 1. Chattanooga, Tenn.
    (1). WILLIAM MILTON COX, b. Memphis, Tenn., June 22, 1872; m. ib. in Oct. 1900, *Florence Riddle* of that place; he is a bookkeeper; 1. Chattanooga, Tenn.
    (2). MATTIE MAY COX, b. Memphis, Tenn., May 12, 1878; 1. Chattanooga, Tenn.
    (3). WILLIAM OSCAR COX, b. Memphis, Tenn., July 8, 1880; 1. Chattanooga, Tenn.
6. MARY WILLIS MILTON, b. Lexington, Ky., Dec. 29, 1849; m. Memphis, Tenn., March 25, 1869, *Deitrich Wintter* (b. Nurnburg, Bavaria, Germany, May 10, 1826; d. Memphis, Tenn., Sept. 14, 1871; he was an architect); 1. Memphis, Tenn.
    (1). DEITRICH WINTTER, b. Memphis, Tenn., March 15, 1870; m. Memphis, Tenn., Nov. 25, 1894, *Mabel Sherman Glisson* (b. ib. April 15, 1871); he is in the cotton business in Memphis.

THE MILTON FAMILY.

   a. MARY EMMA WINTTER, b. ib. April 5, 1896.
   b. ALICE WINTTER, b. ib. May 10, 1898.
   c. WILLIAM ARTHUR WINTTER, b. ib. Nov. 13, 1900.
   (2). WILLIAM MILTON WINTTER, b. ib. Jan. 22, 1872; 1. ib.; he is in the cotton business.
7. WILLIAM ELIJAH MILTON, b. Memphis, Tenn., June 18, 1856; d. Collierville, Tenn., Jan. 5, 1866.
8. KITTY WORLEY MILTON, b. Memphis, Tenn., March 4, 1861; d. ib. in May 1864.

§160   D. JOHN MILTON, b. Prince William County, about 1758; d. "Milton Valley", near Berryville, March 17, 1818; m. *1st.* "Hopewell", Frederick County, July 20, 1782, *Ann Stribling* (for her ancestry see STRIBLING FAMILY, §62); m. *2nd.* near Shenandale, Jefferson County, Feb. 20, 1812, *Mrs. Catherine Washington-Nelson* (b. "Fairfield" about 1765; d. near Millwood, July 1, 1845; she was the daughter of Warner Washington and Hannah Fairfax, and the widow of Dr. Nelson of Maryland, by whom she had eight children. After the death of Mr. Milton, she moved to the Millwood neighborhood to live with her two married daughters). He came from Prince William County to the Valley when quite a young man, and settled near Berryville, then in Frederick County, but now in Clarke, where he built the homestead of "Milton Valley". He soon became one of the foremost men of the community and a leader in all public enterprises. On Dec. 5, 1780 he gave bond for £35,000 as treasurer of the county board of charities, which office he continued to hold for at least twelve years. In 1797 he was president of the same board. He was Justice of the Peace, Vestryman of the Parish in 1785, and Trustee of Battletown, now Berryville, when the village was incorporated in 1798. He was "a man of strong self-reliance, fine moral character, great industry and enterprise". His broad fields of wheat and corn, and the large herds of cattle and sheep that grazed upon his meadows, indicated the success with which his labors were crowned. "The Story of a Long Life", written by his great-granddaughter, Harriot Milton Hammond, while referring primarily to his daughter, Mrs. Bushrod Taylor, gives an excellent description of the beautiful homelife at "Milton Valley", and of the members of the household and those who so frequently shared their hospitality. He had eleven children by his first marriage, as follows:

 I. TALIAFERRO MILTON, b. "Milton Valley", Sept. 13, 1783; d. Staunton, August 12, 1806. He studied law with Judge Holmes of Winchester, and was just beginning to practice at the time of his death.

§161 II. HARRIOT MILTON, b. "Milton Valley", July 23, 1785; d. ib. August 23, 1824; m. *1st.* ib. March 13, 1806, *John McIlhany* (for his ancestry see MCILHANY FAMILY, §129); m. *2nd.* ib. Nov. 11, 1812, *William Taylor* (b. in Kentucky, Feb. 24, 1787; d. "Milton Valley", April 29, 1839; for his ancestry see §185. His home was "Hawthorn", in Clarke County. After the death of her father he purchased "Milton Valley", where he lived till the time of his death). She was a most able woman, and was for some years looked up to by her younger brothers and sisters as the head of the household. During the two years following her first marriage she lived in Loudoun County; then at "Milton Valley" till her second marriage; then till her father's death at "Hawthorn"; and thereafter at "Milton Valley". By her first marriage she had one son, and by her second a son and two daughters, as follows:

  1. TALIAFERRO MILTON MCILHANY; for his descendants see MCILHANY FAMILY, §§129–131.

§162 2. JOHN WILLIAM TAYLOR, b. "Hawthorn", Oct. 24, 1813; d. ib. Nov. 26, 1815.

  3. SARAH ANN MILTON TAYLOR, b. ib. Sept. 22, 1817; d. Winchester, Feb. 2, 1847; e. in Clarke County and at Mrs. Porter's School in Alexandria; m. "Milton Valley", Jan. 20, 1836, *George Washington Hammond* (b. "Happy Retreat", Charlestown, Apr. 14, 1809; d. Baltimore, Md., Jan. 8, 1859; p. Thomas Hammond of "Happy Retreat").

   (1). MARY MILDRED HAMMOND, b. "Happy Retreat", Nov. 3, 1836; e. Winchester; m. ib. Dec. 13, 1856, *Algernon Sidney Sullivan* (b. Madison,

Ind., April 5, 1826; d. New York City, Dec. 4, 1887; p. Jeremiah Sullivan and Charlotte Cutler of Madison, Ind. He was a distinguished lawyer of New York City. A memorial volume of his life has been issued by his son.) She has traveled abroad once, and is a leader in New York society and charitable work; l. New York City.

    a. GEORGE HAMMOND SULLIVAN, b. ib. Nov. 20, 1859; e. Columbia College and Harvard; studied law at the Columbia Law School and is practicing in New York City.

(2). HARRIOT MILTON HAMMOND, b. Charlestown, W. Va., Aug. 28, 1838; e. Winchester, and at the Virginia Female Institute in Staunton; has been abroad several times; l. New York City. She wrote the charming memorial of "Aunt Bet" Taylor mentioned above, §160.

(3). WILLIAM TAYLOR HAMMOND, b. "Shannon Hill", Jefferson County, W. Va., Feb. 14, 1841; d. Dinwiddie County, July 4, 1864, as the result of a wound received in the battle of Reams Station.

(4). THOMAS BUSHROD HAMMOND, b. "Shannon Hill", July 27, 1843; l. Los Angeles, Cal.

(5). HENRY WASHINGTON HAMMOND, b. "Shannon Hill", July 27, 1843; d. Winchester, Sept. 13, 1848.

§163   (6). FLORINDA JONES HAMMOND, b. Winchester, Sept. 17, 1846; m. Berryville, Dec. 15, 1869, *John Boyle Tilford* (b. Lexington, Ky., Dec. 16, 1846; d. Colorado Springs, Col., Feb. 22, 1887; p. John Boyle Tilford and Catherine Hunt; he was a banker in New York City); l. Winchester.

    a. WILLIAM HAMMOND TILFORD, b. New York City, Oct. 31, 1870; d. East Orange, N. J., Nov. 20, 1876.

    b. FRANK VINCIT TILFORD, b. ib. Nov. 30, 1871; m. *1st.* Berryville, June 21, 1893, *Rosalie Warwick Lewis* (b. Clarke County, in 1872; d. ib. Sept. 28, 1895); m. *2nd.* Berry-

ville, *Mary Kownslar Moore* (b. ib. Feb. 27, 1874). He is Asst. Superintendent of a Knitting Mill at Huntsville, Ala.
 c. ELIZABETH TAYLOR TILFORD, b. East Orange, N. J., April 9, 1874; m. Washington, D. C., Feb. 12, 1896, *Carl Bismarck Keferstein* (b. Washington, D. C., July 10, 1867; he is an architect); 1. ib.
  (a). ELIZABETH CARL KEFERSTEIN, b. ib. Nov. 19, 1897.
 d. JOHN BOYLE TILFORD, b. East Orange, N. J., August 31, 1885; d. ib. July 10, 1887.
(7). GEORGE WASHINGTON HAMMOND, b. and d. Winchester, Sept. 17, 1846.
4. FLORINDA ELIZABETH HARRIOT TAYLOR, b. "Milton Valley", July 31, 1821; d. Winchester, April 1, 1846; e. Mrs. Gardner's School in Philadelphia; m. "Shannon Hill", August 1, 1842, *William Strother Jones* (b. "Vaucluse", Frederick County, Dec. 20, 1817; d. Winchester, Jan. 10, 1894; p. William Strother Jones and Anna Maria Marshall of "Vaucluse"; gr. p. Col. Strother Jones and Mary Frances Thornton of "Vaucluse"—Charles Marshall, brother of Chief Justice Marshall, and Lucy Pickett of Warrenton. He married secondly Mary E. Barton of Fredericksburg, by whom he had several children).
 (1). WILLIAM STROTHER JONES, b. "Vaucluse", June 28, 1844; d. ib. Oct. 20, 1851.
III. JOHN MILTON, b. "Milton Valley", Nov. 22, 1787; d. ib. March 20, 1810.
§164 IV. NANCY MILTON, b. ib. May 13, 1790; d. Shelby County, Ky., about 1835; m. "Milton Valley", May 5, 1819, *Presley Davis*, her first cousin; see §180. She had only one child.
 1. TALIAFERRO MILTON DAVIS, b. Shelby County, Ky., about 1821; d. Fayette County, Mo., about April 1871; m. *Amanda L. Polk* of Shelby County, Ky. They moved to the neighborhood of Lexington, Mo., where they died. They had no children.

THE MILTON FAMILY. 199

V. MARGARET MILTON, b. "Milton Valley", June 21, 1792; d. ib. March 20, 1794.

VI. WILLIAM MILTON, b. ib. July 15, 1794; d. ib. Dec. 22, 1797.

§165 VII. RICHARD MILTON, b. ib. June 2, 1796; d. Hannibal, Mo., August 17, 1868; e. Berryville and Mr. Ellzey's School in Loudoun County; m. Winchester, Nov. 11, 1817, *Margaret Rosannah Davisson;* see MCILHANY FAMILY, §116. He was Sheriff of Frederick County and Postmaster at Winchester, and afterwards lived at Hannibal, Mo.

   1. ANN MARGARET MILTON, b. Winchester, Nov. 10, 1818; e. ib.; d. ib. August 14, 1850.

   2. FREDERICK RICHARD MILTON, b. ib. Nov. 9, 1820; e. Loudoun County; d. Hannibal, Mo., July 11, 1873; m. Winchester, April 30, 1850, *Annie Maria Miller* (b. ib. Sept. 6, 1822; d. St. Louis, Mo., March 21, 1902; p. Godfrey Miller and Catharine E. Schultz; gr. p. John and Catharine Schultz). From Winchester he moved to Hannibal, Mo., where he was Sheriff and Assessor.

     (1). MARGARET ANNA MILTON, b. Winchester, Feb. 14, 1851; e. Hannibal, Mo.; d. ib. Oct. 28, 1879; m. ib. Oct. 17, 1872, *Cecil Calvert Kaylor* (b. Newark, Mo., March 4, 1842; d. La Belle, Mo., August 7, 1893; p. William and Emeline Manning Kaylor).

        a. ANNA MILTON KAYLOR, b. Quincy, Ill., Dec. 1, 1878; e. St. Louis, Mo.; l. ib.

     (2). GODFREY MILLER MILTON, b. Winchester, March 1, 1853; e. Hannibal, Mo.; d. ib. July 14, 1882.

§166   (3). BESSIE OTTO MILTON, b. ib. Feb. 13, 1855; e. ib.; m. ib. Jan 21, 1880, *Milton Goodfellow*, her first cousin; see §168; l. St. Louis, Mo.

     (4). ROSANNAH DAVISSON MILTON, b. Hannibal, Mo., Nov. 5, 1858; e. ib.; l. St. Louis, Mo.

     (5). RICHARD STRIBLING MILTON, b. Hannibal, Mo., Oct. 8, 1860; d. ib. July 11, 1864.

     (6). ROBERT EDWARD LEE MILTON, b. ib. Oct. 2, 1862; e. ib.; is chief clerk in the offices of the Wabash R. R. at St. Louis, Mo.

3. JAMES TALIAFERRO THEODORE MILTON, b. Winchester, August 29, 1825; e. Baltimore, Md.; d. Hannibal, Mo., March 5, 1879; m. "Carter's Hall", near Winchester, Nov. 21, 1849, *Mary Elizabeth Carter* (b. ib. about 1830; d. Chicago, Ill., May 9, 1902; p. William Arthur Carter and Sarah Caroline Beeler of "Carter's Hall"). He moved to Missouri in 1854, and was in the furniture business at Hannibal, Mo.

 (1). WILLIAM DAVISSON MILTON, b. "Carter's Hall", Sept. 23, 1850; e. Hannibal, Mo.; m. ib. Aug. 13, 1876, *Annie Tracie Shaffer* (b. ib. May 25, 1858; p. Adam and Mary Shaffer). He was an engineer at Oakwood, Mo.

  a. ESTELLA ELIZABETH MILTON, b. Hannibal, Mo., Dec. 4, 1877.

  b. CHARLES WILLIAM MILTON, b. ib. Jan. 25, 1881; d. ib. Feb. 22, 1881.

  c. JAMES HENRY WICKES MILTON, b. ib. June 16, 1885.

§167 (2). ROSE CARTER MILTON, b. "Carter's Hall", June 9, 1853; e. Hannibal, Mo.; m. ib. Feb. 15, 1872, *Harris Nathan Bennett* (b. Baltic, Conn., Aug. 8, 1845; p. Nathan Bennett and Abby Sarah Manning; gr. p. Amos and Hannah Bennett; he is a lumber merchant); l. Maplewood, Mo.

  a. HARRIS NATHAN BENNETT, b. Hannibal, Mo., Feb. 2, 1873; l. Maplewood, Mo.; he is a lumber merchant.

  b. JAMES WILLIAM BENNETT, b. Hannibal, Mo., Feb. 12, 1874; d. ib. June 12, 1874.

  c. LENA MAY BENNETT, b. ib. March 1, 1876; l. Maplewood, Mo.

  d. FREDERICK DAVISSON BENNETT, b. ib. Feb. 15, 1879; m. Maplewood, Mo., March 26, 1900, *Clara Helen Harrison* of Maplewood; he is in the insurance business.

   (a). RUTH BENNETT.

 (3). MARY ELIZABETH MILTON, b. Hannibal, Mo., Oct. 14, 1855; e. ib.; m. ib. June 14, 1881, *William Barton Smith;* l. Chicago, Ill.

THE MILTON FAMILY.

a. JULIA IRENE SMITH, b. Orlando, Fla., Dec. 15, 1883; m. Chicago, Ill., Dec. 13, 1901, *William Jacolio* of Chicago.

(4). KATHERINE CARTER MILTON, b. Hannibal, Mo., Oct. 7, 1856; e. ib.; m. ib. May 25, 1881, *Silas Wright Snyder;* 1. Chicago, Ill.

    a. NETTIE EDNA SNYDER, b. Burlington, Ia., August 11, 1884; m. Chicago, Ill., July 30, 1901, *Paul Jesse* of Chicago.

    b. EDWIN MILTON SNYDER, b. ib. August 6, 1894.

(5). ANNIE LEE MILTON, b. Hannibal, Mo., Sept. 15, 1865; d. St. Louis, Mo., April 8, 1901; m. Hannibal, Mo., Feb. 3, 1881, *William Wilson Lysle* (b. Mt. Vernon, Penn., Feb. 23, 1844; d. Kansas City, Mo., August 5, 1900; p. William Wilson Lysle and Caroline Beckney Fetterman; he was revising clerk of the Santa Fe R. R. at Kansas City, Mo.).

    a. MILTON CARTER LYSLE, b. ib. Jan. 30, 1882; 1. St. Louis, Mo.

(6). AUGUSTA NETTLETON MILTON, b. Hannibal, Mo., Jan. 29, 1867; d. Chicago, Ill., May 31, 1890.

(7). BETTIE TAYLOR MILTON, b. Hannibal, Mo., Sept. 2, 1876; d. ib. in May, 1882.

§168   4. ELIZABETH HANNAH MILTON, b. Winchester, May 5, 1829; e ib.; d. Pasadena, Cal., Dec. 24, 1887; m. Winchester, Nov. 18, 1852, *Rev. Thomas Miles Goodfellow* (b. Clearfield, Penn., May 15, 1818; d. Arlington Heights, Ill., Dec. 29, 1871; p. Thomas Goodfellow and Ellen Grahame; he served through the Civil War in the 4th Iowa Infantry; he was a Methodist minister).

    (1). MILTON GOODFELLOW, b. Winchester, Oct. 24, 1853; d. Peoria, Ill., Sept. 4, 1890; m. Hannibal, Mo., Jan. 21, 1880, *Bessie Otto Milton*, his first cousin; see §166; he was a hardware merchant.

The Milton Family.

  a. Richard Milton Goodfellow, b. Oshkosh, Wis., March 2, 1881; is clerking in a wholesale dry goods house in St. Louis, Mo.
  b. Howard Davisson Goodfellow, b, Oshkosh, Wis., Jan. 9, 1883; d. ib. Aug. 29, 1883.

(2). Rose Davisson Goodfellow, b. Hannibal, Mo., Oct. 27, 1855; d. Colorado Springs, Col., Nov. 24, 1901; e. Englewood Normal College, Englewood, Ill.; m. Arlington Heights, Ill., Oct. 9, 1877, *Charles Alfred Parsons* (b. Deerfield, Lake County, Ill., May 10, 1852; p. Alfred Parsons and Susan Vedder; gr. p. Stephen and Pena Parsons—Philip Vedder and Margaret Haverly; he is a farmer at Deerfield, Ill.).

  a. Harrie Alfred Parsons, b. ib. Jan. 17, 1879; m. Van Horne, Iowa, July 18, 1901, *Emma Katherine Wagner* of that place; 1. Colorado Springs, Col.
      (a). Alvin Philip Parsons.
  b. Roy Milton Parsons, b. ib. Feb. 7, 1881.
  c. Lura Elizabeth Parsons, b. Arlington Heights, Ill., Sept. 9, 1883.
  d. Virginia Grahame Parsons, b. Deerfield, Ill., Jan. 10, 1886.
  e. Frank Elon Parsons, b. Arlington Heights, Ill., April 15, 1888.

(3). Harry Grahame Goodfellow, b. Council Bluffs, Iowa, March 13, 1858; d. Rollo, Mo., Feb. 8, 1862.

(4). Ellen Grahame Goodfellow, b. Council Bluffs, Iowa. Dec. 12, 1860; e. Arlington Heights, Ill; m. Oshkosh, Wis., Oct. 20, 1881, *George Wallace Fleming* (b. Arlington Heights, Ill., August 15, 1859; p. John Fleming and Eliza Ann Wallace of Arlington Heights; gr. p. Joseph Fleming and Martha Fowler—Robert Wallace and Jane McEldowney; he is a travelling salesman); 1. Olney, Ill.

a. GEORGIA ELIZABETH FLEMING, b. Arlington Heights, Ill., April 2, 1884.
b. ROSE GRAHAME FLEMING, b. Englewood, Ill., August 4, 1886.
c. GERTRUDE WALLACE FLEMING, b. Arlington Heights, Ill., Oct. 5, 1888.
d. JOHN GOODFELLOW FLEMING, b. ib. Feb. 21, 1890.
e. ELLEN MILTON FLEMING, b. Olney, Ill., March 10, 1898.

(5). FRANK HOWARD GOODFELLOW, b. Nashville, Tenn., July 9, 1865; d. Arlington Heights, Ill., Jan. 31. 1886.

(6). GUY CARLTON GOODFELLOW, b. Courtland, Ala., Aug. 30, 1867; m. Peoria, Ill ,Nov. 15,1893, *Ella Irene Chuse* (b. Bloomington, Ill., March 1, 1868; p. Marion Xavier Chuse and Sarah Catharine Shannon of Peoria, Ill.; gr. p. Joseph and Anna Katrina Chuse—William Shannon and Nancy Bronson Ritchy); l. Peoria, Ill.; he is in the insurance business.

a. MARION GOODFELLOW, b. ib. Nov. 6, 1894.
b. THOMAS GOODFELLOW, b. ib. Jan. 6, 1896.
c. SARAH ELIZABETH GOODFELLOW, b. ib. Jan. 10, 1898.
d. FERDINAND GOODFELLOW, b.ib. April 21, 1901.

§169 5. GEORGE ROBERT MILTON, b. Winchester, July 29, 1832; e. V. M. I. and University of Va., and studied medicine with his uncle, Dr. Frederick Davisson at Hillsboro; d. New Florence, Mo., May 31, 1865; m. ib. Nov. 25, 1856, *Betty Washington McIlhany*, a first cousin of his mother; see MCILHANY FAMILY, §141. He was a physician and surgeon of rare skill. He entered the Confederate Army as Major, and after the battle at Lexington, Mo., was made Colonel for bravery shown in leading the charge at that battle.

(1). BENJAMIN BRODIE MILTON, b. Danville, Mo., Sept. 12, 1857; d. ib. Oct. 10, 1857.

THE MILTON FAMILY. 204

(2). HERBERT MILTON, b. ib. Dec. 23, 1860; 1. Lawrence, Kan.

(3). VIRGINIUS FAIRFAX MILTON, b. New Florence, Mo., Sept. 10, 1862; m. El Reno, Okla., April 15, 1894, *Laura Marshall* (b. near Marshall, Mo., April 3, 1872; p. W. T. Marshall and Mary Walton); l. Kingfisher, Okla.

    a. GEORGE ROBERT MILTON, b. ib. Nov. 7, 1898.

    b. MARY CATHERINE MILTON, b. ib. Nov. 20, 1900.

(4). ROSANNAH DAVISSON MILTON, b. New Florence, Mo., August 23, 1864; d. Calloway County, Mo., in Oct. 1867.

6. SLICER WICKES MILTON, b. Winchester, March 7, 1835; e. ib. and Burlington, Ia.; d. Hannibal, Mo, Feb. 5, 1868; m. St. Louis, Mo., Feb. 7, 1864, *Emmeline Catherine Fredrickson* (b. La Porte, Ind., April 9, 1839; p. Henry Fredrickson and Margaret McKeown; l. ib); he was a civil engineer.

(1). RICHARD HENRY MILTON, b. Washington, D. C., Dec. 24, 1865; d. ib. Dec 26, 1865.

(2). FRANK MILTON, b. Hannibal, Mo., May 2, 1867; d. ib. Sept. 25, 1867.

§170. 7. FLORINDA DAVISSON MILTON, b. Loudoun County, June 3, 1845; e. Hannibal and St. Louis, Mo.; m. *1st*. Council Bluffs, Ia., Jan. 21, 1862, *Thomas Jeremiah Latham* (b. Culpeper, March 3, 1827; d. Denver, Col., July 3, 1889; p. Jeremiah Latham and Isabella McNeal. He was commissioner of deeds in Nebraska in 1856, and a member of the Legislature in the same State. As lieutenant of a company of Nebraska Volunteers, he saw some hard service fighting the Indians. Later he was a banker in Washington, D. C.); m. *2nd*. *F. M. Stigers*, a commercial traveller, and is living in Kansas.

(1). HENRY MILTON LATHAM, b. Council Bluffs, Iowa, April 1, 1864; e. near Baltimore, Md.; is now travelling in the west.

THE MILTON FAMILY. 205

(2). FRANCES MABEL LATHAM, b. Washington,
D. C., March 17, 1869; e. Baltimore, Md., and at
the Convent of Notre Dame, Georgetown, D. C.;
m. Washington, D. C., Jan. 24, 1887, *William
Nehemiah Harriss* (b. Wilmington, N. C., Feb. 4,
1865; p. George Harriss and Julia O. Sanders; gr.
p. Dr. William James Harriss and Mary Jennings
—John Sanders and Mary Ellen Nixon. He has
served as Mayor of Wilmington, Consul for
Uruguay, Captain of the Wilmington Light Infantry, and Adjutant of the 2nd Reg. of the N.
C. State Guard; he is a ship broker); l. Wilmington, N. C.
    a. MARION SANDERS HARRISS, b. ib. Jan. 25,
       1889.
    b. ANNA MABEL HARRISS, b. ib. April 28,
       1891; d. ib. Nov. 11, 1891.
    c. GEORGE LATHAM HARRISS, b. near ib.
       July 27, 1895.

§171 VIII. ALEXANDER ROSS MILTON, b. "Milton Valley",
April 30, 1798; e. Berryville Academy, Winchester and at
Mr. Ellzey's School in Loudoun County; d. "Hampton",
near Berryville, Feb. 4, 1862; m. "Upton", Clarke County, April 21, 1819, *Harriet Malvina McCormick* (b. Frederick County, June 22, 1801; d. "Hampton", August 4,
1856; for her ancestry see §204); he was a farmer at
"Hampton".
    1. ANN ELIZABETH MILTON, b. "Upton", Feb. 5,
    1821; e. Col. Smith's School in Winchester; m. "Gal-
    loway", Jefferson County, W. Va., Jan. 9, 1840, *John
    McPherson Lupton* (b. Alexandria, June 20, 1811; d.
    "Hampton", March 15, 1873; p. David Lupton and
    Ann McPherson of Frederick County. He went to
    California in 1849, and spent two years mining for
    gold, but was so unfortunate as to have most of his
    gains stolen. He was afterwards a merchant in Vir-
    ginia); she is living with her children.
        (1). HARRIET ANN LUPTON, b. Winchester,
        August 5, 1841; d. "Hampton", June 20, 1876;
        m. Winchester, Oct. 20, 1874, *Dr. Morgan Brown*

THE MILTON FAMILY.

Campbell (b. Highland County, Jan. 24, 1841; he is a physician at Meadowdale, Highland County).

(2). MARGARETTA MOSS LUPTON, b. Winchester, Dec. 10, 1843; d. Summit Point, August 18, 1845.

(3). MARY ELIZABETH LUPTON, b. Summit Point, Feb. 5, 1846; e. Berryville Female Seminary and in Charlestown; m. Berryville, Oct. 26, 1870, *John Willis* (b. Orange County, July 21, 1844; p. John Willis and Lucy Madison; gr. p. Dr. John Willis and Nelly Madison, niece of President Madison—Major Ambrose Madison, nephew of President Madison, and Jane Willis. He entered the Confederate Army and fought the first battle of Manassas on his seventeenth birthday. He was in active service during the entire war with the exception of the year when he was a prisoner at Point Lookout and Fort Delaware; he is Baggage Manager for the C. & O. Ry. at Gordonsville); 1. near Gordonsville.

 a. LUCIE MADISON WILLIS, b. Orange County, Sept. 24, 1871; e. Central Female Institute, Gordonsville; m. ib. Oct. 16, 1901, *Moncure Robinson Taylor* (b. Jefferson County, W. Va., Feb. 23, 1851; he is great-great-grandson of Thomas Jefferson; is farming in Albemarle County, near Charlottesville).

 b. ELIZABETH MILTON WILLIS, b. Orange County, Oct. 15, 1873.

 c. NELLIE ROSS WILLIS, b. ib. August 1, 1875; d. Gordonsville, April 12, 1893.

 d. JOHN BYRD WILLIS, b. Orange County, March 21, 1877.

 e. ANNIE SCOTT WILLIS, b. ib. Feb. 22, 1879.

 f. WILLIAM TAYLOR WILLIS, b. ib. Sept. 21, 1885.

(4). WILLIAM MILTON LUPTON, b. Summit Point, W. Va., Feb. 11, 1848; e. Berryville; m. *1st.* Washington County, Texas, April 23, 1873, *Elizabeth Tyler Grant* (b. Burleson County, Texas, in 1854;

THE MILTON FAMILY.   207

d. Bryan. Texas, Dec. 24, 1876; p. Joseph F. and
Amanda Grant); m. *2nd.* Grimes County, Texas,
Oct. 25, 1882, *Effie McNeill* (b. Clayton, Ala.,
Sept. 10, 1854; p. John Calvin and Mary Augusta
McNeill). He has lived in Texas for the past
twenty-seven years, and is a merchant at Hempstead, Texas. He had three children by his first
marriage and one by the second.
    a. ELIZABETH TYLER LUPTON, b. Burleson
       County, Texas, Jan. 6, 1875; d. Winchester,
       Va., Sept. 20, 1881.
    b. THOMAS KENNON LUPTON, b. Burleson,
       County, Texas, Sept. 30, 1876; d. Winches-
       ter, Va. Sept. 18, 1881.
    c. GEORGE MACON LUPTON, b. and d. Waller
       County, Texas, Jan. 16, 1884.
    d. WILLIE MACON LUPTON, b. Hempstead,
       Texas, April 30, 1888.
(5). THOMAS MCCORMICK LUPTON, b. Berryville,
August 25, 1851; d. Hempstead, Texas, Jan. 12,
1902; e. Berryville; m. Bell County, Texas, Dec.
18, 1878, *Eudora Munger Punchard* (b. Montgomery County, Texas, Dec. 11, 1857; p. Samuel
Wooster Punchard and Mary C. Munger). She
lives at Rogers, Bell County, Texas.
    a. MARY SOPHRONIA LUPTON, b. ib. Oct. 11,
       1879.
    b. JOHN MCPHERSON LUPTON, b. ib. July 15,
       1882; l. Hempstead, Texas.
    c. WILLIAM PUNCHARD LUPTON, b. Rogers,
       Tex., Oct. 23, 1884; d. Hempstead, Tex.,
       July 27, 1890.
    d. TAYLOR STRIBLING LUPTON, b. Rogers,
       Tex., Nov. 30, 1886; d Hempstead, Tex.,
       Sept. 28, 1894.
    e. THOMAS ROSS LUPTON, b. Rogers, Tex.,
       Oct. 29, 1888.
    f. ANNIE IRENE LUPTON, b. Hempstead,
       Tex., Oct. 4, 1892.

§172   (6). REBECCA MCPHERSON LUPTON, b. Berryville, Sept. 25, 1854; e. Berryville Female Seminary; m. Berryville, Nov. 1, 1876, *Rev. Charles Scott Lingamfelter* (b. Hedgesville, April 1, 1852; p. Walter Hedges Lingamfelter and Margaret Oak Nadenbousch; gr. p John Lingamfelter and Mary Hedges—James Frederick Nadenbousch and Eleanor Collins. He is a graduate of Hampden-Sidney College and Union Theological Seminary; is a Presbyterian minister; has been pastor at Berryville, Poolesville, Md., and Elkins, W. Va., and is now Evangelist of the Lexington Presbytery, with his home at Staunton).

    a. FLORA MILTON LINGAMFELTER. b. Berryville, August 13, 1877; e. Mary Baldwin Seminary, Staunton.

    b. MARGARET OAK LINGAMFELTER, b. Berryville, August 15, 1879; e. Elkins, W.Va.; m. Staunton, Sept. 25, 1901, *William Clarence Huber* (b. Chambersburg, Pa., April 16, 1877; he is in the coal business); 1. Chicago, Ill.

    c. SADIE SCOTT LINGAMFELTER, b. Poolesville. Md , March 29, 1882.

    d. ELIZABETH ROSS LINGAMFELTER, b. ib. Dec. 15, 1884.

    e. WALTER MCPHERSON LINGAMFELTER, b. ib. July 13, 1887.

    f. CHARLES SCOTT LINGAMFELTER, b. ib. May 20, 1890.

    g. FREDERICK NADENBOUSCH LINGAMFELTER, b. Elkins, W. Va., August 8, 1893.

   (7). JOHN TALIAFERRO LUPTON, b. Berryville, Feb. 18, 1857; e. Berryville; is manager of the stationary department of John P. Morton & Co's. publishing house in Louisville, Ky.

2. JOHN WILLIAM MILTON, b. near Berryville, June 20, 1823; d. ib. in Nov. 1832.

3. MARY MILTON. b. "Galloway", Nov. 16, 1828; e. Berryville and Winchester; 1. "Hampton".

THE MILTON FAMILY.

4. TALIAFERRO MILTON, b. "Galloway", Feb. 12, 1831; was drowned in Bear River, in California, July 19, 1850.
5. FRANCIS PROVINCE MILTON, b. "Galloway", Nov. 24, 1833; d. ib. Nov. 29, 1833.
6. SUSAN LLEWELLYN MILTON, b. "Galloway", March 18, 1835; d. ib. April 3, 1846.

§173   7. WILLIAM TAYLOR MILTON, b. "Galloway", July 17, 1838; e. Berryville; m. ib. Oct. 30, 1867, *Frances Calendar Duncan* (b. St. Mary's Parish, La., August 27, 1845; p. Stephen Duncan and Louisa Pollard of St. Mary's Parish; gr. p. Thomas Duncan, Chief Justice of Pennsylvania and Martha Calendar). He served through the Civil War, first as Orderly Sergeant and then as 2nd Lieutenant of Co. I., 2nd. Va. Inft.; then as private in Co. D., 6th Va. Cavalry; and was Serg. Major of the regiment at the close of the war. He was Commissioner of the Revenue for Clarke County for twelve years; and then an insurance agent; l. "Hampton".

   (1). WILLIAM HAMMOND MILTON, b. "Hampton", Oct. 17, 1868; graduated at the V. M. I., and the Theological Seminary of Va. at Alexandria; m. Nottoway, June 12, 1895, *Virginia Lee Epes* (b. Hickman County, Ky., Feb. 17, 1872). He is Rector of St. John's Episcopal Church, Roanoke.

     a. VIRGINIA LEE MILTON, b. Baltimore, Md., April 12, 1896.
     b. WILLIAM HAMMOND MILTON, b. Roanoke, March 2, 1900.

   (2). LOUISA DUNCAN MILTON, b. "Hampton", April 21, 1870; e. Berryville; l. Baltimore, Md., where she is a trained nurse.

   (3). HARRIET ROSS MILTON, b. "Hampton", May 7, 1872; e. Berryville and Miss Worthington's School, "Clarens", near Theological Seminary; m. Berryville, July 8, 1891, *Rev. Robert Kinloch Massie* (b. Charlottesville, Feb. 4, 1864; p. N. H. Massie and Eliza K. Nelson; gr. p. Na-

thaniel Massie—Thomas F. Nelson. He is an
Episcopal minister; was for four years a mission-
ary to Shanghai, China; was rector at Upperville
for one year; and is now Professor of Church History in the Theological Seminary near Alexandria).
    a. ROBERT KINLOCH MASSIE, b. Shanghai,
China, May 21, 1892.
    b. FRANCIS MILTON MASSIE, b. ib. Dec. 23,
1893.
  (4). STEPHEN DUNCAN MILTON, b. "Hampton",
Dec. 10, 1874; e. Berryville, and the Commercial
College at Lexington, Ky.; m. Luray, June 25,
1899, *Sadie Alice Klein* (b. Geardtown, W. Va.,
Dec. 27, 1880); 1. Luray; he is a travelling
salesman.
  (5). TALIAFERRO MILTON, b. "Hampton", March
26, 1877; graduated at the V. M. I. in 1897; was
Commandant of the Military Department of the
University of the South one year; and is now
sub-professor of Chemistry and Electricity at the
V. M. I.
  (6). MARGARETTA DUNCAN MILTON, b. "Hampton", May 23, 1879; e. Hannah More Academy,
near Baltimore; 1. "Hampton".
  (7). MARSHALL MCCORMICK MILTON, b. "Hampton", Sept. 17, 1881; is a cadet at the V. M. I.
  (8). LAWRENCE TAYLOR MILTON, b. "Hampton",
Dec. 15, 1884; 1. ib.
8. FLORINDA HARRIOT MILTON, b. "Galloway", Aug.
2, 1841; e. Berryville; 1. Winchester.
§174 IX. ELIZABETH STRIBLING WRIGHT MILTON, b. "Milton Valley", May 3, 1800; d. New York City, Feb. 15,
1883; e. Berryville and Winchester; m. "Milton Valley",
Nov. 13, 1817, *Bushrod Taylor* (b. in Kentucky in 1793;
d. Winchester, July 14, 1847; see §185. He lived in Clarke
County and then in Winchester, and was a foremost man
in all public enterprises, and a most excellent husband
and citizen). She was commonly known as "Aunt Bet";
and while she had no children of her own, a number of her

orphaned nieces and nephews were brought up in her hospitable home. The story of her long and beautiful life has been charmingly told by one of her adopted children, Harriot Milton Hammond, in "The Story of a Long Life", to which reference has been made.

X. LUCINDA MILTON, b. "Milton Valley", Oct. 28, 1802; d. ib. March 19, 1803.

§175 XI. FLORINDA MILTON. b. ib. Oct. 28, 1802; d. Winchester, April 7, 1836; m. "Milton Valley", Jan. 15, 1824, *Dawson McCormick* (b. "Weehaw", Clarke County, Oct. 19, 1786; d. "Cleremont", March 26, 1834; see §197; he was a farmer at "Cleremont", near Berryville).

    1. EDWARD MCCORMICK, b. "Cleremont", Oct. 26, 1824; d. ib. March 18, 1870; graduated at Princeton about 1845; m. *1st.* "Hopewell", Feb. 4, 1847, *Mary Elizabeth Stribling*, his second cousin (see STRIBLING FAMILY, §37); m. *2nd.* "Ellerslie", Rappahannock County, April 24, 1856, *Ellen Lane Jett* (b. ib. Sept. 27, 1833; p James Jett and Julia M. Lane of "Ellerslie"; gr. p. John Jett and Hannah Calvert; l. "Cleremont"). He was a farmer at "Cleremont". He entered the Civil War as a member of the Clarke County Cavalry. but becoming disabled he served as Commissary at Lynchburg till the close of the war. He had three children by his first wife and six by his second.

        (1). FLORINDA TAYLOR MCCORMICK, b. "Cleremont", July 24, 1848; d. ib. Sept. 10, 1885.

        (2). MARY STRIBLING MCCORMICK, b. ib. in July 1849; d. ib. in 1850.

        (3). ANN MCCORMICK, b. "Glen Owen", Clarke County, Nov. 5, 1852; d. "Cleremont", March 8, 1857.

        (4). EDWARD MCCORMICK, b. "Ellerslie", April 2, 1857; d Amherst County, Sept. 17, 1862.

        (5). ELVIRA JETT MCCORMICK, b. "Cleremont", Nov. 17, 1858; d. ib. June 18, 1882; e. Mr. Wheat's School at Winchester; m. Berryville, April 29, 1880, *Rev. Samuel Scollay Moore, D. D.* (b. Charlestown, W. Va., Sept. 27, 1853; p. Samuel

J. C. Moore and Eleanor Scollay of Charlestown; gr. p. Thomas Moore and a Miss Cramer from Eastern Virginia. He was first a lawyer at Berryville; is now an Episcopal minister at Parkersburg, W. Va., and is married a second time).
    a. EDWARD MOORE, b. Berryville, April 12, 1881; l. St. Joseph, Mo.

§176   (6). DAWSON MCCORMICK, b. "Glen Owen", Aug. 22, 1860;. m. Berryville, Sept. 6, 1883, *Margaretta Moss Broun* (b. Middleburg, Nov. 14, 1860; see §203 ; he is in the real estate business in New York City.
    a. ELVIRA JETT MCCORMICK, b. "Edgewood", Clarke County, August 22, 1884.

(7). ANN HERNDON MCCORMICK, b. "Ellerslie", Oct. 29, 1862; m. Berryville, March 18, 1886, *Goodwin Hulings Williams* (b. Baltimore County, Md., July 7, 1853; p. Goodwin Gardner Williams and Mary Rebecca Hulings; gr. p. Thomas Nottingham Williams and Ann S. Nottingham of Northampton County—David S. Hulings and Maria Patton of Pennsylvania. He practiced law for a while in Baltimore; is now connected with the Union Biscuit Company, Newark, N. J.).
    a. LLOYD WILLIAM WILLIAMS, b. "Nottingham", Clarke County, June 5, 1887.
    b. THOMAS NOTTINGHAM WILLIAMS, b. ib. Nov. 25, 1888.
    c. ELLEN LANE JETT WILLIAMS, b. "Cleremont", Oct. 28, 1890.
    d. NANCY GOODWIN WILLIAMS, b. ib. July 11, 1898.

(8). ALBERT MONTGOMERY DUPUY MCCORMICK, b. ib. March 27, 1866; e. Blackburn's School in Alexandria, and is a graduate of the Medical Department of Maryland University; m. Milwaukee, Wis., Oct. 25, 1894, *Edith Lynde Abbot* (b. Boston, Mass., March 6, 1872; p. Frederick Abbot and Emily Lynde Whiting; gr. p. George and Elizabeth Abbot—Oliver and Elizabeth Whit-

ing); he is a Surgeon in the U. S. Navy, and
lives at Annapolis, Md.
  a. LYNDE DUPUY MCCORMICK, b. ib. August
  12, 1895.
  b. EDITH JETT MCCORMICK, b. ib. May 31,
  1897.
  c. CORA ABBOT MCCORMICK, b. ib. August
  31, 1900.

§177 (9). JAMES JETT MCCORMICK, b. "Cleremont",
Sept 18, 1868; graduated at the V. M. I. and in
the Medical Department of the University of Virginia; m. Berryville. Feb. 17, 1897, *Virginia
Taylor McCormick* (b. "Edgewood", Clarke
County, May 2, 1873; see §203); he is practicing
medicine in Norfolk.

2. WILLIAM MCCORMICK, b. "Cleremont", Sept. 15,
1826; d. ib. March 3, 1855; m. "Montview" at Shenandoah Junction. Nov. 30, 1848, *Sarah Alexander
Neill* (b. ib. in 1833; d. ib. Feb. 24, 1853; p. Lewis
Neill and Corbina Baker of Jefferson County; gr. p.
Corbin Baker and Margaretta Hamilton from Scotland). He was a member of the Frederick Volunteers
during the Mexican War and served through the
war. He was a farmer at "Meadow View" in Clarke
County.

§178 (1). BESSIE TAYLOR MCCORMICK, b. Berryville,
Jan. 1, 1852; e. ib.; m. ib. Dec. 6, 1871, *Province
McCormick* (b. "Hawthorn", Clarke County,
Feb. 18, 1847; see §203. He is a graduate of the
University of Virginia. He entered the Confederate Army at the age of sixteen and served
through the war. For four years he was located
in the West as U. S. Indian Inspector; is now a
a farmer); 1. Berryville.
  a. ANNIE CONWAY MCCORMICK, b. "Hawthorn", April 25, 1873; e. Berryville; m. ib.
  Sept. 9, 1896, *Rev. John Bronaugh Henry* (b.
  Warrenton, Dec. 16, 1870; p. Rev. Edward
  Hugh Henry and a Miss Stone; he is a min-

ister of the Methodist Church and is located at Gardenville, Md.).
- (a). MARGARETTA HOLMES HENRY, b. La Plata, Charles County, Md., June 19, 1897.
- (b). EDWARD HUGH HENRY, b. ib. June 15, 1899.
- (c). ANNA GRAY HENRY, b. Gardenville, Md., Nov. 10, 1901.

b. BESSIE TAYLOR McCORMICK, b. "Hawthorn", May 27, 1886; l. Berryville.

§179   3. ANNE McCORMICK, b. "Cleremont", Nov. 2, 1831; d. ib. in Nov. 1861; m. Winchester, May 17, 1849, *John Wayt Stribling*, her second cousin; for their descendants see STRIBLING FAMILY, §32.

---

§180   E. NANCY MILTON, m. *Jesse Davis* of Prince William County. They removed to Kentucky shortly after the Revolutionary War, and settled in Nelson County. Their children, nearly all of whom married, were:—Edmund, Thomas, Presley (who married three times, his first wife being Nancy Milton, his first cousin; see §164), Jesse, Elizabeth, Nancy, Harriot, Elijah, Wilson, and William (who had one daughter Kate, who married Maj. Alexander Grant of Frankfort, Ky.; issue,—Alexander, James and Belle, who married Lieut. J. W. Walker of the U. S. Navy).

F. FRANCES MILTON, m. *James Davis*, brother of Jesse Davis above. They also moved to Kentucky, and had a large family.

G. .... MILTON, m. a Mr. *Moore;* they lived in Kentucky, and had issue:—Shadrach, Eben, and others.

H. .... MILTON, m. a Mr. *Wilson*, and moved to Kentucky.

I. .... MILTON, m. *Ralph Chew;* they moved to Kentucky, where she died young.

Note 1. Taylor Family.

§181. The following outlines are taken largely from a chart in the possession of Mr. Griffin Milton of Darlington, Md. I have added a few names and dates under the Taylor family, and have made several corrections and additions in other places, but have not attempted to verify the facts in every particular.

Richard Bushrod and Apphia his wife lived in Gloucester County, Virginia. He patented 4,000 acres of land in Westmoreland County in 1663. Their son,

John Bushrod, b. Jan. 30, 1663; d. Feb. 6, 1719, and is buried at the "Bushfield" estate, Westmoreland County, where his tomb may still be seen; m. Hannah Keene, daughter of William and Elizabeth Keene of Northumberland County, and had two sons and four daughters. His daughter Apphia married in 1705 William Faunt Le Roy, ancestor of the family of that name. His son Richard was a Captain in the French and Indian Wars. His son,

John Bushrod lived at "Bushfield", and was a vestryman of Cople Parish in 1755, High Sheriff of Westmoreland County in 1759, and a member of the House of Burgesses, 1748-1755. He probably married his cousin Anne, daughter of Thomas Bushrod; she dying, he married *Jane Corbin* (see §183), and left two daughters, Hannah and Catherine. About 1760 Hannah married John Augustine Washington, a brother of George Washington, and had four children.—Bushrod, Corbin, Mildred and Augustine.

Catherine Bushrod, m. *William Taylor;* see §184.

[See Bishop Meade's "Old Churches and Families of Virginia", Vol. II, pp. 151-153].

---

§182. *Col. Thomas Lowry* of Virginia married Rebecca Jones, who had red hair. Their children were: William (who died unmarried), Thomas (who married Elizabeth Diggs and left issue), Elizabeth (who married a Mr. Richards), and

Sarah Lowry, b. July 21, 1745; d. May 3, 1819. It is said that she became engaged to George Stubblefield, son of George, when about fifteen years of age. To prevent her early marriage,

THE CORBIN FAMILY.   216

her father sent her to school 600 miles from home. Later she returned home and married Col. Raleigh Dangerfield, and had six children, all of whom died in infancy. Two years after his death, she married her first love, *George Stubblefield*. He became a Captain in the Revolutionary Army, and his orderly book is among the printed records of the Virginia Historical Society. Before the close of the War, he rose to the rank of Major. While he was away with the Revolutionary Army, the British soldiers persecuted his wife, who, with her children, was obliged to flee from her home. Her children were,—William Tabb Stubblefield (m. Susan Cannon), John Lowry Stubblefield (m. Fanny Jones), and

Martha Peyton Stubblefield, m. *Bushrod Taylor;* see §187.

———

§183. *Thomas Corbin* of Warwick County, England, b. May 24, 1594; d. in June 1637; m. in 1620, Winefred, daughter of Gawen Grosvenor. His son,

Henry Corbin, b. in 1629; d. Jan. 8, 1675; came to Virginia 1654; settled first in King and Queen County, and later in Westmoreland County; Burgess from Lancaster County in 1659, and a member of the Council as early as 1663; m. July 25, 1645, Alice Eltonhead, daughter of Richard and Ann (Sutton) Eltonhead of Lancaster County, England. Their son,

Gawin Corbin, d. Jan. 1, 1745; Burgess in 1700, 1702, etc.; member of the Council; either by his second wife, Jane Lane, or by his third wife, Martha Bassett, he had

Jane, or Jenny *Corbin*, who married *Col. John Bushrod;* see §181.

[See Dr. Lee's "Lee of Virginia", pp. 83-86; and Bishop Meade's "Old Churches", etc., Vol. II, pp. 145-146].

———

§184. *William Taylor* married *Catherine Bushrod* (§181) about 1762, and settled at "Green Hill", Frederick County, near Berryville, which estate remained in the possession of his descendants till after 1870. It is said that during the Revolutionary War he was captain of the home guard to protect Battletown, now Berryville, from the depredations of British soldiers. Who his ancestors were has never been handed down, but it is thought that he was of the Tayloe family of Westmoreland County, a change of spelling occurring after he removed to Frederick

THE TAYLOR FAMILY.

County. He is said to have been a man of great force of character. He had six children, as follows:

§185 A. *John Bushrod Taylor*, d. Jan. 27, 1834, aged about 70; m. Sarah Kennon, daughter of William Kennon and a Miss Gardener; he was buried at "Green Hill". His five children were—

I. *William Taylor*, b. Feb. 24, 1787; d. April 19, 1839; m. *1st. Mrs. Harriot Milton-McIlhany*, and had three children, John William, Sarah and Florinda (see §§161–163); m. *2nd.* Jan. 26, 1826, *Hannah McCormick* (see §198), by whom he had three children.

    1. *William Taylor*, b. June 30, 1827; d. Dec. 4, 1891; m. May 20, 1849, Gertrude McGuire (b. Oct. 11, 1828; d. April 24, 1894).

        (1). Samuel McCormick Taylor, b. Feb. 9, 1850; m. Fannie Moncure: issue,—Gertrude, Dorothea Ashby, Eliza Tucker, Samuel McCormick, and Hugh McGuire. He is in the real estate and insurance business in Berryville.

        (2). Annie Moss Taylor, b. Dec. 29, 1850; l. Berryville.

        (3). William Taylor, b. August 9, 1854; m. Carrie Hunt: issue,—Gertrude, Charles and Annie Moss. He is ranching near Temple, Texas.

        (4). *Dr. Hugh McGuire Taylor;* m. MARY EDMUNDS WHITCOMB; see §14.

    2. Eliza Taylor, b. Feb. 21, 1829; d. Nov. 7, 1890; m. August 19, 1856, Alfred Bland Tucker (b. Oct. 4, 1830; d. Sept. 25, 1862; he was a physician).

        (1). Alfred Bland Tucker, b. June 23, 1857; he is a physician in New York City.

        (2). William Taylor Tucker, b. Jan. 15, 1859; d. August 10, 1873.

        (3). Ann Evelina Hunter Tucker, b. Nov. 4, 1861; d. Feb. 23, 1862.

    3. Frances Marshall Taylor, b. April 1, 1831; d. Feb. 2, 1847.

II. Benjamin Taylor, b. in 1789; d. August 20, 1835; m. Sarah Howland(?).

  1. Milton Newton Taylor, was a merchant in Baltimore and died about 1895, aged about 80 years.
  2. Sarah Cornelia Taylor.
 III. Harriet Taylor, m. James Ware. Their daughter,
  1. Catherine Ware, m. Dr. William McGuire.
 IV. *Bushrod Taylor*, m. ELIZABETH STRIBLING WRIGHT MILTON; see §174.
 V. Griffin Taylor, was a merchant in Cincinnati, Ohio. His children were:
  1. Mary Taylor, m. a Mr. Miller.
   (1). Griffin Taylor Miller.
  2. Caroline Taylor, m. a Mr. Dickinson.
  3. A third daughter, m. a Mr. York, a naval officer.

§186 B. Col. Griffin Taylor, inherited "Green Hill", his father's estate; m. Mary Kennon, sister of Sarah Kennon, §185. He is said to have been an officer in the Revolutionary War.
 I. Sarah Griffin Taylor, m. David Allen, and lived at "Clifton", near Berryville.
  1. Thomas Allen, m. a Miss Hopper.
   (1). Maitland Allen.
   (2). Emma Allen, m. Bushrod Washington of Charlestown.
  2. Edgar Allen.
  3. Mary Kennon Allen, m. Gen'l. Carlos Butterfield of Mexican fame.
 II. Catherine Taylor, m. about 1819, Gen'l. Thomas Marshall of Kentucky, nephew of Chief Justice Marshall. She died in Kentucky the following year, leaving no issue.
 III. John Bushrod Taylor, m. Susan Orick. He inherited the "Green Hill" plantation. He had one son,
  1. Benjamin Taylor.

§187 C. *Bushrod Taylor*, d. August 26, 1815, aged 43, and was buried at "Green Hill"; m. Jan. 29, 1801, Martha Peyton Stubblefield (b. Feb. 9, 1784; d. in 1853; see §182. On Jan. 7, 1828 she married Thomas Castleman, §191, as his second wife. After his death, she removed in 1835 to Slickaway, Fayette County, Kentucky, where she purchased the plantation of Elijah Milton. She is buried in the Pisgah graveyard, Woodford County, Ky.). His home was at "Morgan Spring", near Berryville. He was a trustee of the town in 1798, Justice of the Peace in 1811, and a soldier of the War of 1812. They had eight children, as follows:

§188. I. *Dr. George William Taylor*, b. Oct. 7, 1802; d. Feb. 26, 1849; m. Nov. 30, 1824, Ann Eliza White (b. in 1807; d. Feb. 29, 1847).
    1. Josiah B. Taylor. b. Sept. 25, 1825.
    2. Eben Taylor, b. Jan. 14, 1827.
    3. *Mary Louisa Taylor*. m. ROBERT JOSIAH THOMAS WHITE; see §123.
    4. *Dr. James William Taylor*, m. SOPHIA ANN DAVISSON; see §117.
    5. Sarah W. Taylor.
    6. Virginia Taylor, m. Judge Whytock, and has two daughters, Virginia and Laura; l. Albert Lea, Minn.
    7. Amanda T. Taylor, m. Dr. Smith; one son, Taylor Smith; l. Midland, Md.
    8. Laura Taylor, m. Dr. Price; no surviving children.

§189 II. *Emily Bushrod Taylor*, b. Feb. 11, 1804; m. EBEN TAYLOR MILTON, her first cousin; see §§153–154.

III. Harriot Lowry Taylor, b. March 14, 1806; d. Oct. 19, 1809.

IV. *Louisa Ann Taylor*, b. Sept. 5, 1807; m. JOHN MILTON, her first cousin; see §§155–156.

§190 V. *Sarah Elizabeth Taylor*, b. Sept. 25, 1809; m. Charles William Castleman; see §191.
    1. Fenton Castleman, d. in infancy.
    2. Thomas Castleman, d. in infancy.
    3. *Bushrod Taylor Castleman*, m. MARTHA JANE MILTON, his second cousin; see §159.
    4. Mary Louisa Castleman, m. Capt. C. C. McNeely of the U. S. Army; l. Newport, Ky.; three children.
    5. Milton Frost Castleman, d. aged 21.
    6. Charles William Castleman; lived at Leesburg, Fla.
    7. David Stubblefield Castleman, d. aged 30.
    8. Anna Virginia Castleman, d. aged 25.
    9. Jacob Price Castleman, d. aged 14.
    10. Martha Peyton Castleman, d. aged 65; m. Alfred Z. Boyer; three children,—Mary Louisa, Alfred Z., and Betsy Taylor.

The Taylor Family.

VI. Catherine Taylor, b. June 2, 1811; m. Henry K. Berry.
   1. Virginia Berry, m. Henry Bullitt of Lexington, Ky.
   2. Benjamin Berry.
   3. Lucy Berry, m. Dr. Henry Blackburn.
   4. Laura Berry, m. a Mr. Fowler.
   5. Eliza Berry, m. Richard Stanhope.
   6. Lavinia Berry, m. Winder Monroe.
   7. Fanny Berry, m. Esten Keller.
   8. Anderson Berry, m. a Miss Keller.
   9. Sarah Elizabeth Berry.
   10. Mary Bullitt Berry.

VII. Addison Bushrod Taylor, b. Feb. 28, 1813; d. unmarried.

VIII. Bushrod Stribling Taylor, b. Sept. 19, 1815; d. Oct. 27, 1836.

§191 D. Eben Taylor, m. Nancy Shipp.
   I. James Taylor.
   II. Griffin Taylor, m. *1st.* Elizabeth Bell; m. *2nd.* Susan Skelton. He lived in Frederick City, Md.
      1. Eugene Taylor; is married and living near Frederick City, Md.
      2. Griffin Taylor; is married and living at Berryville.

E. Elizabeth Taylor, m. Amos Frost.
   I. Patty Frost.
   II. Catherine Frost.
   III. Sarah Frost.
   IV. Dilly Frost.
   V. Hannah Frost, m. Thomas Castleman (see §187).
      1. David Castleman, m. a Miss Freeman.
      2. Thomas Castleman, m. Laura Little.
      3. Louisa Castleman.
      4. Hannah Castleman.
      5. Charles William Castleman, m. Sarah Elizabeth Taylor; see §190.

§192 F. *Catherine Taylor*, m. ELIJAH MILTON; for their descendants see §§151–159.

Note 2. McCormick Family.

§193. *Dr. John McCormick*, who emigrated to Virginia from Ireland between the years 1730 and 1740, was the founder of this family in America. In the Orange County records there is a deed under date of May 21, 1740 from Just Hite to "John McCarmick of Orange County" for 395 acres of land. Subsequently he took up other grants adjoining this property, which was located in that part of Orange County that eventually became Jefferson County, W. Va. It was on this estate, near Summit Point, that in 1740 he built "The White House", which is still standing. "Weehaw" and "Upton" were a part of this property. He was a graduate in medicine of the University of Dublin, and brought with him to this country a large and valuable medical library, which was sold at his death to Dr. Cramer, then the leading physician of Charlestown. He was the most prominent physician in his neighborhood, and left a lasting impression upon the community in which he lived. He died in the year 1768, leaving a wife and eight children. His estate was appraised Feb. 8, 1769. In his will, made May 8, 1768 and recorded Nov. 2, 1768, he mentions his wife Anne, his sons—James, John, Francis, William, George and Andrew, his "daughter Mary Tate, wife to Magnus Tate", and his "daughter Jean Byren, wife to James Byrn". His wife and son James were the executors of his estate. It would seem that he was married before coming to this country; but the maiden name of his wife is unknown. The descendants of his eight children are scattered throughout many States, some of his sons having gone to Pennsylvania and some to the West. His daughter,

Mary McCormick, b. about 1736; d. in 1810; m. *1st*. Ferrill Riley (or Reily, who died in May, 1757. His will, made May 10, 1757 and recorded June 7, 1757, mentions his wife Mary as executrix, and an only son John Riley. Dr. John McCormick was one of the witnesses. The administration account, recorded on Nov. 4, 1760, was signed by Magnus Tate and Mary his wife, executor and executrix); m. *2nd*. Sept. 26, 1759, *Magnus Tate:* for their descendants see §§88–90.

§194. *Francis McCormick*, son of Dr. John and Anne McCormick, was born April 17, 1734. He was married twice, his first wife being a Miss Province(?), the second a Miss Frost. By his first marriage he had eight children, and one child by his second. He was a large land owner, and each of his five sons who settled in Clarke County possessed a valuable farm. They were all men of great strength of character, energetic and enterprising. A short history of the family was published in 1890 in Mr. Norris's "History of the Lower Shenandoah Valley", from which some of the facts given here have been derived, including the following two paragraphs.

"The early members of the McCormick family were singularly unobtrusive people, content in the happiness derived from their own family relations, being extremely clanish......... Both the men and the women of the family............were without guile, strictly honorable, affectionate, domestic and courteous. One of their marked characteristics was their great regard for the truth.

"One of the heir-looms of the family was an old English prayer book, from which much of the data in this article was gleaned. Unfortunately it was destroyed during the late War. This prayer book was given by Francis McCormick to his son Thomas McCormick at the time of his marriage; in it was a family tree on parchment, a very valuable and curious relic. One page represented Dr. John McCormick in a blue broadcloth suit with brass buttons; another, the marriage scene; and yet another, Anne McCormick with a blue bodice and yellow silk or satin skirt, with a branch of something in her hand and a bird; — another a death scene, coffin, etc., and a notice of dates, births and deaths beneath. The dates were all in 1700."

§195 A. Province McCormick, d. March 3, 1826; lived at "Soldier's Retreat", Clarke County. He served in the War of 1812 with the rank of Colonel. He married a Miss Davenport of Jefferson County, and had a family of five sons and two daughters, all of whom moved to the West.

§196 B. *Thomas McCormick*, d. Oct 4, 1816; m. Ann Frost (b. August 18, 1763; d March 26, 1815); his home was "Weehaw".

    I. Charles McCormick, b. August 18, 1784; d. in Feb. 1848. He is said to have been the largest land-owner in Clarke County. His home was at "Cool Spring", which he purchased from Admiral Wormley of the British Navy. He was a very handsome man, and possessed great business ability. He never married.

§197 II. *Dawson McCormick*, b. Oct. 19, 1786; m. FLORINDA
MILTON; see §175.
III. Samuel McCormick, b. March 29, 1789; d. in 1860.
He served in the War of 1812. (; He never married.
IV. Abraham McCormick, b. Nov. 24, 1791; d. in Jan.
1831. He never married.
V. William McCormick, b. May 6, 1794; d. July 29, 1824.
He never married
§198 VI. *Hannah McCormick*, b. Dec. 4, 1796; d. "Elmington",
June 10, 1879; m. *William Taylor*; see §185. "She was
the embodiment of womanly virtues,—beautiful in face and
character".
VII. Thomas McCormick, b. May 30, 1799; d. Aug. 21,
1824. He never married.
§199 VIII. *Francis McCormick*, b. October 20, 1801; m. ROSE
MORTIMER ELLZEY; see §127. He served four years as
Presiding Justice of the County Court, 1856–1860. His
home was first at "Weehaw" and then at "Frankford".
IX. Dr. Cyrus McCormick, b. Sept. 16, 1804; d. in 1861.
He was a graduate of Princeton, and a distinguished physician.
X. *Eliza McCormick*, b. August 17, 1807; d. in 1848; m.
Thomas McCormick, her first cousin; see §200.
§200 C. *Samuel McCormick*, d. in June 1823; m. Margaret Hampton of Clarke County, and lived near White Post.
I. Charles McCormick, died unmarried.
II. *Thomas McCormick*, d. Dec. 29, 1869. He lived at "Elmington", near Berryville. He married three times: *1st*.
Eliza McCormick, his first cousin; see §199; *2nd*. ANN
REBECCA NEILL; see §53; *3rd*. Mary Holliday; see §91.
He had four children by his first marriage.
1. *Hannah Taylor McCormick*, b. Oct. 13, 1840; d. in
Oct. 1868; m. *Col. Frederick William Mackey Holliday;*
see §91.
2. Nannie McCormick, b. Nov. 6, 1842; d. Oct. 9,
1886; m. Jan. 21, 1869, Dr. E. C. Lippitt (b. Jan. 3,
1829; he is a physician; l. "Elmington").
(1). Mary Alexander Lippitt, b. July 10, 1871; m.
Oct. 18, 1899, Charles William Wattles of Alexandria.

a. Thomas Lippitt Wattles. b. July 15, 1900.
(2). Thomas McCormick Lippitt, b. Jan. 18, 1873; is an Assistant Surgeon in the U. S. Navy.
(3). Eliza Lippitt, b. Feb. 4, 1876.
(4). Edward Russell Lippitt, b. Feb. 4, 1876; d. June 30, 1876.
(5). Nannie Fontaine Lippitt, b. Sept. 1, 1878.
(6). Bowles Fontaine Lippitt, b. March 25, 1882.
3. Eliza McCormick; l. "Elmington".

§201 4. *Thomas McCormick*, m. NANNIE FRANK MCCORMICK, his first cousin; see §128.
III. Lucy McCormick; never married.
D. Isaac McCormick, d. April 25, 1817; went to Ohio early in life.
E. John McCormick, d. in 1819; moved to Ohio early in life.
F. Ann McCormick, d. Sept. 8, 1823.
G. A daughter, name unknown.

§202 H. *William McCormick*, d. March 31, 1819; m. *1st*. Elizabeth Rice; m. *2nd*. a Mrs. McDonald. By his first marriage he had four children.
I. Mary McCormick, m. John Culver of Montgomery, Md.; they moved to Kentucky.
1. Anne Culver, m. Robinson Biggs of Ashland, Ky.: issue,—Virginia, Elizabeth and Robinson.
2. William Culver, married twice.
3. Mary Culver, m. William Patterson of Louisville, Ky., and had ten or eleven children.

§203 II. *Province McCormick*, b. Sept. 10, 1799; d. July 4, 1873; m. November 10, 1831, Margaretta Holmes Moss (b. Sept. 28, 1812; d. Nov. 26, 1865; daughter of William Moss of Fairfax County). He was a lawyer in Frederick County, and was a very prominent man in his profession, being Commonwealth's Attorney for twenty-five years.
1. William Moss McCormick, b. in Sept. 1832; d. in 1834.
2. Gertrude Holmes McCormick, b. in 1834; lived only eighteen months.
3. Dr. Charles McCormick, b. March 14, 1836; d. July 14, 1861; was a surgeon in the Confederate Army and

THE MCCORMICK FAMILY. 225

a member of Gen'l. Albert Sidney Johnston's staff. He married Laura Ayres.
   (1). Charles McCormick, b. March 11, 1871; m. Dec. 31, 1893, Lucy W. Lewis; l. Chicago.

4. *Ann R. McCormick*, b. Sept. 28, 1838; m. Dr. J. Conway Broun of Middleburg; l. Berryville.
   (1). *Margaretta Moss Broun*, m. DAWSON MCCORMICK; see §176.
   (2). Charles M. Broun, b. July 14, 1862; m. Nov. 7, 1900.

5. Millicent McCormick, b. in 1840; died in infancy.

6. Evelina Parker McCormick, b. Dec. 15, 1842; d. Dec. 13, 1850.

7. Hugh Holmes McCormick, b. Dec. 31, 1844; d. May 11, 1870; entered the Confederate army at the age of sixteen, and served through. He was a lawyer.

8. *Province McCormick*, m. BESSIE TAYLOR MCCORMICK; see §178.

9. *Marshall McCormick*, b. June 29, 1849; graduated at the University of Virginia; was mayor of Berryville three terms, commonwealth's attorney nine consecutive years, four years a member of the State Senate, and a member of the National Democratic Convention when Cleveland was first nominated. He is a large land-owner in Clarke county; m. Rosalie Taylor of Alexandria.
   (1). *Virginia Taylor McCormick*, m. JAMES JETT MCCORMICK; see §177.
   (2). Margaretta M. H. McCormick, b. July 14, 1874.
   (3). Hugh Holmes McCormick, b. Nov. 3, 1875; m. Nov. 2, 1899, Edith Allen.
   (4). Rosalie L. McCormick. b. July 5, 1877.
   (5). Annie Broun McCormick, b. Feb. 12, 1879; m. Sept. 6, 1899, Dr. Walter Cox, a Surgeon in the U. S. Army.
   (6). Province McCormick. b. Sept. 5, 1881.
   (7). Gertrude M. McCormick, b. Nov. 28, 1883.
   (8). Marshall McCormick, b. August 20, 1888.
   (9). Harriet T. McCormick, b. May 22, 1895.

10. Margaretta Moss McCormick, b. April 12, 1852; d. Dec. 24, 1856.

III. Ann McCormick, m. a Mr. Pogue of Greenup Co., Ky.
1. Henry Pogue, m. a Miss Wood of Maysville, Ky., and had several children.
2. Amanda Pogue, m. a Mr. Jones of Kentucky, and had eight children.

§204 IV. *Harriet Malvina McCormick*, m. ALEXANDER ROSS MILTON; see §171.

I. George McCormick, son of Francis McCormick and his second wife Miss Frost, b. March 27, 1778; d. March 23, 1846; m. Oct. 18, 1810, Harriet Jones Mitchell (b. April 23, 1790; d. Feb. 18, 1829).

I. Eliza Ann McCormick, b. March 11, 1812; m. Dec. 13, 1832, Ackley Bonham of Clarke County: issue,— George, Ann, Albert, Mary, William, Fanny, Kate, Hannah, Elizabeth and Isaac.

II. Albert McCormick, b. Sept. 6, 1813; d. May 19, 1846.

III. Frances Frost McCormick, b. Jan. 25, 1816; d. Nov. 12, 1869; m. May 18, 1841, Henry Newton Grigsby (b. Sept. 9, 1810; d. Nov. 4, 1861; by his first wife, Harriet J. Knight, he had two children, Eliza Frances and George Henry; his home was "Aspen Shade" in Clarke County).

1. Harriet Newton Grigsby, b. Feb. 17, 1842; d. May 26, 1848.
2. Annie McCormick Grigsby, b. April 18, 1844.
3. Sarah Catlett Grigsby, b. June 8, 1846; d. July 19, 1846.
4. Elizabeth Lewis Grigsby, b. June 16, 1847.
5. Ella Somers Grigsby, b. June 17, 1848; d. July 31, 1848.
6. Emma Grigsby, b. June 19, 1849.
7. Henry Newton Grigsby, b. July 25, 1851; d. May 26, 1881.
8. Blanche Grigsby, b. Oct. 23, 1855.
9. Rose Grigsby, b. Oct. 23, 1855; d. Nov. 1, 1870.
10. Ernest Jay Grigsby, b Feb. 5, 1857; d. Sept. 22, 1861.

IV. Isaac William McCormick, b. April 3, 1818; d. Dec. 9, 1849.

§205 V. Mary Mitchell McCormick, b. May 13, 1820; d. August 3, 1886; m. Lewis Fulton Glass (b. Sept. 12, 1816; d. June 8, 1882; his home was "Aldridge" in Clarke County).
1. George Glass, b. August 20, 1844.
2. Elizabeth F. Glass, b. Oct. 25, 1845; d. July 28, 1846.
3. Albert Glass, b. May 11, 1847.
4. Isaac Glass, b. April 29, 1848.
5. Harriet Louisa Glass, b. March 7, 1850.
6. James Glass, b. March 22, 1852.
7. Fulton Glass, b. August 25, 1854; d. June 14, 1856.
8. Eliza Glass, b. December 24, 1856.
9. Frances Glass, b. Nov. 17, 1860.

VI. Benjamin Mitchell McCormick, b. May 2, 1822; d. Feb. 23, 1832.

VII. Harriet Taylor McCormick, b. July 24, 1824; d. July 13, 1887; m. Jan. 25, 1848, Richard Samuel Bryarly (b. August 24, 1820; d. Nov. 22, 1887).
1. Rowland T. Bryarly, b. Nov. 2, 1848; d. April 30, 1881.
2. Eliza McCormick Bryarly, b. Nov. 5, 1850; d. March 12, 1864.
3. Mary Louisa Bryarly, b. Sept. 13, 1852.
4. Susan Fitzhugh Bryarly, b. July 10, 1854.
5. George Bryarly, b. Nov. 22, 1856.
6. Samuel Bryarly, b. Nov. 22, 1856.
7. John Elliott Bryarly, b. May 2, 1859.
8. Hattie Lee Bryarly, b. Dec. 14, 1864; d. May 31, 1891.
9. Richard Samuel Bryarly, b. March 28, 1868.

THE ROGERS FAMILY.

§206. In 1871 Mr. Arthur Lee Rogers (§223) published a short "Sketch of the Rogers Family", the original draft of which was dated at Middleburg. July 10, 1853. He was always deeply interested in the early history of the family, and talked a great deal about it with his grandfather Hugh Rogers, with whom he was a special pet. As this sketch was written by him after a thorough examination of all the facts at his disposal, I cannot do better than quote here its opening paragraphs, with a few alterations.

"For my own satisfaction, as well as for the gratification of my relations on my father's side, I have, at leisure moments, collected from the most reliable sources the following Sketch of the Rogers Family. It has not been my purpose to manufacture for them a long and distinguished pedigree—for to such a distinction they lay no claim—but simply to state, in as few words as possible, such facts in my possession as may not be uninteresting to *them* and *their descendants.*

"I have learned from highly credible traditional authority, that the Rogers' now settled in Loudoun and adjoining counties in Virginia, are descended from a Presbyterian Scotch-Irish family, who resided in the county of Antrim, in the North of Ireland. And I find, from consulting the most approved works on Heraldry, that there was a family of that name in the said county in Ireland, who emigrated thither from Scotland about the middle of the sixteenth century. They are described as being 'Presbyterians, and bitterly opposed to the Roman Catholic faith'. They were not lords or princes, but are said to have been 'remarkably intelligent, highly respectable and moral people'. Some of them distinguished themselves in the wars against the Romanists; and

HUGH ROGERS
210

it is related of the widow of a Captain William Rogers, who was killed in one of these contests, that she called a daughter, born shortly after his decease, *Mailliw* (his name transposed), she being determined that the child should bear the name of her devoted husband, whether boy or girl. Many of them were men of wealth, and, according to the custom of those days, they adopted a coat-of-arms and crest, on which was a spread-eagle and the motto, '*Justum perficito et nihil timeto*'—act justly and fear nothing."

§207. **William Rogers**, a member of this family, married *Jane Rooney* (whose maiden name was *Hamilton*), a widow with one son. "About the year 1720, William Rogers and his wife came over to the United States, and landed at Philadelphia, where in a short time they died, leaving two helpless children, Hamilton and Arthur."

A. HAMILTON ROGERS, "who was old enough to work at the time of his father's death, was sent to Bucks County, Pennsylvania, where he got the office of deputy sheriff, and filled it for several years. He afterwards became a highly useful and business man. He married a Miss *Mary Mains*, and had sons, William, John, Thomas, Hamilton, Joseph and Benjamin; and three daughters, Jane, Elizabeth, and Isabella."

§208 B. ARTHUR ROGERS, "who was called after Sir Arthur Adair, an Irish nobleman, was taken after the death of his parents and raised by a Presbyterian clergyman, named Letty. When he became of age, he moved also to Bucks County, Pennsylvania, where he married Miss *Mary McFall*, and had sons, Hugh, Hamilton, and William, and daughters, Elizabeth and Anne. He afterwards settled in Loudoun County, Va. He lived to a good old age, and, though blind for many years before his death, was distinguished for the amiability of his disposition and his uniform cheerfulness and good humor. He is buried at the Free Church, in Middleburg."

§209 I. ELIZABETH ROGERS, m. *James Beatty:* issue,—
    1. SALLIE BEATTY, m. *Thomas Biscoe:* issue,— Mary, Ann, Elizabeth, James, etc.

2. SILAS BEATTY, m. *Fannie Gulick:* issue,—Elizabeth (m. James Skinner: issue,—Lucy, Jane, and Annie Elizabeth), Lucinda (m. James Skinner as his second wife), Sarah (m. Strechley Chinn: issue,—Walter, Strechley, etc), Amanda (m. Henry Whitlock), John (married twice), and James (married).

3. MARY BEATTY, m. John Bitzer.

$210 II. HUGH ROGERS, b. Bucks County, Penn., May 19, 1768; d. "Stone Hill", near Middleburg, August 15, 1853; m. Loudoun County, in 1792 (the marriage bond between himself and Samuel Coombs, the father of his wife, being dated Nov. 26, 1792) *Mary Coombs* (b. Loudoun County, Sept. 24, 1776; d. Warrenton, Nov. 2, 1863). His home, near Middleburg, was called "Stone Hill", and it was there that he spent the greater part of his long life. An obituary written at the time of his death says in part:

"He died, loved, respected and lamented, alike by the friends whose affection had lasted more than three quarters of a century, and by those of a more recent date—leaving a widow, with whom he had lived in unclouded harmony for three-score years, and a family of ten children, fifty grand-children, and twenty-eight great-grand-children, all living within an hour's ride.

"His was a most patriarchal character. Till lately his snow-white hair was almost the only mark of age about him. Time seemed loth to lay his hand on so goodly and vigourous a frame; and the Destroyer left his heart wholly untouched, and as young as ever. Up to a short time before his death his practice was to visit his children regularly, the most distant thirty miles off, on horseback, and he was daily in the saddle or on foot, with a keen and sagacious interest in all that was going on about him. His health and elastic spirits never failed him until a few months ago, when he was prostrated by paralysis.

"He was a man of more than ordinary vigor and clearness of mind, possessing the gift, comparatively rare, of a sound and discriminating judgment. He was loveable and hospitable. Excellent as a husband, father and master; of integrity, on which the length of nearly a century left no stain, no breath of imputation. He stood up like a man, ever firmly for the right; and though having all those qualities, which fit a man to contend successfully with the world, his heart was never cankered by selfishness, but was ever ready to feel for the troubles, difficulties and distress of others, and his hand was ever open to assist and relieve them, wisely, gently and efficiently.

"Tho' always of moral deportment, he made no public profession of religion till late in life, when, a few years ago, he united with the Baptist church, and he ever afterwards lamented that he had not obeyed the Divine command by making a confession of his faith before the world at an earlier day."

§211. Mary Coombs, wife of Hugh Rogers, was the daughter of Samuel Coombs and Mary Chestnut of Loudoun County. There is a deed on record in the Loudoun court house, dated June 24, 1760, in which Samuel Coombs, who at that time leased "Catoctin Manour", is said to have been thirty years of age, his wife Mary Coombs twenty-seven years old, and his son Samuel Coombs aged one year. He was, perhaps, the son of Joseph Coombs of Overwharton Parish, Stafford County. One of his sons,—perhaps Samuel, born in 1759—, moved to Kentucky, and left a numerous posterity in that State, among whom was General Leslie Coombs.

"Mrs. Rogers had been a consistent member of the Baptist church for more than half a century, and the doctrine of Christ, which she adorned in her walk and conversation, and the hope which cheered her heart through so many years, did not fail to sustain and comfort her in the last hours of life ....

"She had reared a large family of sons and daughters to live and honor her through her long life, and many of her children and children's children were permitted to surround her dying bed and receive her parting blessing. Her numerous descendants, many of whom are now fighting the battles of their country, may well cherish the memory of this excellent woman, whose life was a connecting link between the first and second American revolutions, and who having outlived the Republic, whose birth she witnessed, watched with deep interest an 1 'ervent prayers this second war of independence through which we are now passing."

The members of the early generations of the Rogers family were remarkable for their longevity. Hugh Rogers died in the eighty-sixth year of his age, and his wife in her eighty-eighth year. They had eleven children,—Elizabeth, Samuel, Hamilton, William, Asa, James, Sarah, Ann, Mary Jane, Martha and Susan. With the exception of Samuel, who died in infancy, these children averaged seventy-seven years of age, and five of them averaged eighty-six.

§212   1. ELIZABETH ROGERS, b. "Stone Hill", March 20, 1794; d. "Edgewood", near Middleburg, about 1880; m. "Stone Hill", about 1813, *William Rogers Swart* (b. in Kentucky, Dec. 24, 1787; d. "Box Hill", in Fauquier County, near Middleburg, April 10, 1861; he was a farmer and lived at "Box Hill").

(1). JANE ANNA SWART, b. ib. Sept. 30, 1814; d. Bell Point March 10, 1863; m. "Box Hill", May 26, 1843, *James Adair* (b. Belfast, Parish of Cumber, County Down, Ireland, June 4, 1807; d. Bell Point, August 31, 1868; he was a farmer, and lived at Bell Point, now called Lurich, in Giles County. He emigrated to this country with his father and family Sept. 3, 1817, landing at Norfolk, Oct. 31, 1817).

a. WILLIAM ADAIR, b. Bell Point, March 24, 1844; is farming at Lurich, Va.

b. ELLEN ADAIR, b. Bell Point, March 30, 1845; m. *1st.* ib. March 2, 1865, *Thaddeus Porter Waldo* (b. Taylor County, W. Va., Dec. 3, 1842; d. Roanoke, Lewis County, W. Va., Dec. 8, 1867; he was a farmer); m. *2nd.* Bell Point, May 22, 1872, *Dr. Benjamin Porter Gooch* (b. Charlottesville, July 4, 1842; d. Hinton, W. Va., Feb. 12, 1892; he was a physician and surgeon); l. Hinton, W. Va.; she had one child by the first marriage and three children by the second.

MRS. HUGH ROGERS
§ 211

(a). HARRY CAMDEN WALDO, b. Roanoke, W. Va., June 3, 1867; m. Hinton, W. Va., August 7, 1893, *Carrie Seth Miller* (b. Dangerfield, Titus County, Tex., Jan. 26, 1873); 1. Hinton, W. Va.
    a. PORTER MARION WALDO, b. ib. May 31, 1894.
    b. SHEREL ADAIR WALDO, b. ib. May 13, 1896.
    c. HARRY CAMDEN WALDO, b. ib. Oct. 8, 1898.
    d. ARTHUR WALLACE WALDO, b.ib. June 24, 1900.

(b). JAMES ADAIR GOOCH, b. ib. March 28, 1873; d. Hot Springs, Ark., Oct. 19, 1901; m. Beckley, W. Va., June 26, 1901, *Mrs. Josephine Lewis Morris*, of Beckley, where she now resides; he was a graduate of the Medical Department of the University of Louisville.

(c) CARLOS ALONZO GOOCH, b. Hinton, W. Va., Feb. 12, 1875; m. Oak Hill, W. Va , March 22, 1902, *Effie Luceile Roach* of that place; 1. ib.; he is a physician and surgeon, having graduated at the University of Louisville with his brother.

(d). MARY WILLIE GOOCH, b. Hinton, W. Va., July 13, 1879; d. ib. August 30, 1880.

c. ASA ROGERS ADAIR, b. Bell Point, March 20, 1846; m. Ellis, Kan., Dec. 6, 1888, *Emma May Keyser* of that place; 1. ib.
  (a). HUGH ROGERS ADAIR, b. ib. Sept. 27, 1889.
  (b). WILLIAM WALLACE ADAIR, b. ib. Nov. 27, 1891.
  (c). RUTH MAY ADAIR, b. Kansas City, Mo., July 13, 1895.

(d). ALBERT SIDNEY ADAIR, b. ib. Jan. 23, 1897.

d. ROBERT WALLACE ADAIR, b. Bell Point, April 3, 1848; m. Giles County, Nov. 24, 1870, *Julia Haven Bane* (b. ib. April 24, 1851); he is farming at Cashmere, Monroe County, W. Va.

   (a). WILLIE MAY ALLEN ADAIR, b. White Gate, Giles County, August 19, 1872; is teaching at Cashmere, W. Va.

   (b). NANNIE BANE ADAIR, b. ib. April 1, 1875; 1. ib.

   (c). ASA ANDREW ADAIR, b. White Gate, Feb. 18, 1878; is a merchant at Cashmere, W. Va.

   (d). HUGH HENDERSON ADAIR, b. ib. May 25, 1884.

e. HUGH THOMAS ADAIR, b. Bell Point, Oct. 7, 1849; m. Giles County, May 26, 1897, *Mary Ann Shumate* (b. ib. Oct. 9, 1854); he is farming at Lurich.

f. JOHN ALEXANDER ADAIR, b. Bell Point, June 20, 1851; m. *1st*. Belle Island, Giles County, Dec. 12, 1876, *Sarah Jane McClaugherty* (b. ib. April 6, 1855; d. ib. April 16, 1887); m. *2nd*. Blacksburg, Oct. 10, 1889, *Fannie Wheeler Peck* (b. Green Valley, Giles County, Dec. 16, 1859); he is farming at Lurich; he had four children by the first marriage and seven by the second.

   (a). JAMES ADAIR, b. Belle Island, Dec. 4, 1877.

   (b). CHARLES ROBERT ADAIR, b. Summer County, Kan., Feb. 3, 1880.

   (c). ELIZA JANE ADAIR, b. Bell Point, Dec. 10, 1882.

   (d). ELLA KYLE ADAIR, b. ib. Nov. 16, 1885.

   (e). RACHEL PORTER ADAIR, b. ib. Oct.

29, 1890; d. Princeton, W. Va., June 6, 1892.

(f). JOHN WILLIAM ADAIR, b. Giles County, Nov. 22, 1891; d. ib. Feb. 16, 1892.

(g). ARTHUR CHAPMAN ADAIR, b. Belle Point, Jan. 26, 1893.

(h). BENNETT FULTON ADAIR, b. ib. Jan. 17, 1895.

(i). A boy, b. Cliff Cottage, Giles County, Feb. 28, 1898; d. ib. March 14, 1898.

(j). A girl, b. ib. July 4, 1899; d. ib. August 18, 1899.

(k). JOHN ALEXANDER ADAIR, b. ib. March 2, 1901.

g. MARY JANE ADAIR, b. Bell Point, March 10, 1854; m. ib. Sept. 30, 1873, *Bennett Rivers Dunn* (b. Nortonsville, Albemarle Co., Sept. 15, 1849; d. Lurich, August 8, 1893; he was a civil engineer and for many years Engineer of Roadway of the Atlantic Coast Line, and lived at Wilmington, N. C.); l.ib.

(a). JANIE BENNETT DUNN, b. Hinton, W. Va., March 2, 1878.

(b). WALLACE ADAIR DUNN, b. Albemarle County, April 9, 1883; is a civil engineer.

(c). BENNETT RIVERS DUNN, b. Wilmington, N. C., Nov. 9, 1890.

h. JAMES ARTHUR ADAIR, b. Bell Point, April 9, 1857; is farming at Lurich.

i. MANELIUS CHAPMAN ADAIR, b. Bell Point, June 20, 1863; drowned in a storm on the Behring Sea, June 6, 1900.

§213 (2). HANNAH ISABELLA SWART, b. "Box Hill", Jan. 29, 1817; d. near Hillsboro, Nov. 23, 1849; m. *1st*. "Box Hill", May 16, 1833, *Edward Rector* (b. near Rectortown; d. near Union, Loudoun County; he was a farmer); m. *2nd*. "Box Hill", about 1844, *Thomas Hough* (b. near Hillsboro; d. ib. May 9, 1870; he was a farmer); she had three children by the first marriage, and four by the second.

    a. MARY CATHERINE RECTOR, b. near Rectortown, Feb. 27, 1834; m. "Box Hill", April 28, 1857, *Charles Littler Wood* (b. "Redbud", near Winchester, Nov. 29, 1819; d. ib. Feb. 14, 1878; he was a farmer); l. ib.

        (a). NANNIE WOOD, b. "Redbud", April 2, 1858; m. ib. Nov. 2. 1875, *George Wirgman Bowly* of Winchester; he is a traveling salesman; l. Atlanta, Ga.

            a. ELIZABETH BUTLER BOWLY, b. "Redbud", Dec. 24, 1876; d. ib. Dec. 25, 1876.

            b. LILLIAN HOLLIDAY BOWLY, b. ib. August 21, 1878; m. Atlanta, Ga., June 15, 1898, *Charles Gabriel Beck* (b. Cincinnati, O., March 22, 1870; he is in the life insurance business); l. Americus, Ga.

            c. CHARLES LITTLER WOOD Bowly, b. Winchester, July 6, 1880.

            d. HEYWARD WIRGMAN BOWLY, b. "Redbud", Dec. 7, 1881.

            e. GEORGE McKIM BOWLY, b. ib. Nov. 11, 1883; d. ib. June 23, 1895.

            f. MARSHALL HUBARD BOWLY, b. ib. June 29, 1885.

            g. ELISE WINCHESTER BOWLY, b. ib Sept. 20, 1889; d. ib. June 14, 1891.

            h. MARY WOOD BOWLY, b. ib. May 28, 1892.

            i. DEVEREUX LESLIE BOWLY, b. Atlanta, Ga., Feb. 13, 1898.

        (b). HENRY MOORE BRENT WOOD, b. "Redbud", Feb. 15, 1860; d. ib. Nov. 10, 1860.

THE ROGERS FAMILY. 237

b. ARABELLA RECTOR, b. "Box Hill", Feb. 11, 1836; m. "Edgewood", Fauquier County, Feb. 11, 1868, *Lawrence Scanland* (b. near Middleburg, about 1830; d. in Georgia; he was a farmer; they had no children). She is living in Georgia.

c. WILLIAM EDWARD RECTOR, b. "Box Hill", Sept. 21, 1837; m. near Harper's Ferry, in Loudoun County, *Emily* ...., and died there soon after his marriage.

d. JAMES THOMAS HOUGH, b. Loudoun County, April 15, 1845; d. Middleburg, June 26, 1866.

e. ELIZABETH ANN HOUGH, b. Loudoun County, March 1, 1847; d. Harper's Ferry, W. Va., March 13, 1886; m. Frederick, Md., August 11, 1869, *Samuel George Smith;* l. Harper's Ferry, W. Va.

    (a). NELLIE KATE SMITH, b. Hillsboro, June 25, 1870; l. Harper's Ferry, W. Va.

    (b). PEACH ISABELL SMITH, b. Hillsboro, August 27, 1872; m. Harper's Ferry, W. Va., July 31, 1889, *James Franklin Cassell* (b. York Haven, Penn., Oct. 18, 1866); l. Harper's Ferry, W. Va.

        a. VICTORIA CASSELL, b. ib. May 29, 1890.

        b. NELLIE ANNA CASSELL, b. ib. Dec. 28, 1893.

    (c). CHARLES THOMAS SMITH, b. Hillsboro, Jan. 25, 1875; m. Baltimore, Md., Sept. 16, 1891, *Myrtle Mohler* of Harper's Ferry, W. Va.

    (d). WILLIAM JACOB SMITH, b. Hillsboro, May 18, 1877; l. Harper's Ferry, W. Va.

    (e). JAMES SAMUEL SMITH, b. Hillsboro, Dec. 19, 1879; m. Cumberland, Md.,

The Rogers Family.   238

Sept. 29, 1901, *Nellie Viola Zarger* of that place.

(f). BRISCOE EUGENE SMITH, b. Hillsboro, Jan. 22, 1883; 1. Harper's Ferry, W. Va.

f. ELLEN ISABELLA HOUGH, b. Loudoun County, Nov. 10, 1848; m. "Redbud", Jan. 14, 1869, *Joel Lupton* (b. Applepie Ridge, Frederick County, Feb. 24, 1847; d. ib. Feb. 17, 1884; he was a farmer); 1. near Winchester.

 (a). MARY WOOD LUPTON, b. Applepie Ridge, Dec. 10, 1869; m. Frederick County, Feb. 7, 1895, *George Isaiah Pitzer* (b. Rest, June 26, 1864; is a farmer near Ridgeway).

  a. HENRY PITZER, b. ib. Dec. 19, 1895.

 (b). CHARLES LITTLER WOOD LUPTON, b. Applepie Ridge, Sept. 6, 1871; is farming near Winchester.

 (c). HUGH WIRGMAN LUPTON, b. Applepie Ridge, Oct. 27, 1874; m. Winchester, March 13, 1901, *Evadna Roberts* of Frederick County; he is a farmer near Winchester.

 (d). ANNA GRIFFITH LUPTON, b. Applepie Ridge, Dec. 22, 1876; d. ib. Sept. 6, 1877.

g. JOSEPH HUGH HOUGH, b. Loudoun County, Nov. 10, 1848; d. Aspen, Col., June 17, 1890.

§214 (3). MARY ELIZABETH SWART, b. near Middleburg, March 18, 1819; m. "Box Hill", Nov. 26, 1840, *Jonathan Waters* (b. Rappahannock County, Nov. 14, 1814; d. "Edgewood", Fauquier County, near Middleburg, Sept. 13, 1852; p. Jonathan Waters and Ann Grady; he was a farmer at "Edgewood"); 1. Middleburg.

THE ROGERS FAMILY. 239

a. ELLEN HAMILTON WATERS, b. "Edgewood", Oct. 24, 1841; d. ib. Nov. 20, 1846.
b. JOHN WILLIAM WATERS, b. ib. Feb. 9, 1843; d. ib. Feb. 17, 1843.
c. MARY JANE WATERS, b. ib. Jan. 5, 1844; d. Washington, D. C., April 10, 1899.
d. BETTY ANNA WATERS, b. "Edgewood", Nov. 2, 1845; d. ib. April 5, 1846.
e. WILLIAM ROGERS WATERS, b. ib. April 13, 1847; d. ib. June 7, 1847.
f. THOMAS HUGH WATERS, b. ib. June 13, 1848; m. Washington, D. C., Oct. 17, 1881, *Charlotte Dudley Sisson* (b. Warsaw, Richmond County, July 5, 1848; p. Solomon Sisson and Charlotte Dudley); l. Washington, D. C.; four of his five children died in infancy.
   (a). MARY COCHRAN WATERS, b. Chantilly, Fairfax County, Nov. 29, 1884.
g. EDWARD GRADY WATERS, b. "Edgewood", March 8, 1850; d. Washington, D. C., Oct. 30, 1899; m. *1st.* Butte, Montana, in Nov. 1881, *Mrs. Ann Hughes-Smith* of Pennsylvania; m. *2nd.* Washington, D. C., in 1886, *Anna Belle Sisson* of King George County. He lost three of his four children in infancy.
   (a). LUCEILE WATERS, b. Washington, D. C., in July 1895; l. ib.
h. WILLIAM ALEXANDER WATERS, b. "Edgewood", April 9, 1852; m. Holden, Tex., Apr. 15, 1877, *Lydia Holman* (b. Dallas County, Texas, Oct. 15, 1858); l. Dallas, Tex.

§215 (4). SARAH HAMILTON SWART, b. "Box Hill", Aug. 13, 1822; m. ib. in March 1841, *Hugh Tiffany* (b. Harrisonburg, Feb. 15, 1802; d. Aldie, Loudoun County, May 10, 1875; he was a farmer and lived in Monroe County, W. Va., and later at Aldie, Va.); she is living with her sons.

a. JOHN TIFFANY, b. Monroe County, W. Va., July 12, 1842; wounded at Gettysburg, Pa., July 3, 1863, and d. July 23, 1863.
b. WILLIAM SWART TIFFANY, b. Monroe County, W. Va., Nov. 24, 1845; m. Dover, Feb. 19, 1874, *Tacie Humphrey Hixson* (b. ib. June 12, 1850); he is farming at North Fork, Loudoun County.
   (a). MARY LOUISA TIFFANY, b. Aldie, Nov. 8, 1874; 1. Washington, D. C.
   (b). LIZZIE LEE TIFFANY, b. White Post, Feb. 8, 1876; m. Washington, D. C., Dec. 12, 1895, *Clarence Eugene Schooley;* 1. ib.
      a. ELSIE MAY SCHOOLEY, b. ib. May 23, 1897.
      b. WILLIE EUGENE SCHOOLEY, b. ib. Feb. 8, 1900.
      c. MILLARD LEE SCHOOLEY, b. ib. Nov. 12, 1901; d. ib. Nov. 21, 1901.
   (c). JOHN WILLIAM TIFFANY, b. White Post, March 11, 1878; 1. Washington, D. C.
   (d). ROSA ARABELLA TIFFANY, b. White Post, Dec. 5, 1880.
   (e). HUGH ROBERT TIFFANY, b. Cedarville, April 1, 1883.
   (f). HENRY WALTER TIFFANY, b. Middleburg, July 23, 1885.
   (g). LUCK ADAIR TIFFANY, b. ib. Aug. 13, 1887.
   (h). GARLAND TIFFANY, b. ib. Sept. 29, 1890.
   (i). JENNIE HUMPHREY TIFFANY, b. Leesburg, Dec. 25, 1892.
   (j). ALMA BALDWIN TIFFANY, b. North Fork, August 5, 1895; d. ib. Dec. 5, 1896.
c. MARY LOUISA TIFFANY, b. Monroe Co., W. Va., Nov. 22, 1847; d. ib. about July, 1859.

d. WALLACE NEWTON TIFFANY, b. ib. April 3, 1850; m. "Claremont", Fauquier County, Nov. 12, 1873, *Mary Gertrude Elgin* (b. Leesburg, Jan. 9, 1848; d. Landmark, June 4, 1897); he is farming at Landmark, Fauquier County.
- (a). PARNELIA HAMILTON TIFFANY, b. ib. Feb. 14, 1875.
- (b). CURRELL ELGIN TIFFANY, b. ib. June 27, 1876; is cashier of the Fauquier National Bank at Warrenton.
- (c). HUGH ADAIR TIFFANY, b. Landmark, June 3, 1878; d. ib. Nov. 1, 1880.
- (d). EFFIE TIFFANY, b. ib. Aug. 29, 1880; d. ib. June 18, 1881.
- (e). HUNTON TIFFANY, b. ib. Sept. 20, 1882.
- (f). WALLACE NEWTON TIFFANY, b. ib. May 31, 1885; d. ib. Sept. 1, 1885.

e. FRANKLIN PIERCE TIFFANY, b. Monroe County, W. Va., August 22, 1853; m. near Leesburg, Nov. 15, 1877, *Annie Virginia Ball* (b. ib. Sept. 10, 1850); he is farming at Woodburn, Loudoun County.
- (a). A son, b. and d. near Mt. Gilead, Jan. 6, 1879.
- (b). LILLIE VIRGINIA TIFFANY, b. ib. Jan. 28, 1880.
- (c). CARROLL FRANKLIN TIFFANY, b. ib. Nov. 9, 1882; l. Washington, D. C.
- (d). SARAH ELEANOR TIFFANY, b. Caroline County, March 19, 1886; d. near Mt. Gilead, Oct. 15, 1892.
- (e). A daughter, b. near Woodburn, May 25, 1890; d. ib. June 4, 1890.

f. SARAH JANE TIFFANY, b. Monroe County, W. Va., in July 1856; d. ib. in August, 1859.

g. ALEXANDER HUMPHRIES TIFFANY, b. ib. about 1858; d. Sallisaw, I. T., May 8, 1889; m. Cherokee Nation, I. T., about 1885,

Lucinda Griffin (of Cookson, I. T.; d. Sallisaw, I. T., Nov. 25, 1895); he was a farmer near Sallisaw.
- (a). WALLACE TIFFANY, b. ib. about 1886; l. Salina, I. T.
- (b). ANDREW TIFFANY, b. near Sallisaw, I. T., about 1888; l. Salina, I. T.
- (c). ALEXANDER TIFFANY, b. near Sallisaw, I. T., about 1889; l. Salina, I.T.

h. HUGH SNYDER TIFFANY, b. Monroe County, W. Va., Sept. 29, 1861; m. "Locust Grove" near Landmark, Feb. 2, 1886, *Elizabeth Jane Cochran* (b. ib. June 23, 1858); he is farming at Middleburg.
- (a). WALTER JORDAN TIFFANY, b. "Edgewood", near Middleburg, Dec. 20, 1886.
- (b). HARRY IRVING TIFFANY, b. ib. March 11, 1888.
- (c). LAURA HENRIETTA TIFFANY, b. "Oakendale", near Middleburg, Nov. 17, 1890.
- (d). MARY ELIZABETH TIFFANY, b. ib. March 17, 1892.
- (e). EARL HAMILTON TIFFANY, b. "Utopia", near Mt. Gilead, June 10, 1894.
- (f). ELLEN ADAIR TIFFANY, b. "Stone Hill", Sept. 12, 1899.

§216 (5). SUSAN CATHARINE SWART, b. "Box Hill", June 18, 1826; d. Middleburg, Nov. 22, 1885; m. *1st.* "Box Hill", in Feb. 1846, *William Christopher Alexander* (b. Clarke County, about 1810; d. ib. in August 1850; he was a farmer and lived near Millwood in Clarke County); m. *2nd.* Middleburg, August 1, 1855, *John Emmett Scruggs* of Powhatan County (he died in prison at Johnson's Island in 1863; he was editor of a newspaper); m. *3rd. Archibald Riddell*, who is still living. She had two children by the first marriage and two by the second.

a. JOHN HENRY ALEXANDER, b. Clarke County, Sept. 23, 1846; m. Hamilton, Oct. 1, 1874, *Emma Hughes* (b. Hughesville, Loudoun County, Nov. 15, 1845); he is a lawyer at Leesburg. He served in Mosby's Command in the Confederate Army.
- (a). JOHN ALEXANDER, b. Leesburg, Nov. 20, 1876; d. Hamilton, June 25, 1877.
- (b). ADA LEE ALEXANDER, b. Leesburg, Jan. 19, 1878.
- (c). ELISABETH MORGAN ALEXANDER, b. ib. June 17, 1880.
- (d). JOHN RICHARD HENRY ALEXANDER, b. near Leesburg, August 7, 1882.
- (e). VIOLET DUNCAN ALEXANDER, b. ib. March 25, 1884.
- (f). EMMA HERNDON ALEXANDER, b. ib. April 2, 1886.

b. WILLIAM ROGERS ALEXANDER, b. Clarke County, March 27, 1849; d. Winchester, Dec. 23, 1898; m. Clarksburg, W. Va., in April 1876, *Annie Shuck Willis* (b. Shusta, Cal., in 1856; d. Winchester, Dec. 3, 1886); he was a lawyer at Winchester.
- (a). VIRGINIA ALEXANDER, b. ib. Jan. 18, 1877; m. Clarksburg, W. Va., August 21, 1900, *Guion Victor de Barril*, a civil engineer of Easton, Penn.
  - a. GUION VICTOR DE BARRIL, b. Springfield, W. Va., May 27, 1901; d. Leesburg, Feb. 21, 1902.
- (b). MARY ROGERS ALEXANDER, b. Winchester, July 12, 1879; l. Leesburg.
- (c). WILLIAM CARROLL ALEXANDER, b. Winchester, July 19, 1881; l. Philadelphia, Penn.
- (d). JOHN BALDWIN ALEXANDER, b. Winchester, in April, 1883; d. ib. Aug. 1, 1883.

c. MARIAN SCOTT SCRUGGS, b. Warrenton, Dec. 7, 1857; d. Fauquier County, about 1859.
d. BESSIE HAMILTON SCRUGGS, b. ib. in Apr. 1862; d. Middleburg, in Feb. 1892; m. Leesburg, Dec. 9, 1886, *Charles Eugene Chamberlayne*, who was a physician at Middleburg.
  (a). SUSAN CHAMBERLAYNE, b. and d. ib. in infancy.
  (b). EUGENE CHAMBERLAYNE, b. ib.; is living in Missouri.

§217 (6). HUGH THOMAS SWART, b. "Box Hill", Nov. 7, 1830; d. Calverton, July 10, 1894; m. *1st.* Clarke County, Dec. 7, 1852, *Annie Eliza Sowers* (b. near Berryville, Jan. 1, 1833; d. Elleslie, Clarke County, April 13, 1856); m. *2nd.* Fredrica, Loudoun County, May 19, 1858, *Mary Catharine Fred* (b. ib. Jan. 24, 1832; 1. near Upperville); he was a farmer in Fauquier County; he had three children by each marriage.
  a. WILLIAM AUBREY SWART, b. Elleslie, Sept. 23, 1853; m. "Mountain View", Loudoun County, Dec. 18, 1884, *Roberta Hixson* (b. ib. Jan. 27, 1852); he is farming near Marshall.
    (a). ANNIE WALTON SWART, b. Fauquier County, Oct. 10, 1885.
    (b). MAMIE VALENTINE SWART, b. ib. Jan. 5, 1889.
    (c). LELIA LEE SWART, b. ib. Feb. 1, 1893.
    (d). HUGH THOMAS SWART, b. ib. Sept. 2, 1894.
  b. MARY SWART, b. Elleslie, in Feb. 1855; d. ib. in May, 1856.
  c. DANIEL WEBSTER SWART, b. ib. Feb. 29, 1856; m. Bleake Hill, Fauquier County, Dec. 1, 1886, *Anna Rachel Murray* (b. near The Plains, July 12, 1864); he is farming near Trapp, Loudoun County.

COL. HAMILTON ROGERS
§ 218

(a). VIRGINIA KERFOOT SWART, b. Springfield, Fauquier County, Jan. 20, 1888; d. near Upperville, Jan. 27, 1891.
(b). NELLIE GORDON SWART, b. ib. Sept. 14, 1890.
(c). MURRAY SETTLE SWART, b. ib. Aug. 10, 1893
(d). ANNA RACHEL SWART, b. ib. Nov. 13, 1899.

d. FANNIE FRED SWART, b. "Box Hill", July 29, 1860; d. Middleburg, Jan. 4, 1862.

e. NELLIE ROGERS SWART, b. "Box Hill", Dec. 24, 1862; l. Powhatan County.

f. THOMAS WALTER SWART, b. "Box Hill", Jan. 14, 1868; m. Morrisville, Fauquier Co., June 4, 1895, *Ella Oscar Bennette*, of "Rosedale", Fauquier Co.; l. Washington, D. C.

2. SAMUEL ROGERS, b. "Stone Hill", about 1796; died ib. in infancy.

§218 3. HAMILTON ROGERS, b. "Stone Hill", Nov. 8, 1798; d. "Oakham", August 20, 1882; m. "Springfield", near Leesburg, Oct. 28, 1823, *Mary Hawling* (b. ib. June 14, 1802; d. "Oakham", July 21, 1884; p. William C. Hawling and Jane Sanderson; gr. p. John W.C. and Hannah Hawling; she was a sister of the wife of his brother James; see §226); he was at one time a Colonel of the State Militia; he was also an Elder in the Presbyterian Church at Middleburg. His estate near that place was called "Oakham".

(1). WILLIAM HAWLING ROGERS, b. "Springfield", near Leesburg, August 22, 1824; until a year ago he has lived at "Oakham"; is now at Woodburn.

(2). MARY JANE ROGERS, b. "Springfield", March 22, 1826; d. "Belle Grove", near Leesburg, July 11, 1871; m. "Oakham", Sept. 27, 1848, *John Walter Fairfax* (b. Prospect Hill, near Dumfries, June 30, 1828; l. Freestone Point, Prince William County; p. Henry Fairfax and Elizabeth Lindsay; gr. p. Jonathan Fairfax and Sarah

Wright; he was a Colonel in the Confederate Army on the staff of General Longstreet).
- a. HENRY FAIRFAX, b. Alexandria, May 4, 1850; m. Richmond, June 4, 1896, *Eugenia Baskerville Tennant* (b. Petersburg, Jan. 9, 1873); he graduated at the V. M. I. in 1871; from 1890 to 1901 he was a member of the Virginia Senate, and was a member of the recent Constitutional Convention, being chairman of the Committee on Taxation and Finance; his estate, nine miles from Leesburg, was once the home of President Monroe, and is called "Oak Hill"; he has recently been appointed a member of the Corporation Commission under the new Constitution.
    - (a). EUGENIA TENNANT FAIRFAX, b. ib. June 1, 1897.
    - (b). MARY JANE FAIRFAX, b. ib. June 22, 1898; d. ib. June 30, 1898.
    - (c). ANNE CHAMP FAIRFAX, b. ib. June 22, 1898; d. ib. July 1, 1898.
    - (d). A son, b. and d. ib. March 21, 1901.
- b. HAMILTON ROGERS FAIRFAX, b. Alexandria, March 4, 1852; m. Rye, N. Y., June 1, 1887, *Eleanor Cecilia Van Rensselaer* (b. ib. Nov. 3, 1853); he was formerly in the real estate business in New York City, but for some years has been residing at Stuttgart, Germany, for educational purposes. He is Warden and Treasurer of the English Church there.
    - (a). KATHERINE VAN RENSSELAER FAIRFAX, b. New York City, Oct. 26, 1888.
    - (b). HAMILTON VAN RENSSELAER FAIRFAX, b. ib. Jan. 26, 1891.
- c. JOHN WALTER FAIRFAX, b. "Oak Hill", Oct. 20, 1854; he is a broker in New York City.

d. LINDSAY FAIRFAX, b. "Oak Hill", May 5, 1856; m. New York City, Feb. 14, 1889, *Grace Bradford* (b. ib. Sept. 2, 1868; p. William H. Bradford of New York City and Lenox, Mass.); he has been a broker in New York City, and is now spending several years in England.
    (a). BRADFORD LINDSAY FAIRFAX, b. New York City, Feb. 11, 1892.
    (b). GRACE LINDSAY FAIRFAX, b. Eastbourne, England, April 21, 1898.

e. MARY ELIZABETH FAIRFAX, b. "Oak Hill", Dec. 24, 1858; m. Washington, D.C., April 16, 1884, *Maj. Charles Greenleaf Ayres* (b. Amsterdam, N. Y., Feb. 26, 1854; he is a Major in the 8th U. S. Cavalry; during the War with Spain he was a Captain in the famous 10th Cavalry, and was three times recommended for the Medal of Honor for heroic conduct in Cuba); l. Ft. Riley, Kansas.
    (a). EMILY DEARBORN AYRES, b. Ft. Davis, Texas, Jan. 30, 1885.
    (b). HENRY FAIRFAX AYRES, b. "Oak Hill", April 23, 1886.

§219   (3). HUGH ROGERS, b. "Springfield", August 5, 1828; d. Washington, D. C., Dec. 8, 1899; m. "Levenworth", Loudoun County, Sept. 28, 1851, *Rosalie Dalrymple Powell* (b. ib. Sept. 24, 1833; p. John Leven Powell and Maria Louisa Grady); he was a farmer.

    a. EDWARD GRADY ROGERS, b. Clifton, July 31, 1852; l. Albemarle County.
    b. HENRY WYER ROGERS, b. Clifton, July 24, 1855; d. ib. August 27, 1888.
    c. POWELL ROGERS, b. ib. Oct. 18, 1857; l. Washington, D. C.
    d. ALEXANDER HAMILTON ROGERS, b. Clifton, July 4, 1859; l. Middleburg.
    e. ROBERT LEE ROGERS, b. Clifton, Dec. 26, 1862; l. Washington, D. C.

The Rogers Family.

f. ARMISTEAD CARTER ROGERS, b. Clifton, Sept. 15, 1865; 1. Washington, D. C.

g. JOHN LEVEN ROGERS, b. Clifton, Jan. 15, 1870; 1. Washington, D. C.

(4). ALEXANDER HAMILTON ROGERS, b. "Springfield", April 15, 1830; m. Leesburg, Oct. 12, 1858, *Julia Hawkins Clagett* (b. ib. Sept. 6, 1836; p. Thomas Hawkins Clagett and Christiana Oden); he is farming at Woodburn near Leesburg.

    a. THOMAS CLAGETT ROGERS, b. Leesburg, August 18, 1859; d. ib. August 15, 1860.

    b. ALEXANDER HAMILTON ROGERS, b. Leesburg, Jan. 29, 1861; d. Roanoke, Sept. 23, 1893.

    c. ELIZABETH CLAGETT ROGERS, b. Leesburg, April 11, 1862; m. ib. Oct. 24, 1888, *Dr. Richard Baxter Fishburn* (b. near Waynesboro, May 30, 1848; he is a physician); 1. Leesburg.

        (a). MARGARET LYNN FISHBURN, b. ib. Sept. 29, 1889.

        (b). JULIA CLAGETT FISHBURN, b. ib. Feb. 7, 1891.

        (c). RICHARD FISHBURN, b. ib. May 26, 1894.

    d. HENRY ODEN ROGERS, b. ib. June 10, 1863; 1. Landover, Md.

    e. MARY ODEN ROGERS, b. ib. August 8, 1868; 1. Woodburn.

    f. CHRISTINE ROGERS, b. ib. August 28, 1871; m. Leesburg, Feb. 8, 1893, *Robert Bentley Wildman* (b. ib. Nov. 4, 1849; he is a merchant); 1. ib.

        (a). ROBERT BENTLEY WILDMAN, b. ib. May 8, 1894; d. "Oakham", August 24, 1895.

        (b). ANNA SNOWDEN WILDMAN, b. Leesburg, July 7, 1895.

        (c). CHRISTIANA CLAGETT WILDMAN, b. ib. July 19, 1898.

GENERAL ASA ROGERS
223

THE ROGERS FAMILY. 249

  (d). MARY ODEN WILDMAN, b.ib. March 29, 1901; d. ib. Aug. 14, 1901.
 g. WILLIAM CLAGETT ROGERS, b. Woodburn, Nov. 3, 1873; d. ib. May 5, 1874.
 h. WILLIAM THOMAS CLAGETT ROGERS, b.ib. May 10, 1875; 1. Landover, Md.
 i. JULIAN MORTIMER ROGERS, b. Woodburn, Jan. 25, 1877; is clerking in Baltimore, Md.
(5). ADIN ROGERS, b. "Springfield", March 19, 1832; was killed at the battle of Spotsylvania C. H., May 10, 1864; he was a member of the 1st. Va. Cavalry.

§220 (6). ANNIE DOUGLAS ROGERS, b. "Oakham", April 4, 1835; m. ib. Feb. 9, 1860, *Alexander Keene Phillips* (b. Fredericksburg, Feb. 14, 1807; d. ib. July 5, 1892; he was a commission merchant there; p. Samuel and Sarah Phillips); 1. ib.
 a. MARY HAMILTON PHILLIPS, b. "Oakham", Nov. 29, 1861; m. Fredericksburg, June 1, 1887, *Brainard Henry Warner*, a banker of Washington, D. C.; 1. ib.
  (a). MARGARET DOUGLAS WARNER, b.ib. Sept. 28, 1889.
  (b). ALEXANDER PHILLIPS WARNER, b. ib. August 21, 1892.
  (c). HAMILTON WARNER, b. ib. June 21, 1898.
 b. ALEXANDER KEENE PHILLIPS, b. Fredericksburg, June 9, 1863; m. ib. Nov. 1, 1897, *Nannie Maury Herndon* of that place; he is in the insurance business in Washington, D. C.
  (a). ALEXANDER KEENE PHILLIPS, b. ib. Sept. 4, 1900.
 c. ANNIE DOUGLAS PHILLIPS, b. Fredericksburg, Dec. 9, 1865; m. *1st.* ib. April 9, 1889, *Courtland Smith* of Alexandria; m. *2nd.* Fredericksburg, Jan. 16, 1896, *Col. Daniel Davis Wheeler* of the U. S. Army; 1. San Francisco, Cal.

d. JANE TRAVERS PHILLIPS, b. Fredericksburg, Nov. 2, 1878; 1. ib.

§221 (7). ASA ROGERS, b. "Oakham", August 20, 1836; m. Petersburg, Nov. 20, 1872, *Alice Broocks* (b. ib. August 5, 1849; p. Thomas T. Broocks and Priscilla Hill Gary); 1. ib.; he is Collector of Internal Revenue of the 2nd District of Virginia.
 a. BROOCKS ROGERS, b. ib. July 21, 1873; m. ib. Feb. 11, 1902, *Mattie Eppes Watson* (b. ib. Dec. 20, 1874); 1. ib.; he represents the Virginia Trunk and Bag Company in the South.
 b. HAMILTON ROGERS, b. ib. April 25, 1875; 1. ib.; practicing law.
 c. ASA DOUGLAS ROGERS, b. ib. Sept. 16, 1879; 1. ib.; he is a manufacturer's agent.
 d. HERBERT ROGERS, b. ib. Sept. 9, 1883; 1. ib.; clerking.
 e. WILLIAM MAHONE ROGERS, b. ib. May 8, 1887; 1. ib.

(8). MORTIMER MCILHANY ROGERS, b. "Oakham", Feb. 2, 1839; m. "Buena Vista", near Roanoke, Nov. 18, 1875, *Virginia Tayloe* (b. ib. Jan. 3, 1848; p. Col. Geo. P. Tayloe and Mary Elizabeth Langhorne); he served in the Confederate Army in the 1st. Va. Cavalry, and later as Captain on the staff of Gen. Wm. C. Wickham; he is in the real estate business in Roanoke; 1. "Buena Vista".
 a. MARY TAYLOE ROGERS, b. Baltimore, Md., March 24, 1878.
 b. VIRGINIA MORTIMER ROGERS, b. "Buena Vista", Jan. 14, 1880.
 c. TAYLOE ROGERS, b. ib. July 24, 1881.
 d. MORTIMER HAMILTON ROGERS, b. ib. June 14, 1883.
 e. ROSA THORNTON ROGERS, b. ib. Oct. 27, 1889.

(9). JOHN LOUIS ROGERS, b. "Oakham", Dec. 10, 1842; d. Buchanan, July 24, 1881.

§222   4. WILLIAM ROGERS, b. "Stone Hill", Jan. 1, 1800; d. Dover, Dec. 22, 1888; m. *1st.* ib. Nov. 7, 1822, *Elizabeth Hixson* (b. and d. ib.); m. *2nd.* "Bratton Hill", near Hillsboro, about 1845, *Ruth White* (b. ib. about 1810; d. Dover, Dec. 12, 1874); he was a farmer and lived at Dover; he had one child by each marriage.

   (1). JAMES HAMILTON ROGERS, b. Dover, about 1825; d. ib. April 26, 1888; he studied medicine at the University of Virginia, but had to give up the profession on account of ill health.

   (2). MOLLIE WHITE ROGERS, b. ib. August 30, 1847; m. ib. Jan. 17, 1866, *Milton McIlhany Rogers*, her first cousin; see §229; she is living at Charlottesville.

§223   5. ASA ROGERS, b. near "Stone Hill", June 4, 1802; d. Middleburg, Sept. 20, 1887; m. Leesburg, May 5, 1829, *Eleanor Lee Orr* (b. Clarke County, Nov. 7, 1802; d. Middleburg, Sept. 1, 1862; p. Dr. John Dalrymple Orr and Lucinda Lee; gr. p. John Orr and Susan Grayson—Thomas Ludwell Lee of "Belvue" and Mary Aylett, daughter of Col. William Aylett). He was in public life before the formation of the Whig party, of which he was a conspicuous and influential member throughout its existence. In 1826 he was elected to the House of Delegates from Loudoun County, and was alternately in the Senate and lower house for many years preceding 1860. He was appointed by the Legislature Second Auditor of the State in 1870, and filled that important office till 1880. At one time he was a General of the State Militia.

   (1). JOHN DALRYMPLE ROGERS, b. Middleburg, Feb. 24, 1830; d. Lexington, Nov. 30, 1889; m. *1st.* "Farley", Culpeper County, Oct. 26, 1853, *Parke Farley Wellford* (b. Fredericksburg, Nov. 20, 1830; d. "Farley Vale", King George County, Oct. 23, 1870; p. Dr. William Nelson Wellford and Rebecca Parke Farley Corbin of "Farley"; gr. p. John Spotswood Wellford and Fanny Page

Nelson, daughter of Col. William Nelson of the Revolution); m. *2nd*. "Briery Knowe", Amherst County, Oct. 18, 1882, *Kitty Temple Minor* (daughter of Launcelot Minor and Mary Ann Swann; l. Lexington); he was a farmer for many years in Fauquier County, his estate, near Middleburg, being called "Springfield"; for a few years before his death he was connected with the Richmond and Alleghany Railroad as Traveling Solicitor; he had eight children by the first marriage and three by the second.

 a. WILLIAM WELLFORD ROGERS, b. Middleburg, April 9, 1855; d. ib. Nov. 26, 1855.
 b. FARLEY CORBIN ROGERS, b."Springfield", August 27, 1856; d. ib. Nov. 1, 1861.
 c. ELEANOR ORR ROGERS, b. ib. April 1, 1859; d. ib. Nov. 5, 1861.
 d. ASA ROGERS, b. ib. July 17, 1860; d. ib. in infancy.
 e. PARKE WELLFORD ROGERS, b. ib. Dec. 31, 1861; d. "Farley Vale", Sept. 2, 1870.
 f. LUCY DALRYMPLE ROGERS, b. "Springfield", April 19, 1866; m. Brooklyn, N. Y., Jan. 9, 1901, *Francis Dominick Mead;* he is a broker; l. ib.
  (a). JOHN DALRYMPLE ROGERS MEAD, b. ib. Jan. 16, 1902.
  (b). WILLIAM CARROLL MEAD, b.ib. Jan. 12, 1903.
 g. EDITH GROSVENOR ROGERS, b. "Springfield", May 21, 1867; m. Brooklyn, N. Y., April 16, 1902, *Noel Mack Bush;* he is a salesman; l. ib.
 h. VIRGINIA HETH ROGERS, b. Fredericksburg, Dec. 17, 1869; d. in infancy.
 i. ELLEN LEE ROGERS, b. "Briery Knowe", Oct. 3, 1883.
 j. JOHN DALRYMPLE ROGERS, b. Iron Gate, Dec. 31, 1886.

REV. ARTHUR BARKSDALE KINSOLVING
§ 224

k. KITTY MINOR ROGERS, b. Lexington, August 9, 1889.

(2). ARTHUR LEE ROGERS, b. Middleburg, Oct. 21, 1831; d. ib. Sept. 13, 1871; m. Baltimore, Md., Nov. 23, 1858, *Charlotte Rust* (b. Leesburg, Sept. 22, 1837; p. George Rust and Maria Clagett Marlow; l. Plainfield, N. J.); he graduated in law at the University of Virginia; during the Civil War he was promoted for gallantry to the rank of Major; a severe wound received at the battle of Chancellorsville kept him from continuing the practice of law after the war.

 a. MARIA CLAGETT ROGERS, b. Leesburg, Oct. 20, 1859; l. Plainfield, N. J.

 b. LUCY LEE ROGERS, b. Middleburg, Nov. 20, 1861; d. Charlottesville, Dec. 27, 1863.

 c. ELLEN VIRGINIA ROGERS, b. Lexington, March 5, 1864; l. Plainfield, N. J.

 d. GEORGE RUST ROGERS, b. Middleburg, July 18, 1866; m. Frederick, Md., Oct. 23, 1901, *Caroline Ross* of that place (p. Chas. Worthington and Cornelia Potts Ross); he is a broker in New York City; l. Plainfield, N. J.

 e. LAURA LEE ROGERS, b. Middleburg, June 9, 1868; l. Plainfield, N. J.

 f. CHARLOTTE RUST ROGERS, b. Middleburg, Feb. 13, 1870; m. New York City, Jan. 25, 1894, *Dr. Elihu Hall Richardson*, a physician of Belair, Md.; l. ib.

  (a). ELIHU HALL RICHARDSON, b. ib. May 12, 1897; d. ib. Feb. 6, 1899.

§224 (3). LUCY LEE ROGERS, b. Middleburg, Dec. 8, 1833; d. ib. May 27, 1862; m. ib. Aug. 9, 1859, *Rev. Ovid Americus Kinsolving*, *D. D.* (b. Charlottesville, Dec. 13, 1822; d. Houston, Va., Nov. 24, 1894; p. George W. and Ann Rogers Kinsolving; he was an Episcopal minister. By a former marriage he was the father of the Rt. Rev. George Herbert Kinsolving, D. D., Bishop of Texas.)

a. ARTHUR BARKSDALE KINSOLVING, b. Middleburg. Feb. 20, 1861; m. Richmond, Feb. 5, 1896, *Sally Archer Bruce* (b. ib. Feb. 14, 1876; p. Thomas Seddon Bruce and Mary Anderson); he studied at the University of Virginia and the Virginia Theological Seminary at Alexandria; for thirteen years he has been Rector of Christ Episcopal Church, Brooklyn, N. Y., one of the largest and most influential churches of that city.
    (a). MARY BRUCE KINSOLVING, b. ib. Dec. 5, 1896.
    (b). ARTHUR LEE KINSOLVING, b. Huntington, Long Island, August 24, 1899.
    (c). ELEANOR ROGERS KINSOLVING, b. Brooklyn, N. Y., May 7, 1902.

b. LUCIEN LEE KINSOLVING, b. Middleburg, May 14, 1862; m. Mt. Holly, N. J., Jan. 8, 1892, *Alice Brown* (b. ib. in Sept. 1866; p. Charles and Hannah Brown); he studied at the University of Virginia and the Virginia Theological Seminary; he was one of the two pioneer missionaries of the Episcopal Church to Brazil, and, with the assistance of other workers, in ten years' time founded a national church in that Republic, and was elected its first Bishop; the degree of S. T. D. has been conferred upon him by the University of Pennsylvania; 1. Porto Alegre, Brazil.
    (a). CHARLES MCILVAINE KINSOLVING, b. Rio Grande do Sul, Brazil, Jan. 19, 1893.
    (b). ARTHUR BARKSDALE KINSOLVING, b. ib. Sept. 13, 1895.
    (c). LUCY LEE KINSOLVING, b. Porto Allegre, Brazil, Jan. 7, 1902.

§225   (4). LAURA FRANCES ROGERS, b. Middleburg, Nov. 29, 1835; m. ib. June 27, 1860, *George Lee* (b. Leesburg, May 3, 1831; d. Brooklyn, N. Y.,

April 14, 1892; p. Dr. George Lee and Sally Moore Henderson of Leesburg; he was a merchant, first at Nashville, Tenn., and then in Brooklyn, N. Y.); l. ib.
 a. HUGH DOUGLAS LEE, b. Nashville, Tenn., June 26, 1861; m. Pittsburg, Pa., Dec. 16, 1896, *Heléne Brookbank;* he is a salesman in New York City.
 b. GEORGE LEE, b. Middleburg, Oct. 21, 1863; d. ib. Nov. 9, 1883.
 c. ELEANOR ORR LEE, b. Greensboro, Ala., May 12, 1867; m. Brooklyn, N. Y., June 6, 1899, *Abbott Brisbane Rhett*, originally of South Carolina; he is cashier of the Continental Tobacco Company; l. Brooklyn, N. Y.
  (a). ABBOTT BRISBANE RHETT, b. ib. May 21, 1900.
 d. ASA ROGERS LEE, b. Leesburg, Sept. 20, 1869; m. Brooklyn, N. Y., April 17, 1901, *Mary Rogers*, daughter of Charles Edgar Rogers of that place; he is a dealer in mortgages; l. ib.
  (a). ASA ROGERS LEE, b. ib. Feb. 4, 1902.
 e. ARTHUR LEE, b. ib. Jan. 29, 1874; he is a graduate of the Columbia University Law School, and is practicing in New York City.
 f. BEVERLY RANDOLPH LEE, b. Brooklyn, N. Y., Dec. 23, 1875; d. ib. March 24, 1877.
(5). HUGH HAMILTON ROGERS, b. Middleburg, Nov. 8, 1839; d suddenly on the train near Anderson, S. C., Feb. 9, 1896.

§226 6. JAMES ROGERS, b. "Stone Hill", about 1804; d. Jeffersonton, Culpeper County, Nov. 5, 1883; m. Loudoun County, about 1827, *Martha Hawling* (b. ib. in 1814; d. near Leesburg, May 23, 1882; she was a sister of his brother Hamilton's wife; see §218); he was a farmer and lived in Fauquier County; the latter part of his life he lived in Warrenton.

(1). JANE ROGERS, b. Loudoun County, about 1829; d. ib. unmarried.
(2). HENRIETTA ROGERS, b. Loudoun County, June 24, 1831; d. Fauquier County, March 21, 1889; m. ib Nov. 28, 1855, *Benjamin Elliott Curlette* (b. Clarke County, May 23, 1830; he is a farmer, and lives at "Waverley", near Delaplane; he has married a second time).
    a. MARTHA CURLETTE, b. Fauquier County, Jan. 18, 1857; d. ib. June 11, 1893.
    b. SUSAN ELLIOTT CURLETTE, b. ib. Jan. 2, 1859; m. ib. Nov. 22, 1894, *Henry Clay Bayly* (b. ib. Feb. 1, 1848; he is farming at "Ashleigh" near Delaplane; his first wife was her sister Ann Lee Curlette; see below).
        (a). ANN LEE BAYLY, b. ib. May 12, 1896.
        (b). CORINNE BRUCE BAVLY, b. ib. June 24, 1900.
    c. ANNE LEE CURLETTE, b. Independence, Mo., July 5, 1861; d. Danville, May 17, 1893; m. Fauquier County, Feb. 9, 1881, *Henry Clay Bayly* (he afterwards married her sister Susan; see above).
        (a). WILLIAM ELLIOTT BAYLY, b. "Waverley", June 7, 1883.
        (b). HENRY CLAY BAYLY, b. ib. Sept. 13, 1884.
        (c). ROGERS HINKS BAYLY, b. "Ashleigh", June 6, 1890.
    d. WILLIAM SMITH CURLETTE, b. Independence, Mo., Oct. 13, 1864; m. Oneonto, Ala., Oct. 3, 1895, *Kathleen Clowdur* (b. Village Springs, Ala., Feb. 3, 1873); he is a bookkeeper at South Port, Tenn.
        (a). RICHARD CURLETTE, b. Mt. Pleasant, Tenn., March 22, 1897.
        (b). ROGER CURLETTE, b. Ettaton, Tenn., Feb. 22, 1901.

RT. REV. LUCIEN LEE KINSOLVING
224

THE ROGERS FAMILY. 257

  e. CORINNE CURLETTE, b. Warrenton, Nov.
   8, 1867; 1. Delaplane.
  f. RICHARD ROGERS CURLETTE, b. Warrenton. July 26, 1869; d. Patton, Ala., June 6,
   1893.
  g. JAMES ELLIOTT CURLETTE, b. Warrenton,
   Sept. 27, 1874; d. Fauquier County, Feb.
   7, 1902.
 (3) JOHN MARSHALL ROGERS, b. Fauquier County, about 1834; d. Warrenton, about 1871.
 (4). RICHARD ROGERS, b. Fauquier County, about
  1837; d. St. Louis, Mo., about 1869.
 (5). WILLIAM ROGERS, b. Fauquier County, about
  1840; d. Columbia, Mo., about 1866.
 (6). SUSAN ROGERS, b. Fauquier County, April
  6, 1846; d. Danville, June 7, 1899; m. Washington, D. C., June 20, 1877, *Maj. James William
  Bruce* (b. Albemarle County, Feb. 9, 1834; he is
  a merchant at Danville).
 (7) ROSE ROGERS, b. Fauquier County, about
  1850; d. Danville, Nov. 6, 1887.
 (8). JAMES EDWARD ROGERS, b. Fauquier County,
  about 1855; d. Washington, D. C., in Feb. 1877.
 (9). MARY LEWIS ROGERS, b. Fauquier County,
  March 4, 1863; m. Danville, Feb. 28, 1883, *Dr.
  Charles Dallam* (b. Mayfield, Ky., Feb. 22, 1853;
  he is a druggist); 1. ib.
   a. ELIZABETH WISTON DALLAM, b. Danville,
    July 31, 1885.

§227 7. SARAH ROGERS, b. "Stone Hill", Sept. 24, 1807;
  d. Warrenton, Dec. 20, 1894; m. "Stone Hill", March
  22, 1830, *Theodore Nathaniel Davisson;* for their descendants see MCILHANY FAMILY, §118.

§228 8. ANN ROGERS, b. "Stone Hill", August 4, 1809;
  d. Warrenton, July 5, 1882; m. "Stone Hill",
  Nov. 20, 1827, *Taliaferro Milton McIlhany;* for their
  descendants see MCILHANY FAMILY, §§129–131.

§229 9. MARY JANE ROGERS, b. "Stone Hill", Feb. 29,
  1812; d. Richmond, Jan. 19, 1871; m. "Stone
  Hill", Sept. 23, 1834, *William Hixson Rogers* (b. near

Middleburg, April 7, 1812; d. Richmond, in May 1883; p. Sanford and Margaret Rogers; he was not related to her); they lived at Middleburg and Alexandria until the time of the Civil War, and thereafter at Richmond; he was a merchant.

(1). HENRY JUDSON ROGERS, b. "Stone Hill", April 9, 1836; d. New York City, about 1890; m. Baltimore, Md., Oct. 12, 1865, *Lucia Bayne*, daughter of Lawrence Bayne of New York City. He was a civil engineer. Their twin daughters, born about 1870, lived only a few months.
    a. MARY EDMONIA ROGERS.
    b. DELIA BAYNE ROGERS.

(2). MILTON McILHANY ROGERS, b. Middleburg, Sept. 8, 1837; d. Dover, Oct. 2, 1889; m. Dover, Jan. 17, 1866, *Mollie White Rogers*, his first cousin; see §222; he was a farmer, and lived at Dover.

(3). MARY ROBERTA ROGERS, b. Middleburg, Sept. 20, 1842; d. ib. Nov. 8, 1843.

(4). JAMES PENDLETON ROGERS, b. ib. March 9, 1845; d. Richmond, March 17, 1883; m. ib. Nov. 15, 1866, *Ellen McCance* (b. ib. March 2, 1848; p. Thomas W. McCance and Emeline Gardner; l. ib.); he was in the wholesale grocery business in Richmond.
    a. ELLEN McCANCE ROGERS, b. ib. May 7, 1869; d. ib. June 11, 1898.
    b. HUGH GARDNER ROGERS, b. ib. Nov. 15, 1870; d. Healing Springs, July 8, 1871.
    c. WILLIAM PENDLETON ROGERS, b. Richmond, Nov. 23, 1872; m. Chicago, Ill., June 14, 1902, *Carrie Teasdale*; l. New York City, where he is purchasing agent of the International Steam Pump Company.
    d. MARY EDMONIA ROGERS, b. Richmond, Jan. 18, 1874; l. ib.
    e. EMELINE ROBERTA ROGERS, b. ib. May 1, 1875; d. ib. May 19, 1875.
    f. LUCIA DUNLOP ROGERS, b. ib. Dec. 8, 1876; d. ib. July 6, 1877.

g. ROBERT EMILE ROGERS, b. ib. Dec. 25, 1878; l. ib.

(5). MARY EDMONIA ROGERS, b. Middleburg, July 27, 1847; d. Richmond, Oct. 8, 1870; m. Richmond, April 28, 1868, *James Albert Slaughter* (b. Washington, Va., about 1836; is a broker at Galveston, Tex.).

    a. WILLIAM PENDLETON SLAUGHTER, b. Richmond, May 29, 1869; m. Kenova, W. Va., Nov. 14, 1894, *Mary Rhea Duncan* (b. Ceredo, W. Va., March 1, 1875); he is manager of the Thacker Coal Company, Cincinnati, Ohio.

    b. FRANK SLAUGHTER, b. Richmond, Aug. 1, 1870; d. Roanoke, Nov. 14, 1893.

§230   10. MARTHA ROGERS, b. "Stone Hill" about 1815; d. Warrenton, April 4, 1882; m. "Stone Hill", June 11, 1839, *Daniel Alfred Sowers* (b. Clarke County; d. ib. in May 1852; he was a farmer and lived in Clarke County)

(1). SUSAN IDA SOWERS, b. ib. Oct. 6, 1841; d. Warrenton, March 1, 1867; m. ib. Dec. 21, 1865, *Edward Lemmon Fisher* (b. ib. about 1840; after her death he married again); they lived at Warrenton.

    a. MARY WITHERS FISHER, b. ib. Feb. 28, 1867; d. Campbell County, July 7, 1886.

(2). JAMES KERFOOT SOWERS, b. Clarke County, May 7, 1845; was killed at the battle of Spotsylvania C. H., May 10, 1864.

(3). MARTHA LOUISA SOWERS, b. Middleburg, March 6, 1849; m. *1st*. Warrenton, April 28, 1875, *Francis Washington Jenings* (b. ib. in Jan. 1848; d. ib. May 23, 1880; he was a merchant at Warrenton); m. *2nd*. Washington, D. C., Feb. 11, 1896, *Charles William Smith* (b. Leesburg, Oct. 10, 1857; he is a real estate agent); l. Warrenton.

    a. MARTHA WASHINGTON JENINGS, b. Washington, D. C., Feb. 12, 1876; l. Baltimore, Md.

b. WILLIAM FRANCIS JENINGS, b. Warrenton, Jan. 25, 1878; l. New York City; he is a traveling salesman.

(4). NANNIE SOWERS, b. Clarke County, June 29, 1851; m. Warrenton, Dec. 17, 1873, *James McEvoy* (b. Baltimore, Md., Oct. 20, 1843; he is a 'real estate manager); l. ib.
    a. JAMES McEVOY, b. ib. Dec. 12, 1874; studied law at the University of Maryland, and is practicing in Baltimore, Md.
    b. MARTHA ROGERS McEVOY, b.ib. May 12, 1876; d. Jeffersonton, Culpeper County, Aug. 15, 1877.
    c. PHILIP WILLIAMS McEVOY, b. Baltimore, Md., March 24, 1880; d. ib. March 25, 1880.

§231   11. SUSAN ROGERS, b. "Stone Hill", about 1818; d. Warrenton, March 2, 1874; m. "Stone Hill", about 1843, *John Armistead Spilman* (b. Jeffersonton, Culpeper County, June 4, 1819; d. Warrenton, March 27, 1889; he was a merchant at Warrenton; his home was called "Conway Grove").

(1). WILLIAM MASON SPILMAN, b. Jeffersonton, August 29, 1844; d. Warrenton, Dec. 8, 1898; m. ib. April 21, 1875, *Heningham Lyons Scott* (b. Richmond, April 15, 1851; p. Hon. Robert E. Scott and Heningham Lyons; l. ib.); he was a merchant at Warrenton.
    a. ROBERT SCOTT SPILMAN, b. ib. March 22, 1876; he graduated at the V. M. I., and in the Law Department of the University of Virginia; is practicing at Charleston, W. Va.
    b. JOHN ARMISTEAD SPILMAN, b. Warrenton, April 15, 1878; he graduated at the U. S. Naval Academy, and is now Assistant Naval Constructor at Boston.
    c. HENINGHAM WATKINS SPILMAN, b. Warrenton, March 12, 1880; m. Richmond, Dec. 30, 1902, *Otto Theodore Hess*, a lawyer of New York City; l. ib.

d. SUSAN CONWAY SPILMAN, b. Warrenton,
   Jan. 19, 1882; 1. Richmond.
(2). BETTIE CONWAY SPILMAN, b. Warrenton,
   about 1846; d. ib., aged about two years.
(3). MARY ARMISTEAD SPILMAN, b. ib. Feb. 25,
   1848; m. ib. Nov. 10, 1886, *Rev. Francis Ryland
   Boston* (b. Somerset Co., Md., Dec. 29, 1846; he
   is pastor of the Baptist Church at Warrenton).
      a. JOHN ARMISTEAD BOSTON, b. ib. July 14,
      1889.
      b. FLORENCE FRAZER BOSTON, b. ib. Oct.
      27, 1893.
(4). ANNIE FLORENCE SPILMAN, b.ib. August 20,
   1850; m. ib. June 19, 1873, *Robert Frazer* (b.
   Orange County, May 30, 1840; he has been President of the State Normal School at Farmville,
   and is now connected with the Southern Educational Board as Field Secretary); 1. Warrenton.
(5). HUGH CONWAY SPILMAN, b. ib. Jan. 1, 1852;
   m. ib. Dec. 29, 1887, *Annie Heyward North* (b.
   Norfolk, Va., Jan. 23, 1856); 1. "Conway Grove",
   Warrenton; he is a traveling salesman.
      a. HEYWARD NORTH SPILMAN, b. Warrenton,
      June 17, 1889.
      b. CONWAY SPILMAN, b. ib. Nov. 28, 1890;
      d. ib. Dec. 18, 1890.
      c. HUGH ARMISTEAD SPILMAN, b. ib. Sept.
      30, 1892.
(6). LANDONIA SPILMAN, b. ib. about 1854; d. ib.
   aged about three months.
(7). CLARA FITZGERALD SPILMAN, b. ib. Jan. 1,
   1856; is teaching music at Farmville.

§232 III. HAMILTON ROGERS, b. about 1770; m. *Dinah Gregg*.
They lived in Loudoun County, and had ten children.
   1. THOMAS ROGERS, m. *Elmina S. Chamblin;* ten children.
   2. MARY ROGERS, m. *John Holmes;* four children.
   3. ARTHUR ROGERS, m. *Hannah Nichols;* ten children.
   4. HUGH ROGERS, m. *Mary Simpson;* thirteen children

5. ELIZABETH ROGERS, m. *Elijah Holmes;* nine children.
6. SAMUEL ROGERS, m. *Jane Adams;* five children.
7. WILLIAM ROGERS, died young and unmarried.
8. HAMILTON ROGERS, m. *Ann Hixson;* three children.
9. MARTHA ANN ROGERS, m. *John H. Hughes;* nine children.
10. JOSEPH ROGERS, m. *Mary Eaton;* five children.

§233 IV. ANNE ROGERS, m. June 21, 1795, *Jesse McVeigh* (b. August 30, 1770; p Jonathan and Elizabeth McVeigh; gr. p. Jeremiah McVeigh and Mary Potts of Philadelphia; by a second marriage he had eight children); she lived and died near Middleburg, and had at least six children. The following is an incomplete outline of her descendants.

1. ELI McVEIGH, m. *Jane Hutchinson:* issue,—Luther, Martha (m. a Mr. Rawlings), James and Cornelia.
2. HIRAM McVEIGH, b. Sept. 3, 1798; m. *1st. Jane Elgin;* m. *2nd. Mary Elizabeth White,* and had ten children; see §§120–121. The six children by his first marriage were,—Charles, Frank, Richard (m. a Mrs. Dunbar), Robert, Thomas, and Adelaide (m. a Mr. Price).
3. TOWNSEND McVEIGH, m. *Karen H. Thrift:* issue,—
    (1). HAMILTON McVEIGH, m. *Eliza Whiteman:* issue,—Eliza (m. Lee Cousins), Sallie, John Whiteman, Jennie and Clara (m. Dr. Willetts).
    (2). SALLIE ANN McVEIGH.
    (3). WILLIAM HARVEY McVEIGH, m. *Hattie Rogers:* issue,—Howard (m. Lillie Snyder; l. Parkersburg, W. Va.), Norman (d. young) and Ella Rogers (m. Rev. R. T. Vann).
    (4). AMERICA McVEIGH, m. *Isaac D. Budd:* issue. —William Henry (m. Laura Bell Lykens), Karen Blanche (married; no issue), Townsend McVeigh, Mary Franconia, Norman, Alice (married; two children), and Florence (m. Howard J. Baldwin).
    (5). GEORGIA McVEIGH, m. *Col. V. M. Johnson.*
    (6). COLUMBIA McVEIGH.
    (7). VIRGINIA McVEIGH.

THE ROGERS FAMILY.

  (8). BLANCHE MCVEIGH, m. *William V. Moss:* issue,—George, Marion T., Townsend, Vincent, Carleton and Mary Rust.

  (9). TOWNSEND MCVEIGH, m. *Berta Moss:* issue,—Willie, Blanche, Jesse, George and Townsend.

§234 4. JAMES H. MCVEIGH, m. May 25, 1830, *Cynthia Ariel Guest:* issue,—

  (1). LIZZIE MCVEIGH, m. *Edgar Hutchinson* of Richmond: issue,—Harvey, Lula, Lizzie, Edgar and Grace.

  (2). LOUISA MCVEIGH; l. ib.

  (3). JOB MCVEIGH, m. *Jennie McFarland;* no issue.

  (4). EDGAR MCVEIGH, m. *Bettie English;* l. Rappahannock County.

  (5). BELLE MCVEIGH; l. Richmond.

  (6). NEWTON MCVEIGH, m. *Lillie Tapscott:* issue,—Charles S. and Charlotte Wallace (died young); l. Richmond.

  (7). LAURA MCVEIGH.

  (8). CYNTHIA MCVEIGH; l. ib.

  (9). T. EMORY MCVEIGH; married and living in Lynchburg.

 5. WILLIAM NEWTON MCVEIGH, m. *Jane Chamberlane:* issue,—Mollie (m. G. Powell Hill of Richmond), Maria (m. Charles Baldwin; l. Richmond), William, Llewellyn (m. Charlotte Skelton; one son, Llewellyn) and Harvey:

 6. MARY ANN MCVEIGH, m. *Joshua Gibson:* issue,—Annie, Jesse, John Newton, Armistead and Henry.

§235 V. WILLIAM ROGERS, died unmarried at about twenty-one years of age.

INDEX.

Adair,	232-235
Aisquith,	106
Alexander, J. F.	93
John Henry	243
Morgan	107
William Christopher	242
William Rogers	243
Allder, Albert J.	53
Allen,	69-70, 218
Ambler Family,	29, 81
Anderson, Wm. Franklin	63
Arey,	120-121
Armstrong, Rev. Jas. Edward	131
Ashmore, Dr. W. Frank	92
Atkinson, Roger B.	161
Aylett, Col. William	251
Ayres, Maj. Charles G.	247
Baldwin Family,	110-111
Charles,	263
Barnett, Judge Andrew	189
Barrett, Rev. Robt. S.	79
Barron, Wm. A.	93
Barry,	67-68
Barton,	66-67
Baskerville, H. E. C.	69
Battaile, Capt. John	100
Bayless, Rev. Samuel	186
Bayly, Henry Clay	256
Beatty,	229-230
Beck, Charles G.	236
Beeson, Edward	85
Bell,	19-20
Bennett, H. N.	200
Berry,	220
Best, James	136
Biggs, Robinson	224
Biscoe, Thomas	229

Biser, Capt. C. T.	60
Blair, Rebecca (Trout)	130
Blount, Reading J.	183
Bolen, William Harrison	159
Bond, Richard Thompson	168
Bonham, Ackley	226
Boston, Rev. Francis R.	261
Bowen, Rev. O. R.	117
Bowles, Dr. George F.	56
Bowly, George W.	236
Bowyer,	42-44
Boyd, George W.	109
Boyer, Alfred Z.	219
Boyers, Jacob	132
Braden, R. W.	58
Bradford, William H.	247
Bradley, Henry	165
Britton, Dr. Edward W.	107
Brooke, Robert S.	102
Broun, Dr. J. Conway	225
Browinski, James F.	190
Brown, Bertram	174
Glenn	14
Henry	111
John A.	121
Bruce, Maj. James William	257
Sloan	98
Thomas Seddon	254
Dr. Walter	77
Bryant, William Nicholas	127
Bryarly, Richard Samuel	227
Budd, Isaac D.	262
Burwell, Lewis	29
Bush, Noel Mack	252
Bushrod Family,	215-216
Butcher, Robert Hume	103
Butterfield, Gen. Carlos	218
Byerly, Dr. Wm. H.	116

INDEX.

Cabell, Maj. Charles Ellet	155	Dallam, Dr. Charles	257
Caldwell, John North	81	Dangerfield, Col. Raleigh	216
Calvert, Cornelius	88	Daniel, James W.	9
Campbell, Dr. Morgan B.	205	Daugherty, Joseph	101
Philip Slaughter	191	Samuel	169
Carr, Dr. William P.	163	Dr. Thomas	129
Carter,	162-163	W. T.	106
Cary, William	29	Davis, Clifton	94
Cassell, James F.	237	James	214
Castleman, Alfred	179	Jesse	214
Bushrod Taylor	194, 219	Presley	198
Charles William	219, 220	Solomon	161
Thomas	218, 220	Taliaferro Milton	198
Chamberlain, Jas. Davisson	142	William Louis	61
Chamberlayne, Dr. Chas. Eugene	244	Davisson, Rev. Augustus	142
Chamberlin, Ellis McK.	192	Maj. Daniel	139
Chapman,	13-15	Dr. Frederick Augustus	139
Chastain, Dr. Stephen	31-32	John William	141
Chenoweth, Margaret (Tate)	106	Margaret (Milton)	139, 199
Chesley, Mary (Kinney)	1	Nathaniel	139
Chestnut, Mary (Coombs)	231	Theodore Nathaniel	142, 257
Chilton, Capt. A. W.	54	Dawalt, Jonathan	9
Clark, Rev. Rufus W.	104	Dawson, C. E.	49
Clarkson,	77	De Barril, Guion Victor	243
Clay, Henry	183	Donaghe, Dr. Briscoe Baldwin	102
Dr. John Gillam	146	Donaldson, Wm. Edward	130
Claypool, Mary Anne (Milton)	191	Douthat, Agnes H. (Stribling)	81
Cleveland, L. C.	94	Doyle, Dr. John N.	94, 98
Clifton, Edward	94	Drummond, Sarah (Stribling)	85
Cochran, Col. James C.	103	Dunn, Bennett Rivers	235
Susan Baldwin (Hilleary)	158		
Cockerill, Almond B.	169	Eaton, Theodore H.	104
Coombs Family	230-231	Edmunds, Mary (Kinney)	6
Conway, William	174	Samuel	6
Cooke, Charles L.	118, 119	Edwards, F. M.	40
Corbin Family,	216	Elliott, Dr. Henry Randall	140
Cox, James Oscar	194	Ellzey, Lewis	149
Dr. Walter	225	English,	44-45
Craig, William	26	Epperson, B. C.	72
Crawford,	59-63, 181	Eskridge, Thomas P.	102
Crosby, Admiral Pierce	42		
Crump, Benjamin	27	Fairfax,	245-247
Culver, John	224	Farrar Family,	31-32
Cunningham,	188-189	Fenton, William F.	192
Cupp, Marcus L.	120	Fishburn, Dr. Richard B.	248
Curlette,	256-257	Fisher Family,	28-29
Cuthbert, Henrietta (Stribling)	41	Edward H.	16, 29
		Edward Lemmon	259

INDEX.

Fisher, Mary Ann (Kinney)	6, 29
Robert Haxall	15, 28
Fleming, George Wallace	202
Fletcher, F. A.	109
James William	110
Rev. Patterson	103
Flynt, Walter	172
Ford, George Howard	82
William Warfield	192
Foster, Frank Stribling	42
I. J.	89
James Carrington	16
James Johnston	16
John Hunton	77
Richard Taylor	41
Robert Erskine	16
Frazer, Robert	261
Frazier, Emma L. (Bell)	19
Frost, Amos	220
Fry, Rev. George M.	161
Galt, Jean M. (Kinney)	11
Gardner, Dr. G. W.	96
Garland, John Spotswood	43
George, John	135
Gibbons, Rev. J. H.	63
Gibson, Joshua	263
Glass, Lewis Fulton	227
Gleaves, Albert	43
Gooch,	232-233
Goodfellow,	201-203
Grant, Maj. Alexander	214
Green,	182
Grepe, Stanley	109
Grigsby, Henry Newton	226
Grubb, Ebenezer	135
Grymes, Rev. Charles	99
Guthrie, Dr. L. Van G.	45
Haile, John	87
Haldeman, Bruce	193
Hall, Edward	108
Virginius	15
Hamilton, Jane (Rogers)	229
Hammond,	196-197
Harkey, Josiah	98
Harman, E. V.	12
Harnsberger, William Henry	123

Harper,	124-126
Harriss, William N.	205
Hawkins, James	184
Hawling, William C.	245
Heap,	42-43
Heaton,	54-58
Henderson, Richard Henry	162
Hening, Dr. William H.	142
Henry, Rev. John Bronaugh	213
Hereford,	83
Hess, Otto Theodore	260
Hickman,	130-131
Higginson, James M.	15
Hill, G. Powell	263
Sumpter Brock	127
Hilleary,	157-158
Hohenstein, W. Owen	50
Holleman, Townes	90
Holliday, Col. Fred. W. M.	108, 223
McHenry	11
Dr. R. McKim	108
Holloway Family,	27-28
Holmes,	261
Hough, Thomas	236
Thomas Edwin	153
Hubbard, Charles Francis	39
Huber, William Clarence	208
Hughes, John H.	261
Humphreys, Samuel P.	69
Hunter, Moses	111
Hutchinson, Edgar	263
Ingram,	191-192
Izzard, Prudence (Davisson)	139
Jacolio, William	201
Janney,	57, 136
Jaquelin, Edward	29
Jenings, Francis Washington	259
Jesse, Paul	201
Johnson, John Henry	184
Johnston, Reuben	162
Jones, Charles Scott Dodge	49
Hartwell	92
Mary (Stribling)	89
Samuel	53
William Strother	198
Jordan, Green Berry	98

INDEX.

Jordan, Richard Dudley	60	Kinney, John Chesley	22
Jungbluth, Karl	187	John Crawford	9
		John Marshall	12
Kaylor, Cecil Calvert	199	Kenton Harper	8
Keferstein, Carl B.	198	Leonidas Bell	9
Keech, Eliza (Kilgour)	176	Louis Nicholas	7
Keen, Dr. Thomas F.	147	Mary Edmunds (Chapman)	13
Keene, William	215	Mary Edmunds (Ker)	21
Kemp, John H.	101	Matilda (Stribling)	5, 37
Kennon, William	217	Matilda Ruth (Craig)	26
Ker, Heber	21	Nicholas Cabell	6
James	13	Rebecca Farrar (Richardson)	18
John Chesley	21	Richard Stevenson	22
Richard S.	22	Robert H.	7
Severn Parker	21	Robert Porterfield	8, 17
Kilgour Family,	176	Sarah Holloway	26
Alexander	53, 55, 176	Thomas Colston	11, 12
Charles Jourdan	165, 166, 176	Dr. Thomas Holloway	24
Francis Stribling	54, 58	Thomas Pollard	24
Henry Jourdan	165	Virginia (Whitcomb)	23
James McIlhany	162, 165	William	1, 12, 19, 26
John A. T.	176	William Galt	11
John Mortimer	166	William Nicholas	25, 26
William	53	Kinsolving	253–254
Kilpatrick, B. F.	94	Klein, Barbara (Trout)	114
Kimball,	59	Kownslar,	47, 48
Kincheloe, Cornelius	86		
Kinney Family,	1–32	Lambert Family,	132
Alexander Fisher	11	Lane, Carr W.	28
Ann (Whitesides)	5	George Steptoe	85
Anne Maria (Bell)	19	Susan A. (Kinney)	25, 28
Archibald	25	Latham, Thos. Jeremiah	204
Archibald Stuart	26	Laurie, Benjamin A.	175
Beirne	12	Lawrence, John	92
Cabell Carrington	12	Le Baron, A. C.	68
Maj. Chapman Johnson	11	Lee, Asa Rogers	255
Dr. Charles Porterfield	8	Charles K.	122
Chesley	6, 10, 21	George	254
Clifton C.	22	Hugh Douglas	255
Edward Carrington	12	John William	122
Edwin Taylor	18	Joseph William	122
Eliza Holloway	20	Stephen Archer	123
Elizabeth C. S. P. H.	10	Thomas Ludwell	251
Dr. George Nicholas	10	Lewinski, Maj. Thomas	184
Harry Whitcomb	24	Lewis, Col. Andrew	44
Jacob	3	Col. Charles	44
Jane Eleanor (Taylor)	15	Charles H.	101
Jefferson	23, 25	Edward Parke Custis	107

INDEX.

Lewis, Fisher A.   85, 101
  James B.   101
  Dr. John H.   101
  John Stuart   44, 45
  Lorenzo   156
  Dr. Magnus M.   102
  Robert Vincent   102
  Wm. H. T.   65, 102
Liggett, John R.   19
Lindsay, Elizabeth (Fairfax)   245
Lingamfelter, Rev. Chas. S.   208
Lippitt, Dr. E. C.   223
Littler, Rachel Ann (Stribling)   67
  Rebecca (Stribling)   52
Locke, William Milo   188
Longest, J. L. Hugh   55
Lordan, J. J.   49
Lowery, Thomas M.   94
Lowry Family,   215–216
Luke, David L.   64

Lupton. Hugh W.   238
  Joel   238
  John McPherson   205
  John T.   208
  Thomas M.   207
  William Milton   206
Lyle, S. Bradley   116
Lynn, Charles Wright   171
Lysle, William Wilson   201

Mackey, John   110
  Dr. Robert   108
McCamey, Mary   136
McCance, Thomas W.   258
McCemmie, Thomas   182
McCord, William   132
McCormick Family,   221–227
  Dr. Albert M. Dupuy   212
  Anne (Stribling)   47, 214
  Charles   222, 224, 225
  Dr. Cyrus   154, 223
  Dawson   211, 212, 223
  Edward   52, 211
  Francis   221
  Col. Francis   153, 223
  George   226
  Hannah (Taylor)   217, 223

McCormick, Harriet (Milton)   205, 226
  Isaac   224
  Dr. James Jett   213, 225
  Dr. John   221
  John   224
  Marshall   225
  Mary Riley (Tate)   101, 221
  Province   213, 222, 224, 225
  Samuel   156, 223
  Thomas   66, 155, 222, 223, 224
  William   213, 224
McCue, Col. Franklin   31
McDaniel, Charles Lucian   14
McDonald, Col. Marshall   153
McEvoy, James   260
McFall, Mary (Rogers)   229
McGruder, Charles   23
McGuire, Dr. James M. G.   107
  Joseph Deakins   14
  Dr. William   218
  William David   153
McHam, Samuel   73
McIlhany Family,   133–176
  Anne Louisa (Offutt)   173
  Bettie W. (Milton-Sparr)   173, 203
  Cecilia (Stribling)   52, 162
  Douglas   171
  Edward Washington   168
  Eli Offutt   172
  Elizabeth   156
  Hannah (Parker)   137
  Hannah Ann (Bond)   167
  Henry Johnston   172
  Capt. Hugh Milton   119, 160
  Dr. Hugh Milton   161
  Capt. James   135, 137
  James   162
  Dr. James Stuart   164
  John   133, 136, 156, 167, 196
  John Milton   159
  Dr. John William   158
  Joseph Washington   175
  Louisa (Kilgour)   165
  Rev. Marshall   171
  Mary (Davis-Fry)   161
  Mortimer   167
  Col. Mortimer.   169

INDEX. 269

Nancy (Davisson-White)	139	Miller, James Jones	48
Rachael (White)	135	Robert Tunstall	118
Richard Bond	170	Thomas H.	182
Rev. Robert Bruce	169	Milton Family,	177–227
Rosannah (Ellzey)	149	Alexander Ross	85, 147, 179
Taliaferro Milton	157, 196, 257		205, 226
Thomas	134	Benjamin Taylor	187
William Wallace	168, 170, 171	Bushrod Taylor	191
McKindly, Jane B. (Stribling)	92	Charles Johnson	188
McKinstry, K. T.	45	Rev. Charles Louis	181
McMahan, Lawrence	93	Charles Wilt	179
McMullin,	40–41	David M.	189
McNeely, Capt. C. C.	219	Eben	189
McVeigh Family,	262–263	Eben O.	186
Edgar	263	Eben Taylor	185
Eli	262	Edwin Kirtley	187
Elliot Fletcher	145	Elijah	183, 220
Hamilton	262	Elijah Newton	187
Hiram	144, 145, 262	Elizabeth S. W. (Taylor)	
Hugh Rogers	147		36, 210, 218
James H.	263	Dr. Ellis H.	180
Jesse	145, 262	Florinda (McCormick)	211
Job	263	Frances (Davis)	214
Newton	263	Francis Clark	188
Townsend	263	Frederick Richard	199
William Harvey	262	Dr. George Robert	173, 203
William Newton	263	Griffin Taylor	187
Mains, Mary (Rogers)	229	Harriot (McIlhany-Taylor)	
March, Perrin G.	106		156, 196, 217
Marshall, John, C. J. 29, 160, 198, 218		James Berryman	187
John	78	James Foster Barnet	179
Rebecca Peyton (Stribling)	82	Dr. James Ransom	182
Gen'l Thomas	218	James Taliaferro Theodore	200
Mason, Dr. G. F.	108	John	76, 148, 187, 190, 195
Massengale, Samuel	175	John Brown	193
Massie, Rev. Robert K.	209	John Lewis	190
Mathews, Joseph William	146	John T.	181
Matthews, William Edwin	73	Mary	208
May, Joseph William	62	Matthew Scott	190
Mead, Francis Dominick	252	Miles H.	181
Meade, Dr. Basil	103	Moses	178, 179
John	110	Nancy (Davis)	198, 214
Menefee,	63–65	Noland S.	190
Metzger, Frederick Philip	140	Richard,139, 177, 178, 180, 181, 199	
Miller, Charles Taliaferro	50	Dr. Richard L.	180
Ellwood Stribling	50	Robert L.	181
Frederick Otto	116	Slicer Wickes	204
Harry H.	117	Stephen Duncan	210

Milton, Taliaferro,	210	Nicolson, George Llewellyn	24
Theodore Davisson	148	Reginald Fairfax	43
Thomas	180	Dr. William Perrin	23
Thomas Tidball	186	Nott, Andrew H.	15
Thomas Smith	191	Norris, William	103
Turner Ashby	182		
Virginius Fairfax	204	Offutt,	173–174
William	182, 188, 193	O'Meara, F. W. H.	14
William Agun	193	Opie,	103
William Davisson	200	Orr, Dr. John Dalrymple	251
William H.	181	Page, Rev. T. Carter	110
Rev. William Hammond	209	Parker, Wm. H.	137
William Taylor	209	Parsons, Charles Alfred	202
Zack Green	180	Patterson, Frank	94
Minor, Launcelot	252	William	224
Moffett, Horatio Gates	64	Pennybacker,	69–73
Moncure, Richard C. L.	80	Pettus, Judge William H.	186
Robert Ambler	80	Phillips, Alexander Keene	249
Montague, J. S.	40	Pitzer, George I.	238
Moody, Lynnwood C.	55	Pollard, Mary Todd (Kinney)	24
Moore, Edward Doane	46	Porter, John Alexander	57
Magnus S.	72	Dr. Ralph F. S.	54, 57
Capt. Reuben	27	Porterfield Family,	30–32
Rev. Samuel Scollay	211	Rebecca Farrar (Kinney)	12, 31
Solomon Kingree	72	Poulton,	140–141
Morris Family,	26–27	Powell. Hugh Lee	41
Ann (Kinney)	3	John Leven	247
Morrison, Harry L.	124	Rosalie Dalrymple (Rogers)	247
Moss, Frederick	111	Col. William Levin	154
Margaretta (McCormick)	224	Powers,	109–110
William V.	263	Pratt, William A.	18, 129
Mott, John	56	Preston, Hugh Caperton	110½
Mugg,	181, 182	Priest, James A.	191
Murray, H. Dunbar	25	Province,	222
Muse Family,	101–105	Pyke, Alfred Joseph	81
Myers, Barton	110¼		
Charles James	128	Queen, Rose Ellen (Kilgour)	53
Samuel	131		
		Ralston, Minteo	102
Neale, Mary Nelson (Stribling)	74	Ramirez, Jose Maria	146
Neill. John M. B.	66	Ramsey, Alexander	90
Lewis	65	Rawlinson, L. Seymore	103
Dr. Sigismund Stribling	65, 111	Read, Dr. John La Fayette	142
Nelson, Col. William	252	Recktenwald, E.F.	44
Newell, Riverius	56	Rector,	235–237
Newman, Benjamin P.	131	Reid,	91–92
Nicholas, William Stuart	126	Renahan, J. A.	12
Nicklin, Marshall	85	Rennoe, William Winter	158

INDEX.

Rhett, Abbott Brisbane	255		Sartain, James Knox	146
Ribble, Rev. F. G.	78		Saunders, Rev. Jonathan	88
Richardson, Dr. Elihu Hall	253		Scanland, Lawrence	237
Silas Augustus	18		Scharf, Emil Ludwig	149
William Augustus	18		Schooley, Clarence Eugene	240
Riddell, Archibald	242		Scott, Beverly	164
Riddle, George Reed	103		John C	122
John Thornton	40		Robert E.	260
Riley, Ferrill	221		Scruggs, John Emmett	242
Ritenour, Henry	132		Sehon, Columbus	45
Roach, Philip	51		Shelor,	95-97
Robey, Henry D.	124		Simms,	61, 62
Rogers Family,	228-263		Skinker, James Keith	158
Adin	249		Slaughter, James Albert	259
Alexander Hamilton	248		Sligh,	90, 93
Ann (McIlhany)	157, 257		Sloan, Elizabeth (Stribling)	89
Anne (McVeigh)	262		Smith Family,	99-100
Arthur	229, 261		Charles Thomas	237
Arthur Lee	253		Charles William	259
Asa	250, 251		Courtland	249
Broocks,	250		E. B.	93
Elizabeth (Swart)	232		Edward Jaquelin	108, 109
George Rust	253		Francis Stribling	74
Hamilton	229, 245, 261, 262		Rev. George W.	145
Henry Judson	258		James Samuel	237
Hugh	230, 247, 261		Joseph	102
James	255		Col. Lawrence	99
James Hamilton	251		Richard Buckner	109
James Pendleton	258		Robert Randolph	109
John Dalrymple	251		Samuel George	237
Joseph	262		Sarah (Taliaferro)	100
Martha (Sowers)	259		William	74
Mary Jane (Rogers)	257		William Barton	200
Milton McIlhany	258		William Dickerson	46, 108, 109
Mortimer McIlhany	250		Snapp, Charles Edward	125
Samuel	245, 262		Snickers Family,	107-111
Sarah (Davisson)	142, 257		Snyder, Silas Wright	201
Susan (Spilman)	260		Sowers, Daniel A.	259
Thomas	261		Sparr, Ripley Warren	173
William	229, 251		Sparrow, Thomas Wing	17
William Hawling	245		Spilman,	260-261
William Hixson	257		Stahler, Rev. W. E.	70
William Pendleton	258		Staples, Waller R.	129
Rosamond, Richard	89		Steele, William	96
Ross, Margaret (Milton)	178		Stevenson Family	32
Rust, George	253		Stigers, F. M.	204
Ryan,	115-118		Stribling Family,	33-111
			Ann (Milton)	76, 195

INDEX.

Stribling, Anne Elizabeth	58	Stribling, Otis Francis	84
Benjamin	35	Paul Orlando	91
Benjamin F.	87	Robert	87, 94
Benjamin Haile	87	Col. Robert Mackey	81
Bushrod Taylor	47	Dr. Robert Mackey	76, 83
Charles Arthur	46	Samuel Pettigrew	97
Rev. Charles R.	89	Sigismund	34, 59, 86
Cornelius Kincheloe	88, 89	Sloan Y.	91
David Sloan	94	Taliaferro	35, 74, 76
Edward McCormick	48	Dr. Taliaferro,	48
Erasmus	2, 5, 37-39	Thomas	33, 34, 67, 76, 86, 87
Erasmus Mortimer	56	Thomas Edward	78, 92
Francis	34, 36	Thomas H.	87, 92
Capt. Francis	52, 162	Thomas M.	89, 98
Francis James	55	Thomas Sligh	91
Francis Taliaferro	41, 42	Thomas T.	35
George	35	Warren D.	97
George Thomas	97	Warren Webb	98
George William	74, 75	William	34, 84
Henry Clarkson	82	William Clarkson	77
Jacob Kinney	39	William David	93
Dr. James Harrison	87	William Harrison	92
James Hodges	95	William Jesse	96
James Paul	98	William John	95
Jesse	89	Dr. William Magnus	46
Jesse Cornelius	90	Willis	35
Jesse Dendy	98	Strother, Henry St. Geo. Tucker	136
Jesse Wales	94	Stuart, Col. John	44
Jonathan Heaton	56	Rosannah (McIlhany)	133
John	85	Stubblefield, Maj. George	216
John B.	86	Sullivan, Algernon S.	196
John Lewis	47	Swart,	232-245
John Verner	96		
John Wavt	47, 214	Taliaferro Family,	99
Dr. Joseph S.	97	Tandy,	87, 95
Kate Byers	75	Tate Family,	100-107
Lemuel David	96	Erasmus	105
Llewellyn	92	John Chenoweth	106
Magnus Tate	58	John Humphreys	106
Margaret Perry (Pennybacker)	69	Magnus	100, 101, 105
Mark Mitchell	87	Dr. Magnus A.	106
Marshall Stokes	96-98	Dr. Magnus W.	106
Mary Tate (Crawford)	59	Margaret (Muse)	101
Dr. Matthew Wright	36, 83	Mary (Stribling)	48, 105
Matilda Kinney (Trout)	45	Nancy (Stribling)	36, 101
Nancy (Tate)	86	William	106
Nancy Tate (Neill)	65	Tayloe, Col. George P.	250
Nancy Trimmier (White)	97	Taylor Family,	215-220

Taylor, Benjamin	217
Bushrod	210, 218
Catherine (Milton)	183, 220
Eben	220
Edgar D.	23
Edwin Mygatt	15, 17
Emily Bushrod (Milton)	185, 219
Eugene	220
Dr. Frederick William	140
Dr. George William	219
Griffin	218, 220
Dr. Hugh McGuire	23, 217
James Richards	17
Dr. James William	140, 219
John Bushrod	218
Julius Alexander	61
Louisa Ann (Milton)	187, 219
Moncure Robinson	206
Samuel	108
Samuel McCormick	217
William	196, 216, 217
Tennant, Eugenia B. (Fairfax)	246
Thomson, Dr. Augustus P.	164
Thompson,	49-52
Tidball,	110
Tiffany,	239-242
Tilford,	197
Tousey, Oliver	109
Trapnell, Joseph	110
Tribbey,	137, 138
Trimmier,	86
Trout Family,	112-132
tzer	114
Catherine (Boyers-Ritenour)	132
Daniel	114
David	130
Henry	130, 131
Dr. Hugh H.	129
Isaac	129, 130, 131
Jacob	113, 114
James Edmonds	126
James Russel	127
John Baltzer	113
Joseph	5, 115, 131
Joseph Chesley	126, 127
Joseph Oscar	128
Nicholas Kinney	45, 118
Philip	115
Trout, Philip Henry	127, 129
Wilbur A.	129
William B.	129
William Edgar	128
Tucker, Dr. Alfred Bland	217
Tyndall, Rev. Charles N.	101
Ulrich, A. Louis	68
Vandeventer, Charles Oscar	55
Van Rensselaer, Eleanor Cecilia (Fairfax)	246
Vawters, Ann (Stribling)	35
Vint	128
Waddell, Mary (Bell)	20
Waggener,	75-76
Waldo	232-233
Walke, Rev. Lewis	161
Waller	79-81
Walling, Percy A.	46
Walls, Dr. Charles Bruce	192
Walton,	103-105
Ware Family,	107-108
James	107, 218
Warner, Brainard Henry	249
Washington, Alfred Offutt	152
Bushrod	218
Edward Sanford	150
Fayette	37
George William	150
John Augustine	215
Lewis Ellzey	150
Marshall	151
Mary Ann (McIlhany)	167
Warner	111, 195
Waters,	238-239
Watkins, Bushrod Porter	185
Edward Jefferson	193
Elijah Milton	184
Henry	183
John Hancock	183
Thomas Bodley	183, 184
Wattles, Charles William	223
Wayland, Lewis	31
Rebecca (Kinney)	7, 31
Webb, James M.	92
Wellford, Dr. William Nelson	251
West, Elvira Ann (Crawford)	60

Wheeler,	119–121	Wildman, Robert Bentley	248
Col. Daniel Davis	249	Williams, Goodwin Hulings	212
Whitcomb, H. D.	23, 24	James M.	25
White, Agnes Bratton	143	John Thornton	15
Beneah	136	Thomas	139
B. Frank	97	Willis, John	206
D. Sloan	97	Prof. John C.	181
Henry	182	Willson, Gilpin	20
Henry N.	97	Wilson, Clement L.	117
James	135	Wine, Charles Edward	120
James Alexander	144	Wintter, Dietrich	194
James Bratton	143	Wirt, William	3
John	139	Wood, Charles Littler	236
John H.	135	William Weston	47
John Josiah	143	Woolfolk, Richard C.	184
John Richard	152	Wright, Calvin	96
Joshua	135	Elizabeth (Stribling)	86
Josiah T.	136	Francis	36
Leslie Curtis	72	W. E.	181
Nathan S.	110	Wyatt, Rev. Frederick F.	168
Robert Josiah Thomas	149, 219	Wyly, Thomas B.	97
Thomas	135		
Whitehead	111	Young, James Albert	84
Whitesides,	5, 27, 115	John Wesley	51
Whiting, Francis Beverley	153		
Whytock, Judge	219	Zanone, J. P. L.	18

www.ingramcontent.com/pod-product-compliance
Lightning Source LLC
Chambersburg PA
CBHW031250230426
43670CB00005B/118